JOHN REED

& the Writing
of Revolution

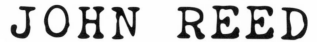

JOHN REED
& the Writing
of Revolution

DANIEL W. LEHMAN

Ohio University Press

Athens

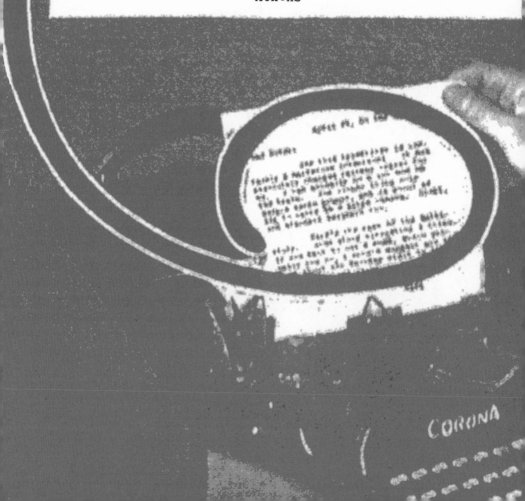

Ohio University Press, Athens, Ohio 45701

Ohio University Press books are printed on acid-free paper ⊗ ™

10 09 08 07 06 05 04 03 02   5 4 3 2 1

Material from the John Reed Papers is quoted by permission of the Houghton Library, Harvard University.

Portions of chapter 1 appeared in somewhat different form in the fall 2001 issue of the *Harvard Library Bulletin* and the fall 2002 issue of *River Teeth: A Journal of Nonfiction Narrative*. A small portion of chapter 3 appeared in substantially different form in *Matters of Fact: Reading Nonfiction over the Edge* (Ohio State University Press, 1997).

Library of Congress Cataloging-in-Publication Data
Lehman, Daniel W. (Daniel Wayne), 1950–
    John Reed and the writing of revolution / Daniel W. Lehman.
        p. cm.
    Includes bibliographical references.
    ISBN 0-8214-1467-4 (cloth : alk. paper) — ISBN 0-8214-1468-2 (pbk. : alk. paper)
        1. Reed, John, 1887–1920—Criticism and interpretation. 2. Revolutionary literature, American—History and criticism. 3. Literature and society—United States—History—20th century. 4. Social problems in literature. I. Title.

PS3535.E2786 Z75 2002
818'.5209—dc21

                                                                        2002072140

This book is for Hadley

and for Barbara Alice Lehman

Contents

Illustrations

Acknowledgments

As a reader and researcher with an inordinate interest in the writings of John Reed, I must confess that nothing quite prepared me for the experience of opening my first folders of his papers. There lay his typescript of the Industrial Workers of the World (IWW) trial—the rhythms of description that I knew so well painstakingly worked over in Reed's strike-outs and pencil corrections. Here were Reed's notes for a new novel, *The Tides of Man,* scrawled in 1920 by his dull pencil on curiously waxy square pages that had been smuggled to Reed's prison cell by sympathetic jailers. Here was Reed's schoolboy copy of Stephen Crane's *George's Mother,* with a list on the flyleaf of his favorite authors. There was a red armband and the pass that made it possible for him to see the Winter Palace stormed. Notebooks, letters, drafts, lists, clippings, poems—they tumbled out into my hands. For that incomparable moment, I wish to thank William Stoneman, director of the Houghton Library at Harvard University, and Leslie Morris, curator of manuscripts for the Houghton Collection. As the recipient of the library's 2000–2001 Stanley J. Kahrl Fellowship in Literary Manuscripts, I can attest to the extraordinary hospitality and helpfulness of the staff; their patience and wisdom in directing my search was beyond compare. Similarly, the staff in the periodicals collection at the Cleveland Public Library helped me find all the copies of *Metropolitan Magazine* in which John Reed's writing appeared. Together we worried over the brittle, yellowing pages of the magazines; their camera produced the copies that I have been reading and considering ever since. Chris Faur, digital media technician at Denison University, went well beyond the call of duty to help me recover Reed material from the *Saturday Evening Post:* my thanks for his assistance as well as that of Mary Prophet and Star Andrews at Denison. Similar help in obtaining and duplicating research materials about Reed was graciously given by Jeff Pinkham, faculty reference librarian at Ashland University.

Ashland University has supported this project with a senior study leave, a summer research grant, and several dean's grants. I particularly thank G. William Benz, Mary Ellen Drushal, John Bee, Fred Yaffe, and John Stratton for their help. English chairs Robert McGovern and Naomi Saslaw offered constant encouragement; Professor Saslaw's ready supply of cookies fueled writing sessions and made up for missed meals. Painstaking transcriptions of Reed's Mexican notebooks were prepared by student researcher and writer extraordinaire R. S. Ross, who just might give John Reed a run for his money some day. And at Ashland, my colleague Joe Mackall—who normally thinks he knows it all—in this case has no idea how much he has taught me about literature and journalism as my co-editor and friend.

At Ohio University Press, senior editor Gillian Berchowitz responded to this project immediately and enthusiastically. She and press director David Sanders encouraged my work on John Reed at every turn and answered all my questions carefully and promptly. Two of my literary heroes, Robert Rosenstone and Barbara Lounsberry, offered wonderfully perceptive readings of the first draft of this study; any improvements I managed can be directly attributed to their wise suggestions. And manuscript editor Nancy Basmajian and marketing manager Sharon Arnold have made me feel that the press values the project as much as I do. The copyeditor, Dennis Marshall, made this a much better book: I treasure his personal and professional interest and the dialogue we established during work on the final manuscript. All remaining errors are mine.

I first learned about John Reed because of his opposition to World War I. I grew up in an Anabaptist Mennonite community in Virginia and recall hearing the stories of older men in my community who had been imprisoned for refusing to fight in that war. Although their pacifism differed in many degrees from that of John Reed, a common instinct joined them. There must be some world out there, they reasoned, in which killing for national pride and profit no longer makes sense. And if that world exists, why not begin living in it now? My parents—both still active editors into their eighties—taught me these and many other lessons in my home.

Barbara Lehman, as always, sets an example for me as a professor and scholar. She and Hadley Lehman are my companions and best friends. Daily they keep me honest—never more needed than now. All thanks to them. To see the world, to believe in the possibility of change, to work for justice and peace —these are our goals together. And finally, to Chet Wenger, you are out there, somewhere, waiting patiently for us to catch up with you. We will ride again some day.

JOHN REED
& the Writing
of Revolution

Introduction

"A slice of intensified history"

> This book is a slice of intensified history—history as I saw it. . . . In the struggle my sympathies were not neutral. But in telling the story of those great days I have tried to see events with the eye of a conscientious reporter, interested in setting down the truth.
>
> —John Reed, *Ten Days That Shook the World*

JOHN REED WAS the author of such powerfully and deeply implicating pieces of nonfictional narrative that his writings on revolution were suppressed in both the Soviet Union and the United States. The subject of at least three federal prosecutions for his on-the-scene reports of a nation skidding toward war, Reed remains a writer almost systematically ignored by literary critics, even if alternately vilified and lionized by historians, biographers, and filmmakers. Reed thus offers the intriguing study of an author whose writing exposed and worked to overcome the contradictions in the relationship of a writer of nonfiction to his subjects—particularly an American writer of some privilege to his exploited foreign subjects. Always the consummate stylist, Reed seemed to learn during his brief career that stories of history can assume the power to shape readers and events. He seemed also to understand that his stories were enfolded within a larger story of economic and political struggle. Perhaps as a result of that recognition, and of his willingness to write about it in increasingly bold terms,

Reed ended his brief career as an author deeply alienated from the cultural, political, and legal power of his homeland. Yet his historical and literary importance assumes threefold significance.[1]

As an author, Reed was early to understand the power of narrative to construct the lives of its subjects. He therefore attempted a historically significant and so far underdocumented break with the journalistic conventions of his time, particularly by challenging the ruling notions of how to cover economic injustice and armed conflict. Moreover, much of Reed's prose styling, particularly his devastatingly drawn character sketches, his sharp eye for ironic detail, and his trademark enumerations, remains fresh nearly a century after it was written and belies the so-called New Journalists' claims to having discovered literary reportage in the 1960s. Reed built his prose on the careful observation of life around him and learned to buttress that observation with research and analysis. Finally, Reed offers an intriguing study because he was a writer who habitually implicated himself and his audience to an uncommon degree. That is, he seemed to think as much about his relationship to the subjects of his writing as he did about the facts of their stories. As his writing matured, Reed became much more willing to own up to that relationship and to weigh the responsibilities attendant on his power to create historical narrative. As a result of his willingness to cut against the political and social grain, Reed paid so dear a price of notoriety that a critical establishment long enamored of detached scholarship could hardly bring itself to read him.

As evidence of the latter point, Reed's historical presence looms large enough that he has been the subject of five full-length biographies and one historical novel (Granville Hicks's *John Reed: The Making of a Revolutionary* [1936]; Barbara Gelb's *So Short a Time* [1973]; Tamara Hovey's *John Reed: Witness to Revolution* [1975]; Robert Rosenstone's *Romantic Revolutionary: A Biography of John Reed* [1975]; Eric Homberger's *John Reed* [1990]; and Alan Cheuse's *The Bohemians* [1982]), as well as at least two feature-length films (Warren Beatty's *Reds* and Sergei Bondarchuk's *Campanas Rojas*), but virtually no serious critical study of his writing. The only book-length treatment that purports to analyze Reed's writing (David C. Duke's *John Reed* [1987]) is written by a historian and is much more useful as a biographical sketch and general survey of Reed's literary career than as criticism. Jim Tuck's *Pancho Villa and John Reed: Two Faces of Romantic Revolution* (1984), while intriguing, focuses more on Villa than Reed and considers only Reed's writings from Mexico. Jim Finnegan's recent doctoral dissertation "Writing to Shake the World" offers to Reed criticism a valuable approach grounded in cultural studies, but it is as much about Don DeLillo and *Spin* magazine's post-punk poetics as it is about Reed.[2] Christopher

P. Wilson offers the best of the relatively scarce shorter criticisms of Reed; particularly helpful are his analyses of Reed's short stories and *Insurgent Mexico*. Meanwhile, John Reed is shut out of the U.S. literary canon, even from recently expanded, multivolume versions such as *The Norton Anthology of American Literature* and *The Heath Anthology of American Literature*.

Moreover, books by and about John Reed rarely are classified as belonging on "literature" shelves, either in libraries or bookstores (in marked contrast to books by and about writers like Stephen Crane and George Orwell). Walter B. Rideout's study *The Radical Novel in the United States, 1900–1954* (1992) concludes, "As far as his influence on the literature of the Left goes, Reed's death was his greatest achievement. . . . Strictly as a literary man, Reed has no place in this volume" (127). The quite comprehensive *Sourcebook of American Literary Journalism* (1992) concludes that he "became an apologist of the [Bolshevik] regime and a political activist, thereby ending his career as a literary journalist" (Humphrey, 159). John C. Hartsock mentions Reed only once in his three-hundred-page *History of American Literary Journalism* (2000), and that in passing; he does, however, provide helpful historical context in which to place Reed's work. Perhaps the most startling snub came from Nathaniel Lande in his otherwise excellent *Dispatches from the Front: A History of the American War Correspondent* (1996): in collecting some eighty writers from the Revolutionary War to the Gulf War, Lande manages to ignore altogether John Reed, who, I hope to demonstrate, is one of the best American writers ever to cover armed conflict and is certainly one of the most complex and theoretically interesting. Finally, Christine Stansell's intriguing recent history of Greenwich Village radicals, *American Moderns: Bohemian New York and the Creation of a New Century* (2000), although insightful about Reed in several instances, mostly treats Reed as an artifact of social history rather than as a literary journalist worthy of careful reading.

John Reed and the Writing of Revolution—in contrast to the brief dismissals by Rideout and Humphrey cited earlier—will consider Reed's work as literary texts worthy of analysis and will approach those texts specifically from the theoretical framework of nonfiction. Along with a handful of other theorists,[3] I have sought to articulate several ideas for reading nonfiction narrative both as literature and as socially and historically implicated text. My earlier study *Matters of Fact: Reading Nonfiction over the Edge* sets out that practice in some detail.

In this context I will cite several theoretical assumptions that guide this study: Nonfiction is a form of communication that purports to reenact for the reader the play of actual characters and events across time. The lives of nonfictional characters thus extend outside the text and compete with the text. Some subjects and other readers will remember stories differently and might wrestle with nonfictional writers over claims, facts, and interpretations. While a reliable truth standard may be insufficient to build an unwavering distinction between fiction and nonfiction, what counts in narrative nonfiction is that events also are available to and experienced by readers and subjects in competing texts. Moreover, the engagement among writer, reader, and subject in an effort to construct meaning around an event "implicates" a nonfictional narrative in the sense that it is "deeply involved, even incriminated" in competing texts of history. This study of Reed, accordingly, will search for the ways that he, his subjects, and his readers are implicated in his goal to reproduce reality in story. Because so many of Reed's narratives present the histories of revolution or armed struggle, the texts' effort to build meaning creates explicitly social and political readings and responses.

Because of this engagement, the writer of nonfiction gains the power and sanctity that a reader might assign to actual lives in exchange for the responsibility of reproducing those lives in text. Readers typically invest meaning in an actual life—making deaths or tragedies emotionally compelling—but a writer has no monopoly on that meaning. The power to read minds, to gain access to characters and their stories, while often taken for granted in standard realistic fiction, assumes theoretical significance in nonfiction. The present study will examine Reed's work for the way it creates, and sometimes manipulates, its characters. Reed's decision to present characters omnisciently, to render their voices, to select and build their historical details into literary imagery, to change or falsify their names, will be measured against his source materials—his notes of conversations and events, his early drafts, his work of editing and rewriting and those of his editors, and the varying texts that he presented as fiction or nonfiction. Reed's works also will be read in the context of their publication venues and in the context of other authors covering the same events. Finally, a nonfiction writer reveals his or her power to reproduce real events compellingly through a writing style. A close reading of nonfiction, therefore, examines literary style within the context of its ability to control meaning for its readers. This book examines Reed's construction of scene, his evocation of detail, and his powers of description to determine how they create the illusion of compelling reality.

Fortunately, the artistic, social, and political context for Reed's writing can be gained through a wealth of source material that has been collected since his death in 1920. By far the most important collection is at Harvard University's Houghton Library (The Papers of John Reed). The papers were donated by Reed's co-reporter and wife, Louise Bryant, and collected by John Stuart for the Harvard John Reed Alumni Committee. These papers were examined and cited by Rosenstone in his comprehensive biography of Reed and, to a somewhat less scholarly extent, by Hicks in his earlier life history. My work using the collection has concentrated on comparing his original notes and correspondence to his journalism and other narrative writing. This study is interested in how Reed puts together a sentence, how he revises and edits his sentences, the rhythms he constructs for his passages, and the imagery he evokes. It also is interested in Reed's reporting: the people he chooses to interview, how he decides whom to quote and how often, how he constructs and manipulates direct quotes, the supporting documents on which he relies, and his notes of meetings and events. I examine the various drafts of Reed's writing as well as the mounds of reporters' notebooks that underpin those drafts. The collection at Harvard provides an opportunity to examine Reed's collection of political tracts and leaflets, the magazines and books he habitually consumed, his college-era textbooks and notes, as well as the stories and articles he wrote while he was still a young man.

Whenever possible, I examine Reed's articles within their original publications. The most important source for original, uncollected articles was *Metropolitan Magazine,* for which Reed wrote between 1913 and 1917. Most of Reed's *Metropolitan* pieces have not been published elsewhere—with the exception of those that Reed himself reprinted in *Insurgent Mexico* and *The War in Eastern Europe*—and many of the articles have never been the source of critical study. Two of these neglected articles, "In the German Trenches" and "Back of Billy Sunday," are reprinted in the appendix to this book so that readers can judge for themselves Reed's performance as a magazine writer and literary journalist. Written on deadline and published in consecutive months during Reed's period of greatest fame, the articles provide ready examples of Reed's knack for description and characterization, his ear for dialogue, and his creation of a subtly ironic narrative persona. I am fortunate in that the Cleveland Public Library, not far from my home, has one of the few complete collections of *Metropolitan,* and I was able to examine at length all the editions during the period that Reed wrote for the magazine. Less hard to obtain, but equally interesting, are Reed's articles for such magazines as *Collier's;* these, too, have not been collected or studied. Others of Reed's writings—particularly hard-to-find essays and articles from his college years or stories for such publications as *Smart Set* or *Trend*—were collected by Reed himself or by members of his family and are available in the Harvard archives.

Eric Homberger and John Biggart have collected many of Reed's hitherto unpublished writings from the period 1917 until his death in 1920 in their 1992 anthology *John Reed and the Russian Revolution: Uncollected Articles, Letters, and Speeches on Russia.* The scope of that collection deepens and complements earlier valuable anthologies of Reed's articles and short stories: the Communist Party's reader *The Education of John Reed* (International Publishers); the Floyd Dell–edited volume, *Daughter of the Revolution and Other Stories;* and the City Lights *Adventures of a Young Man: Short Stories from Life.* James C. Wilson has edited a helpful edition of Reed's writings for *The Masses*—many of which also had been collected by Dell and City Lights—and provides some insightful introductory essays.

Historical context for Reed's life has been provided by the biographies already mentioned—particularly those by Rosenstone, Hicks, and Homberger. Anyone interested at all in Reed or his writing owes a tremendous debt to Robert Rosenstone, whose landmark biography *Romantic Revolutionary* gathers essential source documents and provides an intriguing, comprehensive analysis.[4] I am particularly indebted to the citation by Rosenstone of letters written to Reed that are not available other than in the Lee Gold Archive at the Institute of Marxism-Leninism in Moscow. Hicks's earlier biography of Reed resulted from the assistance of Louise Bryant, the research of John Stuart, and the reminiscences of many of Reed's contemporaries. Those of Reed's colleagues who chose to cooperate with Hicks provided priceless anecdotes that can be found in no other source; Hicks's bibliography of Reed's shorter articles and stories is invaluable to any scholar. Eric Homberger's biography corrects several of Hicks's more doctrinaire observations and offers a coherent explanation of Reed's path through the thicket of left-wing political disputes between 1918 and 1920. Shorter memoirs by Lincoln Steffens, Max Eastman, and Floyd Dell can fill in perspective on many aspects of Reed's literary career—the biography by Tamara Hovey is particularly notable for its citation of correspondence from her father Carl Hovey, Reed's editor at *Metropolitan Magazine.*

I commend any of these biographical sources, particularly Rosenstone, to those interested in an in-depth narrative of Reed's life. Although I have a substantially different duty in this volume, to preface my literary analysis of Reed's work I here present a biographical overview that concentrates on Reed's initial literary influences, on the primary events of his writing life, and on the elements of writing strategy that typify various states of his career.

"I wrote of the things I saw, with a fierce joy of creation"

The overriding theme of John Reed's writing—both early and late—is its deep interest in human relationships within a context of social and political power. In his brief autobiography, "Almost Thirty," written in 1916 when he was recovering from a kidney operation, Reed credits three men for the intertwining passions of history and literature that prepared his writing life: Walter Lippmann, Lincoln Steffens, and Charles Townsend Copeland. Although he would have subsequent quarrels with all three men, Reed recognized in his essay that the three blended his passions for literary narrative and for muckraking, his eye for detail and for keen social analysis, his irrepressible enthusiasm and his empathy.

In his classmate Lippmann, Reed found a way out of the "dry, theoretical" study of the social sciences and embraced the Socialist Club, city elections, the Massachusetts legislature, the organization of Harvard servants, the Men's League for Women's Suffrage, the single tax, and anarchy. (128). Lippmann modeled "reading and thinking and talking about politics and economics, not as dry theoretical studies, but as live forces acting on the world" (136). And Lincoln Steffens—the famous muckraking acquaintance of Reed's father—not only sent important job recommendations Reed's way but encouraged him to look around and capture the world in his writing. Reed recalls a key conversation with Steffens: "'You can do anything you want to,' he said; and I believed him. Since then I have gone to him with my difficulties and troubles, and he has always listened while I solved them myself in the warmth of his understanding. Being with Steffens is to me like flashes of clear light; it is as if I see him, and myself, and the world, with new eyes" (138). Finally, Charles Townsend Copeland, his Harvard English professor, taught Reed to trust his writing instincts. "Professor Copeland, under the pretense of teaching English composition, has stimulated generations of men to find color and strength and beauty in books and in the world, and to express it again" (136), Reed recalls in his essay. In "Copey," Reed found a teacher courageous enough to buck what Reed describes as the prevailing Harvard educational philosophy: "We take young soaring imaginations, consumed with curiosity about the life they see all around, and feed them with dead technique" (129).

Granville Hicks quotes an anecdote in his biography that reveals Reed's drive to enliven dead technique—even in reportage—with literary imagination. Reed and artist Boardman Robinson were together on the Eastern Front in World War I when Robinson challenged Reed's historical accuracy on a writing point. "But it didn't happen that way," Robinson complained. "In reply, Reed seized some of his companion's sketches and announced, 'She didn't have a bundle as big as that,' and 'He didn't have a full beard.' Retorting that he was not interested in photographic accuracy, Robinson claimed to be giving a feeling and impression. 'Exactly,' said Jack, 'that is just what I am trying to do'" (197–98). To Reed, events revealed their importance through their ability to evoke human and emotional response. In "Almost Thirty," Reed roundly sneers at teachers with a small-minded pursuit of "a dull round of dates, acts, half-truths and rules for style, without questioning, without interpreting and without seeing how ridiculously unlike the world their teachings are" (129). To him, the broader emotional truth always outweighed the minutia.

Underpinning Reed's complementary interests in literature and history was his lifelong obsession with the foreign, the exotic, the remote, the "other." He recalls in "Almost Thirty" that he gained that fascination (and sometimes fear) from two sources. One, neatly domesticated by humor and imperialist fantasy, was "my uncle, a romantic figure who played at coffee-planting in Central America, mixed in revolutions, and sometimes blew in, tanned and bearded and speaking 'spigotty' like a *mestizo*" (128). Reed recalls with no small satisfaction that his uncle was said to have helped to lead a revolution that captured Guatemala for a few days, and, when he was made secretary of state of that nation, used the funds of the national treasury to host a grand state ball and to declare war on Germany "because he had flunked his German course in college" (128).[5] The other sources, although economically domesticated at Reed's Portland home in their roles as the family's servants, were Chinese. They offered to young Reed the promise and menace of orientalism, something not fully tamed. "They brought ghosts and superstitions into the house, and the tang of bloody feuds among themselves, idols and foods and drinks, strange customs and ceremonies, half-affectionate, half-contemptuous, wholly independent, and withal outlandish," Reed recalls. "[T]hey have left me a memory of pig-tales and gongs and fluttering red paper" (127). His recollection of a servant named Sing, a wielder of joss sticks and prayer papers, would provide Reed one of his better descriptive profiles in a college essay written for Copeland. He recalls, "I used to go out to the kitchen—we children and the dogs were always welcome—and find Sing washing the dishes, his long pigtail jumping as he simultaneously executed a double-shuffle, at the same time singing Methodist hymns with doleful relish" (bMS Am 1091:1101).

The family's pet name for John Reed was Cobe, chosen as a diminutive of Jacobus, which had followed from the more familiar Jack (bMS Am 1091.3:9). Taught by his mother to read, the young Cobe devoured history books, particularly about knights and kings, and read Bill Nye, Mark Twain, and R. L. Blackmore's *Lorna Doone*. At the age of nine, he began to write his first book, a comic history of the United States, which he attempted to model after Bill Nye. In "Almost Thirty," Reed recalls his father, Charles Jerome Reed, as one of his first heroes, a man with "terrible slashing wit [and] fine scorn of stupidity and cowardice and littleness" (132). The elder Reed was a U.S. marshal during the presidency of Theodore Roosevelt and, with Lincoln Steffens, broke the Oregon Land

Fraud Ring. Some years later, Steffens recalled the toll that the reform activities took on C. J. Reed. Ostracized at his own club, Reed was no longer welcome to sit at a table with the moneyed timber interests who dominated Portland society. Steffens recalls the elder Reed saying, "[T]here at the head of the table, that vacant chair, that's my place. That's where I sat. That's where I stood them off, for fun for years, and then for months in deadly earnest; but gaily, always gaily. I haven't sat in that place since the day I rose and left it. . . . I would like to see which one of them would have the nerve to think that he could take and hold and fill my place. I have heard, and I am glad to see, that it is vacant yet" ("John Reed under the Kremlin").

Reed later said that his father had ruined his health by working so hard to send his sons to Eastern prep schools and then to Harvard College, which Reed entered as a member of the class of 1910. Like his father, John Reed was something of an outsider, at least during the first year at Harvard. He was a classmate of T. S. Eliot's and Walter Lippmann's and began to make a name for himself during his second year, when he successfully tried out for several college publications and made song leader of the cheering squad. That experience clearly had an impact on Reed's life; witness the thrill he felt subsequently when he heard or led mass sing-alongs in venues as various as the Industrial Workers of the World (IWW) pageant in Madison Square Garden, a Billy Sunday evangelical crusade, or the All-Russian Congress of Soviets. "I had the supreme blissful sensation of swaying two thousand voices in great clashing choruses during the big football games" ("Almost Thirty," 134–35), Reed recalls. Reed also turned out to be a copious and satiric writer, penning song lyrics for all the big shows and making sport of college life and cliques.

By his own admission an indifferent student, Reed talked his way into Charles Townsend Copeland's famous English 12, a composition class partially taught by conference and admitting no more than thirty of the college's best writers at a given time. In a biography, *Copey of Harvard,* the veteran writer and editor J. Donald Adams recalls that Copeland's students included such subsequently famous writers as T. S. Eliot, Van Wyck Brooks, Conrad Aiken, Walter Lippmann, Heywood Broun, Robert Benchley, John Dos Passos, Malcolm Cowley, and George Seldes. Generally, Adams remembers, "we were free to write about anything we pleased. At other times there was a definite routine: one week a short story was called for, another an essay, another a book review, and so on. But there was one standing requirement, a brief piece of translation" (152–53). Copeland called students into his office for individual readings and consultations; a favorite Copeland admonition was "Write out of what you know" (157), and—as a former newspaperman and theater critic—he encouraged students to gain as much experience as possible and to write vividly, concretely, and with telling detail.

Copeland's methods, it turns out, divided his more famous students into two camps. One faction included the realists/naturalists such as Reed, who thrilled to Copeland's advice to write from life and to write with emotional detail. The other faction included budding modernists T. S. Eliot and the poet Van Wyck Brooks, who were searching for more lasting literary effect and for the more subtle imagery that Eliot would later identify in his essay on *Hamlet* as "objective correlative." According to Adams, Brooks believed that Copeland relied too much on "vividness without effect" and "going out and seeing life" rather than "staying at home in one's imagination" and searching for the phrase "that is not striking but that haunts the mind" (156).

Adams also unearths an early essay that T. S. Eliot wrote for English 12 about Rudyard Kipling; the manuscript contains Copeland's written responses and delivers additional insight into the differences between developing writers like Reed and Eliot. Although he was describing Kipling (to whom Reed soon would be compared), Eliot may as well have been describing Reed's own more vivid journalism in the essay he wrote for Copeland. "Always more anxious for the appearance of life than for life itself, the appearance of truth more than truth, Mr. Kipling has maintained the pose of a man of the world, a pose of the young and egotistic," Eliot writes. "He has seen everything and done everything. The discursive observer of life, the cosmopolitan like Kipling, often misconsiders that intimacy with sailors, barmen, whores, stokers, thieves, all people of squalid and strange professions—he thinks that such acquaintance gives one a knowledge of life. . . . Mr. Kipling was always more anxious to be striking than to be convincing" (160). To that remark, Copeland rejoins in a penciled note: "Don't you suppose that he expects to convince by striking?" (160) and admonishes Eliot at the end of the essay: "As usual you lean to the unduly harsh. Your opinion of Kipling's faults would carry more weight if you could appreciate without any niggling qualifications [his] masterpieces" (162).[6]

While T. S. Eliot may have had serious qualifications about Copeland, the popular Harvard professor clearly helped Reed's writing become more specific and self-assured. College essays in the Reed archives written before Reed took Copeland's English 12 class tend to be derivative and melodramatic, while those produced later contain glimpses of Reed's trademark sensory detail. Until the two broke over Reed's opposition to U.S. involvement in World War I, Reed remained a favorite of Copeland, always invited to the professor's famous apartment soirees to tell current undergraduates about his latest exploits in Europe or Mexico. Reed subsequently dedicated *Insurgent Mexico* to his Harvard professor, telling Copeland, "I never would have seen what I did see had it not been for your teaching me. I can only add my word to what so many who are writing already have told you: That to listen to you is to learn how to see the hidden beauty of the visible world" (3). And if Eliot fretted about Kipling's intimacy with whores and barmen, Reed was just beginning his exploration of that social stratum when he left Harvard College to write in Greenwich Village. The following long quote from "Almost Thirty" shows the strong influence of Copeland's command to "see life" and captures the full flavor of Reed's responding exuberance:

> New York was an enchanted city to me. It was on an infinitely grander scale than Harvard. Everything was to be found there—it satisfied me utterly. I wandered about the streets, from the soaring imperial towers of downtown, along the East River docks, smelling spices and the clipper ships of the past, through the swarming East Side—alien towns within towns—where the smoky flare of miles of clamorous push carts made a splendor of shabby streets; coming upon sudden shrill markets, dripping blood and fish scales in the light of torches, the big Jewish women bawling their wares under the roaring great bridges; thrilling to the ebb and flow of human tides sweeping to work and back, west and east, south and north. I knew Chinatown, and Little Italy, and the quarter of the Syrians; the marionette theater, Sharkey's and McSorley's saloons, the Bowery lodging houses and the places where the tramps gathered in winter; the Haymarket, the German Village, and all the dives of the Tenderloin. I spent all one summer night on top of a pier of the Williamsburg Bridge; I slept another night in a basket of squid in the Fulton Market, where the red and green and gold sea things glisten in the blue light of the sputtering arcs. The girls that walk the streets were friends of mine, and the drunken sailors off ships new come from the world's end, and the Spanish longshoremen down on West Street. (138–39)

Reed claims to know where to buy drugs, how to hire an assassin, where to gamble the night away, and the dance clubs where the bar girls chat nicely and sway just so. He claims to know Tammany as well as Washington Square and Coney Island as well as Manhattan. In "Almost Thirty," Reed records, "In New York I first loved, and I first wrote of the things I saw, with a fierce joy of creation—and knew at last that I could write" (139–40).

Lincoln Steffens recommended Reed for a job at the *American Magazine,* where Reed read manuscripts and wrote stories and poetry. Despite Copeland's admonitions, many of Reed's stories between 1910 and 1912 were hopelessly derivative, often marked by fantasy and melodrama. When he departed from precise description, Reed descended toward overblown drivel; witness another description of New York that he wrote in 1912. Comparing the city to "the Caliphate of the wise Haroun-al-Raschid"—and strewing allusions as broadly as capital letters—Reed contends that New York is a ring or lamp, "the mere rubbing of which summon all-powerful Jinni to place them at the pinnacle of the world . . . more magnificent than Satan built himself in Hell, more monstrous than the brazen cities of Hindustan, . . . many-hued—dazzling as the servants of Bhanavar the Bountiful. And in the unseeing millions that jostle and hurry him, amid the unceasing roar of human surf, are Sultans and Princes, Calendars and Sailors, Queens, and Peri and Ladies of the Hareem, Prophets and Fakirs and Holy Men who have seen God, and a few—a very few Aladdins" (bMS Am 1091:1137, pp. 1–3). Mercifully, the description was not published, but pieces such as "The Involuntary Ethics of Big Business: A Fable for Pessimists" and "The Peripatetic Prince" did find print in the *Trend* and *Smart Set,* respectively. The former floats on tedious allegory ("Then came the Reformer. 'You are wise,' he remarked, 'to have followed my system.' 'You've called at the wrong asylum,' responded the Rich Man" [289]), while the latter sinks in bombast ("On the barren Andean steppe, swept by the terrible winds that roar between worlds, a heroic granite statue of Peace . . . hang[s] to the bank of the Rio del Real, whose torrential thunder, as it plunges furiously down to the Pacific, makes a booming bass for the never-silent church bells of San Cristobal" [45]).

One problem with this sort of writing was that Reed had neither walked the land of "Sultans and Princes" nor trod the barren Andean steppe. When he sticks to settings he has seen and to people he has observed, Reed's writing delivers a much different sort of world. Two examples from his postcollege period are "The Dinner Guests of Big Tim," published in the *American Magazine,* and "The Harvard Renaissance," written for the same magazine but scrapped when its editors determined the piece might be too controversial for more staid Harvard alumni.

A seventy-three-page typescript, "The Harvard Renaissance" previews the sort of exacting research that would mark Reed's later career. He interviewed scores of students, faculty, and alumni for the piece as he sought to weigh the lasting effect of such innovations as the Socialist Club on the entrenched power of Harvard. Reed's opening salvo reads: "It is rumored that the son of a Cabinet official came home from Cambridge for his vacation and rebuked his mother for keeping a butler in livery—in view of the Brotherhood of Man" (bMS Am 1091:1139, p. 1).[7] With an epigraph from the university's president, "When the young men shall see visions, the dreams of the old men shall come true," Reed's thesis in "The Harvard Renaissance" asks whether the university still prizes the independence and innovation that marks its best moments. "Today it is more restless, more turbulent, a place of more variety of interest, more individuality of thought than ever before," he observes. "Harvard has always been more of a university, and less of a club, than any other American college. You could always find snobs and vulgarians, philosophers and cranks, poets and fanatics among its undergraduates, often solitary, often unknown, they found invariably someone to talk or listen to, and went away, leaving each one his mark upon the many-sided Harvard" (2). And then, through seventy-one additional pages of close reporting, the young writer sets out to prove his thesis.

Although the *American Magazine* chose not to publish his Harvard piece, in "The Dinner Guests of Big Tim" Reed made the most of a routine assignment to cover a free Christmas dinner thrown for indigent New Yorkers by Tammany boss T. D. "Big Tim" Sullivan. On duty by 6:30 A.M., Reed watches "a thousand bent and haggard creatures in a single line that stretched five restless blocks along the Bowery" (101). Reed listens as street peddlers hawk imitation gemstones to dark, foreign sweatshop girls ("Come get your gen-u-yne Brazil di'monds" [102]). Reed smells Bowery dust and bad tobacco, stale beer and cheap coffee, "the foulness of men who have slept in Lower East Side lodging houses" (102). When a man falls out of line, Reed strains at his language, seeming to want to break his reporter's distance to reach out as the man "slumped on the pavement and went rigid, with red foam on his lips. The ghastly crew behind him didn't wait until he was taken out before they surged forward to close up the line," Reed observes. "They stepped over and on his body. After all, they had been waiting four hours" (102). Inside Tammany Hall, Reed sees limping, twitching, slouching men queue for food beneath the two dozen watchful eyes of a dozen Big Tim portraits. Here is a twisted cripple, there a trembling Lear; all sit down to Christmas dinner, while one vagrant, tears streaming down his face, raises his arms in gratitude. "Down at the other end of the room Senator Fitzgerald heard and cried: 'You will not hurry! Take your time, boys'" (104). As he leaves, the young reporter ponders the unseen benevolence of Big Tim Sullivan and asks a deputy: "Where's the Big Fellow? . . . He lifted his face with the same look of reverence as one sees on the faces of medieval saints," Reed observes. "'Oh, he's upstairs,' he whispered. 'He can't be seen.'" Outside, "lights flared up and down the Bowery. There was movement and color, tremendous and unceasing pulse of life on the street. As I passed down the dark stairs, I met a shadowy, blotched line moving wearily up. It had waited long, this line. It was dreary, and dull, and silent; but it had life: it moved up" (104).

Reed marshaled the careful description of "The Dinner Guests of Big Tim" for thematic effect: Big Tim is an unseen deity who throws only scraps to the poor and then expects their gratitude. Unlike the *Smart Set* and *Trend* stories,

Reed mostly allows his material to speak for itself, relying on his access and his senses to bring magazine readers a scene they are unlikely to witness personally. The Tammany story and a subsequent piece about Broadway nightlife for *Metropolitan Magazine* prepared Reed for his next big break, the silk workers' strike at Paterson, New Jersey. Reed parleyed the strike into an unforgettable night in jail as well as major articles for *The Masses* and for *Metropolitan*. Suddenly Reed's career was on its way. The Paterson strike also brought Reed into contact with IWW leaders like Elizabeth Gurley Flynn and William D. "Big Bill" Haywood, and soon he was throwing his energies into the planning of a massive strike pageant at Madison Square Garden. Historian Christine Stansell explains the mutual attraction that drew IWW activists like Flynn and Haywood to Greenwich Village bohemians like Reed and his then-companion Mabel Dodge. "Nonfiction writers were the greatest beneficiaries of the gathering sense of literary importance" (178), writes Stansell in her recent study. "One role that emerged from this notion of purpose was the radical 'writer friend' of the labor movement, a downtown New York invention. Writers touched in some way by this idea of artistic commitment . . . shared one key trait: political engagements shaped by bohemian ideals of friendship and conversational community" (179).

A close reading of Reed's Paterson stories will be saved for my chapter 1; for the present biographical sketch, it is enough to note that the IWW pageant on June 7, 1913, featured a cast of twelve thousand, perhaps the largest for any live theater performance, and mostly was written and directed by Reed. At Madison Square Garden, "[w]ith the subtle line between actor and spectator breached, the crowd was at one with the strikers, booing the police, roaring in unison revolutionary songs, responding to the words of [Carlo] Tresca, Haywood, and Flynn, applauding and shouting approval until the solemn moments of the funeral, when they gazed on raptly while tears ran down many cheeks" (Rosenstone, 129). In a structural foreshadowing of his *Ten Days That Shook the World*, Reed organized the pageant around six dramatic episodes: "The Mills Alive—The Workers Dead," "The Mills Dead—The Workers Alive," "The Funeral of Modestino," "Mass Meeting at Haledon," "May Day," and "Strike Meeting at Town Hall."[8] The pageant program, a rare copy of which survives in the Harvard archives, features lyrics to "The International" and "The Marseillaise" and articles by such IWW luminaries as Flynn, Haywood, Ewald Koettgen, Phillips Russell, the pseudonymous "A Fellow Worker," and a young Britisher who would prove to be enormously influential on Reed's own developing Marxism: Frederick Sumner "Fred" Boyd.

Although the IWW pageant lost money, it helped to establish Reed as one of the rising stars of Bohemian radicalism and fueled his increasing success at

The Masses, a leftist Greenwich Village monthly edited by Max Eastman, and at *Metropolitan Magazine,* a mass-circulated monthly with artistic and socialist pretensions that was underwritten by Henry Payne Whitney, the husband of a Vanderbilt heir and a business associate of the Guggenheim family (Rosenstone, 209). Over the next three years—as chapters 3 and 4 will demonstrate by a close examination of Reed's writings in their wider social context—Reed was to become one of the most famous writers in the United States and a virtual specialist in the literature of foreign and labor conflict.

First in Mexico, then in Colorado, subsequently on the Eastern and Western Fronts of World War I, Reed sought to market his word-pictures of war to a U.S. public eager for vicarious adventure. But within that dominant narrative strategy, born of Reed and nurtured by his *Metropolitan* publicity, a more deeply insurgent impulse was building in John Reed. At first more subtly in the finale of *Insurgent Mexico* and then openly in "The Colorado War," Reed began to understand the local conflicts that he covered so colorfully as part of a larger economic pattern. Hiring Fred Boyd as a research assistant added new toughness to Reed's reporting and strengthened his ideology in ways that proved increasingly unsettling to his *Metropolitan* editors.

It is perhaps too simplistic to see Reed's artistic development during the period from 1914 until 1916 as a battle for supremacy between the sorts of competing influences represented by his friends Bobby Rogers and Fred Boyd. But the contrasting philosophies of these two men, as evidenced by contemporary correspondence and documentation, suggests that Reed often was torn between their different ways of looking at his writing. Robert Emmons "Bobby" Rogers was a Harvard classmate of Reed's who went to New York to write for the *Brooklyn Eagle* and ultimately built a successful career at the Massachusetts Institute of Technology (Rosenstone, 82, 105). Throughout Reed's career, Rogers offered occasional critiques of Reed's work, always advising Reed to drop propaganda for art. On the other hand, Reed had met Frederick Sumner "Fred" Boyd when the young British Marxist was arrested at the Paterson strike. According to Elizabeth Gurley Flynn, Boyd told the Paterson workers: "If you go back to work and you find scabs working alongside of you, you should put a little bit of vinegar on the reed of the loom in order to prevent its operation" (5). For this advice, Boyd was convicted of sabotage.

The reactions of Rogers and Boyd to Reed's increasing activism could hardly have been more different. Rogers called Reed's reporting from the Paterson jail "quick-lunch, emotionally effective propaganda dope" and advised Reed in a 1913 letter to "try and do literature without strings tied to it. The latter for the sake of art, or the first for the sake of Big Bill. You can't do both, as far as I can see" (bMS Am 1091:752). Three years later, as Reed was casting about for something to keep him busy after returning from the Eastern Front of World War I, Rogers wrote:

> I do wish you'd emit a lot of poetry, or a novel, or something beside the *Met* stuff you will do as well. This is not a sermon. . . . We all know now what you can do in the way of reporting life. . . . Why don't you take a winter off and sweat out a novel or a whole of a long poem (even unpublishable) and give us a synthesis? Syntheses are the only things that really count; all the splendid snapshots in the world are snapshots after all. (bMS Am 1091:756)

That Reed took Rogers's admonitions somewhat seriously is revealed by a letter Reed wrote in July 1917 to Louise Bryant at another low moment: "I have discovered with a shock how far I have fallen from the ardent young poet who wrote about Mexico. As Bobby Rogers phrased it, I had 'let myself go.' . . . But please god I intend to get back to poetry and sweetness, some way" (bMS Am 1091:75).

In Fred Boyd, on the other hand, Reed found an intellectual companion far more versed in Marxist theory than he was himself. Max Eastman, Reed's subsequent editor at *The Masses*, described Boyd as a "shy, dry, colorless, narrow-faced, brilliantly rational little Britisher" (quoted in Homberger, 80). Boyd's insurgent credentials were, in fact, sterling; no less a person than Elizabeth Gurley Flynn would pledge in 1916 "to justify our fellow-worker Boyd in everything that he said" (1). When Reed offered Boyd employment as a research assistant in 1914 (Rosenstone, 174), Boyd brought palpable political depth to Reed's reporting, rounding out Reed's word-pictures with effective documentation. Although only a little correspondence between Boyd and Reed survives in the Harvard archives, Reed gives the reader one of his best portraits of his British friend in "Daughter of the Revolution" (explored in detail in chapter 2). In this short story, a character named Fred, obviously based on Boyd, declares that "when the red day comes, I know which side of the Barricades I shall be on" (6) and concludes that "the revolution became sweeter, broader, from generation to generation" (19). Despite the mild irony Reed builds around these somewhat jingoistic observations, the Fred of "Daughter of the Revolution" proves to be what Reed personally coveted: a partisan listener filled with wise observations.[9]

While the letter to Bryant reveals that Reed fretted about competing assessments of his work, Reed's effort to synthesize politics and artistry in narrative writing anchors its lasting value. The chapters in this book about Reed's writing from Mexico and Europe show that Reed learned how to blend effective scene writing with solid, politically informed documentation. While he may not have been able to reconcile Rogers with Boyd, Reed could fashion prose that could serve both parties. His *Ten Days That Shook the World*, as well as several virtually ignored magazine features, answers both Rogers's call for a large-scale canvas rather than individual snapshots and Boyd's drive to make deeper political sense of the human stories Reed finds everywhere around him. Ironically, a literary establishment that, like Rogers, reflexively prizes the "timeless" cast of fiction over the local color of reporting would not know what to make of Reed for at least another half century.[10] Immersing himself in his vivid journalism, Reed would continue to believe he had failed as a poet.

Reed's marriage to Bryant on November 9, 1916—amply documented by any number of Reed's biographers as well as by Warren Beatty's *Reds*—and his outright opposition to World War I provide the stage for the final one-third of Reed's brief writing career. In Bryant, Reed found a woman he loved with whom he could nurture an occasionally spirited competition for stories. "I think I've found her at last," he wrote to his friend Sally Robinson, describing Louise as "wild and brave and straight, and graceful and lovely to look at, A lover of all adventure of spirit and mind, a realist with the most silver scorn of changelessness and fixity. Refuses to be bound, or to bound [bind]" (bMS Am 1091:140). Emotional rather than sexual commitment marked their relationship, the varying success of which is well documented by their letters to each other. In July 1917, at a moment of despair, Reed writes to his wife: "You see, my dearest lover, I was once a free person. I didn't depend on anything. I was as humanly independent as it was possible to be. Then along came women, and they set out deliberately as they always instinctively do, to break something in me" (bMS Am 1091:72). Yet in his last surviving letter to Louise, written from a Finnish prison four months before his death, Reed writes: "Today I learn that the Finnish government will not try me in court, lack of evidence. I am to be freed! . . . It won't be long now, my dearest, that is, in comparison with what has gone. My only object is to see you again as soon as possible" (bMS Am 1091:117).

The papers and possessions that survive in the Harvard archives sketch some lighter touches to the relationship of Reed and Bryant. Together, they collected copies of the *Dial, Little Review, Nation, New Republic,* and many socialist magazines and pamphlets in English, French, and Spanish. Their well-thumbed copy of the *Little Review* of July 1919 contains episode 10 of James Joyce's *Ulysses,* then available only to subscribers of that magazine. The writers collected buttons, armbands, handbills, and train tickets from their travels together. One of Reed's last poems, "To Louise," was dedicated to the reporter who had joined his life and accompanied him to Petrograd to watch the Bolshevik Revolution sweep Russia:

Let my longing lightly rest
On her flower petal breast,
Till the red dawn set me free,
To be with my sweet,
Ever and forever. (223)

Chapters 4 and 5 of this book detail Reed's opposition to World War I and his reporting of the Bolshevik Revolution in November 1917. This section of the book does so, in part, by examining Reed's reporting for *Metropolitan Magazine* within the context of the magazine's political and aesthetic philosophy. Reed's war opposition devastated his conventional reporting career, even as revolutionary developments in Russia provided his most emotionally connected writing and his most lasting fame. Like many radical writers and labor activists, Reed faced various federal indictments from 1918 to 1920 when he covered these stories, and he had to fight to gain control of his notes and other written records.

By 1917, the United States had curtailed domestic free speech more tightly than ever before in its history. The Espionage Act of June 15, 1917, fined and imprisoned anyone who would willfully obstruct the recruiting of soldiers for the armed forces and prohibited the mailing of any newspaper or magazine that published such sentiments. In Kansas City, Rose Pastor Stokes was sentenced under the act to ten years in prison for writing, in a letter to the *Kansas City Star,* "I am for the people while the government is for the profiteer" (Homberger and Biggart, 102). The Sedition Act of May 16, 1918, prohibited "any disloyal, profane, scurrilous or abusive language about the form of government of the United States or the Constitution, military or naval forces, flag, or the uniform of the army or navy of the United States"; any language that would bring these institutions "into contempt, scorn, contumely, or disrepute" was prohibited on pain of stiff fines and federal imprisonment. The U.S. Postal Service could deny without hearings any mailings it believed fitted these standards, then subsequently disqualify such a magazine from further postal delivery because it had missed a mailing and no longer was a regular publication (Mott, 623–24). As chapters 4 and 5 demonstrate, Reed's publishing outlets were effectively suppressed by these tactics, even as mainstream magazines like *Metropolitan* backed away from him because he broke with their editorial policy. For better or worse, Reed believed that the war in Europe was the private battle of competing capitalist nations; he proclaimed his beliefs and urged working people not to supply the war with their bodies. For those beliefs he was indicted in September 1917, and his papers and notes were seized.

Only a year or so earlier, Reed had been able to command a personal meeting with President Woodrow Wilson in the White House; he had been able to meet with a cabinet member at his official residence to discuss his views on Mexico or on other topics of public interest; he had been able to command his choice of stories—Billy Sunday, Henry Ford, heavyweight champion Jess Willard, labor boss Samuel Gompers. Reed's opinions had been sought and prized. For example, he had started a petition to President Wilson in defense of birth-control activist Margaret Sanger in which Reed argued that "the poor are forced by the religious and moral pressure of society to bear and bear and keep on bearing children; so that there may be a great, hungry flood of unemployed to regulate the labor market" (bMS Am 1091:1156). Now, Reed's country appeared to have turned its back on him. He faced prison for his ideas and found few editors who dared to publish him. Reed's private poetry reflected his reaction:

My country, my America!
. . . .
She called me—my lost one, my first lover.
I love thee no more, love no more, love no more.

(bMS Am 1091:1277)

From this perspective, revolutionary developments in Russia were all the more appealing. Arriving in Petrograd after the March overthrow of the czar, Reed shared his impressions in a letter to his old friend Boardman Robinson, with whom in 1915 he had covered the Eastern Front of World War I and had shared a prison cell in Cholm, Poland. "The old town has changed!" Reed writes of Petrograd. "Joy where there was gloom and gloom where there was joy. We are in the middle of things, and believe me it's thrilling. There is so much dramatic to write that I don't know where to begin—but I'll have a tale to unfold if ever . . . For color and terror and grandeur this makes Mexico look pale" (bMS Am 1091:136; Reed's ellipsis). A month later, less than two weeks before the Bolsheviks seized power, Reed would write again to Robinson: "I have so far learned one lesson, I think; and that is, that as long as this world exists, the working class and the employing class have nothing in common" (1091:137).

Now, Reed was to discover that he had more access to Bolshevik leaders in Russia than he had to the president and cabinet of the United States. The Reed archives contain a set of notes that Reed prepared for a speech at the Second Congress of the Communist International (bMS Am 1091:1228). "Comrade Lenin," Reed wrote to the Bolshevik chairman. "Do you want me to say something about the American Negroes? I am also on the Trade Union Commission and so was late. Reed." Lenin's handwritten response: "Yes, absolutely. I do include you in the list of speakers. Lenin" (Gold, 8–9). Reed surprised Leon Trotsky by his eagerness to return to America to stand trial for sedition with fellow editors of *The Masses*—in part for articles that Reed wrote condemning the war draft. Back in the United States, Reed had time to visit Socialist leader Eugene V. Debs, also under federal indictment for an antiwar speech he made in Canton, Ohio, and to cover the IWW trial in which Big Bill Haywood was sentenced to twenty years in prison. In September, in a speech in the Bronx, New York, Reed openly declared his opposition to U.S. intervention in Russia and was arrested the following morning for sedition (Homberger and Biggart, 103).

When Reed's notes on the Russian Revolution were returned to him in November, Reed began writing *Ten Days That Shook the World* in a rented room above a Greenwich Village restaurant. His old friend and *The Masses* editor Max Eastman recalls meeting Reed in the middle of New York's Sheridan Square, during the period when Reed was holed up writing the book:

> He wrote *Ten Days That Shook the World*—wrote it in another ten days and ten nights or a little more. He was gaunt, unshaven, greasy-skinned, a stark sleepless half-crazy look on his slightly potato-like face—had just come down after a night's work for a cup of coffee. "Max, don't tell anybody where I am. I'm writing the Russian revolution in a book. I've got all the placards and papers up there in a little room and a Russian dictionary, and I'm working all day and all night. I haven't shut my eyes for thirty-six hours. I'll finish the whole thing in two weeks. And I've got the name for it too—*Ten Days That Shook the World*. Goodby, I've got to get some coffee. Don't for God's sake tell anybody where I am." Do you wonder why I emphasize his brains? Not so many feats can be found in American literature to surpass what he did there in those two or three weeks in that little room with those piled-up papers, in a half-known tongue, piled clear up to the ceiling, and a small dog-eared dictionary, and a memory, and a determination to get it right, and a gorgeous imagination to paint it with when he got it. But what I wanted to comment on now was the unqualified, concentrated joy in his mad eyes that morning. He was doing what he was made to do, writing a great book. (78)

Ten Days was published in March 1919. Despite its controversial endorsement of the Bolsheviks, it sold much better than any Reed book ever had. By early 1920, Reed had been placed under two more federal indictments, one for exciting riot and a second for conspiracy to overthrow the government by force. He worked his way to Europe as a steamship stoker, using an assumed name, lived in Moscow in a working-class district, and on his return from Russia in February 1920 was arrested in Norway under the name of James Gormley. At the time of his arrest, Reed was carrying more than $15,000 in diamonds (Rosenstone, *Visions of the Past,* 103), as well as letters from Lenin and Trotsky. Four months in a Finnish prison gave Reed time to outline several novels on stolen bits of waxy paper, but ruined his health. When he was released in July 1920, his normally robust frame had shrunk to a shadow. Back in Russia, Reed became a vocal player in Comintern politics, addressing the Second Congress on July 23. Reed contracted typhus on a trip to Baku at the Congress of the Oppressed People of the East. He died on October 17, 1920, a little less than three years after he had witnessed the birth in Petrograd of what he was sure would be the new revolutionary world. The following day, the *New York Call*—one of the last daily newspapers to publish Reed's work in the United States—broke the news on its front page:

> John Reed, famous American writer and social reformer, is dead of typhus in Moscow, according to a special dispatch from that city to the *New York Call* today. Henry G. Reed, Portland bond man, received word Sunday of the death of his brother, who was born in Portland and lived here for many years. The report, he said, was sent by Louise Bryant Reed, his wife. Details other than the bare announcement that typhus was responsible were not given.

At his death, Reed had broken with his country. Whether he would ever have been willing or able to repair the fracture had he lived beyond the age of thirty-three, it is impossible to say. The United States' entry into World War I had prompted a patriotic revival as strong as that which, later, would follow the 1941 attack on Pearl Harbor or the September 11, 2001, attacks on the Pentagon and World Trade Center. Reed made himself an outspoken dissident and an articulate spokesman for worldwide communism at a time when it was profoundly unpopular for him to do so. That fact is impossible to ignore—then or now. To gain a flavor of the challenge that this writer ultimately represented to mainstream opinion between the years of 1916 and 1920, one needs only to imagine what the equivalent might be after September 2001—an articulate, outspoken U.S. writer who, say, would write passionately and persuasively about radical Islam in the shadow of the World Trade Center's twisted remains.

Reed's last dispatch from Russia was received at the offices of the *Liberator* in New York on the day of his death. Published as "Soviet Russia Now" in the December 1920 and January 1921 issues of the journal, Reed's dispatch is anxious to make the case for the success of the new Bolshevik government, but it also contains generous slices of Reed's trademark description. He tells of waiting at a train junction for a day and a night for a train stranded by a blizzard. "I managed to climb into the box car of an empty military train going West, together with two soldiers, a railroad worker going home on a visit with a large broken clock for his only baggage, and an old peasant woman who carried a cage with a dead parrot in it," Reed writes. "We built a fire on the floor of the car and, except for the smoke, were quite comfortable until the bottom of the car burnt out" (271). Reed travels to Russian towns ravaged by a typhus epidemic, visits factories and party rallies, listens to the voices of everyday Russians. "Now, Russians can stand more cold than anyone else in the world," he observes. "But all through the day came peasants' sleighs driven out of the west, carrying what I first took to be logs of wood, but which turned out to be the stiff bodies of Red soldiers, frozen where they had grown too tired to walk any longer. Three hundred of them, piled like cordwood on the station platform" (271).

In a waiting room at a remote Russian train station, Reed finds a young solder who may have reminded Reed a bit of himself. Surrounded by bright lanterns, red banners, and revolutionary posters, the soldier "was agitating for the Communist Party, pleading with the soldiers to join it." To his listeners, "their flat, bearded faces with an expression of strained attention," the young soldier speaks: "'Long must we still suffer,' he said. 'And perhaps even worse things than we suffer now. . . . But through that darkness we must go, comrades, though all of us die, so that the world of our children will be a happy, free world.' And they cheered, those half-frozen skeletons, waving their hats, their sunken eyes shining" (271–72).

John Reed as Literary Journalist

> The thing that made John Reed's character so unusual in the
> life of our times is that although he was gifted with the power
> to use ideas emotionally and paint them with the colors of
> flame—he *was* a poet, he *was* an idealist—nevertheless he was
> never deluded by the emotional coloring of ideas into ignor-
> ing their real meaning when translated into the terms of ac-
> tion upon the matters of fact.
>
> —Max Eastman, editor of *The Masses*,
> at John Reed's funeral

IN HIS TIME, no one ever thought of defending John Reed's writing. Some
things—like Ty Cobb's hitting or Jack Dempsey's two-fisted fury or John Reed's
genius for the descriptive sentence—simply held true without debate. By the
age of twenty-six, Reed was filing battlefield reports from the 1913 Mexican
Revolution for New York's *Metropolitan Magazine* and was the brightest star in
that magazine's constellation of writers, a fiery grouping that included Joseph
Conrad, Susan Glaspell, D. H. Lawrence, Rudyard Kipling, and George Bernard
Shaw. Already, Reed was one of the most highly paid and widely read journalists in the United States. Walter Lippmann, a Harvard classmate and sometimes
bitter political sparring partner of Reed's, wrote in a letter to Reed in 1914: "It's
kind of embarrassing to tell a fellow you know that he's a genius. You have perfect eyes and your power of telling leaves nothing to be desired. If all history

had been reported as you are doing this, Lord—I say that with Jack Reed reporting begins" (bMS Am 1091:568).

Reed's shrewd character sketches and his sparkling descriptions remain, nearly a century after their writing, fresh and compelling. His writing and reporting would snatch the eye of any present-day New York editor and would move Reed to the head of the class in any of today's creative nonfiction workshops. Yet his writing rarely is read.

One reason for the current neglect of Reed's work stems from holdover genre politics within the literary criticism establishment. Even after several decades of canon reformulation, the chief manner by which a nonfiction writer is read seriously today is if he or she has published some measure of acclaimed fiction. How else to explain why the literary reporting of Stephen Crane, George Orwell, and Ernest Hemingway is anthologized in composition readers and accessible in libraries and bookstores, while arguably better work by John Reed, Dorothy Day, and Richard Harding Davis is not? As Phyllis Frus has noted, this phenomenon depends "on the elevation of literature to a transcendent category . . . and the concomitant linking of nonfiction forms like journalism with the mundane world of factuality, thereby defining them as only of temporal interest" (54). In this hierarchy, prose nonfiction writers are ranked by the relative excellence of their fiction. A comparable absurdity would emerge if, say, novelists were ranked by their ability to write poetry or if scholars felt free to dismiss Wallace Stevens or Walt Whitman because they had never written a great novel.

Another reason for the relative neglect of Reed's writing stems from his personal and political notoriety. As a cofounder of the American Communist Party and as one of only four Americans to be buried in front of the Soviet Kremlin, Reed lived a life that demanded social and political response, not detached appreciation. Ironically, in the present era, when literary critics generally have turned from formal studies of artistic technique to more socially implicated critique, new critical work on Reed might benefit, at least initially, from an unprecedented dose of old-fashioned close reading. By understanding Reed's meticulous craft, contemporary readers might open a new pathway toward the meaning of his narratives. Reed's work always will implicate itself socially; indeed, his historical presence during the era of the cold war loomed so large that few readers, then or now, have bothered to study his writing carefully. My study certainly has no intention to remove Reed from his larger social and political mission. Other chapters will consider Reed fully within his historical context; in fact, chapter 4 produces a long reading of Reed's journalism with a specific cultural study of *Metropolitan Magazine*. But, for a time, I want to concentrate on that most neglected topic: John Reed's writing and artistry.

The Standards of Literary Nonfiction

To place that artistry in context, a contemporary reader might assess how Reed's writing measures up against the best current practice in literary nonfiction and reporting. Although Reed predates Philip Gerard, the contemporary nonfiction writer and professor, by nearly a century, we can turn to Gerard for assistance in analyzing the craft of narratives such as those Reed wrote. In his *Creative Nonfiction: Researching and Crafting the Stories of Real Life,* Gerard describes effective nonfictional craft as accurate diction; skillful turns of phrase; fresh metaphors; lively, scenic presentation; lyricism; and rhythm. Great writing shuns clichés and obvious endings and maintains control over nuance and tone (11). Such narratives will tell a good story and will go beyond immediate research to reflect on larger truths (7–11).

We can also turn to Tom Wolfe, who asserts that effective narrative journalism will construct scenes, relay convincing dialogue, experiment with point of view, and report the status details of everyday life that will characterize individuals and social groups (Wolfe, 31–32). Root and Steinberg, in their analysis of effective nonfictional writing, look for narratives that establish personal presence and self-discovery, that use a flexibility of form, and that are both literary and true (24–27). Finally, veteran journalist Mark Kramer, co-editor of the influential *Literary Journalism* and director of the Neiman Narrative Journalism Program at Harvard University, finds that effective literary journalism is built on immersion reporting; accuracy; a fresh, human, sometimes ironic voice; stylistic grace; structural savvy; and a sure sense of reader reaction (22–33). My own *Matters of Fact: Reading Nonfiction over the Edge* has concentrated on the relationship between the author and subject in narratives that claim to be true. I have explored the manner by which the author positions himself in relation to his subject—that is, whether he or she is willing to reveal the power relationships that accompany the reporting project. Such elements of nonfiction as access to characters and scenes, the use and positioning of direct quotes, and decisions about whether to enter the points of view of one character over another are examples of authorial decisions that produce both stylistic and social effects.[1]

Reed's writing of course predates all the above analyses; yet his literary reportage remains fresh, skillful, and compelling. The hallmarks of Reed's literary style are shrewd character sketches drawn from social and speaking mannerisms; close, lyrical descriptions built on cascading details; a narrative voice capable of both interpretation and irony; and a sense of the textuality of history, which results in his willingness to reveal history's constructedness to his readers. I will demonstrate these concepts first by examining Reed's long profile of the American evangelist Billy Sunday, originally published in the May 1915 edition of *Metropolitan Magazine,* but never reprinted. "Back of Billy Sunday" contains some of Reed's best descriptive and investigative writing and reveals his knack for framing riveting scenes and compelling personal portraits within a larger political context. As a supplement to this reading, I will discuss three other representative narratives: Reed's exposé of conditions in the Paterson jail after the 1913 New Jersey silk mill strike; his harrowing record of "Goutchevo and the Valley of Corpses" on the Eastern Front of World War I; and his coverage of the 1918 sedition trial of the Industrial Workers of the World in the Chicago courtroom of Judge Kenesaw Mountain Landis. Finally, to show the extraordinary way in which Reed reveals the construction of his texts to his reader, I will present another case study—this one a profile that Reed did of William Jennings Bryan for *Collier's.*

Billy Sunday and the Price of Sawdust Salvation: A Case Study

> Billy Sunday, the sweat pouring from his red face, his trembling tense left leg thrust out behind, both arms stretched wide, as he leaned out over the vast crowd like a diver, shouted hoarsely: "Say, it would milk any bishop dry to stand here and preach eight or nine weeks! If you don't believe me, try it." And twenty thousand people, worked up to the point of hysterics by loathsome descriptions, funny stories, and the uncanny, long-drawn "O-o-o-o-oh, come to Jesus!" broke the tension in a mighty shout of laughter. (10)

Reed's "Back of Billy Sunday" is a twelve-thousand-word tour de force that is nearly as raucous and complex as one of Billy Sunday's own sermons. And probably no more than a couple of dozen people have had the opportunity to read it in the last eighty or so years. In "Back of Billy Sunday," Reed watches spellbound as the legendary evangelist mesmerizes two tent-meeting audiences of twenty thousand in a single day. By turns, the journalist Reed leaps to his feet to roar a gospel hymn and shout "Hallelujah!" with the masses and outwits the overprotective Ma Sunday to gain a private audience with her revivalist husband while Sunday enjoys a rubdown from his bodyguard, a former prizefighter. Reed carefully details the capitalist clout that paves the evangelist's sawdust trail as well as the ready cash that flows to Billy and Ma Sunday from goodwill offerings and the relentless hawking of songbooks and religious memorabilia.

Throughout, Reed anticipates the advice of Wolfe and Kramer by creating descriptive scenes to reproduce the color and cadences of the revival campaign. Reed describes for his readers the ballplayer-turned-evangelist, a former player for the Chicago White Stockings, who was said to have converted more than three hundred thousand men and women among the millions he preached to in his lifetime and who served as a model for late-twentieth-century preacher Billy Graham.

> "Sing!" cried Sunday, thrusting his left leg out behind him. "I don't care if you don't know a note from a horse-fly. Sing 'Ring the Bells of Heaven for There's Joy To-day,' and you'll start the heavenly harmonies a-jangling." He was . . . climbing on the pulpit, sliding from one end of the platform to the other, crouching like a runner, leaping, crouching, every movement as graceful as a wolf's. His lithe, springy body beneath his clothes was as beautiful as a Greek runner's. When he wrenched himself into a contortion twenty thousand heads and shoulders involuntarily followed. (71)[2]

Typically, Reed's vivid verbs *(thrusting, climbing, sliding, leaping, crouching)* jostle with bursts of colorful quotes to capture Sunday's style. "I tell you, it was no common sauerkraut, wienerwurst, pretzel and lager beer crowd that was invited that night. It was the real goods," says Sunday of the night that "old Bel" (the Babylonian King Belshazzer) read God's handwriting on the wall. Sometimes writing from stenographer's notes (his own and sometimes others) and sometimes from his keen memory and an instinct for a subject's speaking style, Reed sprinkles his articles with such quotes, using each one to reveal something unique about the subject.

One of the more interesting anecdotes in the Billy Sunday piece concerns Reed's effort to break through Sunday's protective entourage to steal a few words with the minister. Sunday's first line of defense is Homer W. Rodeheaver, his chorister and general chairman, whom Reed captures in an acerbic aside: "Mr. Rodeheaver came in, a short, stocky man with a deep, sanctimonious voice, suspicious eyes, and the kind of clammy hand that won't let yours go" (10). Rodeheaver refuses to allow Reed access to Sunday but defers to Helen "Ma" Sunday, the evangelist's wife, for final permission. Yet to get to Ma Sunday, Reed has to go through the Rev. George W. Bickley, vice chair of the Philadelphia ministerial committee. The interchange between Reed and Bickley shows the author's willingness to relay convincing dialogue and experience with unique point of view (as Wolfe recommends). Reed characterizes himself and recreates swaths of conversation that reveal to the reader both the manner by which the reporter gains his information and his sometimes contentious interplay with the subject of his research.

"[D]oes Sunday's preaching have any particular effect on social and political conditions?" Reed asks Bickley. "I mean, will it help make politics any better in Philadelphia? Will it help the workingmen to get a living wage? Will it help clean up the Third Ward, where 130,000 people live packed in one-room tenements in the worst square mile in the world?"

"It will," Bickley replies. "It will redeem men from the improvidence that comes from drinking. Slums, you know, are largely the fault of those who live there—dirty, disreputable, vicious people" (10–11). The reverend goes on to tell Reed of a mill owner, the son of a millionaire, who was converted by Sunday and gave up a life of "vile women and viler amusements in the low places of Philadelphia."

"Did he raise wages after being converted?" Reed wonders.

"N-o," Bickley admits. " . . . You don't seem to understand; raising wages is a question of economics, not of religion" (11).

When Bickley proves unable to deliver Reed to Billy Sunday, the writer takes up his quest with Ma Sunday herself, whom he deftly characterizes as "scrutinizing us sharply with her alert brown eyes—a good-looking woman of middle age, handsomely dressed, of quick, certain movements, and an air of thorough practicality." Ma Sunday tells Reed that "every one of Mr. Sunday's movements—and mine—are directed by God" and that "there are twenty-five thousand new people in Philadelphia today living according to the dictates of Jesus Christ." At that moment the telephone rings and Ma Sunday excuses herself to take the call in the room's phone booth. Reed eavesdrops: "'Hello!' we heard her say. 'Who is this? Oh, yes, the agents. No, I tell you I wouldn't sell for less than twelve thousand. That's the fourth time in two weeks you've called me up to offer a low figure. . . . No, I told you before I won't sell for less than twelve thousand'" (12).

Following the call, Reed and Ma Sunday engage in a bit more byplay, during which Reed presses his question about whether a redeemed businessman will be more likely to raise workers' wages. Ma replies that a saved worker doesn't need a raise because "[w]hen these men get to be good Christians they take that money they have spent on books and cigarettes and buy loaves of bread for their families" (12). Ma Sunday then excuses herself to meet a delegation of ministers from Richmond, Virginia. As they gather to debate whether Sunday "should preach a Jim Crow heaven" in his upcoming Richmond crusade, Ma Sunday warns the arriving ministers: "Say, don't you gentlemen speak a word to those two reporters [Reed and his illustrator George Bellows]. They're slick" (12).

Reed does, indeed, prove his slickness in the next stage of his quest for Billy Sunday when he befriends Jack Cardiff, "ex-prizefighter, ex-actor, and now physical trainer and rubber-down to the evangelist" (12). Reed simply plies Cardiff with friendly questions and listens to the garrulous bodyguard talk about his conversion from a hard-drinking, $800-a-week fighter. "Yes, I sure gave up something for my Savior," Cardiff tells Reed, "but it was worth it. I've been with Billy now about a year, sparring with him and rubbing him down. He's a great man!" (66). Reed warms up Cardiff by encouraging him to talk about his father—a seventy-five-year-old Irishman who can still go six rounds, smokes everyday, and has drunk enough whiskey to swim in it back to Ireland —then asks Cardiff if he'll take Reed and his illustrator in to see Billy Sunday. "Sure, just wait till I get my shirt on," Cardiff replies, and soon the reporters are in "a front room where, robed in white pajamas, in the midst of an enormous bed, Billy Sunday lay reading a book by the light of an electric lamp over his shoulder" (66). Then follows what readers have come to expect of Reed: what Gerard calls "scenic presentation" laced with Wolfe's "status details." Reed deftly distills the unique components of character:

> Billy lifted his head with the swift movement of an animal and looked at us with eyes in which cordiality, appraisal, doubt, and fear of ridicule chased themselves like wind on water. The upper part of his face was extraordinarily alive and expressive; his mouth was strong, mobile, enthusiastic—trembling into a kind of embarrassed grin. He looked at us as if he thought that perhaps we had come to persecute him. . . . The gray thin hair on top of his head was almost invisible, making his face seem incredibly boyish—for Billy Sunday is fifty-two. Since the sermon, a gray stubble had sprouted on his cheeks and chin, and there were sagging pouches of flesh and tired lines at the corners of his mouth. (66)

With all their differences, Sunday and Reed soon find one area of common ground. At the time of the interview, Reed had just returned from Russia and the Balkans, where he had been covering the Eastern Front of World War I for *Metropolitan Magazine*. "Say," says Sunday, "there's too many bullets flying around over there for me. A fellow's got to have a good deal of courage to go over there now, hasn't he?" Then Sunday's eyes fill with tears as he reflects on the war in brief conversation with Reed, who already was writing articles against U.S. involvement and military conscription. "I think [the war] is the most horrible, awful thing in the whole world," says Sunday, only to be cut off by Ma Sunday, who bustles into the room and shouts, "You villains! Didn't I tell you you couldn't see Billy? What have they been doing, Billy—pumping you?" (66).

What sets apart Reed's profile of Billy Sunday from many lesser articles, both then and now, is his blending of such descriptive scene writing with some rather hard-nosed investigative reporting of the economic structure of the Sunday campaign team. The reporter anticipates Gerard's call for writing and research that seeks out larger trends and deeper truths, that gets beyond simple research to develop meaningful context. Reed also meets Root and Steinberg's call for narratives that are both literary and true. The reporter takes the trouble to learn the identities of the evangelist's Philadelphia backers, a roster of forty-four industrialists and Main Liners that includes retailer John W. Wannemaker and Mrs. Anthony Drexel Biddle, as well as Baldwin Locomotive's Alba B. Johnson. Typically, Reed captures Johnson physically and also reveals for his readers the setting and the ground rules of their interview. "He is a large, well-fed man of slow deliberate movements, a ruthless mouth, and the coldest, most business-like eyes behind his spectacles that I ever saw," says Reed of Johnson. "I did not take stenographic notes [of the interview], but as he talked directly at an open window, behind which his stenographer was concealed, these remarks can doubtless be verified" (11). Reed and Johnson joust over the causes of unemployment and whether Christian business interests are helping or hurting the working man.

Not content simply to relay the interview, which he presents in running dialogue, Reed later visits the headquarters of the labor union that has attempted to organize Johnson's plants, finding that a man with a family makes $13 a week at Baldwin Locomotive and that some workers make as little as $1.50 a day. Many of the workers have been injured by unsafe working conditions at the plant, Reed reports. "Strike after strike, broken with private detectives, armed guards, the blacklist, testify to the workers' hopeless fight for the right to organize" (11). And beyond Johnson's plant, Reed carefully draws out the connections between the Billy Sunday backers and the Penrose-Vare-McNicholl mob that had been exposed by muckraker Lincoln Steffens in his "Philadelphia, Corrupt and Contented."

Why, Reed wonders, would Sunday stand for a citizens' committee that includes the very liquor profiteers against whom he rails in his nightly sermons? What would align a Protestant religious establishment behind a populist street preacher who regularly excoriates main-line churches in his hellfire sermons? Patiently, Reed shows how each group profits from the other: how the ministers and business people guarantee $50,000 in up-front money to the crusade, how the pledge cards signed by each of the two hundred thousand revival converts directs them to attend and financially support their local churches, how a goodwill thank-you offering nets the Billy Sunday crusade more than $100,000 in cash, and how crusade hawkers sell more than a thousand hymnbooks a day to eager attendees at a dollar apiece. The captains of industry give their workers time off to attend the campaigns, Reed reports, constructing scenes inside the tabernacle during which the company attendees are recognized by name and encouraged to engage in friendly competition to see who can sing the loudest and present the most generous gifts (a canvas bag of money, a religious painting, a sixteen-bore shotgun) to Sunday. What the bosses get for their troubles, Reed says, is a workforce specifically instructed by Billy Sunday during the revival crusade to cease union activity and to do their jobs without complaining.

Still, Reed is too good a writer merely to dismiss Billy Sunday in the piece as a one-dimensional villain. Instead, he is after what Kramer describes as "a fresh, human, sometimes ironic voice" (23, 28) built on immersion reporting. Reed culminates the article with a description of a revival service in Sunday's tabernacle that meets the standards for scene construction advanced by Wolfe and Kramer and that quotes long sections of Sunday's sermon. Whether Reed was writing from stenography notes or simply relying on his memory and sense of Sunday's style, the sermon reproductions are extraordinary. They reveal that Reed really listened to the evangelist, that he was able to evoke the imagery and cadences that made the sermons successful, and that his own emotions were swayed rather powerfully by the strength of Sunday's appeal. A relatively long quote will demonstrate:

> He strode up and down the platform for a minute, walking quickly and more quickly. Suddenly he wheeled and shot his arm out at the people. "My text tonight," he cried, in a high, harsh, tense voice, is "Woman, is it well with thee? Is it well with thy husband? Is it well with the child?" He snapped off his voice, but held his arm extended like a menace. There was not a sound in the huge auditorium. "Could it be well with you if the police were hunting for you?" He let his voice drop, then suddenly shook both fists above his head and lifted his right knee almost up to his chin, roaring: "Then how could it be well with thee if the powers of Heaven are against you? I tell you, it don't make a difference what you've done if you repent! I tell you, it don't make any difference whether you're ignorant or not if you don't repent! You'll go down to flaming hell to fry on the coals forever. . . . This is the last chance for Philadelphia! This is the last chance for Philadelphia! Repent or you are lost!" He kneeled on top of the pulpit and lifted his hands above them. "If you want your sin"—his voice dropped again—"well, you can just take your devil and go to the devil with him! Huh," he said, grinning, and then shouted: "O-o-o-o-oh men and women, don't let God go! Just let me tell you, you be good and scared of God." (70)

Sunday tells the story of a prideful young "scotchman" who had been raised with religious education and wealth but turns out to be an atheist and refuses Sunday's personal call to salvation ("You can't convince me. There is no God").

Years later, the evangelist recounts, the man was dying of "loathsome disease," his body "a mass of putrefaction. His nose had rotted away. Diseased matter was oozing from his eyes. . . . He recognized me, and he said, 'Billy you were right. I want you to introduce me to Christ.'"

Sunday then slides across the stage like a ballplayer hurtling into second base, snarling, bawling, screaming. "It's too late, Philadelphia! . . . Why do you swell up like poisoned pups?" he howls at the clergyman's bench. "Don't you know that when you sneer at revivals you spit in the face of God, that you jab your hands in the bloody palms and feet and side of Jesus Christ?" (70–71). In the midst of the sermon, Sunday suddenly commands the audience to sing: here, says Reed, "the swinging emotional unity of the great crowd intoxicated one—as mob excitement always does. We found ourselves roaring gospel hymns with the best of them. 'Hallelujah!' cried voices all over the tabernacle. Women fainted here and there and were carried out" (71).

After a riveting rendition of Belshazzar's last feast ("Chariots drawn by fiery-eyed steeds stamped and reared and plunged . . . as thousands of lords and ladies, dressed in the glories of that Assyrian age, came to the banquet"), suddenly Sunday shook the crowd, Reed says, "by a long-drawn bestial howl: 'It's too late, Philadelphia! . . . Turn a polecat loose in the parlor, and see which'll change first. . . . No, you big mutt, go home and look in the looking-glass and say to God, "There's the sinner!"'" Reed, who only two years before had rallied some sixteen thousand Paterson silk workers to stage the historic IWW pageant at Madison Square Garden, is moved by Sunday's power to command his masses of listeners, even if the reporter believes that the evangelist's mission is mistaken. No doubt Reed can identify Sunday's charisma with his own leading of the Harvard student cheering section. And only two years after the Sunday campaign, Reed would take the opportunity to watch Vladimir Lenin rally the Second All-Russian Congress of Soviets in Saint Petersburg amid "a thundering wave of cheers" (*Ten Days*, 697).

The reader of "Back of Billy Sunday" will discover many echoes between the descriptions of Sunday and those of perhaps the most famous scene of Reed's writing career: his portrait of Lenin as he "proceed[s] to construct the Socialist order" at the Congress of Soviets: "A short, stocky figure with a big head set down on his shoulders, bald and bulging," says Reed of Lenin. "Little eyes, a snubbish nose, wide generous mouth, and heavy chin; clean-shaven now but already beginning to bristle with the well-known beard of his past and future . . . letting his little winking eyes travel over the crowd as he stood there waiting, apparently oblivious to the long-rolling ovation, which lasted several minutes" (*Ten Days*, 697–98).

If Reed would have to wait those two years until he found a mass move-ment that he believed was worth his own supreme sacrifice, he takes pains to construct for his readers the powerful conclusion of the Billy Sunday campaign: the call from the altar to go down the sawdust trail to salvation. A quote at some length will show Reed's effort to capture emotion through specific human detail:

> "Who's coming to Jesus Christ!" [Sunday] made one leap across the platform, jerked open the trapdoor, and dropped into the little pit. The sermon was over. A dirty old man without a collar stumbled up the aisle with the dazed look of one hypnotized; a little boy about eleven years old followed him, weep-ing bitterly; a tall girl in white furs with a white drawn face staggered after him. Everywhere all over the tremendous hall you could see the Voluntary Church Workers hustling people into the aisle, turning them forward as they went to-ward the exit, climbing over the benches and plucking the shaken ones from their seats and leading them forward. An endless steady trickle of hysterical women, children and men of all conditions and ages poured along the Saw-dust Trail. They flooded into the open space in front of the platform weeping, hardly knowing what they did. Billy leaned down from his pit, keeping up a steady stream of wild, incoherent talk, an exultant smile on his face, the sweat pouring from him. Guided by the church workers they filled up the Glory Benches up front, row after row, their eyes fixed steadily and glowingly upon Billy, moving unconsciously as he moved, bursting into shouts of "Hallelujah!" until there were more than six hundred of them. (72)

The strategy of the scene is one to which Reed will return often in his writ-ing. Beginning with the snapshots of individual men and women that pull the reader into human interaction and emotion, Reed slowly withdraws his writerly eye toward the longer shot that will construct the scene's social significance. Throughout, the narrative is built on vivid action verbs that capture the out-pouring of religious emotion and answer Gerard's call for precise diction: *jerked, dropped, stumbled, leading, weeping, staggered, flooded, bursting.*

Reed believes that Billy Sunday's potentially incendiary populist appeal has been blunted by colluding business interests both inside and outside his campaign organization. Therefore, his article takes pains to unearth the cam-paign's financial backing, to understand its significance, and to reveal its re-sulting contradictions. Sunday is likely to curse the system that promotes child labor, yet he is equally scornful of workers on strike. Sunday believes that the greed of rich men and the envy of poor men are equal sins (10). For his part, Reed does all he can as a writer to bring the preacher to life in his text, to kindle his power and passion, and to understand the Sunday campaign both as the work of an extraordinary individual as well as a deeply entrenched political and economic phenomenon. "Is Billy Sunday sincere? I think he is," Reed concludes. "I do not believe he could put the fire and passion and enthusiasm into his words and actions if he were not sincere. He is generous, even reckless, with his money—he seems to have no idea of its value. Everyone who talks with him loves him. As to the social, economic and political relations of the world about him, I think he is just ignorant, that's all" (66).

The Elements of John Reed's Style

The Construction of Character

Turning from this relatively lengthy examination of one of Reed's texts, I now wish to document specifically four of Reed's notable writing strategies. These strategies can be documented against the evidence of three other articles spanning Reed's career: his coverage in 1913 of jail conditions in Paterson, New Jersey; his account in 1915 of a bloody Serbian battle in World War I; and his record of the 1918 sedition trial in Chicago. These three pieces show how Reed relies on shrewd character sketches drawn from social and speaking mannerisms; on close, lyrical descriptions built on cascading details; on a narrative voice capable of both interpretation and irony; and on his sense of the textuality of history and his willingness to reveal history's constructedness to his readers.

The examples from "Back of Billy Sunday" have already begun to demonstrate Reed's knack for a quick character sketch built on a subject's mannerisms, or what Wolfe calls "status details" (32): for example, Homer W. Rodeheaver's clammy, lingering handshake, Ma Sunday's quick, certain movements, Alba B. Johnson's ruthless mouth, and Billy Sunday's "eyes in which cordiality, appraisal, doubt and fear of ridicule chased themselves like wind on water" (66). The evidence among Reed's manuscripts and typescripts at Harvard's Houghton Library reveals that Reed anticipates Gerard's call for lyricism and rhythm. He constructed his descriptions quite carefully, often prowling over them again and again to achieve exactly the motion and wording for which he was searching. For example, consider the following passage from Reed's "The I.W.W. in Court," wherein Reed sketches one of the more colorful characters of the early twentieth century: Judge Kenesaw Mountain Landis, federal jurist and commissioner of major-league baseball following the Chicago "Black Sox" scandal of 1919. A year before assuming the baseball commissioner's office, Judge Landis presided at the federal sedition trial of members of the IWW, which Reed covered for the *Liberator*, a New York radical monthly. Ninety-three IWW leaders were charged with conspiring to violate the criminal syndicalist laws and subsequently were given federal sentences ranging from four to thirty-eight years (*The Education of John Reed,* 176, editor's note). At the trial, Reed sweeps his eyes across a courtroom bas relief to rest on the federal judge:

> Heroic priests of Israel veil their faces, while Moses elevates the Tables of the Law against a background of clouds and flame. Small on the huge bench sits a wasted man with untidy white hair, an emaciated face in which two burning eyes are set like jewels, parchment skin split by a crack for a month; the face of Andrew Jackson three years dead. This is Judge Kenesaw Mountain Landis, named for a battle—a fighter and a sport, according to his lights, and as just as he knows how to be. . . . Upon this man has devolved the historic role of trying the Social Revolution. He is doing it like a gentleman. Not that he admits the existence of a Social Revolution. (*The Education of John Reed,* 176)

From the evidence in his collected papers, Reed pounded out the passage on an upright manual typewriter, striking over the passages that he wished to edit out with a row of ampersands and inking corrections by hand. In the Judge Landis passage, Reed's hand corrections reveal his extraordinary attention to the rhythm of a sentence. The courtroom detail that begins the scene is improved by economy. Reed's initial phrase, "heroic figures of the priests of Israel draw back and veil their faces," becomes "heroic priests of Israel veil their faces" so as to set up a rhythm for the remainder of the sentence, where "Moses elevates the Tables of the Law against a background of clouds and flame." As Reed turns his attention to Landis, a "wasted little thin-faced man" becomes "a wasted man." Reed seems to be struck by Landis's wrinkled, translucent skin, which reminds the reporter of parchment. Reed works his way through several attempts at the parchment metaphor before he gets his sentence just right. First there is a "parchment-thin face," then an "emaciated face in whose parchment-like skin," then simply "parchment skin split by a crack for a mouth." The revised phrase achieves a subtle dactylic rhythm to punch the words *split, crack,* and *mouth: parch*ment skin *split* by a *crack* for a *mouth.* Reed similarly achieves improved rhythm by changing "like Andrew Jackson three years dead" to "the face of Andrew Jackson three years dead." The sentence, revised four times, thus reads: "Small on the huge bench sits a wasted man with untidy white hair, an emaciated face in which two burning eyes are set like jewels, parchment skin split by a crack for a mouth; the face of Andrew Jackson three years dead" (176). The revisions satisfy Gerard's call for fresh turns of phrase and metaphors, liveliness, and nuance. The passage, in addition to scanning more gracefully, now pits rare value (jewels, parchment) against decay (wasted, untidy, emaciated, burning, dead), thereby to enact the personal struggle that Reed perceives between Judge Landis's rare penchant for simple human kindness against his commitment to a legal system that Reed believes to be corrupt and dying.

Typically, Reed observes the judge with care to draw out significant details for the reader. Reed notes that Landis has dispensed with the "All rise!" ceremony each time he enters the courtroom and that he disdains the wearing of robes in favor of an ordinary business suit. The judge, Reed reports, "often leaves the bench to come down and perch on the step of the jury box" and by judicial decree has placed spittoons by the IWW prisoners' seats "so they can while away the day with a chaw" (177). Moreover, he allows the prisoners to take off their coats, move freely around the courtroom, and read newspapers. Despite the judge's human compassion, Reed notes that Landis stands firm on federal procedure, in one case ruling out (with an irony that Reed appreciates) a piece of IWW evidence because it is "as irrelevant as the Holy Bible" (177). The judge, Reed finally concludes, is part of a much larger economic and governmental structure that has immersed the United States in war. The reporter describes the phenomenon by building from the individual details he sees about him toward a broader social context, just as he did in the Billy Sunday profile:

> And I looked through the great windows and saw, in the windows of the office buildings that ringed us round, the lawyers, the agents, the brokers at their desks, weaving the fabric of this civilization of ours, which drives men to revolt and dream, and then crushes them. From the street came roaring up the ceaseless thunder of Chicago, and a military band went blaring down invisible ways of war. (178–79)

That intermingling of description and social context proves to be a hallmark of Reed's reporting from his first published articles until his death. In 1913, near the beginning of his career as a New York reporter, Reed had been arrested while covering a silk workers' strike in Paterson, New Jersey, and used the experience to write two freelance articles. One piece concentrated on his arrest and was published as "War in Paterson" in *The Masses,* a radical monthly at which Reed was to become a senior editor. The second, published in *Metropolitan Magazine* as "Sheriff Radcliff's Hotel," was a profile of the Paterson jail and marked Reed's first major breakthrough to the mainstream press. Both articles are fine examples of what Kramer calls immersion reporting. Perhaps because it has been reprinted in several Reed anthologies, the article for *The Masses* has been read more closely; meanwhile, as with the other uncollected articles from Reed's *Metropolitan Magazine* days, "Sheriff Radcliff's Hotel" virtually has been ignored. Yet, Reed's trademark descriptions are everywhere evident in both pieces; and, in the *Metropolitan* piece, Reed manages to pen several characterizations of prisoners that remain starkly effective.

As we saw above, Reed typically starts with his subject's facial features, expands to include other physical characteristics, then relays a snatch of direct quote to bestow on the subject a sense of voice. In each case, Reed searches out the odd detail of appearance or speech that distinguishes the particular subject. For example, one of the Paterson prisoners is a large man who hoards food despite every evidence that it is riddled with maggots. "On the end of the seat sat a giant of a man who held a crutch under his arm," Reed reports. "His thin, stubby face was a ghastly gray, the gray of desperate lines. He gouged out his quarter loaf of bread and thrust the piece of meat in it. After lunch he took it and surreptitiously hid it in his cell, with the pathetic hoarding instinct of a wild animal against the time when he should be hungry" (15). Another prisoner "with loose folds of skin lying in the hollows of his face" finds himself unable to eat the food, pushing away his plate "with a groan. 'I can't,' he said, almost weeping. 'I can't. It sorta takes away my appetite. I been here a month and lost twenty pounds'" (15). Yet another prisoner is the mentally disturbed Billy Mack, who was "rational enough" when he was first jailed on flimsy charges of highway robbery. "I caught a glimpse of him through the bars that divided the two 'sides' —a gaunt man with a big jaw, stalking dreadfully around with two lighted cigarettes in his mouth." To the facial portrait Reed then adds the music of Mack's speech: "He kept up a monotonous deep-voiced shouting day and night, like the bay of bloodhounds," Reed reports. "'Hello, Louisiana! Hello, Jimsie! Hello, Georgiana! Forty-nine! One hundred and sixty-two.' The other prisoners followed him, the high walls echoing with their coarse laughter" (15).

Reed's most disturbing profile in the piece is that of Eddy, a lad of about eighteen the authorities found chained to a post by his father. The town of Paterson jailed Eddy and his brother Ellsie as potential witnesses in the father's abuse trial and kept them incarcerated "because nobody knew what to do with them" (59) after the father was sentenced to six months for cruelty. "Eddy sat upon a bench surrounded by a crowd of laughing prisoners," Reed observes. "They were teasing him. One would say, 'Meat, Eddy, meat!' and he would repeat spasmodically, 'Meat! Meat!' showing his teeth and growling like an animal" (59). Horrified, Reed continues to watch as the prisoners torment the teenager. "Then they would dangle a piece of meat in front of him; with a roar he'd go for it, slavering at the mouth, the lower part of his face twitching and jerking. But he never could catch it, for his feet were flat and twisted in toward each other. He shuffled wildly along, then stopped whimpering." While the other inmates would slap their thighs with delight, Eddy would look "vaguely from one to the other; his face dead-white, browless, chinless, with a curiously earnest expression—baffled but intent, as if he had missed the answer to some terribly important problem" (59).

In his personal portraits, Reed seems to understand almost instinctively a concept that nonfiction theorists have been arriving at only over the last decade or so: that is, readers consuming a story they believe to be true are drawn by the construction of character and their sense that these characters cast a shadow that falls off the printed page. Why else would Reed's readers react so strongly to the plight of an eighteen-year-old prisoner tormented in a cage that he cannot comprehend if not for the readers' sense that a *person*, not simply a character, is suffering these indignities? His editors at *Metropolitan Magazine* were quick to understand that power. In an editorial printed in the same issue of *Metropolitan* as "Sheriff Radcliff's Hotel" (September 1913), Reed's editor Carl Hovey described the magazine's best writing as follows: "wise, temperate, picturesque, human, giving in a most attractive style the essential information. . . . This policy is to present [to *Metropolitan* readers] the real and the vitally interesting" (3). Throughout his career, Reed seemed to understand that his best articles would only be as strong as their human touches and that human touches come from careful observation of details unique to individuals.

Despite this gift, at the beginning of his writing career (as "Sheriff Radcliff's Hotel" demonstrates) Reed could fall into a discourse that made jail inmates or working people into noble (or even ignorant) savages—a stereotype that played into standard reader expectations of the time. But after witnessing the Russian Revolution in 1917 and by the time he covered the IWW trial in 1918, Reed's portrayals of working people had become more mature and even-handed. In any event, Reed's article on the Paterson jail for *Metropolitan* launched a string of successes at the magazine that carried over the next three years. Hardly a month went by without one or two Reed pieces, each one built on the spine of characterization, whereby the reader comes to understand a social situation by the people who inhabit the situation.

Reed's Lyrical Description

Reed was a poet before he was ever a reporter, and although his early verses were marked by a derivatively romantic style, he reached his more mature voice through the careful reading of his senses. At its best, Reed's poetry draws from the same spring as his best prose; he listens, watches, hears, feels, and smells— then finds specific, concrete words to pass on those sensations. He reads people's bodies and finds a context for their actions. One of Reed's best poems, and an insight to his descriptive prose style, is the never-completed three-hundred-line opus "America 1918," which he wrote that year, while traveling in Russia and Norway, as an homage to a nation whose people he loved. Bristling with concrete description and owing an obvious debt to Walt Whitman, the poem also reveals Reed's careful attention to the rhythm of language.

> By my free boyhood in the wide West,
> The powerful sweet river, fish-wheels, log-rafts,
> Ships from behind the sunset, Lascar-manned,
> Chinatown, throbbing with mysterious gongs,
> The blue thunderous Pacific, blaring sunsets,
> Black smoking forests on surf-beaten headlands,
> Lost beaches, camp-fires, wail of hunting cougars . . .
> By the rolling range, and the flat sun-smitten desert,
> Night with coyotes yapping, domed with burst of stars,
> The gray herd moving eastward, towering dust,
> Ropes whistling in slow coils, hats flapping. Yells . . .
> By miles of yellow wheat rippling in the Chinook,
> Orchards forever endless, deep in blooming,
> Green-golden orange groves and snow-peaks looming over . . .
> By raw audacious cities sprung from nothing,
> Brawling and bragging in their careless youth . . .
> I know thee America!   (bMS Am 1091:1277; Reed's ellipses)

It is easy to see a direct connection between the lyrical descriptions of Reed's poetry and a similar use of enumeration in his prose reporting, particularly in "With Gene Debs on The Fourth," an article penned for the *Liberator* in 1918 after Reed visited Eugene V. Debs, Socialist candidate for president and, like Reed, an opponent of World War I. Reed stopped in Debs's hometown of Terre Haute, Indiana, on an eastward train excursion and used the occasion to capture the Indiana heartland:

> Going through that country on the train I can never resist the feeling that after all, *this* is real America. Trim villages, white farmhouses set in trees, fields of tasseled corn; shallow rivers flowing between earthen banks, little rolling hills spotted with lazy cows, bare-legged children; the church spires and graveyards of New England, transported hither by Protestant folk, mellowed and grown more spacious by contact with the South and the West; rural school houses, and everywhere hideous and beloved monuments commemorating the Civil War; locusts jarring in the sycamores, and almost overwhelming fertility rioting in the black earth, steaming in the procreative heat of flat-country summer, and distilling a local sweetness that is distinctively American—sentimental and humorous. (188)

As is common in Reed's best work, the poet never writes for long without casting his eyes toward people and relaying the details of their activity and appearance. In each of the groups that he enumerates in "America 1918," Reed strives to capture particular mannerisms (a swaggering, tobacco-chewing brakeman atop a boxcar or a gold-flush prospector buying his happiness in a barroom) as a means of suggesting the wider social significance of people at work or at play. The strength of a nation or of a piece of writing, Reed suggests by this strategy, derives from the human beings that inhabit it and give it life:

> Fishermen putting out from Astoria in the foggy dawn their double-bowed boats,
> Lean cow-punchers jogging south from Burns, with faces burned leathery and silent,
> Stringy old prospectors trudging behind reluctant pack-horses, across the Nevada alkali,
> Hunters coming out of the brush at night-fall on the brink of the Lewis and Clark canyon,
> Grunting as they slide off their fifty-pound packs and look around for a place to make camp,
> Forest rangers standing on a bald peak and sweeping the wilderness for smoke,
> Big-gloved brakemen walking the top of a swaying freight, spanner in hand, biting off a hunk of plug,
> Lumbermen with spiked boots and timber-hook, riding the broken jam in white water,
> Indians on the street-corner in Pocatello, pulling out chin-whiskers with a pair of tweezers and a pocket-mirror,
> Or down on the Siuslaw, squatting behind their summer lodges listening to Caruso on a two-hundred-dollar phonograph,
> Loud-roaring Alaska miners, smashing looking-glasses, throwing the waiter a five-dollar gold piece for a shot of whiskey and telling him to keep the change,
> Keepers of dance-halls in construction camps, bar-keeps, prostitutes,
> Bums riding the rods, wobblies singing their defiant songs, unafraid of death,
> Card-sharps and real-estate agents, timber-kings, wheat-kings, cattle-kings . . .
> I know ye, Americans!   (bMS Am 1091:1277; Reed's ellipsis)

It is easy to see how Reed built on a similar poetic strategy in the prose piece "The Social Revolution in Court," where he surveys the federal courtroom and describes one by one the defendant "wobblies singing their defiant songs." In a portion of the article collected in *Daughter of the Revolution* and abridged from *The Education of John Reed,* Reed finds that the radical defendants "aren't afraid of anything" and are the kind of men that "the capitalist points to as he drives past some great building they are putting up, or some huge bridge they are throwing over a river" (163). Reed watches as they file into the courtroom, greeting their comrades in the gallery and hailing other friends who are brought in from a holding cell. The reporter shifts to the present tense and introduces each defendant with a short sketch similar to the cadences he establishes in "America 1918." Reed relishes the sound of their names and rolls them off his tongue:

> There goes Big Bill Haywood, with his black Stetson above a face like a scarred mountain; Ralph Chaplin, looking like Jack London in his youth; Reddy Doran, of kindly pugnacious countenance, and mop of bright red hair falling over the green eye-shade he always wears; Harrison George, whose forehead is lined with hard thinking; Sam Scarlett, who might have been a yeoman at Crechy; George Andreytchine, his eyes full of Slav storm; Charley Ashleigh, fastidious, sophisticated, with the expression of a well-bred Puck; Grover Perry, young, stony-faced after the manner of the West; Jim Thompson, John Foss, J. A. MacDonald; Boose, Prancner, Rothfisher, Johanson, Lossiev. (163)[3]

Reed watches the men inside the court rail: reading papers, crowded, rolling up their shirtsleeves, a few stretched out in sleep. He sees "the faces of workers and fighters . . . the faces of orators, of poets, the sensitive and passionate faces of foreigners—but all strong faces, all faces of men inspired, somehow; many scarred, few bitter" (163).

The enumerations of names and characters as well as the specific descriptions that mark Reed's writing apparently result from careful preparation. From the evidence of his work papers, Reed relied on copious note taking and journaling to summon the details that made his writing most descriptive. He immersed himself in the lives of his characters and strove for accuracy and truth (Kramer, 22–23; Root and Steinberg, 26). An excellent example is his Mexican notebooks, which Reed relied on as source material for the finished articles that he sent back to *Metropolitan Magazine* in 1913 from the Mexican Revolution. Each evening, after riding long days on horseback or in a primitive buggy across the Mexican outback, Reed took the time to enter a handwritten page or two in his journal. One example, as nearly as it can be deciphered from the tattered notes that survive, shows how carefully Reed fashioned the source material that he would then nurse through several more rewrites before committing to the magazine. As usual, even in his initial notes, he concentrates on specific, active verbs and vivid metaphors:

The sun went down suddenly behind the western mountains that crinkled so lightly across the sky ahead of us, and the sky became a sail of watered silk stained with the most startling blood-fire, and the mountains were curtains of deep blue velvet. The stars swarmed out through the branches of a giant alamo tree like a shower of diamonds. And we rode along through the darkness odorous with sage, Mac beating the mules and cursing them after the fashion of the natives. (bMS Am 1091:1316)

In a finished piece like "Sheriff Radcliff's Hotel," Reed's careful preparation and eye for scene pays off with a passage such as the one he pens of a race between a champion cockroach named Deputy, owned by Harvey, an enormous inmate, and any challenger cockroach that the other inmates could find. First, Reed creates a specific setting: a long, narrow corridor that separates a double tier of cells from a towering brick wall. A table in the corridor can hold about sixty prisoners. Above them is a "small skylight, through which thin light filtered down upon the center of the table. Both ends lay in gloom, illuminated only by gas jets" (14). Reed then turns his attention to tactile, auditory, and olfactory details before introducing characters to the sketch. "Steam pipes along the wall snapped with damp heat. Each black, barred cell gave out a foul reek . . . [the] tiny skylight was the only ventilation" (14). Within this forbidding setting, the inmate Harvey "would produce 'Deputy' from his cigar box; another roach would be caught, and the course marked out with pencil on the table. What excited swearing, what prodding with pencils, what guiding of steeds with dirty thumbs!" reports Reed. "Then when Deputy romped home a winner, as he invariably did, a wonderfully profane battle of words followed" (16). Harvey's masterful cursing was surpassed only by an inmate dubbed Pork Chops, possessed of an inventively profane vocabulary and a "genius at lightning calculation. When I played checkers with him he would say, 'I'll give you thirteen moves.' And thirteen moves was all I could make before he won the game" (16).

A more tragic piece that also builds from Reed's careful reporting is "Goutchevo and the Valley of Corpses," his account of the Serbs' battle against the Austrians on the Eastern Front of World War I. First published in *Metropolitan Magazine* in October 1915 under the title "At the Serbian Front," the article was among many collected in Reed's book *The War in Eastern Europe;* it was also published by the *World,* the New York newspaper, on April 22, 1917, as "The Most Tragic Incident I Saw in the War." "Goutchevo and the Valley of Corpses" benefits from what I have called Reed's strategy of cascading detail; he builds a series of sensory impressions that verges on redundancy, but saves itself by interlocking the impressions in a portrait of wider social significance.[4] In the article, Reed travels on horseback with a genial young Serbian captain from Loznitza, Serbia, to the summit of Goutchevo Mountain. The mountain summit was the site of a fifty-four-day battle that ended with a Serbian retreat. Once the Austrians captured the summit, at the cost of an estimated ten thousand lives on both sides, they simply abandoned their stronghold. The battle for Reed thus epitomizes the tremendous waste that was World War I. To him, the "Great War" was fought by working people in the service of state interests they little understood and from which they never profited.

Throughout the piece, Reed contrasts the sparkling natural beauty of the Serbian mountains against the horror of human-generated conflict. In the high valley fed by the waters of the Emin River, Reed finds "the white houses of a village [lying] half hidden in a sea of riotous plum blossoms," but the beauty of the countryside soon is marred by the mourning wails of women weeping for their dead (365). Reed and the young captain spur forward through golden silence and humming bees as the wailing fades in the distance. "The path wound upward along the flank of the mountain and through a leaping stream which we waded," Reed recounts. "Here it ceased; but on the other side the deeply scored hillside rose almost straight for five hundred feet. We dismounted and led the stumbling, winded mountain horses, zigzagging from shelf to shelf of earth and crumbling rock" (365). Brass cartridge shells, trace leathers, bits of Serbian uniforms, and the wheels of shattered cannon timbers litter the forest floor as Reed and his companion approach the battle zone. There, "half the forest lifted gaunt, broken spikes where the vicious hail of bullets had torn off their tops—and then came trees naked of branches." At the top of the mountain are two trenches, only twenty yards apart, where thousands of Serbians and Austrians did battle and "where now nothing but jagged stumps studded with glistening lead remained" (367).

A lengthy quote is necessary to do justice to Reed's descriptive strategy, which is as harrowing a piece of literary journalism as any ever penned. In its layers of specifics, it prefigures Joan Didion's description in *Salvador* of the Puerto del Diablo body dump outside San Salvador. In both narratives, the reporters are forced to walk through what Didion called "what is left of the bodies, pecked and maggoty masses of flesh, bone, hair" (21). In Reed's case, the scene includes eerie packs of snarling wild dogs and bodies leaching into blood-sodden earth.

> Here and there both trenches merged into immense pits, forty feet around and fifty feet deep, where the enemy had undermined and dynamited them. The ground between was humped into irregular piles of earth. Looking closer, we saw a ghastly thing: from these little mounds protruded pieces of uniform, skulls with draggled hair, upon which shreds of flesh still hung; white bones

with rotting hands at the end, bloody bones sticking from boots such as soldiers wear. An awful smell hung over the place. Bands of half-wild dogs slunk at the end of the forest, and far away we could see two tearing at something that lay half-covered on the ground. Without a word the captain pulled out his revolver and shot. One dog staggered and fell thrashing, then lay still—the other fled howling into the trees; and instantly from the depths of the wood all around came a wolfish, eerie howling in answer, dying away along the edge of the battle-field for miles. We walked on the dead, so thick were they—sometimes our feet sank through into pits of rotting flesh, crunching bones. Little holes opened suddenly, leading deep down and swarming with gray maggots. Most of the bodies were covered only with a film of earth, partly washed away by the rain—many were not buried at all. Piles of Austrians lay as they had fallen in desperate charge, heaped along the ground in attitudes of terrible action. Serbians were among them. In one place the half-eaten skeletons of an Austrian and a Serbian were entangled, their arms and legs wrapped about each other in a death-grip that even now could not be loosened. (367–68)

The powerful images in the scene need no amplification, and Reed's writing remains relatively restrained, considering its subject. As the scene progresses, he adopts layers of description, moving from half-focused glimpses of human carnage closer and closer until he fixes on the picture of the Austrian-Serbian death grip that he extends into a metaphor for the entire war. The soundtrack for the scene comes from the bands of feral dogs that snarl and tear at flesh and whose howls echo across the death fields. Reed's descriptions of half-buried bodies, here amassed in cascading description, were to recur throughout his World War I coverage, as we shall see in a later chapter when we turn to the publication and reception of Reed's war writing.

While he is descending the peaks of Goutchevo, Reed returns to the juxtaposition of war's horror and nature's beauty and draws out an image that both extends to the entire piece its social significance and meets Gerard's criteria for reflective significance and deeper truths (7–11). If the paradigm of war is ignorant armies clashing without a sense of why they fight or why they need the land for which they die, Reed suggests that such human folly is capable of poisoning the land that might otherwise offer human beings some hope for redemption. An excellent example of Reed's cascading description comes as mountain streams splash down toward the valleys. Adding layer on layer *(through, between, under)*, Reed imagines the waters dousing an unspoiled Eden with human evil. "We rode through fruit orchards heavy with blossoms, between great forests of oaks and beeches and blooming chestnuts; under high wooded hills, whose slopes broke into a hundred rippling mountain meadows that caught the sun like silk," says Reed of his return from Goutchevo with the young captain. "Everywhere springs poured from the hollows, and clear streams leaped down canyons choked with verdure" (368). The mountain springs of Goutchevo, tainted by decaying human flesh, flow down the mountainside to spoil the land's fertility. "All of this part of Serbia was watered by the springs of Goutchevo, and on the other side they flowed into the Drina, thence into the Save and the Danube," Reed reports, "through lands where millions of people drank and washed and fished in them. To the Black Sea flowed the poison of Goutchevo" (368).

Reed's Narrative Voice

John Reed, the writer, is a constant companion to the readers of his descriptive prose. In virtually every scene, we accompany Reed as he watches the events around him and comments on their significance. We eavesdrop as he talks to his subjects, often hearing the exact questions he asks and the responses that the questions elicit. In part, Reed merely is reflecting the journalistic customs of his time; today's practice of customarily effacing the reporter's point of view was not the standard in journalism then. Yet Reed went further in his writing, not only offering himself as a central intelligence or guide for the reader, but often constructing a gently ironic persona who does not always interpret accurately everything he sees. I develop this theme more deeply in the next chapter when I travel to the borderlands of Reed's fictional and nonfictional tales. For now, I examine how the construction of persona enhances the writer's ability to add life and voice to his scenes. I believe that Reed skillfully predates Kramer's call for writers who can fashion an intimate voice—fresh, informal, frank, human, and ironic—to guide the reader (22, 28).

In the Paterson jail narrative, as in his behind-the-scenes coverage of Billy Sunday, Reed uses his own character and immersion journalism to provide readers with access to a normally forbidden world—one that they otherwise could not see. In this case, Reed engineered his own arrest so as to gain the jail material that later became the articles "War in Paterson," in *The Masses,* and "Sheriff Radcliff's Hotel," in *Metropolitan.* Max Eastman, Reed's editor at *The Masses,* recalled in a memoir that Reed hectored a police officer until the officer agreed to arrest him. Eastman quoted the officer as follows: "So he moves into the county jail. But he no more than sits down there than he starts writing articles . . . describing how there's vermin all over the place and decayed vegetables and spoiled meat in the soup, and insects in the salt and pepper boxes" (71). The more direct description of Reed's arrest is contained in *The Masses* article, which Reed opens with the silk-mill strikers gathering for an early-morning demonstration under a light rain. A squadron of police soon arrives and orders everyone off the street. Reed takes shelter on the porch of a house, but when a police officer learns that it is not Reed's house, he tells him to leave. Reed refuses to go and challenges the officer to arrest him if he is committing a crime. This sets up a verbal confrontation:

> "I've got your number," said I sweetly. "Now will you tell me your name?"
> "Yes," he bellowed, "an I got *your* number! I'll arrest you." He took me by the arm and marched me up the street. (41)

The police officer, who in fact is named McCormack, continues to curse and threaten Reed, but the reporter insists, with some irony, that for his part he "returned airy persiflage" to the threats. As McCormack continues the verbal abuse, he is joined by two other policemen, who "supplied fresh epithets. I soon found them repeating themselves, however, and told them so." Reed continues, "'I had to come all the way to Paterson to put one over on a cop!' I said. Eureka! They had at last found a crime! When I was arraigned in the Recorder's Court that remark of mine was the charge against me!" (41).

Reed concentrates on the IWW political inmates in the jail scenes of his *Masses* piece, including William D. "Big Bill" Haywood, one of the IWW's founders, whose "massive, rugged face, seamed and scarred like a mountain, and as calm, radiated strength" (44). Of the convicted room (quarters where prisoners were held after trial), which was to become the focus of the *Metropolitan Magazine* piece, Reed provides only a brief physical description in *The Masses,* and he remarks, "I shan't attempt to describe the horrors I saw in that room" (45). Reed saved those horrors, of course, for a much wider audience and characterized himself playing checkers and racing cockroaches with the inmates so as to give his reporting an authority and immediacy it otherwise would not have had.

One of the initial scenes of the *Metropolitan* version, which is subtitled "What One Man Saw in a County Jail," relays the reception that Reed met when he entered the "convicted room" on the other side of the jail from many of the political detainees. His description relies on the reader's seeing him as an outsider who ultimately earns a welcome from the other prisoners. "Then a voice bellowed my name and I passed into the 'sentenced' room. The sour stench of the place was like a blow," Reed reports. "Between groups of men I passed—all sorts of men, in the common mediocrity of prison clothes. They fell silent, instinctively hostile, as dogs are to a strange dog" (14). The men remain hostile until Reed defies jail policy and keeps his hat on during the dinner hour. "'Take off your hat,' hissed a dozen warningly, glancing furtively at where the keeper sat enthroned. 'You can't wear a hat at table!' I was no longer a stranger," says Reed to his readers, thereby asserting his ability to get the inside story of inmate life. "I wore the common uniform. I was one of them, stamped with the insignia of the terrible, incomprehensible law" (14).

Reed uses his new-found status to befriend—and to relay the stories of—two older vagrants in the jail: Charlie and Willy. Discharged from a hospital despite a badly wounded leg and trying to raise ten cents for a flophouse bed, Charlie was arrested for panhandling and was sentenced to six months in jail. He unwraps his bandages for Reed to see, pokes at four badly festering sores on his feet, then wipes his hands on "the common towel" that Reed notes sardonically is shared by forty men. Willy, a "gentle philosopher with drooping mustache and a bald head surrounded with a fringe of white hair," lived in the New Jersey woods and built rustic furniture that he carried on his back into Paterson to sell. One winter night, Reed reports, Willy got drunk, passed out in the snow, and froze his hands and feet. Reed finds the prisoner, somehow convicted of housebreaking for a crime he doesn't remember, to be pale and weakened by jail life, hardly able to walk and unable to resume his trade because his frostbitten hands no longer work.

Presented with these portraits of suffering, Reed writes a short, understated paragraph that reveals how he relies on his own character to measure an appropriate response. Listening to Willy recount his troubles, Reed says, "I lay there in the upper bunk of the cell while his slow, deliberate talk floated up with the strong fumes of his pipe, and all the bugs in the world paraded across the ceiling above my head" (15). The author here relies on what Root and Steinberg describe as "personal presence" and "self-discovery" (xxiv–xxv) to lead the reader toward a flash of understanding.[5]

At the IWW trial in Chicago, Reed again builds a narrative from the manner by which he processes information: first surveying the courtroom friezes of the signing of the Magna Carta and Moses's hoisting of the Ten Commandments, then describing Judge Landis and the defendants in the case, and finally listening carefully as, one by one, the Wobbly defendants tell their stories to the judge. In the evidence portion, the narrative assumes the cadences of a testimonial: "I heard Frank Rogers, a youth grown black and bitter, with eyes full of vengeance, tell briefly and drily of the Speculator mine fire, and how hundreds of men burned to death because the company would not put doors in the bulkheads" (184). The IWW testimony grows in waves: an attempted hanging of a labor organizer in Montana by company vigilantes, the tar-and-feathering of workers in Oklahoma, the killing of five workers outside Seattle. "I sat for the better part of two days listening to A. S. Embree telling over again the astounding narrative of the Arizona deportations," says Reed, eventually finding a visual detail to buttress his testimony, "and as I listened, looked at photographs of the miners being marched across the arid country, between rows of men who carried rifles in the hollow of their arms, and wore white handkerchiefs about their wrists" (184).

Finally, says Reed, "I sat listening to a very simple fellow named Eggel." Eggel recounts how vigilantes hunted IWW farmhands in South Dakota, beat them with two-by-fours notched with criss-crossed ridges, and tore up their union cards. In a subtle echo to the article's opening image of Moses elevating the tables of the law above the chosen people, Reed advises his readers to "listen to the scriptural simplicity" of Eggel's story. "There's no use tearing that card up, we can get duplicates," the union worker tells a vigilante. "Well," the deputy says, "we can tear the duplicates up too." The worker replies: "Yes, but you can't tear it out of my heart" (185).

Reed's tactic in each of the articles—as well as in the Goutchevo Mountain piece during which he hears the bones of the deceased "crunch" under his feet—is to present himself as a mediating presence in the text, a conduit through which his descriptions assume a human dimension. The shortcomings of such a strategy might be that it reveals where Reed's sympathies lie and thus might rob the pieces of some measure of credibility if the reader believes Reed's judgment to be skewed. But the strength of Reed's policy perhaps outweighs the disadvantages in that many readers tend naturally to identify with a first-person narrator who proves to be a generous and literate companion—particularly when Reed remembers to show flashes of humor and self-effacement, as when he admits that Billy Sunday's hallelujahs brought him shouting to his feet or that he richly enjoyed hectoring the Paterson police or that he responded warmly despite his misgivings at Judge Landis's canny, short-sleeved style. The narrative presence that the reporter constructs for himself proves to be an effective part of Reed's overall writing strategy.

Reed and the Making of History

The fourth characteristic of Reed's literary reporting may be the one in which he was most ahead of his time. To a degree that anticipated some of the more adventurous nonfiction writers of the latter half of the twentieth century, Reed seems willing to unmask the manner by which the textuality of history destabilizes its presence. We have already seen in "Back of Billy Sunday" how Reed makes the effort he took to gain access to Billy Sunday an important part of his story. Reed also reveals in "Back of Billy Sunday" how he eavesdropped on the telephone call between Ma Sunday and the land broker and raises the question of whether he will be able to quote the comments of industrialist Alba B. Johnson accurately enough to match the record taken by Johnson's stenographer hiding outside the room. In each case, Reed invites his readers to understand the manner by which their access to information depends on a complicated relationship between the reporter and his subjects and how differently history might read depending on who does the telling. These decisions reveal what I mean (*Matters of Fact*, 135) when I call for "implicated" readings that examine the manner by which a writer constructs a nonfictional account. Readers are expected to see how the historical record will vary depending on the writer's access to information, the way that information is arranged and presented, and the social positioning of the author. In this way, Reed deepens the historical presence he constructs in his narratives beyond the stylistic strategy outlined in the previous section. Here, the reporter deliberately presents history as an intersubjective transaction and attempts to make visible his own role in that transaction.[6]

One example is from Reed's "The I.W.W. Trial in Chicago," during which he charges that the daily press "has hushed up or perverted utterly the story of the I.W.W. trial." Were the trial to be reported openly, Reed asserts, "publicity could not help but win the case for the Wobblies," and so "newspapers ignore the most dramatic legal battle since Dred Scott [the 1857 Supreme Court case that upheld slavery]—one whose implications are as serious" (184). Were Reed to stop there, his tactics could be dismissed as the carping of a writer who believes the real story is being wrongly ignored by editors to whom he has no access. But Reed goes further in the article to show that history is inescapably intertwined with ideology; that is, that the social allegiance of the teller provides the context through which history is created.[7] At the end of the piece, in a section anthologized only in *Daughter of the Revolution and Other Stories*, Reed dramatizes that concept by imagining how the IWW trial would be different were the working classes in control of the narrative rather than what he believes are the corporate interests represented by Judge Landis and the federal prosecutors. In his self-characterization, he reveals to the reader that he has recently returned from Russia, where he had witnessed the creation of the Bolshevik state. In the Chicago courtroom, Reed allows his mind to wander toward a new, and substantially different, narrative:

> There could not be gathered together in America one hundred and one men more fit to stand for the Social Revolution. People going into that courtroom say, "It's more like a convention than a trial!" To me, fresh from Russia, the

scene was strangely familiar. For a long time I was puzzled at the feeling of having witnessed it all before; suddenly it flashed upon me. The I.W.W. trial in the Federal courtroom of Chicago looked like a meeting of the Central Executive Committee of the All-Russian Soviets of Workers Deputies in Petrograd! I could not get it into my head that these men were on trial. They were not at all cringing, or frightened, but confident, interested, humanly understanding . . . like the Bolshevik Revolutionary Tribunal. . . . For a moment it seemed to me that I was watching the Central Committee of the American Soviets trying Judge Landis for—well, say counter-revolution. (163–64; Reed's ellipses)

The point that Reed is reaching for here stems only in part from his contention that the IWW defendants are more law-abiding than a federal judicial system that, Reed believes, effaces its violence behind institutional power. Within a competing ideology, Landis's judgment of the IWW defendants could be read as their judging the judge in an emerging class struggle. Not only does Reed reveal his own political ideology, but he reveals how his underlying perspective gains the power to construct meaning and invites the reader to react to that construction.

Similarly, in a remarkable passage near the end of "Sheriff Radcliff's Hotel," Reed shows how the master narrative of American law infects those members of society who find themselves on the wrong side of the bars. The prisoners, Reed asserts, lose their power to transform themselves when they are swallowed by the story that the ruling interests would make out of them. "If imprisonment in Paterson jail filled men with hate, we might have some hope of change," says Reed, "for anything that men hate will sooner or later have to go. But it doesn't. It simply saps their strength and their intelligence" (60). The result, says Reed, is that the prisoners accept their roles in the history written for them; they are convinced they are wrong and the law is right. "They believed in a God and feared him—the Law, whose ways are past human understanding and whose decrees are merciless and unalterable. . . . Society greets them coldly and suspiciously. 'You have done wrong,' says Society. 'You are guilty until you prove yourself innocent. We cannot shake your hand until you gain respectability'" (60).

The endings of Reed's two Paterson jail narratives reveal how nimbly Reed can construct his own historical presence to achieve the narrative effect he desires. In "War in Paterson," it suits Reed's interests to convince his readers that he has been personally accepted by the IWW radicals who were in jail with him. In reality, Reed had been mistaken for a police informant when he entered the Paterson jail: he had been shunned by the radical inmates until he was personally greeted by Big Bill Haywood (Rosenstone, 120–21). The reporter suppressed that information in "War in Paterson," ending the piece with a scene similar to ones we will find in *Insurgent Mexico*—as much about Reed's passage into political manhood as about the political events he is describing. "When it came time for me to go out I said good-by to all those gentle, alert, brave men, ennobled by something greater than themselves. *They* were the strike—not Bill Haywood, not Gurley Flynn, not any other individual," Reed recounts. "And as I passed out through the front room they crowded around me again, patting my sleeve and my hand, friendly, warm-hearted, trusting, eloquent. . . . 'You go out,' they said softly. 'That's nice. Glad you go out. Pretty soon we go out. Then we go back on picket line" (46–47).

Contrary to the few scholarly readers of Reed's early writing (Stuart; Duke), I find *Metropolitan Magazine*'s "Sheriff Radcliff's Hotel" to be the superior ending journalistically. Rather than confining himself rather narcissistically to his own release and political coming-of-age, Reed in the *Metropolitan* piece shifts to the third person, exploring the effects of the jail experience on a prisoner and showing how a master narrative can control the historical experience of those who submit to it. "And so, when he takes his final bath, and puts on his shabby clothes and walks out into the sunlight, he stands for a moment on the corner, watching the happy, free people go about their business." Reed imagines the released prisoner cut out of the "wonderful machinery" that society reserves for the respectable—churches, city halls, theaters, automobiles— and forced to live on the margin of a life controlled by others. "What place in all this is there for a man who has lived six months in Paterson jail?" he asks. "So he turns away from a system which has no place for the sick men it manufactures and goes back to the society of panhandlers and petty criminals, who, being weak, understand weakness" (60).

Reed and "the Great Commoner" Make History: A Case Study of Textual Implication

A fascinating aspect of narrative nonfiction is the complex and sometimes troubled relationship that can develop between author and character. Unlike the characters of fiction—who reside more or less in the universe of an author's imagination—characters in nonfiction cast shadows and talk back. They sometimes contest their authors over matters of fact and interpretation, especially if they perceive that the narratives are likely to assume some public sway over their lives outside the texts. Although very little work had been done in the theory of nonfictional narrative when Reed wrote, he seemed instinctively to understand the way nonfiction implicates its writers and readers; moreover—as I have already shown—he proves willing to reveal that contest over meaning.

An extended case study of this sort of uneasy relationship between a non-fiction author and his character is drawn from the John Reed archives at Harvard in a folio entitled "What Mr. Bryan Said." The folio material details a series of strained negotiations between Reed and William Jennings Bryan, "the Great Commoner." Recently returned from covering the Eastern Front of World War I and a little more than a year away from his *Ten Days That Shook the World* reporting of the Bolshevik Revolution, Reed traveled for *Collier's* magazine to Palatka, Florida, in February 1916 to interview Bryan, who six months earlier had quit his job as Woodrow Wilson's secretary of state because he disagreed with Wilson's response to Germany following the sinking of the *Lusitania* (Rosenstone, 242).

Barred from the Western Front of World War I for firing a German gun in the general direction of the French front, Reed was writing domestic pieces during most of 1916, producing long profiles of Henry Ford, Billy Sunday, boxer Jess Willard, and labor organizer Samuel Gompers, as well as Bryan. None of these articles, several of which remain startlingly contemporary, has appeared in any subsequent John Reed collection. To interview Bryan, Reed traveled by train through the Deep South, writing to his lover Louise Bryant: "All the whites in this section look mean and cruel and vain. Have you ever seen Jim Crow cars, colored waiting rooms in stations, etc.? I had seen them before, so they don't shake me as much as they did. Just make me feel sick. That's the south. I have no wish now but to see Bryan, get through with it and get back to my dearest old harp" (bMS Am 1091:25).

"What Mr. Bryan Said" reveals a dispute between Reed and Bryan over quotes that Reed attributed to the former secretary of state following their meeting in Florida. Out of deference to Bryan, Reed did something that most editors would warn reporters not to do: he submitted typed transcripts of Bryan's quotes for the former secretary's approval before *Collier's* published the article, which appeared in the May 20, 1916, edition as "Bryan on Tour." The resulting interchange reveals strained feelings between the men. Bryan was disturbed that Reed was prepared to quote him so liberally, especially because the reporter had gained some of the material while Bryan's guard was down during a boating trip on the Saint Johns River. In a Feb. 18, 1916, letter contained in the Houghton archives, Bryan wrote the journalist:

> I am returning corrected interview and have only stricken out that part which you understood was not for publication. It is not entirely accurate, but there is no reason for correcting it because it is not to be used. I am surprised that you should reduce it to writing. . . . I gave this interview to you at your request and

gave you more time and material than I have given anyone else and you understood from the beginning that only those subjects were to be treated which I was willing to discuss. (bMS Am 1091:234)

For his part, Reed apparently had not anticipated Bryan's taking such umbrage at the quotes. The "Bryan on Tour" typescripts at the Houghton Library show that Reed had written the article for *Collier's* before he contacted Bryan about the quotes. When Bryan objected to the quotes, Reed made most of the resulting last-minute changes to the typescript by hand before he shipped it off to his magazine publishers; on four leaves, the changes were so great that Reed had to retype the pages entirely (bMS Am 1091:1161).

Reed's profile of the Great Commoner, nearly ten thousand words long, had been built on just the sort of close status detail, extended dialogue, and detailed scene construction that Tom Wolfe would claim to have pioneered fifty years later in his New Journalism. Beginning with an intimate portrayal of Bryan's residence in Washington, D.C., before he resigned as secretary of state, continuing with a finely drawn scene of Bryan's oratorical skill, and culminating with the boating expedition on the "wide, sluggish" (40) Saint Johns River, Reed's literary strategy in "Bryan on Tour" depended on exactly the type of unguarded revelations that his subject was desperate to forestall. Although Reed's direct communications to Bryan do not survive, he apparently was not pleased by Bryan's prepublication interference, as Bryan acknowledges in a follow-up letter to the reporter dated Feb. 26, 1916. "My Dear Mr. Reed," Bryan wrote, "it distresses me not to be able to substitute your judgment for mine as to subjects we discussed, but experience has taught me the importance of confining discussion to subjects which I am prepared to defend without departing from my line of march. . . . Possibly we shall both be the wiser for the interview and know better what to do next time" (bMS Am 1091:236).

Though he may have bridled at doing so, Reed scrupulously adhered to Bryan's wishes and struck the offending quotes from his article. But in a move that anticipates the metanarrative aspects of some contemporary nonfiction, Reed also revealed to his *Collier's* readers exactly the manner by which Bryan had attempted to affect his own portrayal. "Don't you admire sensual beauty in art, Mr. Bryan?" Reed quotes himself as asking Bryan in one of the retyped manuscript pages (bMS Am 1091:1161, p. 31a) that made the final *Collier's* piece. "His answer I am forbidden to give here. Also his opinions upon the censorship of painting, literature, and the theatre, upon the right of the people to judge questions of morality, upon the nude in painting, the beauty of the human body, and modern dances" (45). Reed then tells his readers about the exchange of

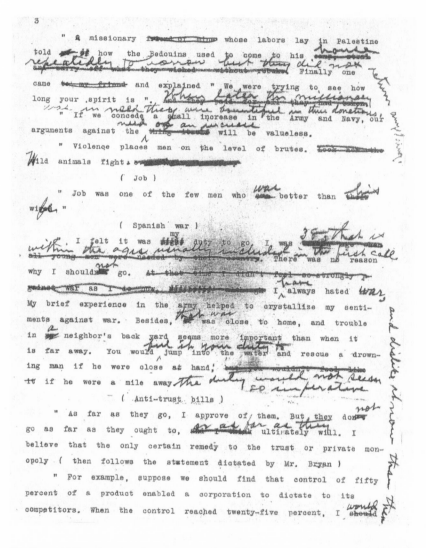

3

" A missionary ~~friend of mine~~ whose labors lay in Palestine told ~~me~~ ## how the Bedouins used to come to his ~~camp~~ *house* *repeatedly to ~~~~ but they did not* ~~and carry what they wicked without rebuke~~ Finally one came ~~to my friend~~ and explained " We were trying to see how long your spirit is ". *When later the missionary ~~~~* ~~and they ~~~~ they ~~~~ ~~ *was in need they were bountiful in their donations*

" If we concede a small increase in the Army and Navy, our *need an increase* arguments against the ~~thing items~~ will be valueless.

" Violence places men on the level of brutes. ~~Look at the~~ *W*ild animals fight ~~~~

(Job)

" Job was one of the few men who *was* ~~was~~ better than ~~their~~ *his* wif~~e~~. "

(Spanish war)

within I felt it was ~~~~ my duty to go, I was *38 that is* ~~the age usually included in the first call~~ ~~all young men were needed by their country.~~ There was *not* reason why I should~~n't~~ go. ~~At that time I didn't feel so strongly~~ *have* ~~against war as I do now.~~ ~~~~ I always hated *war* My brief experience in the army helped to crystallize my senti- *for war* ments against war. Besides, ~~it was~~ close to home, and trouble *a* in ~~a~~ neighbor's back yard seems more important than when it *put it your duty to* is far away. You would jump into the water and rescue a drown- ing man if he were close at hand, ~~but~~ ~~wouldn't feel like~~ *the duty would not seem* ~~it~~ if he were a mile away *so imperative*

(Anti-trust bills)

" As far as they go, I approve of them. But, they do~~n't~~ *not* go as far as they ought to, ~~as at far as they~~ ~~and I~~ ultimately will. I believe that the only certain remedy to the trust or private mon- opoly (then follows the statement dictated by Mr. Bryan)

" For example, suppose we should find that control of fifty percent of a product enabled a corporation to dictate to its competitors. When the control reached twenty-five percent, I ~~should~~ *would*

Reed sent William Jennings Bryan a typescript of direct quotes that Reed had gleaned from a fishing trip with Bryan in Florida in February 1916. In his own hand, Bryan produced an exacting pencil edit of the quotes. His changes range from uncoupling Reed's contractions to eliminating entire sentences ("At that time I didn't feel so strongly against war as I do now") that Reed believed had captured the Great Commoner's ruminations on such topics as militarism and economic policy. *(Houghton bMS Am 1091:1162. By permission of Houghton Library, Harvard University.)*

letters between him and Bryan ("I did not understand that this part of our talk was not for publication" [45]) and quotes at length Bryan's refusal to be quoted on the issues of art, morality, and censorship: "I have not time to enter upon the answering of questions or of arguments on these subjects. I am engaged in work which seems to me important and cannot turn aside for other things" (45).

Had Reed confined his profile of Bryan to this sort of interchange, he might have been justifiably criticized for following up questionable reporting with cheap-shot writing. Yet what emerges from the entire article is a surprisingly touching portrayal of the former secretary of state in which Reed demonstrates through the interchange that Bryan's greatest strength—his rock-ribbed self-possession—also proves to be Bryan's political undoing. Bryan's attempts to manage his own reputation become in the article a central way to understand his character. Reed relies on his powers of observation and on his understanding of Bryan's voice and mannerisms to make his case. He moves from the personal, through the political, and back to the personal to show his readers how Bryan's deep empathy for common Americans was undermined by his often-frustrated desire for control.

Reed's original typescript opens with an anecdote that *Collier's* chose not to publish: a fairly lengthy recollection of Reed's first meeting with Bryan in June 1914 at the then-secretary's official residence in Washington, D.C. At the time one of the most popular and highly-paid journalists in America, Reed had just returned from covering Pancho Villa in the 1913 Mexican Revolution and had gained audiences with President Wilson and with Bryan to relay his views on the Mexican situation. Reed describes Bryan's house in terms that link the secretary of state to the common people whom he professes to serve: "It was a hot Sunday. Tennis rackets, a baby carriage and a row of assorted rubbers littered the front porch, and through the screen door were wafted odors of a dinner recently consumed." Reed is admitted to the house by a "capable" house-keeper, who is humming the hymn "Lead Kindly Light." Juxtaposed against this portrait of average American domesticity, however, Reed constructs a meticulous scene that emphasizes Bryan as the sort of man who strews statues and oil paintings of himself around his house:

> Two enormous Oriental vases flanked the mantle-piece, at whose center sat a large bronze bust of William Jennings Bryan. There were other busts of him scattered about—of wood, marble, granite, cast-iron, and silver-gilt metal. Incongruous rugs lay upon the carpet, and several tall oil-paintings caught the eye—portraits of third-rate rajahs and obscure sultans, such as stare down

upon the country visitor from the walls of the State Department corridors. The furniture was hair-cloth, of the best period. And I retain an impression of lace window curtains.... In a short time Mr. Bryan appeared, wearing that famous cutaway of his, those famous half-glasses on the wide statesman's black ribbon, the well-known clerical white bow tie, and that familiar and appealing smile. His noble head rose massively from a wave of hair projecting behind. He looked the way I always thought a statesman ought to look, and he talked in the way a statesman should—slowly, impressively, with massive seriousness. (bMS Am 1091:1161, pp. 1–2)

Reed deftly weaves these glimpses of Bryan throughout passages that, by contrast, emphasize the statesman's "succession of forlorn hopes" for the commoner. Bryan is for free silver and for populism, for low taxes, for disarmament. He is anti-rum, antiimperialist, and antitrust: preaching the principles of Thomas Jefferson and of old-time Christian virtues. "[E]ach time [he] went down in crashing defeat," Reed observes, "and each time [he] bobbed up again, a bourgeois Don Quixote.... Politics did not corrupt him; defeat did not change his way of life" (3).

In the section of Reed's piece that *Collier's* chose for its lead, Reed manages to capture all of Bryan's contradictory impulses in a single scene. He meets Bryan in the hotel dining room in Palatka, where Reed notes that not a detail of Bryan's appearance has changed since his departure from the cabinet, "even to the statesman's cutaway coat and the black ministerial tie he substituted for the white one in the evening" (11). Bryan converses easily and confidently on the latest political news that Reed brings with him from Washington, a man firmly in possession of his calling and his self-discipline. Reed, however, always is on the look-out for the detail that undercuts Bryan's pretensions and reveals his human qualities. The statesman's grandson John accompanies the party and at one point bounces up from the table and shouts: "'Grandma! At lunch grandpa ate two pieces of pie and drank a whole bottle of grape juice!' 'Billy,' said Mrs. Bryan reproachfully, eyeing her husband, who looked ashamed of himself. 'You know you oughtn't to.' He mumbled something to the waiter, but she interrupted: 'You don't eat this kind of soup, dear'" (11).

That night, Reed goes to the Palatka Opera House, where several hundred retired Confederate soldiers, Yankee tourists, and "blond, fluffy-haired Southern beauties" (11) have paid fifty cents apiece to listen to the former secretary of state speak on the current state of government affairs. Reed presents long passages of the speech verbatim, aided by his own dictation and by two reprints of earlier speeches that Reed read carefully and underlined copiously in his own hand (bMS Am 1091:1161; loose notes and material). At the opera house, the reporter reads the crowd as carefully as he does Bryan; they regard the defrocked cabinet officer with a combination of amused tolerance and occasional disbelief. But the crowd is moved in spite of itself as Bryan warms to his speech, which Reed says he presents "firstly, secondly, and thirdly like a sermon . . . sonorous periods of Cicero improved by Daniel Webster, and sparks of homely common sense, like the talk of farmers among themselves" (12). Carefully, Bryan makes the case against preparedness as the nation teeters toward its involvement in World War I, arguing that tax money would be better spent to build roads and to make loans to hard-working Americans striving to improve their lives. "And if in a moment of excitement one of the madmen of Europe were to challenge us, I think we would be justified in answering 'No!'" Bryan thunders. "We have the welfare of a hundred million people to guard and priceless ideals to preserve, and we will not get down with you and wallow in the mire of human blood just to conform to a false standard of honor." Reed then turns his eyes to the audience and reports: "That got them. Not the idea, not the principle of the thing. But the resounding phrases and dramatic delivery" (12).

Certainly, this is the portion of Reed's article that would have most pleased Bryan and the portion that most reporters of Reed's time—schooled in their duty to report the public affairs of public men—would be content to portray. But Reed attempted to go much further and thus earned something of Bryan's wrath. The occasion for some of the sharpest insights in the piece, as well as the centerpiece of the dispute over Reed's quoting, is the boating expedition on the Saint Johns River that gives Reed the occasion to observe closely the Bryan of everyday life while listening as the statesman holds forth on events of the day. As they float through the swampland along the narrow river, the topic turns to impending U.S. involvement in the war. Reed's artistry shines through the resulting passage, redeeming what would otherwise be a workmanlike profile. He pits Bryan's efforts to master the political climate of his time against the unwillingness of Bryan's peers to be manipulated by him. Reed's lyrical metaphor for Bryan's effort to plow through political opposition becomes the Florida swampland itself—liquid, riotous, dense, ultimately unmoved—altered only temporarily by Bryan's slow-moving vessel. Reed observes:

> As we talked the boat swung toward the dense tropical forest, which opened miraculously in a narrow channel, scarcely wider than the vessel, winding so tortuously that we crept at half-speed, twisting and turning almost completely around as we doubled the corners. On both sides was swamp choked with riotous vegetation, cedars draped with long Spanish moss, creepers, tall leaning palms, and spiky palmettos. Our keel scraped bottom incessantly and we plowed through masses of water hyacinth. (40)

Like Bryan, Reed was deeply opposed to U.S. participation in the war, but unlike Bryan, Reed's objection stemmed from his adherence to the principles of international socialism rather than from Bryan's rather isolationist pacifism. While the two men relax on the boat, Reed takes the opportunity to question Bryan about his beliefs, apparently in a manner that Bryan did not realize would lead to direct quotation. "What would you do, Mr. Bryan, if the United States were to undertake an unjust war?" (40), Reed asks. When Bryan refuses to answer the hypothetical question, Reed probes Bryan's own enlistment in the Spanish War. Bryan's reply proves to be one of the quotes contested in the subsequent dispute preserved in "What Mr. Bryan Said."

Reed apparently was not taking notes openly at the time; otherwise, Bryan could not have professed surprise that Reed was prepared to quote him. Whether Reed produced the quotes from surreptitious notes or from memory, the typed quotes he sent to Bryan read:

> I felt it was my duty to go. I was of an age when all men were needed by their country. There was no reason why I shouldn't go. At that time I didn't feel so strongly against war as I do now. (bMS Am 1091:1162, p. 3)

Bryan's handwritten changes are intriguing. First, he gets rid of the phrase "of an age when all men were needed by their country," perhaps because it might stir in *Collier's* readers some feelings of patriotism that Bryan did not wish to incite. He also replaces "at that time I didn't feel so strongly against war" with "I have always hated war, and dislike it now [more] than then," a phrase that tends to make Bryan appear more resolute and less inconsistent in his beliefs. And finally, in a schoolmarm-like touch that no doubt rankled a Reed finally attuned to the cadence of actual speech, Bryan uncoupled all the contractions *(shouldn't, didn't)* in Reed's version (bMS Am 1091:1162, p. 3). Bryan's version of the quote thus reads:

> I felt it was my duty to go. I was 38, that is, within the ages usually included in the first call. There was no reason why I should not go. I have always hated war, and dislike it now [more] than then. (bMS Am 1091:1162, p. 3)

Reed acquiesced to Bryan's version of the quotes in the final *Collier's* piece, but did not use them all and interjected descriptive phrases so as to reassert the author's control over the nonfictional text. Reed weaves quotes into a believable scene and links quotes from widely separated passages in the "What Mr. Bryan Said" transcript, while upholding his agreement to use quotes that Bryan had approved. The final *Collier's* version:

"There was no reason why I should not go," he answered slowly. "I was thirty-eight, that is within the ages usually included in the first call." He hesitated. "Besides, that war was close to home, and trouble in a neighbor's back yard seems more important than when it is far away." . . . He interrupted himself to shout to his grandson: "Look, John! There's an alligator." (41)

Bryan's meddling with the quotes only confirmed an aspect of the former secretary's personality of which Reed was keenly aware before the exchange of letters. In the typed draft of "Bryan on Tour" completed before Reed was forced to alter the quotes, the journalist already had written a passage that revealed Bryan's attempts to assert his mastery of language. The exchange, which made it into the final *Collier's* article, also concerns Bryan's thoughts on war. Reed asks the former secretary if he would be prepared to use warfare to enforce treaties. Citing Thomas Carlyle, Bryan launches into a defense of the axiom that "history proves that force is not a sufficient basis for peace" (41). Reed quotes Bryan at length, ending Bryan's treatise as follows: "Love is the only weapon for which there is no shield. And it must guide nations to peace as it guides individuals to peace" (41). In another metanarrative aside, Reed muses on Bryan's self-calculation, the way his language turns aside deeper feelings, perhaps as surely as the yacht scrapes bottom or plows through fragile water flowers. "He was greatly moved as he said this, uplifted and sure," said Reed of Bryan's dissertation on the power of love. "But he spoke as a public man, in the careful phrasing of an address, and I had a sudden feeling of impatience with him. Hardly ever did he say a natural, impulsive thing; and when he did, he quickly revised it, made it formal and lifeless" (41).

That Reed considered this revelation important is revealed by the pains he took with the passage. Reed's first draft read: "I had a sudden impatience because I could never get from Bryan the natural reaction of a natural human being," before Reed toned down the phrasing a bit with a hand correction (bMS Am 1091:1161, p. 23). One can imagine, then, how Reed felt when Bryan later started meddling with the quotes Reed was at pains to garner from the statesman's more unguarded moments.

In the time of action on the yacht, Reed resorts to attempts to surprise Bryan into extemporaneous reactions, such as when one of the passengers spots an alligator half-submerged in the water. As the other passengers scrambled from Bryan's circle to look, Bryan remarks that he had shot an alligator only a week before. Reed baits him: "I remarked jocularly that I'd bet that alligator wished he'd had a peace treaty with Mr. Bryan, providing for a year's investigation of their differences before war was declared. This did not seem to please him" (41). Reed then returns to the extended metaphor that he has constructed to reveal the Great Commoner's uncommon urge to master the universe. Reed's description mingles lyricism and irony:

> Below the somber water long predatory fish flitted across white sand patches; solemn rows of great turtles decorated the fallen tree trunks; strange, bright-hued birds like flame shot through the gloomy gray of the jungle; and alligators flopped from their sunning places at our approach. Through that savage hot death struggle, that wild anarchy of tropical nature, moved William Jennings Bryan on a gasoline yacht, in black statesmanlike cutaway, white clerical tie, light gray fedora hat, his hands clasped across his stomach, benevolently bringing love and order into his simple world. (41)

Another example of Reed's examination of Bryan's sometimes contradictory nature concerns a brief speech that the former secretary makes at a settlement along the Saint Johns in Orange Springs Landing. The passage reveals how Reed worked up his material from longhand notes, creating a voice for Bryan out of his scribblings and memory, and then contesting with Bryan over that voice in the final text. The yacht begins to emerge from the swampland into back-country orange groves, "showers of golden globes shining in the rich green leaves" (44). A tall, shambling man with one suspender hails the boat and tells its passengers that a crowd has gathered around the bend, eager to hear Bryan speak. "We tooted our whistle as we rounded the bend, and Orange Springs Landing lay before us, thronged with citizens," Reed reports sardonically. "I counted twenty-nine." Among them are orange farmers "vigorously chewing plug," several well-dressed women, a few African Americans, and a northern tourist (44).

Reed's notes of the speech, wherein Bryan forwards Florida's Silver Springs as a model of piety and purity, accompanies the "Bryan on Tour" typescript in the Houghton Library archives. In Reed's hand, on folded stationery from the Harrison Hall Hotel in Ocala, is written: "my friends," "Silver Springs," "like an upright life," "clear and pure and rushing forth an abundance of goodness," "while a stagnant town is like a sinful life, all sluggishness and choked with evil," "a tarnished life" (bMS Am 1091:1161). What Reed makes of these notes in the *Collier's* article is: "And now, my friends, I want to say that to me Silver Springs is like an upright life, pure and clear and pouring forth an abundance of goodness. The opposite, of course, is a stagnant pool, which is like a sinful life, sluggish and choked with evil" (45).

Because Bryan was speaking in a public forum in which Reed openly was taking notes, Reed didn't bother to check this quote with the former secretary.

A reader can see how Reed smooths his notes into an intelligible line, occasionally improving the sentence's rhythm and striving to capture his subject in words. Indeed, if Reed's long article has an obvious flaw, it is perhaps overquoting. Many long passages from Bryan's speeches and conversations are rendered, and they are always improved when Reed remembers to intersperse them with insights and local color. In the Orange Springs Landing speech, Reed's description frames the text, again revealing the power of the nonfiction author to build context and, in this case, a gentle layer of irony. In Reed's eyes, Bryan's display of eloquence fails to move his listeners, perhaps in part because he dares to cite Abraham Lincoln, whose birth date it is, before a largely Southern crowd. "Several persons giggled shamefacedly, others lifted their hats, but there was no spark of intelligence upon any face," Reed observes. "We whistled again and backed out of the mud, turning once more down the river; as long as we were in sight the audience stood like statues, gaping after us" (45).

Given that William Jennings Bryan was perhaps to be best known for opposing the theory of evolution and for helping to prosecute the 1925 John T. Scopes trial, it is interesting that Reed ends his long article with another speech, this time in Ocala, where Bryan decries evolution. In Reed's words, Bryan "sneered at the Darwinian theory, saying that if some people liked to believe they were descended from monkeys, well he didn't." The journalist then directly quotes Bryan to the effect that "Darwinian theory has done more to paralyze Christian ethics than any other thing in the world" (47). After the speech, Reed tells his readers that he "cornered" Bryan in the hotel lobby and asked Bryan about the higher criticism of the Bible then fashionable in progressive theological circles. Reed presents Bryan's answer as if spoken at the moment. In fact, Bryan flatly rejected Reed's memory of the quote in the typescript "What Mr. Bryan Said" and penned an entirely new statement on the back of a leaf, which Reed dutifully reproduced in the *Collier's* article verbatim (bMS Am 1091:1162, p. 8).

Shining through these somewhat contentious passages is Reed's genuine liking for the principles for which Bryan stood. Reed and the Great Commoner were joined by contempt for war profiteers, by distaste for "jingoists" anxious to send American youths into battle, by suspicion of the machinations of Wall Street and the banking industry, and by a genuine admiration of working people and their interests. Both men also were on record for their support of women's suffrage. Reed during this period raised money for the defense of Margaret Sanger (bMS Am 1191:1156) and wrote specifically of his admiration for Mary Baird Bryan, telling his *Collier's* readers that her marriage to Bryan forced her into "a life of abnegation and devotedness and of immeasurable aid to her husband." Reed concludes, with a touch of irony toward the man who was anxious to edit his own work: "She has always revised and edited his speeches and articles. She studied law and was admitted to the bar in order to understand his interests. Her mind, I think, entertains more than his, and the habit of public life has not dulled her natural reaction to things as it has his" (45).

The libertine Reed, however, was ill-matched temperamentally to either Mary Baird Bryan or her husband. So it is no surprise that Bryan flatly refused during their conversations to be drawn into the topic of "sensual beauty in art" or "the nude in art" and crossed out what quotes that Reed had managed to garner on the topics in the "What Mr. Bryan Said" transcript (bMS Am 1091:1162, p. 6). Meanwhile, the journalist himself was substantially less discreet. On the trip to Florida, Reed was writing letters to Louise Bryant: "My little lover. I become more and more gloomy and mournful to think I'm not going to sleep all over you in our scandalous and sinful voluptuous bed" (bMS Am 1091:24). One can only imagine what William Jennings Bryan would have made of that; for his part he contented himself with a futile effort to save Reed's soul. In the Feb. 18, 1916, letter that accompanied Bryan's objection to Reed's quotes, Bryan ordered Reed a copy of a religious pamphlet to give the writer "more consideration to the faith in which you were raised," and added: "It is the example of Christ at which we should look, not at the frail and faulty human beings who profess to follow him." After this bit of fatherly advice, Bryan adds, "Send me a copy of your article when published. Shall be pleased to see myself from your point of view" (bMS Am 1091:234). No record survives as to whether Bryan was pleased or dismayed when he actually picked up the May 20, 1916, issue of *Collier's* and encountered Reed's evocation of his life. But it is not likely that the Great Commoner forgot his encounter with the brash young journalist who shared his belief that the United States could be a much greater place if it invested more power in the people who toiled at its heart.

Reed saves his most unambiguous tribute to Bryan until near the end of the resulting *Collier's* article. In the final scene, the two men talk late into the night after Bryan's Ocala speech, Reed contemplating the "romance" of Bryan's life and "his steady power over common men." Despite the frustration that already was building in Reed's mind over Bryan's attempt to master the unfolding narrative, Reed thinks of all the principles that the two men shared, and concludes:

> After all, whatever is said, Bryan has always been on the side of democracy. Remember that he was talking popular government twenty years ago and getting called anarchist for it; remember that he advocated such things as the in-

come tax, the popular election of senators, railroad regulation, low tariff, the destruction of private monopoly, and the initiative and referendum when such things were considered the dreams of an idiot; and remember that he is not yet done. (47)

What separated the men was equally profound: their differing beliefs about what sort of power could ignite a spark of genuine renewal in the United States, what sort of power could halt a nation skidding toward war, and what sort of power could kindle strength and autonomy in common people. For Bryan it was faith in the Higher Power and resolute character-building by means of religious training and application. For Reed it was the promise of worldwide revolutionary socialism. And, as it turned out, each man was to discover the potential and limitations of his dreams in the years to come.

FROM THIS EXAMINATION of John Reed's literary reporting, we can see that in general he predated those standards advanced by contemporary nonfiction writers, editors, and teachers. Reed writes with lively, crafted diction; builds immediate description into larger truths; constructs effective scenes from skillful dialogue; manipulates point of view and structure effectively; establishes his personal presence to guide his readers toward self-discovery; and reveals the power of his stories to affect his subjects and readers. Nevertheless, like other writers of the late nineteenth and early twentieth centuries (Stephen Crane, George Ade, Richard Harding Davis), Reed sometimes blurred the fictional and/or nonfictional status of his stories.

In the next chapter, I examine carefully a series of such stories—mostly drawn from Reed's early writing for *The Masses*—so as to examine what Reed learned about nonfiction from writing fiction. My contention is that Reed reversed the process that canon literature has taught a generation of critics to anticipate and venerate—that is, that skillful nonfictional storytelling can lay the basis for lasting fiction. Unlike Crane or Hemingway—who tended to use their reporting experience to sharpen the realistic underpinnings of their stories and novels—Reed's early experiments in fiction taught him how to write complex and nuanced nonfictional narratives. Particularly in the development of a narrator persona capable of ironic distance and in his ability to build lasting themes from the events of history, Reed's early writing of fiction prepared him for what was clearly to be his métier—extended nonfictional narratives based on fine writing and in-depth reporting.

Fact and Fiction in John Reed's Tales

THE STANDARD NARRATIVE about realistic fiction of the late nineteenth and early twentieth centuries informs us that the greatest American novelists learned their observational skills and writing craft from the nonfiction they produced early in their careers. According to this story, the observation of life, combined with the press of journalistic deadline and its premium on terse, economical writing, hones a writer later capable of discarding the localities of journalism for the timeless quality of fiction. Shelley Fisher Fishkin's study of Mark Twain, Theodore Dreiser, Ernest Hemingway, and John Dos Passos typifies this approach to the journalist/novelist relationship. "Early apprenticeship in journalism exposed each writer to a vast range of experience that would ultimately form the core of his greatest imaginative works," Fishkin asserts in her study, *From Fact to Fiction: Journalism and Imaginative Writing in America.* "It forced him to become a precise observer, nurtured in him a respect for fact, and taught him lessons about style that would shape his greatest literary creations. It taught him to be mistrustful of rhetoric, abstractions, hypocrisy, and cant; it taught him to be suspicious of secondhand accounts and to insist on seeing with his own eyes" (4).

Fishkin suggests that writers like Twain and Hemingway turned from journalism because they tired of the formulaic approaches required by newspaper discourse. "The conventional nonfiction narratives they wrote as journalists were designed to be taken at face value by passive readers who would trust what they read," Fishkin says. "The self-effacing, open-ended, fiction-blasting fictions they wrote as poets or novelists were designed to create active readers capable of questioning everything they read and of constructing new patterns of meaning on their own" (9). It was not until Tom Wolfe and the New Journalists, Fishkin concludes, that nonfiction writers brought to their journalism the techniques associated with America's great novelists. "When Tom Wolfe and other writers grew impatient with the limits of conventional journalism in the 1960s, their goal was the same as that which propelled [earlier] writers from fact to fictions: they wanted, as Wolfe put it, 'to excite the reader both intellectually and emotionally' in ways that conventional journalism could not. But unlike these earlier writers, they saw no need to turn away from the world of fact" (9).

Most likely this paradigmatic reading of the relationship between journalism and fiction fits only because the critics who advance it tend to ignore those early-twentieth-century prose writers who did not quite follow the authorized career path from nonfiction toward the fictional realm of "timeless artistry." The production of critically acclaimed novels continues to be the standard by which early-twentieth-century prose writers normally are judged, and those writers who lie outside that paradigm often are discounted. Because many literary critics tend to study novelists most seriously, they overlook those writers who contradict their analyses; thus the privileging of realistic fiction and its underlying ideology produces the very phenomenon that it claims to describe.

The career of John Reed offers a fascinating antidote to dominant prose criticism in that Reed started his career by writing poetry and short stories and developed it toward the publication of three books of literary nonfiction: *Insurgent Mexico, The War in Eastern Europe,* and *Ten Days That Shook the World.* Rather than applying the lessons learned in his journalism to the production of novels, Reed used his poetic voice and the sketches he created and marketed as fictional tales to develop the descriptive power and sense of dialogue that he was to use successfully in his nonfiction. By applying the fictional techniques developed early in his writing career to his nonfiction, Reed anticipated many of the formal initiatives that Wolfe and other New Journalists claimed to have developed a half-century later. Chief among the accomplishments that Reed seems to have transferred from his fiction toward his nonfiction was the development of a first-person narrator capable of well-honed irony and expressive detail: in short, a mediator, but one that Reed used to add depth to his narratives as well as to reveal the textuality and construction of historical meaning. Reed also developed from his fiction an ability to write convincing dialogue and to reveal character through dialogue and close description. To prove those points, I intend to read quite closely a group of short stories that Reed produced between 1913 and 1916. Many of the stories were published in *The Masses*, the Greenwich Village monthly that Reed edited with Max Eastman and Floyd Dell.

Only four critics—James C. Wilson, David C. Duke, Christopher P. Wilson, and Jim Finnegan—have written about the stories at any length, and none has read them specifically for the ways that Reed's fictional output prepared him for his more sustained and developed nonfiction. For his part, James C. Wilson simply conflates the two types of writing: discussing the stories as if they were nonfiction, calling them "articles," and suggesting that Reed "took occasional liberties with the facts in order to enhance the artistic integrity of his creations" (8). Wilson is correct in noting that Reed "shaped dialogue, reorganized chronologies, and constructed plots" (8), but he seems to miss the ways by which Reed deliberately understood his stories as something substantially different from the articles that he wrote during the same period—for example, "War in Paterson," "Sheriff Radcliff's Hotel," or "Back of Billy Sunday."

Although the fictional/nonfictional status of some of the narratives in *The Masses* is murky by contemporary standards, Floyd Dell—the man who likely served as editor for most of the stories discussed in this chapter—provides some clue by classifying them as "tales," rather than "journalistic accounts," in *Daughter of the Revolution and Other Stories,* the 1927 collection of Reed's writing that Dell edited. Although both forms of narrative rely on descriptive detail, lively scenes, and realistic dialogue, the articles discussed in the preceding chapter assert a much stronger propositional quality than the short stories discussed here.[1] In the articles, Reed exposes specific industrial and public institutions, outlines financing schemes, and describes recognizable and often notorious characters. He obviously means such characters as Billy Sunday, Alba B. Johnson, Sheriff Radcliff, and Big Bill Haywood to signify and interplay with the histories of real people and to assert truths about these characters that will affect the reputations of people outside the text. I am not insisting on a fixed generic boundary between all of Reed's tales and articles. Like Jim Finnegan, I believe that Reed's narratives "reflect a conscious experimentation with formal structures, crossing boundaries between traditional literary genres and whole disciplines" (162), but I also believe that discussing each Reed text as if it were of identical status might cause readers to miss much of the subtlety of Reed's writing as well as the way he used fiction specifically to prepare himself for his more adventurous nonfiction.

Duke seems to be correct in noting that Reed's tales are "cast as fiction [and] generated by his own sensitive observations" (81–82) of real life. Duke also understands that Reed's best stories are marked not by sophisticated or even well-developed plots but by a level of irony often generated by the narrator's discovery of "subtleties about the lives of his characters that give added twists to unresolved conclusions" (81). What both James C. Wilson and Duke appear to miss, however, is the distance that Reed is able to achieve between himself as a writer and the alter ego that he chooses to serve as the narrator of his tales. Wilson misses that distancing because he chooses to read the stories as relatively simplistic, if often embellished, nonfiction. Even though Duke is on the track of the stories' irony, he tends to undervalue the distancing effect because he concludes that "Reed himself" (81) normally is the narrator of the tales and habitually refers to the unnamed first-person narrators as "Reed" (78–79).

Christopher P. Wilson and Jim Finnegan offer perhaps the most sophisticated readings of the group of stories that Wilson classifies as Reed's "city tales." Asserting that Reed owes a strong debt to Stephen Crane's tales of New York, Wilson's essay "Broadway Nights: John Reed and the City" suggests a valuable direction for the criticism of Reed's short stories by concentrating on the sometimes ironic interrelation between the author and the first-person narrator in Reed's best stories. Wilson says that "Reed turns the problem of subjectivity . . . into a pointed examination of a viewer's inability to see because of where he stands in a sociopolitical system" (287). Similarly, Finnegan focuses on Reed's "anxiety about feeling the power of possessing cultural knowledge, yet of being marginalized by the very culture that he wrote both of and for" (203). My study answers Wilson's and Finnegan's challenges and explores even more deeply the way that Reed uses first-person narrators for ironic and artistic effect; I also examine specific borderline texts from Reed's original typescripts to sort out the differing and sometimes complementary ways that Reed wrote stories he claims to be true as opposed to those for which he made less specific propositional assertions.

Reed's Fictional Narrators and the Rhetoric of Distance

> I took his arm and guided him into the white door of an all-night lunchroom. I sat him at a table, where he dropped into a dead sleep. I set before him roast beef, and mashed potatoes and two ham sandwiches, and a cup of coffee, and bread and butter, and a big piece of pie. And then I woke him up. He looked up at me with a dawning meaning in his expression. The look of humble gratitude, love, devotion was almost canine in its intensity. I felt a warm thrill of Christian brotherhood all through my veins. I sat back and watched him eat. ("Another Case of Ingratitude," 150)

Published in 1913, "Another Case of Ingratitude" is limited to a chance meeting between an unnamed protagonist and an out-of-work bricklayer whom the protagonist-narrator "saves" from starvation with a hot meal at an all-night restaurant. Although its plot is simple, the story epitomizes the degree of irony that Reed is able to achieve by pitting the values of the first-person narrator against the values that the author has designed the overall story to express.

Confident that he has revived the bricklayer, the narrator basks in the warm glow of Christian charity and expects that his reward will be the opportunity to possess the story of the bricklayer's life. When the bricklayer proves to be reluctant to answer his questions ("Wot do you t'ink I am, a polygraft?" [151]), the narrator is offended and insists that he was only trying to make conversation. "Naw, you wasn't. You t'ought just because you give me a hand-out, I'd do a sob-story all over you," replies the bricklayer. "Wot right have you got to ask me all them questions? I know you fellers. Just because you got money you t'ink you can buy me with a meal" (152). The narrator responds that he stood for the free meal "perfectly unselfishly," but both the bricklayer and the reader see that that is not the case. "You get all you want," the bricklayer replies. "Come on now, don't it make you feel good all over to save a poor starvin' bum's life? God! You're pure and holy for a week" (152). At the end of the story, the narrator concludes that the bricklayer doesn't have "a bit of gratitude" in him and repairs for home "to wake up Drusilla, who alone understands me" (152).[2]

The story's final line, as well as its title, cements the distance between the story's author and the narrator whom author Reed has chosen to relate the tale. The narrator's fragile ego has been reduced so greatly by his encounter with the bricklayer that, in need of "understanding," he resorts to awakening his female friend. The reader is expected to see that his relationship with Drusilla is probably as exploitative as the one he seeks to have with the bricklayer. The narrator's narcissism requires both that he see his "warm thrill of Christian brotherhood" reflected in the bricklayer's gratitude and his supposed sensitivity reflected in Drusilla's support—even if he has to wake her to receive it. And via the use of the word *another* in the story's title, the reader is expected to understand that the protagonist replays his drama of insecurity again and again.

It is no wonder that Reed makes thematic use of the bricklayer's confusion between a phonograph and a polygraph. The narrator wants to consume the bricklayer for entertainment, as though he were a phonograph; the bricklayer, however, instead reveals a difficult truth, as would a polygraph. Although the story may have been based on a real incident, Reed's protagonist appears to share more of the preening sensibility of a Ma Sunday or a Homer W. Rodeheaver than that of the author. If any part of the narrator's hypocrisy cuts close to Reed's, it might be the narrator's need to consume the story of the out-of-work bricklayer in return for his charity. As a journalist and writer who in 1913 regularly roamed the streets of New York (and the jails of Paterson, New Jersey) in search of stories to nourish his freelance career, Reed could be expected to understand the thin line between easing the grief of another and profiting from that grief.

Similar in theme to "Another Case of Ingratitude" but more complex in both plot and narration is "The Capitalist," a story that although printed in the April 1916 edition of *The Masses* was written in 1912, according to Dell, Reed's editor. "The Capitalist" differs from "Another Case of Ingratitude" in that its protagonist, William Booth Wrenn, is not the narrator of the story, although, as in "Another Case of Ingratitude," the story ends with a plot reversal that exposes Wrenn's lack of self-awareness. Wrenn, marooned on Washington Square one November night after what appears to be a day of unsuccessful job hunting, is accosted by a woman named Mrs. Trimball, who needs money for a room and a drink. Although the reader soon understands that Wrenn is not much better off than Mrs. Trimball, he takes on the airs of a higher caste. "Yer a Cap'tal'st," she responds, a cigarette trembling in her lips. "Ye wouldn't be so p'lite to me if you didn't want sumpin" (109). Later, Wrenn tells the woman that he is "Courcey dePeyster Stuyvesant," a name he recalls from the society pages. "Didn't I tell ye?" the old lady replies. "I know ye (hic). I'll have no truck wid ye! You gettin' yer money from yer pa, and me workin' on me knees seven days out o' the week" (111–12). Eventually, Wrenn gives the woman and an elderly hobo sixty of the sixty-five cents he has in his pocket.

"You're a good young feller for a Cap'tal'st," Mrs. Trimball tells him. "You got the stuff in you. All you want is a little hard work."

"If you working people weren't so extravagant, you'd save enough to make you comfortable in your old age" (112), Wrenn replies.

After the woman leaves, William Booth Wrenn continues through Washington Square, a chill working through his thin clothing. The capitalist airs he has put on amount to nothing when he is confronted by a police officer who tells him to move on. "My man, don't you know who I am?" Wrenn asks the officer. "Yes," the officer replies. "I know who you are. You're the guy I chased out of here twice already last night. Now git, or I'll fan you" (113).

As with "Another Case of Ingratitude," the story explores the less-than-ideal motivations displayed by those who give charity to others. Despite his apparently reduced circumstances, Wrenn desires the aura of class and privilege in exchange for the sixty cents he bestows on the vagrants, only to have his social position dashed by the police officer, who treats him as no better than a common bum. James C. Wilson, who follows Christopher P. Wilson in noting the story's debt to Stephen Crane's New York tales, assumes that Wrenn actually is in reduced circumstances and that the story exposes "Wrenn's psychological need to patronize the old woman and lecture her on the 'extravagance' of working people" (9). Similarly, John S. Bak concludes that Wrenn enjoys playing the capitalist that the woman takes him to be. Wrenn therefore "gives her the money he has made that day, not out of charity (as he needs it as much as she) but because he enjoys the romantic idea of possibly being Mr. Courcey DePeyster Stuyvesant" (21).

These interpretations are on target, but the story assumes a much deeper irony if the reader considers the possibility that Wrenn may be only pretending to be a bum, thus providing Reed with the opportunity to draw a more provocative link between "The Capitalist" and the writing of Stephen Crane. Perhaps Reed meant "The Capitalist" to be a direct response to Crane's famous narrative "An Experiment in Misery," in which Crane pretended to be a vagrant in New York's City Hall Park in order to report the inside story of vagrancy in the big city. Consider the openings of the two stories. First Crane:[3]

> It was late at night, and a fine rain was swirling softly down, causing the pavements to glisten with hue of steel and blue and glow in the rays of the innumerable lights. A youth was trudging slowly, without enthusiasm, with his hands buried deep in his trousers' pockets, toward the downtown places where beds can be hired for coppers. He was clothed in a ragged and tattered suit, and his derby was a marvel of dust-covered crown and torn rim. He was going forth to eat as a wanderer may eat and sleep as the homeless sleep. ("An Experiment in Misery," 283)

Reed's opening is:

> You know how Washington Square looks in a wet mist on November nights; that gray, luminous pastel atmosphere, softening incredibly the hard outlines of bare trees and iron railings, obliterating the sharp edges of shadows, and casting a silver halo about each high electric globe. All the straight concrete walks are black onyx, jewelled in every little unevenness with pools of steely rain-water. An imperceptible rain fills the air; your cheeks and the backs of your hands are damp and cool. And yet you can walk three times around the Square with your raincoat open and not get wet at all. It was on such a night that William Booth Wrenn, strolling from somewhere to nowhere in particular, stopped under the two arc lights near Washington Arch to count his wealth. . . . A hasty glance at Mr. Wrenn, if you are not particularly observant, would have convinced you that he was an ordinary young man in ordinary circumstances . . . [b]ut if you had looked closer, you might have noticed that his high collar was frayed and smudgy-looking . . . [o]r that the English hat was fast ungluing in the wet. ("The Capitalist," 105–6)

My contention is that Reed's deepest irony in the story develops when we read it specifically as his critique of Crane's "An Experiment in Misery." In Crane's tale (marketed as "a wonderfully vivid picture of a strange phase of New York Life" in the April 22, 1894, edition of the *New York Press* [Bowers, 861–62]), Crane pretends to be an indigent wanderer who spends a night as a Bowery area bum so as to craft a portrait of life there.[4] Although Crane does not name himself in the narrative, he was identified by the *New York Press* as "the author of *Maggie*" (Bowers, 892) and states early in the story that "he was going forth to eat as a wanderer may eat and sleep as the homeless sleep" (283). The reporter (I shall call him Crane since Crane was the author of *Maggie: A Girl of the Streets*) gives a hobo, whom he terms "an assassin steeped in crimes," three pennies to be taken to a "gloom shrouded" flophouse where he can spend the night. What he finds there turns his liver white as he meets "strange and unspeakable odors that assailed him like malignant diseases with wings" (287). Throughout the night, Crane lies awake and watches the other men in the flophouse beds: "the tawny hues of naked flesh, limbs thrust into the darkness, projecting beyond the cots; up-reared knees; arms hanging, long and thin, over the cot edges. For the most part they were statuesque, carven, dead" (288). Some men thrash and moan. Since he cannot sleep, Crane lies there, "carving biographies for these men from his meager experience" (289).

In the morning, Crane escapes from the flophouse and hurries down the street. Accosted by one of the flophouse men, Crane at first denies that he had spent the night there, then agrees to stand the man a breakfast. Two bowls of soup and a few crusts of bread appear to cement the bond between Crane and the hobo, and they wander off together to City Hall Park, there to sit on the benches, huddled in their rags, "slumberously conscious of the march of the hours which for them had no meaning" (293). Crane feels a sudden awe at the indifference with which the middle and upper classes regard him. "They expressed to the young man his infinite distance from all that he valued. Social position, comfort, the pleasures of living, were unconquerable kingdoms" (293), and at the end of the story Crane confesses himself an outcast.

Reed's deviations from Crane's well-known tale are interesting. In addition to providing his protagonist with a name (William Booth Wrenn) not his own, Reed has Wrenn use another alias (Stuyvesant) within the tale, which further complicates naming and identity. As in Crane's "Experiment in Misery," the chief action of the story consists of the protagonist's various interactions with those who truly are down-and-out as well as with those in authority. And also as in Crane's story, the protagonist somehow has more money, seems more educated, and speaks with less broken dialect than the indigents who surround him. Finally, in both stories the protagonists seem to be losing their grip on the upper rungs of society that once were in their possession. Both now are treated as bums because they look like bums and are defined by the ruling powers as bums.

Yet Crane never truly surrenders his superior power as an outside observer in his "Experiment in Misery." Despite the "unconquerable kingdoms" he feels at the story's end, he successfully markets his experience to a New York newspaper and reasserts his position. He is identified in the story's larger discourse as the author of *Maggie* and thus remains secure as a writer and reporter for the *New York Press.* By contrast, Reed's protagonist is less clearly defined. Is he Courcey dePeyster Stuyvesant or William Booth Wrenn? Or perhaps some stand-in for the author himself? Whatever the case, he is threatened and chased off by a police officer (113). No larger discourse redeems him. It is possible that Wrenn might be a young man slightly above the bum, a capitalist on the way down parting with his last spare change, thereby earning sympathy from the reader in the rather poignant ending. But Wrenn also could be an actual bum who is putting on airs or, perhaps, some experience-hungry interloper who is pretending to be a bum putting on airs. If the latter is true—as it was for Crane—the police officer's threats of violence will force Wrenn to a decision not faced by Crane in his tale: will he retain his cover so as to continue his experience or will he reveal himself so as to reassert his rightful place in society? Whichever it is, Reed challenges the veneer of social identity much more explicitly and fundamentally than does Crane. "My man, do you know who I am?" (113), Wrenn asks the police officer at story's end. Neither the officer nor the reader can say for sure.

Reed's effect can be seen more clearly when "The Capitalist" is contrasted to a story where Reed grounds his identity more securely. "A Taste of Justice"— a New York tale written immediately following "The Capitalist" and published in *The Masses* in April 1913—is the only story in which Reed uses his own name. Yet the narrator that the author constructs is not precisely Reed himself, for the narrator appears willing to trade more readily on social position than the thematic norms of the story would endorse. In the brief story, a protagonist-narrator finds himself on the corner of Irving Place and Fifteenth Street, where he observes the ladies of the evening, his ears "full of low whisperings and the soft scuff of their feet" (20). Eventually the narrator is told to move on by a police officer in virtually the same terms as was William Booth Wrenn: "Now git along, or I'll fan ye" (21). Arrested by the officer when he refuses to move, the narrator is taken to night court, where he witnesses loitering prostitutes sentenced indiscriminately to ten days on Riker's Island. When it is the narrator's turn to be processed and the charge of resisting an officer is read, the judge looks up, nods, and smiles. "'Hello, Reed!' he said. He venomously regarded the Cop. 'Next time you pull a friend of mine—' suggestively, he left the threat unfinished. Then to me, 'Want to sit up on the bench for a while?'" (130).

Reed uses his self-named alter ego in the story to build the irony of the story's title: "A Taste of Justice." As all of the story's readers have noticed, what is delivered at the end is anything but justice (Duke, 77; James C. Wilson, 8; Christopher P. Wilson, 287; Rosenstone, 118). The author's "Reed" trades on his privilege, with the help of his friend the judge, and gets one over on the working-class police officer who arrested him. And Finnegan gets to a deeper level of analysis: "By withholding the privileged identity of the (seemingly) fictional, first-person narrator till the end, Reed forces the reader to reconsider and scrutinize the narrator's role in the story more closely, causing us to take notice of how that narrator moves from first *watching* the scene from a 'safe' distance to actually *precipitating* the action of his own story" (200; Finnegan's emphases).

What no critic has so far discussed, however, is the story's relationship to "The Capitalist," where the protagonist's class identity and ultimate rescue is considerably less assured. Beyond the aesthetic gains Reed makes as he learns to complicate his experience and writes more complex and multilayered scenes, each of these stories concerns class, identity, observation, and privilege. That ambiguity raises pertinent questions: How much comfort can one reasonably expect to trade for experience? How much does one exploit the subjects that one uses for that experience? When does one intervene in the "material" that one observes, and when is it proper to alter that material in an effort to make a difference? Is it possible to shed the trappings of power, or will one always be trapped by a name, identified as a "Reed," a Harvard man, and invited to rejoin the ruling class? Although these are questions that Reed ponders in his fiction, each has specific relevance to his developing nonfiction. As we shall see in upcoming chapters of this study, these questions continue to reverberate for Reed. And as the author experiments with varying ways to portray a protagonist in his fictional tales, he is building experience about the manner by which similarly complex portrayals can work in his journalism.

In the preceding chapter, I demonstrated how Reed was able to construct subtly shifting narrative personae in "War in Paterson" and "Sheriff Radcliff's Hotel" with journalistic technique ahead of its time. In the present context, we can observe the fictional workshop wherein he learned his lessons. In his New York tales, Reed can alter his perceptions ironically within those of an unnamed narrator ("Another Case of Ingratitude"); he can destabilize his identity and privilege entirely in a manner not quite envisioned by Stephen Crane ("The

Capitalist"); he can name himself, but implicate that very naming by questioning his own rank and privilege ("A Taste of Justice").

Reed's story "Seeing Is Believing" further complicates the question of narrative identity that Reed was exploring in his New York tales. Reminiscent of Henry James's "The Real Thing," the story's protagonist is George, an upper-class bounder and acquaintance of the story's first-person narrator (the narrator does not participate in the story's action other than to relate it). George has met a girl who is either a fresh-faced innocent from Chillicothe, Ohio, or a street-wise hustler who knows how to pretend to be a fresh-faced innocent from Chillicothe, Ohio. Throughout the story, Reed's narrator, a habitué of a midtown club, is certain that the girl is a hustler, though Reed generally is careful to distinguish his narrator's perceptions from his own. For example, the narrator declaims piously that the police should arrest any shabbily dressed girl walking alone on the streets of New York near his upscale club, then a moment later says, "Why, we *never* pick up a girl in front of our club" (133).

With the unctuous hypocrisy of his narrator thus established, Reed has him relate George's encounter with the unnamed girl, who talks George out of a twenty-dollar ticket to return to Chillicothe, then mysteriously reappears on the New York streets. Her reappearance delights George's friends, particularly one Burgess, who has bet George five dollars that the ticket purchase was a scam. When George confronts the girl about his ticket money, she tells him the rather implausible tale that she met a man on the train who convinced her to return to New York. She now needs ten dollars more for a new suit, the girl tells George, because the man had mistaken her for a prostitute, and she thus can no longer honorably wear the clothes the man had purchased for her. "Do you know what any man would have thought?" George asks the girl. "Yes," she says, unsmilingly, "Just what you thought. And he'd do pretty much what you're doing, too. I'm not afraid of you" (138).

When George relates the story to his friends, they "guyed him to death for a sentimental sucker" (140) and seemingly are unimpressed by his impressions of the girl's breathtaking innocence and of her capacity for hope. Reed describes her hopefulness lyrically:

"Tried to get a job? Me? Why no!" she looked surprised. "I don't want to work here. I want to see things. And O, there are so many millions of things to see and feel! Yesterday I walked—a long distance I walked, from early in the morning until almost noon. I went up a long shining street that climbed the roofs of the houses, between enormous quivering steel spider webs, until at last I could look down on miles and miles of smoky city spread flat—where all the streets boiled over with children. Think of it! All that to see—and I didn't know it was there at all." (145)

George confesses to his friends that he, too, doubts that such innocence is possible and that he finally "told her just what he thought of her" (146)—presumably that she is a prostitute. The reaction of the girl, he tells his friends, was to tilt her head bird-like to the side and to say that the two will meet again when she most needs him. George claims to be cynical, but Burgess nevertheless tells him he'll donate five of the ten dollars. Reed writes, "'What ten?' snapped George. 'That ten you gave her to pay for her suit,' and Burgess held out the bill." Here the narrator tells us that "George stood there, getting redder and redder, looking at all of us to see if we were laughing at him. Then he said 'Thanks' in a stifled voice and took it" (146).

The story's richly humorous and ironic ending leaves the reader with the same pair of possibilities that face George, and although his narrator chooses a cynical interpretation, Reed refuses to endorse that interpretation. In the alienated city, Reed suggests, seeing *is* believing; nothing is certain; perceptions may rule realities. A girl with a romantic possibility for hope or with a story line that makes such a possibility believable can achieve almost anything—at least if there are enough bounders willing to trade in their cynicism to share vicariously in that capacity for hope. Although he undercuts him at every turn, Reed seems to share George's wistfulness for the excitement of experience that the girl says motivates her: "George says he had the strangest, most irrational sensation—for a moment he actually believed the girl. He seemed to look into a world whose existence he had never dreamed of—a world from which he was externally excluded, because he knew too much! It hurt. The girl might have been a little *white flame burning in him*" (145; emphasis added).

The complex range of distances that Reed is able to achieve in "Seeing Is Believing" between his own sensibilities, those of his narrator, and those of George were to prepare him directly for the complex irony of his subsequent journalism, as I show in the next chapter when discussing the enigmatic finale of *Insurgent Mexico* at the pageant of Santa Maria del Oro. There, in Mexico, amid the "*white, burning* moonlight" (256; emphasis added), Reed will encounter another people with an unlimited capacity for hope, and—like the ironic narrators he developed for "Another Case of Ingratitude" or "Seeing Is Believing"—in the nonfictional *Insurgent Mexico* he will explore the possibility that his own nonfictional persona might be something of a jaded Lucifer in their midst.

On the Borders of Fiction/Nonfiction:
Case Study of "Shot at Sunrise"

After developing such complex narrators, Reed turned toward hybrid narratives as he became increasingly immersed in the production of nonfiction accounts. During this period, Reed habitually treads the borderlines of fiction and nonfiction, learning the craft of each form of narrative and eventually applying those lessons in all their force to the adventurous nonfiction that marks his best-known books and articles. To assess the norms that Reed adopted for the writing of variously fictional and nonfictional narratives, contemporary readers can be guided by the example of two little-known and never-published manuscripts in the Reed archives, cataloged under the title "Shot at Sunrise," versions 1 and 2 (bMS Am 1091:1152 and 1153).

Drawn from an experience that Reed had with fellow reporter Robert Dunn of the New York *Evening Post*, "Shot at Sunrise" recounts the arrest of two U.S. correspondents in September 1914. The two men have traveled to the French front lines near Marne against the strict policy of the Allied armies. Taking its title from the threatened execution of the newspapermen, Reed first conceived the narrative as a nonfictional dispatch for *Metropolitan*, but he told his editor, Carl Hovey, "I have never done such awful work, I know" (bMS Am 1091:130). Reed's biographer Robert Rosenstone describes the never-completed typescripts as a "confused mass of material" (401n) and dismisses their importance.

While the two versions of "Shot at Sunrise" certainly were not completed and may be of limited biographical interest, they do offer an excellent opportunity to study Reed's writing at the borderlines of fact and fiction. One of the manuscripts (bMS Am 1091:1153) sticks rather firmly to what we know of the historical record, while the other (bMS Am 1091:1152) reads like either fiction or more fully developed literary nonfiction. Although the more developed draft is cataloged first by Reed's bibliographers, the evidence from the texts is that the expanded narrative may in fact have been written subsequent to the more terse account.[5]

Whatever the chronology, the two drafts can give the reader a very specific example of how Reed built fictional techniques into his nonfictional texts. The texts show the advantages Reed gained by doing this as well as the issues of credibility that his techniques raise. An initial contrasting of the two texts shows how Reed reworked his material to build a more effective immediate scene and much more convincing dialogue:

> "We came to ask your permission to go to the front," I began.
> "How did you get in the British lines?" he said severely. "You already know

more than we want known. I am obliged to place you upon parole not to leave Coulommiers until you are permitted. Your case will be dealt with later. You know perfectly well that no correspondents are permitted within the British lines, and I must tell you that this is a very serious offense."

Thunderstruck, we retired. (bMS Am 1091:1153, p. 19)

The other man, a tall dry-faced Englishman with drooping walrus whiskers, busied himself with the maps for a moment. Then he carefully placed a monocle in his left eye and walked to the edge of the platform, coldly scrutinizing us.

"You are the prisoners?" he drawled.

"We are not prisoners," said Dunn indignantly. "We came here of our own free will, to ask permission to go to the front. We are Americans."

"Eh?" the Provost removed his monocle and examined us as if we were specimens of a new fauna. "Just so, I beg pardon. May I ask, without offense, what the devil you are doing here?"

"We are correspondents, and we want—"

"Just so. We will consider your wants later. Are you aware that unauthorized civilians are not allowed within the lines?"

"No, we were not informed. No one told us—"

He stared at us with cold, flat blue eyes, polishing the monocle with his handkerchief. "It is an official army order that unauthorized civilians should not enter the lines. As pressmen, you should be acquainted with that order. . . ."

"What?" cried Dunn. "Do you mean that we are arrested? We came here—"

The Provost had turned away and was shifting the maps on his table. "Your case will come up at two o'clock," he flung over his shoulder. (bMS Am 1091:1152, pp. 11–13)

In the latter excerpt, Reed introduces elements normally associated with standard realistic fiction to improve the immediacy of his scene. What is an anonymous man in the first excerpt becomes a dry-faced Englishman with whiskers and a monocle in the second. Flat statements—"I am obliged to place you upon parole not to leave"—in the first excerpt are inflected with subtle sarcasm and specific verbal mannerisms in the second: "Just so, I beg pardon. May I ask, without offense, what the devil you are doing here?" Visual particulars—"busied himself with the maps," "carefully placed a monocle in his left eye," "polishing the monocle with his handkerchief," "was shifting the maps on the table"—are inserted for pacing and to catch the mind's eye.

This study already has considered how Reed two years later would use the sorts of details normally associated with standard realistic fiction to develop his William Jennings Bryan profile. Working from the sort of strategy I am examining here, Reed built an immediacy of dialogue as well as the details of fishing on the Saint Johns River, even though the Bryan piece was presented in

Collier's as nonfiction and even though Reed could use only the quotes and wording that Bryan had approved. Some of the early lessons that prepared Reed for his coverage of Bryan may have been learned in such texts as the "Shot at Sunrise" variations.

The two typescripts of "Shot at Sunrise" also demonstrate a subsidiary effect in the development of Reed's narrative craft: the questions of credibility raised by his revisions. Although both versions feature a historical name (Reed's co-reporter Robert Dunn) for an independent character who happens to be a real reporter, the expanded version departs rather more significantly from the historical record in characterizing Dunn and his scheme to get the reporters into restricted war territory. Another contrast between the versions:

> Bobby and I rented an automobile on the ninth of September, and procured a pass from the Prefecture of Police, which one had to have in order to leave the fortifications of Paris, saying that we were going to Nice for our health; Bobby, having angina pectoris in his family, knew the symptoms, and consented to be the *malade* if one was needed. (bMS Am 1091:1153, p. 2)

> He [Bobby Dunn] suggested that we hire an automobile and get a pass to take a sick man to Nice for his health. After passing the Porte de Charenton we could throw Nice overboard and take our chances on getting North and East. We settled on epilepsy as a convenient disease, because one of Bobby's relatives had once had it, and he knew the symptoms. But in order to make the illusion perfect, we hunted out a doctor who agreed to finish him off for the modest sum of ten francs. It was a bargain. All one afternoon the doctor rehearsed Bobby; shouting, as he thrashed about on the floor, overturning chairs and tables, "*Plus d'ecume, mon ami!* More foam at the mouth! *Abandon! Abandon!*"
> Afterwards we went to the Prefecture of Police. The Sub-Prefect was rather cynical; he wanted to know which of us was the sick man.
> "I am the nurse," I said. Suddenly the Sub-Prefect turned pale. Dunn had fixed him with a vacant stare, swayed gently backward and forward, and bubbled a little.
> "It's all right!" cried the Sub-Prefect. "Quick! A blank pass, somebody! Monsieur had better get his friend into the air—he is unwell." (bMS Am 1091:1152, p. 3)

Since we know from the historical record that Dunn's family malady was, in fact, angina pectoris (Rosenstone, 401), we can begin to assess how Reed crosses the boundary line from factual toward fictional narrative in the revised passage. The shift from angina to epilepsy is accompanied by a deepening of the reporters' plotting. Not only do they "settle on a convenient disease" rather than an actual medical history, but Reed now interjects a fully fictional scene wherein a theatrical doctor schools Bobby, for a price, on how to throw a convincing epileptic fit.

The subsequent dialogue between Reed and the subprefect solves one problem but creates another: Reed fills out the scene wonderfully toward its humorous culmination, but also raises questions of truth and genre. Although many writers and reporters currently practicing the art of literary journalism might be tempted to look the other way at the simple substitution of epilepsy for angina, most modern journalists would judge that Reed has crossed the line into fiction by his wholesale invention of the scene with the theatrical doctor.[6] Because Reed's "Shot at Sunrise" was never published, it is difficult for present-day readers to assess his narrative intentions for the piece; certainly, the shorter piece was sent to his editor Carl Hovey with a *Metropolitan* dateline, but it is not clear that the expanded piece ever was sent anywhere. Moreover, it is entirely possible that Reed meant the piece to be read as fiction. To some extent, with the exception of its use of Dunn's real name, it reads like some of the historically based narratives from France or Mexico that editor Dell classified as tales ("The World Well Lost"; "The Rights of Small Nations"; "The Thing to Do"; "The Head of the Family"). Those four stories are set during moments of Reed's travels that we know to be factual—his visits to Serbia and Bucharest or people he met on his railway trip from Oregon to New York—but they (unlike "Shot at Sunrise") do not cite a real-life protagonist by his real name.

The intertwining of the historical Robert Dunn with an obviously invented scene in the drafts raises interesting theoretical questions. Certainly, Reed did use real names in other pieces of his fiction, but generally he cites only first names (Mac, in "Mac-American"; Fred, for F. Sumner "Fred" Boyd, in "Daughter of the Revolution"). When Reed labels major characters in his narratives with their full names (Pancho Villa, Billy Sunday, Henry Ford, Eugene V. Debs), he seems to intend that these names make specific claims about people and events in history, in narratives that generally are classified as nonfiction. As we shall see in chapter 3, Reed clearly did not intend to tell the whole truth about Mac in "Mac-American": he hid the most important feature of his relationship with Mac. Thus, he shortened Mac's name in the story and masked his real identity.

By contrast, Reed clearly evokes the historical Robert Dunn in "Shot at Sunrise." Reed writes of the scheme to enter restricted war space, "The idea wasn't mine. Bobby Dunn thought of it. Bobby Dunn, the only war correspondent in the world who always gets expelled from every belligerent country during the war" (bMS Am 1091:1152, pp. 2–3). Reed could count on many contemporary readers of his piece to know the reputation of Dunn, a veteran correspondent and explorer who had traveled to the Far East, Alaska, and Mexico and already had a popular book to his credit.[7] So this evocation of the historical Dunn now calls into question the way Reed embellished his tale.[8]

It is ironic that the theme of story embellishment becomes part of the plot of the expanded "Shot at Sunrise." The piece opens with a scene at the Taverne Royale in Paris, where disgruntled war correspondents are nursing drinks, gossiping, and "gnawing their futile writing muscles." One correspondent says, 'Huh! I read that thing Richard Harding Davis wrote about his arrest in Belgium. It sounded faked to me. I don't believe he ever got out of Brussels'" (bMS Am 1091:1152, p. 1). Another correspondent adds that a photographer working with a reporter named E. Alexander Powell told him that Powell never was within two hundred miles of the battle he claimed to witness.[9]

In the scene, Reed wants to satirize the sort of inventive journalism that typified war reporting in the early twentieth century as well as to capture the naked ambition and competition that typifies the working press. Naming Richard Harding Davis, his rival reporter, is an interesting tactic; the reference apparently was based on a real incident. In the same letter in which he had described his own work as "awful," Reed had written to his editor: "Richard Harding Davis, Morgan, and all the other correspondents got arrested . . . and the field is definitely closed to newspapermen" (bMS Am 1091:129). The remarks about Davis or Powell, however, would have been typical digs by a rival newspaperman; neither reporter is characterized further in the piece. By contrast, Robert Dunn virtually is the piece's protagonist; he generates the idea to sneak into forbidden territory and is the most vocal character in the piece. In altering the facts of Dunn's scheme and inventing whole scenes around it, Reed, therefore, was engaging in just the sort of invention and embellishment that his characters attribute to Powell and Davis. Whether Reed intended this irony or not is not clear from the drafts; later I present evidence that Reed's subsequent nonfictional narratives variously reveal unintended irony of this sort *(Insurgent Mexico)* or make effective use of deliberate irony *(Ten Days That Shook the World)*.

An example of how Reed further developed Dunn in the expanded typescript can be seen in yet another comparison of the two versions of "Shot at Sunrise." In the more clearly nonfictional version, Reed builds a scene around his and Dunn's incarceration with three British reporters who, like them, had been picked up in restricted territory. One of them is a stout man who warns the Americans:

"The British army will treat you like dogs, gentlemen, like dogs." Here he gave a ferocious look at the officer, who did not notice him. Just then entered two other civilians, Englishmen, with dirty collars, and a look of sleeplessness and general discomfort.

"*Voila*, the rest of the prisoners!" said the big man bitterly, "Mr. Sanders of the *Daily Mail*—Mr. England of the *Mirror*. I," he continued, twisting his mustaches. "I am Tom Smith, of the *Times*."

He paused to let this sink in.

"Ah, the *Times*," said Bobby, interestedly. "London or New York?"

Mr. Smith snorted, "I am not in the habit of writing for American periodicals, sir," he said. (bMS Am 1091:1153, p. 25)

This is one of the most detailed scenes in the less-developed account, and Reed builds on it in the expanded version, giving to Dunn a more pugnacious role and enhancing the descriptions of the incarceration. Rather than making the setting a simple room inhabited by three dour Englishmen, the expanded version takes Reed and Dunn "down long winding steps into a musty place lighted by tiny barred windows up under the ceiling," and the inmates are more developed, too. As the Americans' eyes adjust to the darkness, Dunn soon will be baiting his British cellmates:

"Anyway," said Dunn nervously. "We are not prisoners."

From the bowels of the place hollow laughter responded. We made out dimly the figures of three beings slouched upon boxes in various attitudes of dejection, and another advancing slowly toward us—a huge corpulent figure in a green velvet hat; his large, round face was garnished with a prodigious grey mustache and an imperial, and he carried a thick cane hung from his elbow.

"Napoleon the Third after Sedan!" cried Dunn, peering at him. "Hello, Louie!"

"Americans!" said the figure in a deep, dignified contemptuous voice. "My name is not Louie, sir! I am John Borden of the *Times*."

"New York, or London?" said I, politely.

"The *Times*, sir, the *Times*! Good God!" (bMS Am 1091:1152, pp. 13–14)

Beyond changing the reporter's name from Smith to Borden, Reed develops an extended argument between the British and American reporters that is resolved only when both sides agree to save their hostilities for the British soldiers who are detaining them. Throughout the argument, Dunn gets off repeatedly snide quips, eventually pulling a more reluctant Reed into the fray.

" New York, or London ? " said I, politely.

" The *Times* , sir, the *Times* ! Good God ! "

We introduced ourselves. " I think I've heard your name somewhere " ventured Dunn.

" No doubt. No doubt. " boomed ~~$$$~~ Mr. ~~$$$~~ Borden/ with heavy sarcasm. " No doubt you have also heard of Gladstone, and Cecil Rhodes, and Chinese Gordon - " A stifled snicker came from ~~$$$$$~~ behind, and he wheeled around furiously " As for you, Mr. Wight, I have remarked in you a lack of respect to which I am not accustomed!"

" It's all right, Louie " said Dunn " Don't get yourself all heated up "

A double gasp from ~~the darkness testified to the horror of the other two prisoners.~~

" O I say - " expostulated a modulated English voice. A ~~$$$$$~~ short, dark man ~~$$$$$$$$$$$$$$$$$$$$$~~ with drooping black moustaches emerged ~~$$$$~~ into the light. " I say - really. That's a bit strong, isn't it, - what ? Really. This is the famous John Borden, you know.... I am Jeliffe, also of the *Times* "

" What did he ever do to make him famous ? " I asked defiantly.

" I - " began the old man with a snort. But there was an interruption. ~~$$$$$$$$$$~~

A clear voice from the gloom ~~announced solemnly.~~ said " He has been the principal figure in every great war since the Second Punic. He has advised all the victorious generals of antiquity how to -."

" Enough ! " thundered the irate Borden, pounding the floor with his cane " Insolence ! "

A third character joined us languidly, - a ~~$$$$$$~~ slender youth ~~$$$$$$$$$$$$$$$$$$$$$$$$$$$$$$$$$$$~~ exquisitely dressed, with

The typescript of Reed's revised "Shot at Sunrise" (1914) demonstrates his typical self-editing strategy. He revised during two stages of the writing process. While typing he used ampersands, percentage marks, or dollar signs to strike over passages for improved diction or sentence structure. His subsequent written corrections or strike-outs completed the process. Though Reed presented most of his work as nonfiction, the evidence in his work papers shows that he was not averse to altering and editing the direct quotes of real-life characters. *(Houghton bMS Am 1091:1152. By permission of Houghton Library, Harvard University.)*

What we have seen by comparing the factual status of the two "Shot at Sunrise" typescripts is how Reed consistently moves to deepen and complicate his reporting narrative. As his career progresses—in direct contradiction to what critics believe to be the ruling paradigm of early-twentieth-century American letters—Reed borrows the techniques he already knew would work in his fiction and directly applies them to his nonfiction. As he does so, new theoretical problems arise when he plays loose with facts in nonfiction—some of which had plagued him in *Insurgent Mexico* and would not be resolved until *Ten Days That Shook the World*.

Having established this trend, I will conclude my discussion of "Shot at Sunrise" by examining two more hallmarks of Reed's fictional discourse that seem to have migrated toward his nonfiction: a quality of descriptive writing able to carry substantial symbolic weight as well as the development of an ironic first-person narrator who is "Reed," but not precisely the author. Both drafts of "Shot at Sunrise" create a scene around Reed's and Dunn's visit to the village of Courtecan. Reed's less-expansive draft reads:

> [S]uddenly we came smack into the most terrible evidence of war we had yet seen. It was the village of Courtecan, a beautiful little French place of about a dozen houses—sacked, looted, and still burning. *As I remember it,* there was only one house which had not been gutted by fire. Bottles, bed-clothes, broken furniture lay in fouled trails from the cottage doors to the streets. Tall columns of smoke mounted straight into the still air, and there was a sound of crackling flames. We pulled up beside a group of old women *standing dumbly* beside the road, looking southward where their men had fled with the wagons when the Germans first came in sight. The Germans had only left Courtecan the night before, they said, at the approach of a company of Highlanders. (bMS Am 1091:1153, p. 10; emphases added)

Reed's more developed draft—whether it is to be read as fiction or nonfiction—presents the scene directly and dramatically. No longer are the women "standing dumbly"; the reader now hears a woman's exact words and precise complaint. Gone are the qualifications ("as I remember it") that intervene between reporter and the present scene. Generic observations now are presented as precise, evocative description:

> The road was empty. A few minutes later, we were gliding through a demolished village, the house-roofs smashed and vacant to the sky, low walls smouldering, thick clouds of smoke still rising from them. A group of bowed old women stood gossiping dazedly before the ruins of the cafe, amid a litter of broken window glass and bottles.

"The Germans? They were here this morning. They went that way when the English cavalry came." All pointed north. "*Mon dieu,* they took my little daughter." We saw a man with a rifle on his shoulder come limping down the road. We did not wait for her to finish.

Beyond the village was a trampled field strewn with hay, and scarred with the ashes of fires where the Germans had bivouacked. In a meadow, peasants were dragging the body of a horse toward a pit they had dug. Other dead horses lay in the ditch along the road, their legs stiffly erect. By the roots of a tree was the limp figure of a man in the field-gray of the Uhlans, his broken lance across his legs, his spurs still upon his boots. The ditch on both sides was pitted with little individual trenches where the Germans had lain to cover the retreat with rifle fire. (bMS Am 1091:1152, p. 5)

Reed's removal of the filter of his potentially imperfect memories from the second narrative seems to free him to make a more complex use of his own character in this expanded version. Because Reed allows his reader to face scenes directly rather than through the observer's memory, that observer now stands ready for more subtle service. In the case of "Shot at Sunrise," the character of "Reed" develops in the same sort of gently ironic manner that we have come to expect from the narrators of Reed's fictional tales like "Another Case of Ingratitude" or "A Taste of Justice." The "Reed" of the narrative—whether it be fictional or nonfictional—does not precisely share the sensibilities of Reed the writer. The gap created by this tactic allows Reed a wealth of possibilities.

In the scene that opens the expanded "Shot at Sunrise," Reed interrupts the conversation of the bored reporters with an observation directly from his narrator: "What else was there to do in Paris during the early days of September? The Germans were rolling down upon us forty miles a day. South and west continuous crawling trains of box-cars, flat-cars, freight-cars bore hundreds of thousands fleeing from the city" (bMS Am 1091:1152, p. 1). The irony, of course, is that Reed's question answers itself. Instead of sitting around gossiping and sniping at rivals, the reporters—Reed included—might be concentrating on the human misery that is all around them. Certainly, among the thousands abandoning lives and property in Paris, there would be one or two who have a story if only the reporters will bother to check. Reed the writer seems to understand this, while Reed the character seems to want only an easy story and a good meal. Later, when a waiter reports yet another rumor of imminent German attack, Reed's narrator observes, "These things ceased any longer to attract. We were blase from weeks of all the preliminary thrills and horrors of a siege. Paris was empty. The chefs had all been mobilized, and you couldn't get a decent meal. . . . And the town was empty of all save concierges, military, and war *correspondents who could not correspond*" (2; emphasis added).

Finally, when Reed and Dunn are about to be detained by the Allied troops, Reed's blustering narrative alter ego responds: "'We'll stay right here,' I added confidently. 'I have a hunch that we're going to see the whole war if we just stick around'" (10). The upshot of the narrative, of course, is that the reporters are going to see nothing but the inside of the prison that they share with three obstreperous British reporters who have had no more success at covering the war than have Reed and Dunn.

As these three examples begin to prove, the development of a subtly ironic narrative presence was another important lesson that Reed would learn from his early fictional tales. While "Shot at Sunrise" admittedly is an early and less-than-successful workshop, the typescripts present a fascinating snapshot in the evolution of Reed's work. In the more-developed draft, Reed creates himself as a subtly ironic character and presents scenes directly and forcefully. Together with Reed's more specific descriptions and extended characterizations, these snapshots reveal a young man becoming a writer and reporter "gifted with the power to use ideas emotionally and paint them with the colors of flame" (Eastman, quoted in Dell, vi).

"Daughter of the Revolution": Reed's Conflict in Fictional Form

Having established the germination of some of Reed's fictional techniques and having begun to demonstrate how those techniques migrate toward his non-fiction, I conclude this discussion of Reed's early fictional tales with an extended reading of one of his better-known stories, "Daughter of the Revolution." Although Reed's first-person narrator only briefly appears as a character, I believe that "Daughter of the Revolution" reveals an aspect of Reed's personal dilemma as a writer and reporter that was to dominate his career.

Like the young female protagonist in "Daughter of the Revolution," Reed seems to be torn between conflicting impulses. In one of them lies his loyalty to paternal perquisites of class, in the other, Reed's instinct to hurl himself into revolutionary change. Written in 1914, the tale achieves significant irony and affords a fictional glimpse at the greatest single theme of Reed's nonfiction—a theme that we shall trace across Mexico, through his reporting of World War I, and finally to its culmination in Russia. Typically, Reed seems first to confront in fiction what he ultimately writes to much deeper purpose and effect in his nonfiction.

"Daughter of the Revolution" apparently grows out of a conversation that Reed and F. Sumner "Fred" Boyd had with a young Parisian prostitute shortly after Reed arrived in Paris in 1914 to cover the war. The story's opening resembles that of "The Capitalist." Although variously set in Washington Square Park and at a cafe in the Rotonde, both tales feature a rainy mist that suffuses the streets without really wetting them, perhaps symbolizing the fog of blurred identity that each protagonist will face. In both cases, a major character who appears to be one thing turns out to be another. Indeed, both stories explore the crisis of identity and the themes of class and freedom. Reed sets up the differing poles of wealth/social acceptance (gold) and annihilation/freedom (blackness) through the contrasting images that surround the sidewalk cafe: "The yellow lights flooded us, and splashed the shining black streets with gold" (3). Marcelle, the prostitute, first tells her companions that she is the daughter of "a very rich and highly respectable family" and that she became a prostitute after being ravished by a duke. That confession prompts Reed's narrator to conclude, rather self-righteously: "A strain of recklessness and unashamed love of life held only a little longer. Marcelle was already soiled with too much handling" (4).

As usual, however, Reed the writer has created a distance between himself and his first-person narrator, and we come to understand that the narrator's initial conclusion misses a deeper complexity. When she hears Fred, the narrator's companion, whistle a revolutionary song, Marcelle confesses that her family really spans four generations of revolutionists and Parisian communards. Her stonemason grandfather was stabbed with a bayonet while hiding from soldiers during a strike, and her father has been bloodied repeatedly at the Creusot strike and for leading a labor action at Thirion's coal yard. "He used to come home at night every week after the meeting of the Union, his eyes shining like stars, roaring blasphemies through the streets," Marcelle recalls. "He was a terrible man. He was always the leader" (11). As for her brother, when they would go to church to pray "he would suddenly jump up and run shouting around the church, kicking over chairs and smashing the candles burning in the chapels" (13). Her brother, Marcelle says, would walk into a cabaret, sing the "Internationale," and yell "Down with the Capitalists! A bas the police! To the Lanterne with the flics!" (14). Even the brother's child is a revolutionary in the cradle.

Marcelle's story prompts cries of understanding from both Fred and the story's narrator. "When the red day comes I'll know which side of the barricades I shall be on" (6), says Fred, as Marcelle begins her story. For his part, the narrator seems to turn to the reader directly, concluding of Marcelle's family: "Three generations of fierce, free blood, struggling indefatigably for a dim dream of liberty. And now a fourth in the cradle! Did they know why they struggled? No matter. It was a thing deeper than reason, an instinct of the human spirit which neither force nor argument could ever uproot" (15). But Reed the writer has prepared a deeper and more complex lesson than Reed the narrator understands; like that afforded William Booth Wrenn in "The Capitalist," the lesson is not so easily stated. Marcelle, it turns out, has become a prostitute because she could not bear the family's destitution, the endless privation, the endless sacrifice for a greater cause. "I always craved joy and happiness," she confesses. "I always wanted to laugh, be gay, even when I was a baby. I used to imagine drinking champagne, and going to the theater, and I wanted jewels, fine dresses, automobiles" (15). Her father's reaction to her desires is simple: he will disown her. "[T]he first fault you commit, I'll put you out the door and call you my daughter no more" (15).

Marcelle's recollection of her father's threat prompts a revised interpretation from Fred and the narrator. "We started, Fred and I. 'Free!' Wasn't that what the old man had fought for so bitterly" (16). Marcelle's brother, despite his firebrand radicalism, seems to understand her deeper motivations as well. "We are of the same blood," he tells Marcelle. "It would do no good to argue with you, or to force you. Each human being must work out his own life. You shall go and do whatever you please. But I want you to know that whenever you are hungry, or discouraged, or deserted, my house is always open to you—that you will always be welcome here, as long as you live" (17).

That solidarity aside, the heart of the story—and the dilemma that was to assume a deep resonance for Reed's own artistic and political life—concerns two chance meetings between Marcelle and her father. The first occurs after Marcelle declares herself free to seek a better way of life. She becomes the mistress of a rich Argentine and—dressed in the high-heeled slippers, the white gloves, the ostrich-feather hat, and the veil that are the Argentine's love gifts—chances to meet her father one day on the street near the door of her brother's tenement. "*Va t'en!*" he shouts, without recognizing her. "What is your kind doing here, in a workingman's house? What do you mean by coming here and insulting us with your silks and your feathers, sweated out of poor men in mills and their consumptive wives, their dying children? Go away, you whore" (18). The second meeting with the father comes after the Argentine has dissolved into a series of other lovers and Marcelle perhaps is less fresh and finely dressed. She chances to meet her father near Saint Denis, with his lunch pail, going to work early in the morning. "He had not seen my face," Marcelle recalls. "There was nothing to do but walk down the street ahead of him. . . . Then he said in a low voice, 'Mademoiselle, wait for me. We are going in the same direction, *hein?*' I hurried. 'You are pretty, mademoiselle. And I am not old. Can't we get together some place?'" (18).

Reed achieves a nice complexity to the tale by drawing its conflicts against predictable types. While the story appears to uphold revolutionary values, the reader comes to understand that the veteran revolutionist—Marcelle's father—exhibits a blind inflexibility that is as tyrannical in its way as any mill owner's. The reader also understands that Marcelle's desire for freedom, which the story might be willing to endorse, will surely kill her. The men she depends on for material possessions will use her as their material possession. Against these negatives, Reed draws the genuinely mutual relationship between Marcelle and her brother; his insurgency contains a human understanding that makes it possible for him to uphold his sister, even though he disagrees with her actions.

Several of the story's perceptive critical readers concentrate on the way that Marcelle symbolizes Reed's romantic drive for inner fulfillment. "[Reed] was displaying a faith that one person's liberty might be another's slavery and a belief that true liberation must be self-defined" (208), says biographer Rosenstone. David C. Duke, who believes the story to be one of Reed's best, writes: "Marcelle's brother understands her radicalism and realizes that they are both seeking a different kind of freedom. Her rebellion was personal, the kind with which Reed was most comfortable. Like Marcelle, he too was a radical but one still closely tied to the Village ethos of freeing the individual from smothering middle-class constraints" (81).

These conclusions certainly square with the conclusions made by Reed's narrator and his friend in the story, but I believe that Reed the writer is after something a little deeper and more subtle. An often-forgotten detail of the story is that Marcelle's brother has been forced into the army to fight the Great War at the time of the story's action: "And now he must go to kill the *Boches* [Germans], like the others. Perhaps he himself is dead; I do not know—I have heard nothing" (15). Marcelle's brother, clearly the story's most heroic character, therefore is trapped in just as deadly a system of class violence as is Marcelle. Personal fulfillment, while important, pales against the brutality of violent systems, Reed suggests. Reed's dilemma, as well as the dilemma of his characters, is how to balance the competing claims of collective action and individual fulfillment. Reed's narrator and his friend Fred seem only dimly to understand that dilemma at the end of the story. As Finnegan notes, "While Fred sees both the father and Marcelle as suffering from the same false consciousness of bourgeois sexism and repressive morality, the final irony of the story turns on Fred and *his* condescending assumptions about feminism and women's freedom" (196; Finnegan's emphasis).

Even more interesting in this context are the twin scenes of rejection and seduction that Reed prepares for Marcelle in her complicated relationship with her father. Although the initial rejection moves in an opposite class direction, the father's charge that she insulted the family with her "silks and feathers" suggests the sort of ruling paternal values that rejected Reed for daring to challenge ruling class assumptions in his work. That Reed chooses to build a class image around Marcelle's silk is intriguing, since it was the strike at the Paterson silk mill that gave Reed his first big break as a reporter and activist. And he achieves an even more eerie effect at the end of the story when the father attempts to pick up a prostitute that he does not understand to be his daughter. Here, the daughter represents a material commodity to a man who earlier has criticized explicitly her materialism as containing the effaced violence of worker exploitation. The father now says, "We are going in the same direction.... Can't we get together some place?" (18). Both statements contain an unintended irony on the father's part. The daughter and her father both are going the same direction, locked in a self-destructive rebelliousness that short-circuits collective action. Were they to understand this, they might "get together some place" and gain an understanding of their common plight. Instead, they are trapped by a paternal economic system that both exploits them and would make the daughter an instrument of her father's illicit desire. No wonder Marcelle recalls, "I was so full of horror and of fear that he might see my face! I did not dare turn up a side street, for he would have seen my profile. So I walked straight ahead —straight ahead for hours, for miles" (18–19).

The compromised relationship between father and daughter teases out a deeper meaning to the story's title and reveals its threshold stakes for Reed. If Marcelle is a daughter of the "revolution," the title would seem to equate her father with that revolution, and his twin attractions of menace and desire with those of the revolutionary urge. It almost goes without saying that Reed himself was deeply attracted to revolution and yet menaced by its challenge to his personal and material stability. Both in Mexico and in his World War I journalism, Reed was aware of revolution's differing aspects of seduction and danger. As the next chapter will demonstrate, the Mac character, in "Mac-American," whom Reed met in Mexico, places Reed precisely in the same position to profit from or be menaced by paternal U.S. power as Marcelle is placed in near the end of Reed's fictional tale. Mac offers Reed a career opportunity in exchange for Reed's covert acquiescence to a sell-out that Reed cannot admit publicly. After Mexico, as the remainder of this book will demonstrate, Reed spent much of his career resolving his problematic relationship to power. How he changes and how he achieves that change is perhaps the most important single theme of Reed's writing. Two points link this discussion to the present chapter: Reed is not afraid to drive a thematic wedge between the conclusions of his narrator and deeper norms that the author designs the story to express; and Reed uses the occasion of his *fictional* "Daughter of the Revolution" to explore a theme that will gain its fullest expression in his *nonfiction*. Reed thus travels the opposite direction of the prevailing literary norm that generations of critics have used to describe his peers.

Thematically, Reed's divided mind is revealed by his genuine understanding of the plight that Marcelle faces at the end of the story. The narrator and Fred are anxious to absolve her of responsibility. "Your father—fighting all his life for liberty—yet turned you out because you wanted *your* liberty!" (19; Reed's emphasis), Fred cries, adding that women will need another generation to attain the same revolutionary freedoms as men. Marcelle demurs from Fred's analysis: "Oh but you don't understand. . . . I did wrong. I am bad. If I had a daughter who was like me, I should do the same thing" (19). In making this claim, Marcelle falls back on an old paternal standard that women are to be "respectable" and must help to contain the runaway sexuality of men rather than encourage it. Yet an insurgency runs through her veins not easily tamed by her ruling values. The narrator asks if she regrets her decision to rebel against her family: "'Regret my life?' she flashed back, tossing her head proudly. '*Dame*, no. I'm free!'" (19). The record shows that Reed was more successful at expanding these complicated themes in his nonfiction than he ever would be again in his fiction.

Serial "Dynamite" and the Wages of Compromise

For a final consideration of Reed's fiction, I want to examine how "Dynamite," the dramatic serial that Reed wrote in 1916 for *Collier's*, reaches across the literary divide to echo "Daughter of the Revolution"—perhaps Reed's best-known and most artistically successful short story. The four-part "Dynamite" probably made Reed more money than any other piece of his fiction, yet it routinely is dismissed as pulp fiction and is ignored by his critical readers. Certainly "Dynamite" suffers from all the worst elements of serial fiction: cliffhangers at the end of each section, stereotypical characters, a contrived and melodramatic plot. Still, its underlying theme of seduction and rebellion intertwines with Reed's more ambitious fiction and sheds additional light on Reed's political and artistic contradictions.

In "Dynamite," a young secretary, Anita, and her fiancé Tom stumble onto a complicated stock-manipulation plot in which Anita's boss attempts to make a financial killing by killing, literally, a corporate takeover artist on the eve of a lucrative merger deal. Without belaboring the plot, I want to show how the characters of "Dynamite" roughly correspond with those of "Daughter of the Revolution" and how the fictional series explores similar themes. Like Marcelle, Anita and Tom in "Dynamite" are anxious to improve their class status; they need more money so as to marry and to gain personal fulfillment. To do so, Anita must defy her scheming boss, T. Mordecai, and his values in something of the same way that Marcelle had to defy her father's values. Both stories contain scenes of "discovery" in which the father figure surprises the rebellious parties in the midst of a transformation to new values. Both father figures also attempt seduction (in the case of "Dynamite," T. Mordecai offers a no-work job and a regular paycheck, even if it comes at the price of keeping quiet). In both stories, rebellious parties are disciplined for their insurgency—although Anita and Tom are punished (abducted, beaten, bound to a chair, etc.) in a much more melodramatic manner. Most importantly, in both stories the protagonists face a critical decision: whether to acquiesce to a system they know to be corrupt or to go down fighting it, even at great risk to health and class stability. Menace and seduction, therefore, are closely intertwined in both cases, although more predictably in the serial.

Intriguingly, "Daughter of the Revolution" and "Dynamite" even share having a young hero more radical than the protagonists—one who at first seems subservient to the enemies of the protagonists, but who transforms under pressure into a true revolutionary. Both of these characters—Marcelle's brother, in "Daughter of the Revolution," and Rhadiatchine, in "Dynamite"—emerge heroic, but suffer for their rebellion. Both at first seem to be impulsive and self-destructive, but prove loyal to the heroes at their time of greatest need. Eventually, however, Marcelle's brother is trapped in a worldwide traders' war, never to be heard from again; while Rhadiatchine disappears after he is critically wounded in a knife fight. The publication of "Daughter of the Revolution" in a radical periodical (*The Masses*) allows Reed to portray Marcelle's revolutionary brother much more realistically; in the *Collier's* story, he had to take care not to make a world revolutionist too sympathetic. At first he sets up the Marxist plotter to be the story's stock villain, then cleverly reverses field to show that Rhadiatchine has been deceived by even more nefarious capitalist profiteers.

Finally, in both stories Reed explores how financial reward affects his protagonists. We have already seen how the silks and feathers in which Marcelle wraps herself become as confining as a funeral shroud, even though they initially are the instruments of her freedom. In the conventions of "Dynamite," Reed must reward Tom and Anita for their refusal to knuckle under to Mordecai's scheming. But he faces a dilemma: How can he deliver that reward in a way that will uphold the values of his *Collier's* readers without selling out his personal beliefs? In a manner that is typical of Reed's most compromised writing, Reed turns to self-irony.

Reed's early biographer, the Marxist critic Granville Hicks, describes Reed's tactic. "'And they all lived happily ever after,' he concluded in the story, lest anyone should fail to realize that his tongue was in his cheek" (222), Hicks observes. While that is true, it is interesting to note that Reed places Tom and Anita in precisely the same position that the writer himself faced by selling his potboiler serial to *Collier's*. That is, he allows Tom and Anita to profit (Reed financed a kidney operation and a summer in Provincetown with the serial), but not in so lavish a way as to undermine their deeper values. Reed thereby manages to expose the evils of war profiteering at the same time he permits his heroes short-term gains against a long-term promise not to do it again. To foil Mordecai's plot, Tom and Anita ally themselves with a war profiteer and reap a stock tip that could make them truly wealthy. Instead, Tom sells at a relatively modest $13,000 profit. He has his regrets when the stock subsequently soars, but Anita's values are deeper and more enduring. "[M]uch as Tom wished he had held on to his [stock], Anita soon bullied him into a reluctant belief that he had done right. And before they married he had to swear a solemn oath that he would never again play the stock market" (chapter 4, 28). Perhaps the deal that Reed made to finance his own summer on the Cape with "Dynamite" was similarly circumscribed.

In the context of this chapter's argument, however, the relationship of "Dynamite" to the earlier "Daughter of the Revolution" helps to illustrate two points: rebellion and capitulation were both seductive and terrifying to John Reed. Additionally, Reed uses fiction to prepare himself for more-adventurous nonfiction. By this latter tactic, Reed cuts against the grain of the U.S. writers who surround him: Twain, Dreiser, Hemingway, and Dos Passos. The crucible of Reed's early fiction—its nimble narrators, its richly developed descriptions, its themes of seduction and menace—prepare Reed for more deeply developed and serious nonfiction. Meanwhile, Reed would not devote any great effort to the fiction he wrote during the second half of his career. For that decision, Reed pays a price as dear to his literary reputation as the insurgency practiced by Marcelle's brother or by Rhadiatchine. For nearly a century, those few scholars of English who have bothered to read Reed seem to have decided that his career path reveals an overall failure of imagination. To that way of thinking, Reed thus forfeits his place in the literary canon represented by such arbiters as *The Norton Anthology of American Literature* or by the thousands of course syllabi distributed in universities each year.

In the chapters that follow, I want to take a look at Reed's greatest non-fiction both for its artistry and for its fuller cultural context. How will Reed resolve the competing instincts for insurgency and self-preservation that are revealed by such tales as "Daughter of the Revolution" and "Dynamite"? Similarly, what will Reed disclose about the deals and compromises that provide his access to material? Will he mourn when living characters die for the cause of his compelling war narratives? What distance will Reed create between the author and teller of the nonfiction tale? And what are the subtle effects of that distance? Where does Reed's journalism find its place in the larger narrative of magazine editorials and advertisements? Can Reed craft a nonfictional world sufficient to his purpose? Reed himself said:

> I can extract from the richness of my life something beautiful and strong. . . .
> In my rambles about the city, I couldn't help but observe the ugliness of poverty and all its train of evil, the cruel inequality between rich people who had too many motor cars and poor people who didn't have enough to eat. It didn't come to me from books that the workers produced all the wealth of the world, which went to those who did not earn it. ("Almost Thirty," 140)

To fashion the sort of book sufficient to expose "the ugliness of poverty and all its train of evil," Reed sets aside his fiction to breathe new life into the non-fictional form.

An Insurgent in Mexico

JOHN REED IS best known today for his *Ten Days That Shook the World* account of the Bolshevik Revolution, but the book that made his contemporary reputation was *Insurgent Mexico*. Reed went to Mexico in December 1913 as an untested freelance reporter. He emerged four months later as a $500-a-week literary superstar and the self-styled confidant of Mexican rebel Pancho Villa. Published in 1914 by Appleton & Co., *Insurgent Mexico* is a brash, uneven, wonderfully written book brimming with intriguing puzzles.

A close reading of the book against Reed's original notes in the Harvard archives reveals that Reed lied about his access to material, transferred actual characters into fiction, and made up fictional roles for characters to fill the gaps in his nonfiction. As I have argued elsewhere (Lehman, 97), Reed seemingly could not accept the contradiction of his marketing the experience of Mexico's insurgents to a magazine bankrolled by North American business interests, specifically the Vanderbilt and Guggenheim connections of Henry Payne Whitney. In a perhaps unwitting textual reenactment of that contradiction, Reed inflates his acceptance by rebel Mexicans at the same time he effaces a pragmatic arrangement he made with a U.S. war profiteer. Yet despite this problem, Reed manages a significant break in *Insurgent Mexico* from the ruling notion of how to cover alien culture and armed conflict that was established by Stephen Crane and Richard Harding Davis, his contemporary role models and sometime rivals. Across the pages of the book and hidden in its enigmatic ending is compelling evidence that Reed was beginning to understand the ethical implications of reproducing human life and death and of marketing war misery to voyeuristic readers. In this way, *Insurgent Mexico* becomes an important transitional text for Reed: it is the book where he first glimpses the possibility of writing sustained and socially informed literary nonfiction, even as he shies from the full acceptance of that possibility to protect his writing market and to nurture his growing literary reputation.

In exploring this transition, I follow the lead of John J. Pauly, a communications scholar who recommends that nonfictional narrative be examined for "the way the reporting process implicates writer, subjects, and readers in relationships beyond the text," even as one also reads inside the text for its "play of meaning" (112). This strategy brings to the nonfictional text the fullest possible resources of what literary scholars traditionally have done (narrative and textual analysis, close reading, and the like) as well as broader models of cultural studies and communication theory. This chapter reads *Insurgent Mexico* for the manner in which it implicates its author historically and examines the narrator of the text (located by close reading and other traditions of literary analysis) against the grain of what is known of its actual author (produced by social and historical analysis of such competing texts as Reed's Mexican notes).

As I have demonstrated in earlier studies (Lehman, *Matters of Fact: Reading Nonfiction over the Edge*), many of the properties and powers we routinely grant to a narrator in fiction—an ability to read minds, to foretell the future, to be everywhere, to reproduce speech verbatim, to construct and arrange scenes—raise intriguing problems in nonfiction. Reed cannot control a public character like Pancho Villa quite so neatly as if he were inventing him purely from his imagination. A narrative that purports to present the thoughts or "exact words" of a nonfictional character who, inexplicably and against all evidence, turns out to think and speak just like the author has, in fact, raised the sorts of questions about his methodology that implicate him, that cut against the grain of his voiced intent, and that reveal his ideology. Similarly, decisions about what characters to quote in what order, what events to dramatize, what factual details to elevate to the status of symbols, and so forth, expose not only the factual status of the narrative but also its social positioning.

My intent in reading *Insurgent Mexico* and other nonfictional texts is not to transfer the narrative into the category of "fiction" as soon as discrepancies of intent and practice are revealed. It is rather to examine those discrepancies for what they say about the cultural relationship of Reed, his Mexican subjects, and the readers—then and now—who are attracted to these stories. How does an author approach his subjects? Does he or she dominate them or liberate them? Is he frightened by them or does he celebrate them? In extreme cases, certainly, the gaps we find between stated intent and actual practice might cause us to close the book or to read it as fiction or fantasy. In a nonfictional text like *Insurgent Mexico,* however, such a reading can bring more complex appreciation for the way the book works to reenact the experience of actuality in narrative form and for the book's place in the cultural history of literary journalism. The cultural and artistic conflict revealed by a close reading demonstrates that the Reed of *Insurgent Mexico* could never shed the recognition that he—as a gringo journalist trading on the wealth and rights of North American power—was implicated by the very terms of his project. He thus leaves, wittingly or unwittingly, unacknowledged "traces" of his manipulating presence throughout the text, most notably in the liberties he takes with the historical record and, ultimately, in his construction of the morality play that makes up the book's final scene.

To make that case, this chapter will examine carefully Reed's Mexican notebooks, a series of handwritten scrawls on reporter's notepads that survive among Reed's papers at Harvard and that form the first written text from which ultimately came *Insurgent Mexico.* As in earlier chapters, I will examine the source materials to see how Reed builds characters, scenes, and quotes from his initial observations and jottings. But in this chapter the examination goes further, ferreting out discrepancies between notes and finished text to unearth the author's manipulation and distortion. Having established the cultural ramifications of Reed's subterfuge, the chapter then turns to passages of *Insurgent Mexico* in which the author mounts an effective attack on the ruling assumptions of war and war representation in the pre–World War I era. To do this, the tradition in which Reed wrote is examined: how Stephen Crane and Richard Harding Davis covered Spanish-American battles at the turn of the century and how Reed significantly adjusted that received tradition. The chapter specifically studies at some length the contradictions contained in Crane's earlier reporting from Mexico and the way that Reed approaches a partially successful resolution of the contradictions. Finally, the study of *Insurgent Mexico* produces a fresh reading of the enigmatic last chapter of the book, suggesting an underlying irony that predicts Reed's subsequent development as a socially implicated reporter and writer.

The Mexican Notebooks and the Birth of a Book

Insurgent Mexico consists of six parts presented in nonchronological order and anchored by vivid coverage of two battles (the routing of the revolutionary Tropa unit by a band of loyalist *colorados* and Pancho Villa's successful assault on the northern Mexican city of Torreon). The book also contains interviews and sketches of Villa and "First Chief" Venustiano Carranza, as well as extended portraits of Mexican life in the northern Durango towns of Las Nieves, Valle Allegre, and Santa Maria del Oro. Nine portions of the book were first published in *Metropolitan Magazine* between February and September 1914; two shorter sketches first appeared in *The Masses* in July and August 1914. In addition, Reed sent seven dispatches from the battle of Torreon to the *World,* a New York daily, during March and April 1914. Front-page exclusive interviews with Pancho Villa and Venustiano Carranza appeared in the *World* on March 1 and 4, 1914— pieces that cemented Reed's reputation as a foreign correspondent. Reed also wrote the short story "Mac-American" for *The Masses* based on an experience in Chihuahua City.

The events of the book concern revolutionary fighting in Mexico after a constitutionalist regime led by Francisco Madero had been toppled during a military coup in February 1913. Madero had seized power from Mexico's long-time dictator Porfirio Diaz and had instituted a measure of land and political reform in Mexico before being captured and shot in the military coup engineered by the reactionary Victoriano Huerta. In battles covered by Reed's book, Huerta's federalist troops are first attacked by irregular revolutionaries, called the Tropa, fighting in the Mexican state of Durango under the command of General Tomas Urbina and later by Francisco Villa's regular revolutionary army as it makes a successful assault in February 1914 on Gomez Palacio and Torreon, a strategic federalist city in the state of Chihuahua. By 1914, the revolutionary interests in Mexico had coalesced around forces led by Emiliano Zapata in the south and former outlaw Francisco Villa, who commanded the Division del Norte in the north. Both revolutionary generals were loosely aligned with Venustiana Carranza, the self-proclaimed First Chief of the Revolution, and the governor of the Mexican state of Coahuila. In *Insurgent Mexico,* Reed's sympathies clearly lie more with Villa than with Carranza: "Villa, with a well-armed, well-disciplined force of 10,000 men, was entering on the Torreon campaign," Reed reports. "All this was accomplished almost single-handedly by Villa. Carranza seems to have contributed nothing but congratulations" (*Insurgent Mexico,* 221).

As he would demonstrate elsewhere during his career as a journalist, Reed's political instincts were sound. Despite his many flaws, Villa offered the best hope for the Mexican Revolution because he proved to be a brilliant strategist, on one occasion commandeering a federalist train and sneaking into Cuidad Juarez with two thousand rebel troops. The key border city had fallen to the invading revolutionaries before loyalist defenders could fire a shot. Villa also perfected night raids and surprise attacks that met with uncommon success, particularly during late 1913 and most of 1914. "Villa emerged as a consensus candidate to reestablish the coalition of lower- and middle-class forces that had brought Madero to power" (204), concludes Friedrich Katz, the foremost historical authority on Villa and the Mexican Revolution. Fortunately for Reed, Pancho Villa took a shine to the young, pug-nosed reporter, fresh from New York and eager to make a journalistic splash.

The structure of *Insurgent Mexico* is problematic: Reed presents scenes out of order, leaves vast gaps in the chronology of his travels, and shows up in widely differing locations without any indication as to how he got there.[1] Given that the book is nonsequential, one is tempted to assign great significance to the order in which Reed arranges the six major parts of *Insurgent Mexico*. The truth, however, is that for the most part *Insurgent Mexico* is structured as it originally appeared in *Metropolitan*. The magazine first published "With *La Tropa*," in April 1914; the following month it published "The Battle of La Cadena," and in June printed a long profile of Villa under the title of "Francisco Villa—The Man of Destiny." These *Metropolitan* pieces correspond to the first two long parts of *Insurgent Mexico:* "Desert War" and "Francisco Villa," although Reed also wrote a new chapter, entitled "Elizabetta," specifically for the book. Parts 4 and 5 and a portion of part 6 of *Insurgent Mexico* had initially appeared in *Metropolitan* between July 1914 and September 1914. Although Reed's newspaper profiles of Villa and Carranza had been published in the *World* only three days apart, *Metropolitan* separated its versions of the profiles by three months. Undoubtedly, the sequence resulted from *Metropolitan*'s recognition that Pancho Villa simply made better copy. The magazine had expended considerable capital on its construction of Villa as a colorful revolutionary outlaw and on Reed as the man to cover him. Reed's profile of the more mainstream Carranza —which appears as part 5 of *Insurgent Mexico* and depicts Carranza as a remote, moody reformer—clearly drew less priority from *Metropolitan*. Reed's subsequent book maintains the sequence established by the magazine.

Despite this relatively simple explanation for *Insurgent Mexico*'s chronology, the most provocative additions to Reed's book form part 3 of *Insurgent Mexico* ("Jimenez and Points West") and the final two chapters of part 6 ("Happy Valley" and "Los Pastores"). In part 3, Reed inserts accounts drawn from his journey to meet Villa *after* the book already has presented the long profile of the revolutionary general. And the rural Mexican chapters of part 6 that end the book actually took place *before* the dramatic battles at Gomez Palacio and the fall of Torreon that Reed depicts in part 5.

Drawn from sketches that Reed wrote both for *The Masses* and for *Metropolitan*, the nonsequential sections of the book reveal something of Reed's overall conception of *Insurgent Mexico.* The reporter intersperses his profiles and his two major battle scenes (the intensely personal account of his adventures with Tropa revolutionary irregulars and the Villa army's successful assault on Torreon) with scenes of Mexican domesticity, the most vivid of which ends the book. Christopher P. Wilson correctly notes that the overall structure of the book thus undercuts what was then the ruling U.S. opinion—that a political movement led by the reformer Carranza might usher Mexico into a successful junior partnership with the United States. In Wilson's words, "The book's final underscoring of the localized collectivity of village culture also countermanded the U.S. media's recurring tendency to anoint a singular (bourgeois) Moses—in this case, Carranza—to lead his people to the promised values of the United States" (355). The final shaping of *Insurgent Mexico,* according to Wilson, "is by and large a movement *back* in actual and mythic time, away from geopolitics and literally into the hills" (353; Wilson's emphasis).

This chapter generally accepts the explanation that Wilson provides for Reed's structure in *Insurgent Mexico,* but it produces a much closer reading of Reed's first book than any that has been done before. I explicitly compare the original notes that Reed brought back from Mexico with his finished writing. Most of Reed's most vivid scenes in *Insurgent Mexico* can be traced to first drafts in his Mexican notebooks, handwritten accounts of his experiences now collected in the John Reed Papers at Harvard University. Some 116 pages of Reed's notes survive from the four months he spent in Durango riding with the irregular revolutionist Tropa and accompanying Pancho Villa around the state of Chihuahua. Nearly one hundred years later, the pages of the three-by-five-inch notebooks have separated from their string bindings and must be painstakingly arranged into a semblance of order; some pages are torn, and significant sections of Reed's Mexican experience seem to be missing. Yet what remains presents a fascinating, and sometimes incriminating, glimpse of Reed's reporting and writing style.

In 1913, as he traveled to Presidio County, Texas, with Mabel Dodge, who at that time was his lover, Reed seemed as much a prototypical gonzo journalist or Tom Wolfe dandy as serious political writer. Dressed in a bright orange corduroy suit and indulging, with Dodge and her money, in several days of hard partying as the train wound its way toward Texas, Reed arrived in El Paso to find a border town bristling with Yankee profiteers, soldiers, outlaws, and gunrunners. Davis, perhaps the most famous war correspondent of the day and, with Crane, the star reporter of the Spanish-American War, was already there for the New York *Tribune* (Hicks, 112), as were other journalists and photographers.

Competition was intense as the writers and photographers scrambled for angles. The Mexican Revolution was the first war to be covered by photographers capable of shooting action scenes for quick newsprint reproduction, an innovation that extended what seemed like an insatiable public appetite for war representation. The development and efficient transmission of halftone photos by the outbreak of the Mexican Revolution in 1910 had transformed war photography from a collection of staged scenes and stills to action shots. The Mexican Revolution soon became the laboratory for the new photographic techniques, and competition intensified. Editors searched for writers capable of constructing strong narrative word-pictures that could compete with and support photographic reproduction. Photographer George Leighton recalled some thirty years later that pictorial reproduction was so fashionable during the 1920s that even Pancho Villa hired an artist to ride along with him to chronicle the triumphs of the revolution and indulged the Mutual Film Company, which had offered him money to stage a sham battle for their cameras, by hurrying preparations for a real battle and fighting it while the camera crank turned (Brenner and Leighton, 192).[2]

For his part, Reed was more than ready to take up the challenge of creating word-pictures, and his palm-sized notebooks were the first step in that literary production. Although he carried a camera until he dropped it in headlong flight from colorado loyalists while he was riding with the Tropa (*Insurgent Mexico*, 75), Reed primarily depended on his gift for verbal description to capture Villa for his North American readers. For example, a section of the Mexican notebooks bears the following in Reed's rapid scrawl from the reporter's first meeting with the revolutionary on December 26, 1913:

> V's actions and movements were like those of a wild animal. When he stood up, he was awkward and stiffish below the knees, from much horse-back riding. Above the waist, with hands and arms and trunk, he moved with the unconscious swiftness and sureness of a coyote. His mouth hung open, and when it did not smile, his face looked good-natured, almost simple. His eyes, dark, perfectly round, blood-shot, shallow, were really the desperate things about him. Absolutely hot and steely. Did not say much. Spoke very little, and then sticks by it. Wearing business suit, felt hat. He's never been in uniform until Christmas day. (bMS Am 1091:1316)

Reed is too good a reporter and writer simply to regurgitate these notes into finished print, but one sees his painstaking observation of Villa bear fruit when he describes the revolutionary general in action. Little pieces of the characterizations that began in Reed's notes (Villa's posture, his mannerisms, his clothing, his half-smiles, his animal grace, his steely resolve) make their way

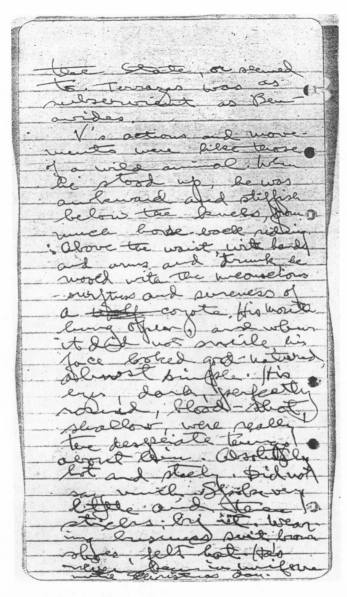

This page from the notebook that Reed kept during his travels in Mexico in 1913–14 contains some of his earliest and most vivid impressions of the revolutionary general Pancho Villa. Reed's relatively careful handwriting here indicates that he most likely wrote these impressions in journal form. When he was conducting interviews or reporting on the scene, his handwriting tended to become sprawling and haphazard. *(Houghton bMS Am 1091:1316. By permission of Houghton Library, Harvard University.)*

into more active descriptions. Here is Villa in *Insurgent Mexico* walking into a meeting of his artillery corps: "He walked a little pigeon-toed, humped over, with his hands in his trousers pockets. As he entered the aisle between the rigid lines of soldiers he seemed slightly embarrassed, and grinned and nodded to a *compadre* here and there in the ranks" (96). Or Villa bullfighting: "Villa would walk right up to the pawing, infuriated animal, and, with his double cape, slap him insolently across the face. . . . Sometimes the sawed-off horns of the bull would catch Villa in the seat of his trousers and propel him violently across the ring; then he would turn and grab the bull by the head and wrestle him with the sweat streaming down his face" (111). Or Villa on a troop train: "Often I have seen him slouched on his cot in the little red caboose, . . . cracking jokes familiarly with twenty ragged privates sprawled on the floor, chairs, and tables. . . . Villa personally would be on hand in a dirty old suit, without a collar, kicking mules in the stomach and pushing horses in and out of the stock cars. Getting thirsty all of a sudden, he would grab some soldier's canteen and drain it" (120).

The section of the Mexican notebooks that most closely parallels the finished *Insurgent Mexico* is the description of Villa's army at Yermo on the eve of the successful invasion of Torreon. In his original notes, Reed wrote: "Yermo —flat desert to the northeast and south. To the west, also, with notched mountains in the distance. Desert mesquite and sage-brush" (bMS Am 1091:1316). Crafting the final draft of his word-picture, Reed improved the rhythm and deepened the imagery: "At Yermo there is nothing but leagues and leagues of sandy desert, sparsely covered with scrubby mesquite and dwarf cactus, stretching away on the west to jagged, tawny mountains and on the east to a quivering skyline of plain" (147).

Building from notes to finished form, Reed evokes Villa's revolutionary troops as a modern-day Children of Israel embarked on a desert exodus. "Twenty-one trains lying in the desert. Pillars of smoke by day. Fire by night," read the original notes. In the final draft, Reed alters the passage slightly, enhancing it to increase the sense of the army's wandering isolation. "There is no water to speak of for forty miles," *Insurgent Mexico* tells the reader. "There is no grass for animals. For three months in the spring, bitter, parching winds drive the yellow dust across it. Along the single track in the middle of the desert lay ten enormous trains, pillars of fire by night and of black smoke by day, stretching back northward farther than the eye could reach" (147). A simple, final line in the notebook—"Even God aids General Villa. Wednesday. Dust cloud seven miles long"—infuses a brief scene in the book with specific visual imagery:

> Above the place a mighty cloud of dust, seven miles long and a mile wide, towered up into the still, hot air, and, with the black smoke of the engines, struck

wonder and terror into the Federal outposts. . . . Out into the desert so far that finally they were mere pinpoints of flame stretched the innumerable camp-fires of the army, half obscured by the thick, billowing dust. "Even God," re-marked Major Leyva, "even God is on the side of Francisco Villa!" (148–49)

In chapter 2, we saw how Reed had improved the detail of his prose, added specific color, dialogue, and imagery when he rewrote the nonfictional "Shot at Sunrise" as a more fictionalized version. In *Insurgent Mexico*, Reed takes his effort in an interesting direction. Here the transformation from notes to finished text works to create a *nonfictional* narrative that is as vivid as any fiction. Reed creates his protagonists as a modern diaspora traveling through the Wilderness in search of a Promised Land (or at least the land promised them by agrarian reform). Rather than depending on a higher power, Reed suggests that the power available to them is their ability to work together for a common goal. When the train is stopped by enemy sabotage, Reed depicts four hundred men working shoulder to shoulder, "shouts, and hammering steel, and the thud of falling ties" (171) on the instrument of their own salvation, rather than waiting for some high priest to bring them a sign of God's blessing. Therefore, Reed's panoramic scenes of flood, drought, poison waters, pillars of fire and smoke unify what otherwise might be disjointed scenes.

Reed spent his time on Villa's train either riding on the cowcatcher or perched on the breech of Villa's largest cannon, dubbed El Nino, which Villa had commandeered from the federalists in one of his most important victories. The sections of the book that describe the train's jolting progress are based on pages of notes in which Reed's handwriting becomes virtually indecipherable. On one occasion, the jolted penmanship improves as Villa's train pulls into the village of Brittingham and stops. Villa and his staff gallop into the village on horses, and Reed's notes report an extended conversation that builds a second important allusion in the passage: Villa as a latter-day Robin Hood trickster. Reed's original notes:

> "Have you seen Pancho Villa around?"
> "No, some Federals last night."
> "Do you know what kind of a guy he is? What he looks like?"
> "No."
> "Too bad because I want to catch that *basquariado bandide*. Have you met him?"
> "No, and we don't want to."

Here is how Reed enhances the scene for *Insurgent Mexico*, building its dialogue and injecting strong, active verbs:

At the village of Brittingham the great line halted, while Villa and his staff galloped up to the peons watching from their little mound. "*Oyez!*" said Villa. "Have any troops passed through here lately?"

"*Si, senor!*" answered several men at once. "Some of Don Carlo Argumedo's *gente* went by yesterday pretty fast."

"Hum," Villa meditated. "Have you seen that bandit Pancho Villa around here?"

"No, *senor!*" they chorused.

"Well, he's the fellow I'm looking for. If I catch that *diablo* it will go hard with him!"

"We wish you all success!" cried the *pacificos*, politely.

"You never saw him, did you?"

"No, God forbid!" they said fervently.

"Well!" grinned Villa. "In the future when people ask if you know him you will have to admit the shameful fact! I am Pancho Villa!" And with that he spurred away, and all the army followed. (169–70)

When Villa's constitutionalists engage the federal troops at Gomez Palacio outside of Torreon, Reed's notes are there to capture the sights and sounds: "Big guns booming like bells. Hellish chatter of musketry fire. Woodpecker stabs of machine guns. Shrapnel. Leaden rain." In several passages of the book, Reed's notes pay off in powerfully personified verbs and participles (yelling, vomited, crackling, hammering) that capture as well as any writer ever has the horrors of war.

[T]here wasn't a sign of the shooting—not even smoke, except when a shrapnel shell burst yelling down in the first row of trees a mile ahead and vomited a puff of white. The cracking rip of rifle fire and the staccato machine guns and even the hammering cannon didn't reveal themselves at all. The flat, dusty plain, the trees and chimneys of Gomez, and the stony hill, lay quietly in the heat. From the *alamos* off to the right came the careless song of birds. (179–80)

Here Reed pauses, but he can find his metaphors only in nightmare: "It was an incredible dream, through which the grotesque procession of wounded filtered like ghosts in the dust" (180). Then he is back to his scene, again anchored by vivid aural and visual detail:

Down front the rifle fire had frittered away to ragged sputtering and the machine guns were silent. And then four booms floated to us, and, simultaneously, the enemy's shells, which had been exploding desultorily over the line of trees nearest the city, marched out into the open desert and leaped toward us in four tremendous explosions, each nearer. . . . Crash—Wheeeeaa! Over our heads, snapping viciously in the leafy trees, sang the rain of lead. (179–80, 183)

Reed manages to illustrate his overarching theme of war's brutality and futility through the close observation of individual human beings on the battlefield. His notes as he walks near the hospital train at Gomez Palacio record: "Cottonwoods, streams, fertile green fields. Fires with bloody men around them. Dead bodies. Wounded straggling back." In the book, Reed fills out the passage and adds clinching details. He sees a boy carrying his dead father on his back; he sees a man slouched on a mule, "screaming mechanically" every time the mule took a step. Nearby, "under two tall cottonwood trees beside an irrigation ditch a little fire glowed"; "beside the fire sat a man holding with both hands his leg straight out to the warmth. It was a perfectly good leg as far as the ankle—there it ended in a ragged, oozing mess of trousers and shattered flesh. The man simply sat looking at it. He didn't even stir as we came near, and yet his chest rose and fell with calm breathing, and his mouth was slightly open as if he were daydreaming." Yet another man holds out a hand where a soft lead bullet had "hollowed out a bloody cave" between his middle fingers. "He had wrapped a rag around a little piece of stick," says Reed, "and was unconcernedly dipping it in the water and gouging out the wound" (177). Reed here presses the sort of detailed narrative he had written in his early fiction into the service of his nonfiction— a story meant to capture for his readers the drama and implications of the Villa army's attempts to win Torreon from the federalists.

Reed's Manipulated Truth: How Mac-American Became Antonio Montoya

Despite the apparent artistry of such scenes, on other occasions a comparison of Reed's Mexican notebooks to the finished *Insurgent Mexico* undermines the author's credibility. It seems that Reed lied about his manner of access to rebel troops in his article entitled "Jimenez and Beyond." First published in the August 1914 edition of *The Masses*, the material forms portions of the "Saved by a Wristwatch" and "Symbols of Mexico" chapters of *Insurgent Mexico*'s part 3— some of the book's most compelling sections. I have discussed this incident in a slightly different context in *Matters of Fact: Reading Nonfiction over the Edge* (98–102); here I present a more sustained analysis.

The notebooks show that without a U.S. war profiteer and gunrunner with the surname of MacDonald, whom Reed had met in Chihuahua City and persuaded to take him to meet Villa's army near Magistral, Reed may never have ridden with the rebel Tropa. MacDonald, or Mac, first shows up in Reed's notes in an entry dated Jan. 1 [1914], a day after Reed met him at a bar near his hotel. "Last night was New Year's Eve," the entry reads. "MacDonald (who is taking me down to Magistral) . . . went up to the Chin Lee saloon and drank the New Year in with Tom and Jerrys." Thus fortified with cocktails, Mac and Reed saw the New Year in amid cathedral bells and gunfire from the barracks along the rim of the town and out in the desert. Later, the notes reveal, Mac and Reed met "five drunken officers of the constitutionalist army, armed to the teeth and looking for trouble. They told us afterward that they had come in [to town] to kill a gringo. But we were so courteous, and sat with our arms around their necks for so long, that we parted great friends." Reed adds, somewhat sardonically, "We had to get drunk to do it" (bMS Am 1091:1316).

In *Insurgent Mexico,* Reed says it was one of the five officers, Antonio Montoya, who took him to meet the rebel troops. Reed's actual conduit, the gunrunner MacDonald, is banished from Reed's nonfiction accounts and shows up only in the deeply ironic short story "Mac-American" (published in the April 1914 issue of *The Masses*). Although, as I have demonstrated in the preceding chapter, the fiction/nonfiction status of some of Reed's tales is murky, Floyd Dell, Reed's fellow editor at *The Masses* and the editor most likely to have supervised the publication of Reed's dispatches from Mexico, classified "Mac-American" as one of Reed's "stories"—that is, not among his "journalistic accounts." Dell makes this classification in *Daughter of the Revolution and Other Stories,* his 1927 collection of Reed's narratives; along with Reed's use of a first-person narrator who certainly does not share the author's views about U.S. patriotism, it provides convincing evidence that Reed meant the story to be read as an ironic fiction.

In the short story, Mac is presented as the prototypical ugly American: crude, misogynistic, chauvinistic: Reed calls him an "American in the raw" (43). In the story, this Mac, having met the fictional narrator in a bar on New Year's Eve, says that all Mexican women are "whores," that Mexican men are "dirty skunks and greasers" (44), and that "the greatest sport in the world is hunting niggers" (47). In contrast to these slurs are Mac's self-styled noble ideas about American womanhood: "If any man dared to dirty the fair name of the American Woman to me, I think I'd kill him. . . . She is a Pure Ideal, and we've got to keep her so. I'd like to hear anybody talk rotten about a woman in my hearing" (45).

Mac remembers when, as a Southern deputy sheriff, he was writing a letter to his beloved sister (presumably one of the American Women whom he wished to protect) and he joined a bloodhound hunt of a black man through cotton fields, woods, and rivers. "'Say, did you ever hear a *bloodhound when he's after a human?* It's like a bugle! . . . Of course,' he said, 'when we got up to him, the dogs had just about torn that coon to pieces'" (48–49; Reed's emphasis). The story ends with Mac saying: "I wouldn't like to live here in Mexico. The people haven't got any Heart. I like people to be friendly, like Americans" (49). Although the first-person narrator is never fully developed, his sensibility is certainly not that of Reed, for the narrator tells the reader that Mac is "a breath from home" and that he and his companions listen to Mac with "the solemn righteousness of a convention of Galahads" (43, 45). Reed, as author, certainly expects his readers to conclude that Mac is anything but a friendly or gallant American.

Reed thus presents as a repulsive and presumably fictional character his actual conduit to the revolutionaries, while in his "nonfictional" *Insurgent Mexico,* Reed places the Mexican officer, Montoya, in Mac's place. More importantly, Reed consigns these narratives to the "Symbols of Mexico" sections near midbook, rather than placing them in the early chronology, where they could leave a more certain trace of the reporter's access to the revolutionaries. This analysis of Reed's structure for *Insurgent Mexico,* therefore, presents a somewhat different spin on the positioning of part 3 than that provided by critics like Jim Tuck or Christopher P. Wilson. To understand the depth and ramifications of Reed's subterfuge, therefore, one might contrast the following passages from Reed's "nonfictional" account of the trip to meet Villa's army.

Reed and Mac traveled with a muleteer named Primitivo Aguilar, whose job it was to provide watch at night, but who was chronically sleepy. In his notebooks, Reed wrote: "Mac threatened to kill [Primitivo] if he didn't keep proper watch. Woke up at 3 A.M. found Primitivo asleep. 'Primitivo!' Sleep. 'Primitivo!' Nothing but snores. Kick him. Still sleep. Kick him hard several times. Primitivo suddenly alert. 'Quien vive?'" (bMS Am 1091:1316).

By contrast, Reed's scene, although it fills out details with the effective artistry that we have seen in earlier analyses, assigns the bullying role in the completed *Insurgent Mexico* to Montoya, who was not even along on the trip:

> After a dinner of chopped-up meat and peppers, tortillas, beans and black coffee, Antonio [Montoya] and I gave Primitivo his instructions. He was to keep watch beside the fire with Antonio's revolver and, if he heard anything, was to wake us. But on no account was he to go to sleep. If he did we would kill him. Primitivo said, "*Si, senor,*" very gravely, opened his eyes wide, and gripped the pistol. Antonio and I rolled up in our blankets by the fire.
>
> I must have gone to sleep at once, because when I was wakened by Antonio's rising, my watch showed only half an hour later. From the place where Primitivo had been placed on guard came a series of hearty snores. The lieutenant walked over to him.
>
> "Primitivo," he said.
>
> No answer.

"Primitivo, you fool!" Our sentinel stirred in his sleep and turned over with noises indicative of comfort.

"Primitivo!" shouted Antonio, violently kicking him.

He gave absolutely no response.

Antonio drew back and launched a kick at his back that lifted him several feet into the air. With a start Primitivo woke. He started up alertly, waving the revolver.

"Quien vive?" cried Primitivo. (139)

While one might be tempted to conclude that Reed interjected the sleeping watchman scene merely for comic relief or perhaps to illustrate symbolically the efforts of a political insurgent like Montoya to wake a nominally apolitical Mexican peasant to action, Reed's substitution of Montoya for MacDonald undercuts both of those explanations. More likely, Reed, aware that portions of his North American audience enjoy reading about simple, sleepy Mexicans, provides a scene that will please them. He will not go so far, however, as to disclose the true cultural politics of the scene. As we saw in the two versions of "Shot at Sunrise" in chapter 2, Reed's alterations both improve the scenic immediacy of the passage and raise serious questions of credibility. The intent of this sort of reading is not to transfer the narrative away from the pristine realm of "nonfiction" as soon as irregularities are discovered, but to examine those irregularities for what they reveal about the scene's cultural construction—in this case, the relationship among Reed, his Mexican subjects, and his readers. It clearly does not suit Reed's rhetorical purpose to have two North American men force a Mexican to stay up all night to do their watch duty, nor does it suit him to make sport of a North American war profiteer's viciously kicking a sleeping Mexican. So Reed assigns the brutal task of disciplining Primitivo to the Mexican officer Montoya, whom he lifted from another incident in the book.

Interestingly, that episode also reveals more than Reed might wish us to see about his strategy of coaxing "simple Mexicans" to accede to his wishes. In the "Saved by a Wristwatch" chapter of *Insurgent Mexico,* Montoya is presented as "a pock-marked officer with a big revolver" who threatens to kill Reed, the gringo. The reporter buys off Montoya with his two-dollar wristwatch and observes as with "parted lips and absorbed attention he watched it delightedly, as a child watches the operation of some new mechanical toy. 'Ah *compadre,*' he cried emotionally." A few moments later, according to *Insurgent Mexico,* Reed approached Montoya with the idea of the trip across the desert. "'I am going to drive to Magistral. I need a *mozo.* I will pay three dollars a week.' '*Sta bueno!*' cried Lt. Montoya. 'Whatever you wish, so that I can go with my *amigo!*'" (136–37). The negotiation, of course, never happened. Reed's true conveyance was the chauvinist gunrunner MacDonald.

A long, analytical passage in the notebooks that Reed did not reproduce directly in *Insurgent Mexico* explains the reporter's penchant for buying friendship, even if he does not always disclose that fact to readers of his finished work. Alleging that Mexican life is saturated by graft, Reed opines that Mexicans are "natural anarchists" whose politics are entirely personal. "[T]he official uses his power to punish his enemies and reward his friends," Reed writes in his notes:

> It springs, this graft, from the extremely warm and gracious thing that friendship is in Mexico. If you can give a Mexican some gift that pleases him, he is such a child that he takes a violent fancy to you. As a matter of fact, a Mexican will share with you his last crust. Generous, impulsive, they will do anything for you if you pour out yourself to them in any way. Law, justice, government are incomprehensible to the Mexican. (bMS Am 1091:1316)

As an example, Reed cites in his notebooks the story of a Mexican friend of Mac's named Antonio Garcia, who clearly is a prototype for the character who becomes Antonio Montoya in *Insurgent Mexico*. Garcia, it seems, is known for "savage rage and cold-blooded cruelty": he once shot forty-five prisoners point-blank with his pistol, "only pausing to load every few minutes." Reed tells us that he left Garcia and Mac drinking in a bar to catch some rest in his room. "Pretty soon they came up to the room," Reed writes in his notes. "Garcia saw my wrist watch lying on the table and admired it so covetously that I insisted that he take it. He finally did and embraced me as he left, pouring himself out in a way that showed me how really hotly he was my friend. He said he would be with Villa, and would help me when we went south" (bMS Am 1091:1316).

Reed's retooling of this incident in the "Saved by a Wristwatch" section of *Insurgent Mexico* echoes several other scenes in the book important to Reed's self-depiction as a North American able to establish genuine friendships with Mexicans. The stakes seem high for the reporter. Because Reed knew that his own reporting trip partially was financed by Vanderbilt and Guggenheim money, he must have flinched at what that money could buy in Mexico. In an unpublished sketch he called "El Paso," Reed writes that in every hotel and lodging house near the Mexican border, "cigar-smoking representatives of William Randolph Hearst and the Guggenheims discuss impossible plans and slip mysterious checks to equally mysterious persons" (bMS Am 1091:1147, p. 1). Mine owners, railroad presidents, ambassadors, and State Department agents all are lurking about El Paso, each with his own intrigue afoot, Reed reports. But in his finished *Metropolitan* narratives and subsequent book, Reed was anxious to distance himself from the sources of his reporting access (whether Guggenheim or MacDonald) and instead creates many scenes in which Mexicans accept him as a friend rather than labeling him a war profiteer.

For example, early in the book, while he is riding with the Tropa, Reed is threatened by a hothead named Julian Reyes, who taunts him for refusing to carry weapons and fight with the Mexicans. "We want no correspondents," says Reyes. "We want no words printed in a book. We want rifles and killing." Reed is saved by Lieutenant Longinos "Gino" Guereca, who tells Reyes: "This *campanero* comes thousands of miles by the sea and the land to tell his countrymen the truth of the fight for Liberty. He goes into battle without arms, he's braver than you are, because you have a rifle." Guereca then tells Reed that the two will be compadres, will "sleep in the same blankets, and always be together" (47). An even more serious challenge comes a few days later when a Major Salazar accuses Reed of being "an agent of American businessmen who have vast interests in Mexico. I know *all* about American business," Salazar charges. "You are an agent of the trusts. You come down here to spy upon the movement of our troops, and then you will secretly send word" (61). Salazar recommends that Reed be shot, perhaps coming closer than he realizes to the source of Reed's funding, but once more the correspondent is saved by his friend Guereco.

Reed thus presents several convincing scenes of genuine friendship with soldiers such as Guereca and Luis Martinez, with whom he talks late into the night about "the world, our girls, and what we were going to be and to do when we really got at it" (59); however, his stereotyping of the Mexican penchant for graft and bribery undermines those scenes. This feature of Reed's character is closer to the nakedly ambitious journalist who surfaces in a June 10, 1914, letter to *Metropolitan* editor Carl Hovey. With characteristic braggadocio and startling candor, Reed informs Hovey that he has "bought [rebel leader] Villa a saddle and a rifle with a gold name plate upon it and a Maxim silencer. He is hugely delighted and will do almost anything for me now. The story is going to be not only exciting to the limit, but the greatest human document you have ever seen. It is a beat on the whole world" (from the Lee Gold Archive in the former Institute of Marxism-Leninism, Moscow, quoted in Rosenstone, 163). The idea of Villa eating out of Reed's hand for the price of a saddle, rifle, and silencer is, of course, also silenced from the pages of *Insurgent Mexico,* replaced by scenes of Villa's seemingly genuine liking for the pug-nosed *muchacho* reporter (182).

Reed's biographers, even so astute a historian as Rosenstone, tend to explain away Reed's alterations of the truth in *Insurgent Mexico,* perhaps because they, like most readers, are so taken by the book's overall depth of insight. Although Rosenstone recognizes that the "brutish American" Mac "is hardly a suitable companion for the narrator as revolutionary sympathizer," he explains the substitution of Montoya for Mac as "more dramatic" (168). Choosing not to make an issue of the price for which Montoya's friendship was purchased, Rosenstone also sees Montoya as evidence of Reed's "ability to be embraced even by people who hated gringos" (168). Jim Tuck, who concentrates on Reed's Mexican reporting in his *Pancho Villa and John Reed: Two Faces of Romantic Revolution,* says the incident "is the only one where Reed was caught red-handed juggling fact and fiction," but adds that "none of these flaws vitiated Reed's ability to get at important essences" (105) in his Mexican reporting. Two other commentators who have written briefly on the issues, David C. Duke and James C. Wilson, are even more forgiving. Wilson argues that Reed introduces Montoya to the pages of *Insurgent Mexico* to "personify both the revolution and the Mexican people" (69), while Duke says that Reed simply employs "a little literary license" (88) to add narrative excitement. Duke suggests that Reed's "Mac-American" story illustrates that "Mac is no different from the many other Americans he had met in Mexico. With their ugly nationalism and predatory instincts, their only goal was the pursuit of the dollar. For these 'friendly Americans' Mexico was a country to be exploited" (79–80). While this is an effective reading of "Mac-American," the commentary neglects Reed's complicity; it underestimates the way that Reed, too, had traveled to Mexico to pursue both fame and fortune and also had exploited the revolution, with Mac's assistance, to build his journalistic capital.

Reed's Critique of War Representation

Despite these important ethical and reportorial shortcomings, Reed achieves a powerful message in *Insurgent Mexico.* His recognition that warfare is brutal, banal, and boring stands in sharp contrast to the jingoistic coverage of south-of-the-border skirmishes that fueled newspaper circulation at the end of the nineteenth and in the early twentieth centuries. In addition, Reed seems to be almost alone among his contemporaries to recognize the media's power to alter as well as to document the events they record. Given that his account of the Mexican Revolution is not presented strictly chronologically, it seems important, therefore, that Reed devoted so many of the early and late pages of *Insurgent Mexico* to a narrative critique of the interaction between reality and its representation. Even if *Metropolitan's* publishing schedule suggested the book's opening sequence, it was Reed who decided to end the book the way he did. Some of Reed's critique seems startlingly contemporary today and is a feature missing from such competing accounts as Davis's *Notes of a War Correspondent.*

For example, Reed observes that one of the most booming businesses in the Texas border town of Presidio was the taking of photographic portraits; these images, which were normally sold on the installment plan, were the medium through which the locals liked to prove their existence. Reed becomes involved in taking photographs of a revolutionary general, Tomas Urbina (who later would be executed by Villa's militia for stealing thousands of pounds of gold from the Division of the North's war chest [Atkin, 254–55]). In *Insurgent Mexico*, Reed includes a vignette of the general. It is strikingly drawn—a virtual prototype of the ironically surreal set pieces that Joan Didion was to use to her advantage some six decades later in her reportage from San Salvador and Miami. Reed, like Didion, draws a strong subtheme of the interrelation between macho posturing and its media representation.

When Reed first meets Urbina, the general is talking to his mistress, "a beautiful, aristocratic-looking woman with a voice like a hand-saw" (26). Reed, having agreed to take photographs of Urbina and his family, finds that, as the days pass and the photographs pile up, Urbina is growing suspicious of the young reporter's impatience to reach the front. The general asks Reed whether he is unhappy with the hospitality he is being given: does he want a woman, a pistol, a horse, money? Urbina throws a handful of silver dollars at Reed's feet in a gesture the reporter interprets as far more menacing than munificent. "I said: 'Nowhere in Mexico am I so happy and contented as in this house.' And I was prepared to go further," Reed reports. For the next hour, the reporter takes photographs of General Urbina: "General Urbina on foot, with and without sword; General Urbina on three different horses; General Urbina with and without his family; General Urbina's three children, on horseback and off; General Urbina's mother, and his mistress; the entire family, armed with swords and revolvers, including the phonograph, produced for the purpose, one of the children holding a placard upon which was inked: 'General Tomas Urbina R.'" (27).

Through the artful construction of himself as a mediating presence, Reed reveals to the reader how he came to gain access to his subject; for making the general pictorially immortal, Urbina allowed Reed to ride with the Tropa, the reporter's first big scoop in his Mexican reporting. Reed's refreshingly ironic self-representation ("'Nowhere in Mexico am I so happy and contented as in this house.' And I was prepared to go further") demonstrates the narrative range he had learned from the narrators of his earlier fictional sketches and shows the sort of honest self-criticism of which he is capable, but which is missing from Reed's reporting about MacDonald and Antonio Montoya.

Later in the book, under fire during the "Bloody Dawn" invasion of Torreon, Reed has time for a sardonic anecdote about the symbiosis between war and those correspondents who cover it. In a scene that, except for the horse, would not be out of place in Michael Herr's *Dispatches,* Reed draws a portrait of one Captain Marinelli, a stout Italian soldier of fortune who, under a burst of federal shrapnel, wheels his horse, "steering as near the newspapermen as possible, with a serious Napoleonic look on his face. He glanced once or twice at the camera man, smiling graciously, but the latter coldly looked away," Reed reports. "With a workmanlike flourish [the Italian] ordered the wheeling of his gun into position and sighted it himself. Just then a shell burst deafeningly about a hundred yards in front." Marinelli's response is to bound away from his cannon, mount his horse, and come "galloping dramatically back with his gun rumbling along at a dead retreat. Pulling up his foaming charger in front of the cameraman he flung himself to the ground and took a position. 'Now,' he said, 'you can take my picture.' 'Go to hell,' said the camera man and a great shout of laughter went up along the line" (183–84).

While it was easy to make fun of such media posturing, Reed was not above profiting from the same impulse, though he may not have been directly responsible for the hype. When his first dispatches were published in *Metropolitan Magazine,* the magazine advertised the series in newspapers with a drawing of Reed outfitted in sombrero, revolver, and gunbelts. The advertising copy read: "Word pictures of war by an American Kipling . . . What Stephen Crane and Richard Harding Davis did for the Spanish American War in 1898, John Reed, 26 years old, has done for Mexico" (Rosenstone, 166).

Still, Reed seemed considerably less enamored with the capacity of reporters and photographers to *do* anything for a war effort, as can be seen in a blistering send-up of journalists on the train car hired by Robert Dorman, who later would become the general manager of Acme News Pictures. Dorman had himself been a soldier of fortune until he learned that shooting pictures of war might be more profitable than shooting bullets (Leighton, 290); he manages to hitch the carload of correspondents, among them Reed and several of his drinking buddies, to Villa's troop train. Reed spares neither his fellow correspondents nor himself from his acid reporting when the train car comes under fire. He notes that the reporters began to drink neat whiskey and "to congratulate each other . . . for being so brave as to stay by the car under artillery fire. Our courage increased as the firing grew far between and finally quit altogether" (215). The journalists curse passing Mexicans, and two reporters fall into a booze-addled conversation that would do the racist MacDonald proud. Reed faithfully recounts their slurs: "A Mexican greaser hasn't got any guts! One American can lick fifty Mexicans! Why, did you see how they ran this afternoon when the shells hit that grove? And how we—hic—stayed by the car?" (216).

Reed's coverage of the Mexican fighting differs strikingly from that which either Crane or Davis had produced during the Spanish-American War—his editor's name-dropping marketing strategy notwithstanding. For example, the two more famous writers, fine reporters and deft stylists that they were, had displayed a "rah-rah" sensibility in covering the Battle of San Juan Hill in Cuba some fifteen years earlier that it is impossible to imagine Reed emulating. And to the extent that Davis and Crane concerned themselves with photographic coverage of the Cuban battle, it was only to establish their own talent. Both reporters were careful to establish their superiority over the "picture papers," but, unlike Reed, neither critiques the complicity between war and its media representation. The following, relatively long quotes from Davis, Crane, and Reed establish the significant break that the latter made from his elders.

Davis, the most famous correspondent of his time, writes of the U.S. Army charge up San Juan Hill:

> General Hawkins, with hair as white as snow and yet far in advance of men thirty years his junior, was so noble a sight that you felt inclined to pray for his safety; on the other hand, Roosevelt, mounted high on horseback, and charging the rifle-pits at a gallop and quite alone, made you feel you would like to cheer. He wore on his sombrero a blue polka-dot handkerchief, *a la* Havelock, which, as he advanced, floated out strait behind his head like a guidon. . . . I have seen many illustrations and pictures of this charge on the San Juan hills, but none of them seem to show it just as I remember it. In the picture-papers the men are running uphill swiftly and gallantly, in regular formation, rank after rank, with flags flying, their eyes aflame, and their hair streaming, their bayonets fixed, in long, brilliant lines an invincible, overpowering weight of numbers. Instead of which I think the thing which impressed one the most, when our men started from cover, was that they were so few. It seemed as if some one had made an awful and terrible mistake. One's instinct was to call to them to come back. (*Cuba,* 96–97)

Compare that with Crane's coverage of the same battle for the New York *World* —a dispatch reprinted in the *Chicago Tribune,* the *Boston Globe,* and *Harper's Weekly* under the headline "Stephen Crane's Vivid Story of the Battle of San Juan":

> No doubt when history begins to grind out her story we will find that many a thundering, fine, grand order was given for that day's work; but after all there will be no harm in contending that the fighting line, the men and their regimental officers, took the hill chiefly because they knew they could take it, some having no orders and others disobeying whatever orders they had. In civil life the newspapers would have called it a grand, popular movement. It will never

be forgotten as long as America has a military history. . . . One saw a thin line of black figures moving across a field. They disappeared in the forest. The enemy was keeping up a terrific fire. Then suddenly somebody yelled: "By God, there go our boys up the hill!" There is many a good American who would give an arm to get the thrill of patriotic insanity that coursed through us when we heard that yell. Yes, they were going up the hill, up the hill. It was the best moment of anybody's life. (*Reports of War*, 155, 158)

Reed, depicting Pancho Villa's successful invasion of Torreon, presents a scenario far different than that described by Davis and Crane at San Juan Hill. Certainly, Reed makes it no secret that he wishes Villa to prevail; therefore, Villa's invasion might be the occasion when one might expect a "best moment of anybody's life" tone to emerge in Reed's writing. Instead, he devotes scenes to the irony and immediacy of death and limits his heroes to those ragged soldiers in ditches who have the creativity and moxie to celebrate their struggle in impromptu song. First, as the battle interrupts the card games in the trenches, it becomes a desperate gamble, with death the reward for a losing hand. There is no time to mourn the fallen in this battle scene, which is presented with Reed's customary eye for detail. A quote the same length as Davis's or Crane's illustrates the sharp contrast between Reed and the other two writers:

Bullets roofed the heavens with whistling steel—drummed the smoking dust up until a yellow curtain of whirling cloud veiled us from the horses and the tank. We could see our friend [one of two constitutionalist soldiers Reed has been describing] running low along the ground, the sleepy man following, standing erect, still rubbing his eyes. Behind strung out the gamblers, squabbling yet. Somewhere in the rear a bugle blew. The sharpshooter running in front stopped suddenly, swaying, as if he had run against a solid wall. His left leg doubled under him and he sank crazily to one knee in the exposed flat, whipping up his rifle with a yell. "————the dirty monkeys!" he screamed, firing rapidly into the dust. "I'll show the————! The cropped heads! The jailbirds!" He shook his head impatiently, like a dog with a hurt ear. Blood drops flew from it. Bellowing with rage, he shot the rest of his clip and then slumped to the ground and thrashed to and fro for a minute. The others passed him with scarcely a look. (188)

The heavens in Reed's battle scene are cut off from earth by a "roof of bullets." The "hero" lies dead, pumping his bullets into the ground in an ineffectual death reflex.

Eventually, the land and the peons who work the land rouse themselves to begin anew, and Reed allows himself a moment of genuine, if more than a little patronizing, tribute: "The sun went gloriously down behind the notched purple mountains in front of us, and for a minute a clear fan of quivering light poured up the high arc of stainless sky. The birds awoke in the trees; leaves rustled," he reports. "The fertile land exhaled a pearly mist" (195). Soon, a dozen ragged soldiers lying close to each other begin to improvise a song about the battle of Torreon, a new ballad on the spot. "I felt my whole feeling going out to these gentle, simple people—so lovable they were" (195), Reed concludes.

Even this redemptive scene, however, soon is undercut by three vignettes that establish the poison, the randomness, and finally the terrible boredom of war. First, Reed, like many of Villa's soldiers, drinks water from an arsenic-laced ditch and "rolled very sick on the ground" (197). Second, Reed and a news photographer (a significant detail given Reed's ongoing critique of the media's role in the war) are fired upon by a random, and indeed almost aimless, sniper: "'By God,' said the photographer. 'Some beggar's sniping at us.' Instinctively we both sprinted. The rifle shots came faster. It was a long distance across the plain," Reed recalls. "After a while we reduced it to a jog-trot. Finally we walked along, with the dust spurting up as before, and a feeling that, after all, it wouldn't do any good to run. Then we forgot it" (204). Third, with a thousand dead and a thousand wounded in the days before the fall of Gomez Palacio, Reed shares the last words of the battle chapters between a wry observation of his own and a quote from a common soldier: In a droll voice, the soldier says, "How brave we Mexicans are.... Killing each other like this!" For his part, says Reed, "I soon went back to camp, sick with boredom. A battle is the most boring thing in the world if it lasts any length of time. It is all the same.... And in the morning I went to get the news at headquarters. We had captured Lerdo, but the Cerro, the Corral and the cuartel were still the enemy's. All that slaughter for nothing!" (211).

"The most worthless literature": Stephen Crane's Mexican Precedent

A closer examination of the Mexican reporting of Stephen Crane can serve to place John Reed's later coverage of Mexico in wider historical context. Like Reed, Crane also had deeply ambivalent reservations about the demands that newspaper editors made on him to glorify war and to exploit foreign peoples to an American public hungry for second-hand exoticism. And, like Reed, Crane saved some of his most astute observations for his private writing. Therefore, Crane apparently never attempted to publish his most trenchant criticism of foreign reporting. "It perhaps might be said—if anyone dared—that the most worthless literature of the world has been that which has been written by the men of one nation concerning the men of another," Crane writes in an unpublished sketch known as "The Mexican Lower Classes" (*Tales, Sketches, and Reports,* 436). The passage is a startling admission from a writer who, like Reed, had built his contemporary reputation in large part from his reporting of foreign cultures and conflicts to readers in the United States. And, as it turns out, Crane hid these opinions effectively. Fredson Bowers, the editor of Crane's collected works, reports "so far as is known no typescript was made" from Crane's opinions on foreign reporting, "nor did Crane, so far as is known, ever attempt to publish" (891).[3]

Perhaps small wonder, for while Crane might have been tempted privately to confess the worthlessness of imperial reportage, like Reed he was dependent on marketing its potential wealth to U.S. publishers back home. Crane's contract for Mexican coverage was with Irving Bacheller and his syndicate of North American newspapers during an era when an increasingly literate U.S. public evidenced a willingness to attach substantial market "worth" to reports from foreign lands. Crane's unpublished essay (probably penned in April 1895 during a several-month trip to the Old West and Mexico at Bacheller's expense) merits close reading because its blend of sensitivity and voyeurism reveals Crane's anxiety. He seems to be concerned about the ethics of doing the very thing that his editors were paying him to do—market alien culture.

Crane's ambivalence appears to have been generated in part by contradictions within the reporting industry, wherein nonfiction narrative is produced each day for mass consumption. The industry—then and now—adopts terms that betray the economic underpinnings of journalistic narrative, whereby events are considered to have more or less "news value" for their power to draw reader interest into the lives of others: events are assessed debits and credits in the daily "budget" of the news product. The industry responds in a more direct, but similar, way to the narrative effects that draw a reader to nominally "literary" nonfiction—effects that are produced when readers encounter real-life "others" in a story. Journalism has codified those sensations into enduring standards of news value: conflict, unusualness, impact, prominence, proximity, and timeliness—variations of which have ruled newsrooms in both Crane's time and ours. These standards are what makes news "fit to print" (to impose a little on the *Times* slogan). The first four standards (conflict, unusualness, impact, and prominence) succinctly define the power of the "real-life other," the markers of the past that historiographer Hayden White calls "alien, exotic, or strange" (89), while the last two standards (proximity and timeliness) promise to bring the textual power to the consumer/reader with its juices still hot.

Consider, for example, the cascading headlines by which the Bacheller syndicate marketed Crane's reporting from Mexico in the May 19, 1895, edition of the *Philadelphia Press:* "Mexican Sights and Street Scenes / The Author of 'The Red Badge of Courage' in the Aztec Capital / Pathetic Patient Burros / A City Where Many Things Are Passing Strange, but Where You Can, After All, Get a Manhattan Cocktail" (Bowers, "Tales, Sketches," 891–92). The *Philadelphia Press* headlines foreground the exoticism and "passing strangeness" of Crane's subject matter while reminding readers of the sustaining power of North American meaning and commerce. Small wonder that Crane may have been tempted to leave unpublished his private musings about the ramifications of such power. "It seems that a man must not devote himself for a time to attempts at psychological perception," Crane says in the unpublished essay about the lower classes of Mexico that he wrote during the two months that he was filing articles from Mexico for Bacheller. "He can be sure of two things, form and color. Let him then see all he can, but let him not sit in literary judgment on this or that manner of the people" (436). And then Crane, at least in those journalistic accounts he permitted the Bacheller syndicate to market, proceeds to do just what he has said his conscience will prohibit. For example, in a report printed in five major U.S. newspapers (the report for which, above, I have cited the *Philadelphia Press* headline), Crane uses a vignette of six "stolid and unworried" peasants moving a piano along a Mexico City street to build an overtly psychological perception of the manner by which the "natives" manage their burros. Musing with evident irony on the peasants' proud pedigree from Aztec scientists and inventors, Crane says their ancestry allows the Indians to swear creatively and to "hammer the everlasting daylights out of the donkey" ("Stephen Crane in Mexico—I," 439).

The overall tone of "Stephen Crane in Mexico—I" is not so far from that of Crane's short fiction about Mexico, a tone that leads critic Raymond Paredes to conclude that "there are few characteristics of the Mexican in serious American literature less flattering than Crane's" (quoted in Robertson, 122). Robertson, for his part, notes that in each of Crane's Mexican short stories, "a white American male is the innocent target of unprovoked Mexican threats. The Mexicans are blustering, sneaky, and aggressive, but they are also cowardly, afraid of even the implication of Anglo violence" (122–23). Indeed, as R. W. Stallman notes, Crane often embellished on his nonfiction to make his criticism of Mexicans more biting in his fiction. For example, when a "Bowery fellow" told Crane that he had shot a band of Mexicans who tried to run him off his land, Crane (in the story "A Man and Some Others") reversed the plot by having the Mexicans shoot the outmanned former Bowery saloon-bouncer. Intriguingly, the juxtaposition of Reed's fictional "Mac-American" with its nonfictional counterpart works in the other direction. The chauvinistic blindness of the gringo that is revealed in the fictional story is transferred to a Mexican in Reed's nonfiction, the better to hide Reed's complicity.

Crane appears less willing to stereotype the Mexican people in his nonfiction than in his fiction, perhaps because of the manner by which the nonfiction form normally holds its authors to a more exacting standard of proof and makes it more difficult for the author entirely to control the subject within the text. Moreover, Crane's reluctance to engage in "attempts at psychological perception," which he cites in his earlier unpublished essay, reveals that Crane did think about one of the more theoretically interesting aspects of nonfiction narrative: the benefits and costs of writing omnisciently. One can sense Crane straining at the leash in his unpublished "Mexican Lower Classes" in a remarkable passage wherein he contrasts the apparent thoughts of the North American working class to their brothers and sisters in Mexico. Crane writes of the U.S. poor in a way it is impossible to imagine Reed echoing. To Crane, the poor are menacing aliens:

> The people of the slums of our own cities fill a man with awe. That vast army with its countless faces immovably cynical, that vast army that silently confronts eternal defeat, it makes one afraid. One listens for the first thunder of rebellion, the moment when this silence shall be broken by a roar of war. Meanwhile one fears this class, their numbers, their wickedness, their might—even their laughter. They have it in their power to become terrible. And their silence suggests everything. (436)

Crane says he will not yield to the temptation to read the minds of the Mexican peasant, nor will he conclude that rebellion never occurs to them. "As far as I can perceive him, he is singularly meek and submissive. He has not enough information to be unhappy over his state. Nobody seems to provide him with it. He is born, he works, he worships, he dies, all on less money than would buy a thoroughbred Newfoundland dog, and who dares to enlighten him?" (437). Crane says he refuses even to pity the Mexican poor. "[T]heir faces have almost always a certain smoothness, a certain lack of pain, a serene faith. I can feel the superiority of their contentment" (438).

Crane travels some of the same narrative ground here that Reed was to use to great effectiveness in *Insurgent Mexico:* that is, he seems genuinely impressed by Mexicans' inner spiritualism. But Crane never attempted to publish this observation, nor would he stake his reputation to a public praising of the Mexican people. Crane's well-honed irony makes it difficult to position his writing stance with certainty, but his eight published newspaper articles from Mexico reveal that, despite his assurances, Crane normally presented Mexicans as inferior to other North Americans. In an article published in six Bacheller newspapers during August 1895, Crane reaches for stereotypes while writing of the milky-green Mexican drink *pulque,* the fermented juice of the maguey plant and a poorer cousin of tequila. "Unless there are some Americans around to be robbed, [the Mexican] is obliged to rustle very savagely for his *pulque* money. When he gets it he is happy and the straight line he makes for one of the flaming shops has never been outdone by any metropolitan iceman that drinks" ("A Jug of Pulque Is Heavy," 458). Elsewhere, in "Hats, Shirts, and Spurs in Mexico," Crane writes that the Mexican "is a mystic and silent figure of the darkness. He has two great creeds. One is that *pulque* as a beverage is finer than the melted blue of the sky. The other is that Americans are eternally wealthy and immortally stupid. If the world were really of the size that he believes it to be, you could put his hat over it" (468).

Perhaps the least culturally chauvinistic of Crane's published Mexican articles is a piece dubbed "Stephen Crane in Mexico—II," in which Crane assumes the third-person persona of an archeologist, a ploy that seems to free Crane to build the ironical voice that narrows the gap between the more sensitive, private Crane of the unpublished "Mexican Lower Classes" and the rather predictable, public Crane of the other published Mexican pieces. The story takes place in a train compartment, where the archeologist is conversing with a capitalist. The pair see "a black outline of a man" against the backdrop of the crimson rays of a house fire: "His legs were crossed, his arms were folded in his *serape,* his hat resembled a charlotte *russe.* He leaned negligently against a doorpost" (450). Although the scene itself is as stereotypical as the one Crane penned for "Hats, Shirts, and Spurs in Mexico," the writer is able to distance himself from his archeologist persona and his capitalist companion to chide them for their response to the dozing man. "This figure justified to them all their preconceptions. . . . The two travelers, hungry for color, form, action, strove to penetrate with their glances these black curtains of darkness which intervened between them and the new and strange life" (451). Crane writes with evident irony, noting that it is not long before the capitalist gives up and settles for discussing "the extraordinary attributes" of his children back in the United States.

It is easy to see how such reporting strongly influenced Reed. Here, Crane is using the sort of subtle self-criticism and genuine empathy that would mark Reed's best writing from Mexico. Even though his descriptions of Mexicans are unfailingly narrow (dejected women, dusky shepherds, careless urchins, persistent beggars, catcalling hoodlums, white-teethed peons, sleepy peasants), Crane's piece ends with the most effective scene writing of his Mexican journalism. His descriptions seem vivid and sure as the train climbs up toward the peaks of Popocatepetl and Ixtaccihuatl through "a vast plain of green and yellow fields spread out like a checkered cloth toward the sun-smitten peaks," whose snow fields are cloaked in rose-hued shadow. "At last there came a depot heavily fringed with people, an omnibus, a dozen cabs and a soldier in a uniform that fitted him like a bird cage," Crane writes. "White dust arose high toward the blue sky. In some tall grass on the other side of the track, a little cricket suddenly chirped. The two travelers with shining eyes climbed out of the car. 'A-a-ah,' they said in a prolonged sigh of delight. The city of the Aztecs was in their power" (456).

Crane understands here that, despite the optimism of the capitalist and his archeologist alter ego, the city of the Aztecs will never submit its meaning unambiguously to the foreign journalist. But it is a relatively rare lesson in Crane's published Mexican articles. In the Bacheller pieces, Crane normally surrenders to relatively simple stereotypes in his depiction of Mexican people and is careful not to be implicated by prolonged interaction. In these articles, he remains at the level of top-down voyeuristic discourse described by Mary Louise Pratt in "Scratches in the Face of the Country," her analysis of colonial travel narrative. Pratt calls such discourse "informational": "textually producing the Other without an explicit anchoring either in an observing self or in a particular encounter in which contact with the Other takes place" (140). By contrast, Crane's more emotional interactions are restricted to the relative safety of unpublished discourse, wherein he sometimes seems able to escape from the stereotypes that at the turn of the twentieth century dominated U.S. journalism about foreign lands.

Reed Encounters His Reporting Subjects

Although, as I have demonstrated, Reed's reporting from Mexico was subject to many of the same limitations that marked Crane's nonfiction production, Reed did manage to answer one of Pratt's challenges to imperial reporting: that of "constructing a compelling, observant self . . . a particular encounter in which contact with the Other takes place" (140). In this regard, *Insurgent Mexico* can be read as an elaborate coming of age of the young writer. Reed learns that war reporting is not so romantic as he thought and that the "material" that will sell so well to his readers will be purchased by the death of his friends. Slowly, in the narrative Reed's young first-person reporter works his way into the graces of not only Pancho Villa but, even more importantly, the Tropa soldiers with whom he shares a camp. Reed learns to drink the fiery *sotol* of the Mexicans (35), eats the *carne crudo* ("we ripped meat from the carcass and ate it raw" [41]), argues the meaning of liberty and self-interest (37–38), dances until dawn, and watches the *campanieros* fight the bulls. The scenes of genuine friendship between Reed, the gentle Guereca, and the soulful Subteniente Martinez set up the Tropa's ambush by the loyalist colorados and render the deaths of Guereca, Martinez, and their comrades in that battle all the more poignant.

The Tropa revolutionaries are ambushed along the Santa Domingo Road by loyalists riding like black specks "through the chaparral; the desert swarmed with them" (73). Reed loads his camera and hurries out to watch the battle, later to report: "Above the umber rise of desert loomed a mighty cloud of white dust, shining in the sun, like the biblical pillar of smoke. . . . Five struck spurs into their horses, and sped furiously toward the Puerta—without arms, without hope. It was magnificent" (72). In what are to be the last words Reed will hear from his friend Guereca, Gino shouts back over his shoulder that his promise to show Reed the lost mines of the Spaniards will have to wait for another day (71).

Although the Tropa's doomed charge is "magnificent," Reed quickly learns that war is not nearly so romantic as he thought. "I suddenly discovered that I had been hearing shooting for some time. It sounded immensely far away—like nothing so much as a clicking typewriter," Reed says. "Even while it held our attention, it grew" (73). The federalists now are upon the rebel outpost, "a ring of galloping, shooting, yelling men; and as far as the eye could reach, on every rise of the desert, came more" (74). Symbolically, Reed sheds the instruments of both civilization and media representation as he runs for his life from the colorados: "My camera got between my legs. I dropped it. My overcoat became a terrible weight. I shook it off. . . . I ran on—ran and ran and ran, until I could run no more. Then I walked a few steps and ran again. I was sobbing instead of breathing" (75).

As no portions of the Mexican notebooks survive from the ambush on the Santa Domingo Road, it is likely that, along with his camera and coat, Reed also dropped his notebook, and perhaps his writing instruments. At first he confesses to feeling like a character in someone else's narrative, then consoles himself with having gained reportable material. "I ran. I wondered what time it was. I wasn't very frightened," Reed writes in the completed *Insurgent Mexico.* "Everything still was so unreal, like a page out of Richard Harding Davis. It just seemed to me that if I didn't get away I wouldn't be doing my job very well. I kept thinking to myself: 'Well, this is certainly an experience. I'm going to have something to write about'" (75–76).

Ultimately, Reed recognizes that the nonfictional narrative he seeks to market back to *Metropolitan Magazine* in the United States will be purchased at the price of his friends. Both Gino and Martinez have been shot, and Reed shifts his ruminations from material to mortality: "I felt sick. Sick to think of so many deaths. . . . Blithe, beautiful Martinez; Gino Guereca, whom I learned to love so much" (82). At great personal risk to himself, a *pacifico* offers the fleeing Reed sanctuary and a bath "because a stranger might be God, as we say" (81). The correspondent sinks into the bath's healing waters, sharing the hot spring with a traveling priest, with whom he talks philosophy as "the fierce sky cooled slowly, and the rich sunlight climbed little by little up the pink wall" (80). That night, in an episode written especially for *Insurgent Mexico* and absent from the original *Metropolitan* articles, Reed shares a bed with a woman named Elizabetta, who has lost her own man to the war that day. The villagers, mistakenly thinking that Elizabetta and the reporter are to consummate their love, serenade them as newlyweds. But the two do not have sex; instead, "[h]er hand reached for mine. She snuggled against my body for the comforting human warmth of it. . . . And calmly, sweetly, sleep came to me" (90).[4]

With its ironic echo of Richard Harding Davis, its surrender to the solace of bath and platonic bed, the reporter's travels with the Tropa are meant to establish for the reader not only Reed's narrative presence in the book, but also his flesh-and-blood presence as a foreign writer and journalist. The ambush on the Santa Domingo Road—which teaches the journalist not to subsume actual human beings to narrative "material"—plays much the same role as does the essay on the "Mexican poor" that Crane consigned to his "unpublished" files. Fleeing alone, Reed might have written any script for himself that he wanted. Because his notes did not survive the experience, it is impossible for readers today to assess the script we do have against a competing script. Still, it is significant that Reed chooses a narrative scene that begins with his dropping his camera from between his legs—a phallic instrument of representation—and ends in a womb-like acceptance of his mortality. The passage draws its lasting strength from Reed's declaration of love for two soldiers, his recognition of his implication in their deaths, and his chaste night with a grieving widow. Whether these elements are strictly true or not, they show the extent to which Reed was willing to rewrite the script he had inherited from Crane and Davis—the script of what it might mean to be a heroic witness in time of war.

Still Reed—with some significant exceptions—makes it easy for his readers back home to swallow their complicity in Mexico's struggles, even as Reed avoids some of his own deeper complicity in the "Macs" and "Mac-attitudes" that make his reporting possible. By concentrating on Pancho Villa's human side, his fierce individualism, his Robin Hood method of operations, and the ability of other North Americans to take advantage of Mexicans by buying themselves into the "natural friendliness" of their neighbors to the south, Reed ensured himself a book that could be popular with most of his readers in the United States, despite the significant break it represented from the prevailing examples of war correspondents like Crane and Davis. Reed most likely recognized many of the ways in which his reporting methods sometimes compromised his ideals, particularly the contradiction of a reporter writing about social revolution in a magazine bankrolled by Guggenheim and Vanderbilt money. Some of these contradictions he hid; others he acknowledged. And some traces of that conflict are buried skillfully in the text, as is Reed's construction of the *pastorellas* morality play that makes up the book's final chapter and is one of its most gorgeous and unsettling sections.

In the White Moonlight with Lucifer

As mentioned early in this chapter, Reed departs from chronology to place the *pastorellas* at the end of the book, although it most likely took place before he ever met up with the Tropa or watched Villa storm the Gomez Palacio. It is tempting, therefore, to invest special symbolic significance in the chapter, the action of which takes place in the ancient gold-mining village of Santa Maria del Oro, that very region of lost mines to which his friend Gino Guereca had promised to take him. "The Spaniards enslaved the Indians of the region, of course, and the torrent-worn, narrow valleys are still sinister with legend," Reed reports. "Almost anybody around Santa Maria del Oro can tell you stories of the old days when men were flogged to death in the mines, and the Spanish overseers lived like princes" (253).

In this historic place, the villagers gather for an ancient miracle play, a slice of Elizabethia in rural Mexico, "handed down by word of mouth from mother to daughter, from the remotest antiquity" (255). The play is called "Luzbel," Reed tells his reader, "Spanish for Lucifer, and depicts Perverse Man in the Midst of His Deadly Sin" (255). The description of the setting and of the crowd that gathers for the *pastorellas* represents Reed's writing at its best. It is worth quoting at length to show the emotional detail that the reporter invested in the scene. Its white, burning moonlight echoes the little white flame that burned in the breast of Reed's protagonist in the short story "Seeing Is Believing"—the pure capacity for spiritual wonder amid an increasingly material world.

White, burning moonlight flooded the place. The patio sloped upward along the side of the mountain, where there was no wall to stop the view of great planes of shining upland, tilted to meet the shallow jade sky. To the low roof of the house a canopy of canvas drooped out over a flat place, supported by slanting poles, like the pavilion of a Bedouin king. Its shadow cut the moonlight blacker than night. Six torches stuck in the ground around the outside of the place sent up thin lines of pitchy smoke. There was no other light under the canopy, except the restless gleams of innumerable cigarettes. Along the wall of the house stood black-robed women with black *mantillas* over their heads, the menfolks squatting at their feet. Wherever there was space between their knees were children. Men and women alike smoked their *cigarros,* handing them placidly down so that the little ones might take a puff. It was a quiet audience, speaking little and softly, perfectly content to wait, watching the moonlight in the patio, and listening to the music, which sounded far away in the arch. A nightingale burst into song somewhere among the shrubs, and all of us fell ecstatically silent, listening to it. (256–57)

Reed approvingly notes that Lucifer (played by a woman, as are all the roles in the play) wears the leather costume of an imperial Roman or Spanish legionnaire. Lucifer laments his lost paradise in words that resonate for the American writer:

"Light am I, as my name proclaims—and the light of my fall kindled all the great abyss," Lucifer says in words translated from the Spanish by Reed. "Because I would not humble myself, I, who was the Captain General, be it known to all men, am today the accursed of God" (260). As Lucifer laments his lost station, one irrepressible audience member yells: "That's the way Huerta is going to feel when the Maderistas enter Mexico City" (260). Reed, who less than a year earlier had organized the IWW pageant at Madison Square Garden, thrills to such breaches of the wall that convention erects between performers and audience. Onlookers "joined violently in the discussion" of the play's themes, "hurling the words of the play back and forward—men and women drawing together in two solid hostile bodies" (263). At one juncture, the play is interrupted outright when a hatless youth rushes in and reports a rebel victory in Mapimi. "Even the performers stopped singing . . . and a whirlwind of questions beat upon the newcomer" (266), Reed reports. As Harry Henderson notes, the play is "fully and spontaneously entered into by the audience. The performance creates itself as an art form which has authentic and direct function to the lives of the people" (427).

Amid the hubbub, under the moonlight against a ring of mountain slopes, Reed inserts into his account an ironic detail. Two rustics steal a basket of food and a bottle of wine and consume it amid much hilarity from the audience. Lucifer returns in disguise and is invited to join the feast. Pressed by Lucifer to speculate on the theft of food and wine, the villagers begin "little by little to place the blame upon a stranger whom they all agreed to have seen," Reed reports. "Of course, they meant Lucifer, but, upon being invited to describe him, they depicted a monster a thousand times more repulsive than reality" (265). As the only gringo in the audience, and with his intent to capture his slice of Elizabethan Mexico for readers north of the border, Reed appears to savor the rich irony of his next sentence: "None suspected that the apparently amiable stranger seated in their midst was Lucifer" (265). The observation of course might suggest the reporter himself; whether or not Reed specifically intended this interpretation, its ironic significance is there to be grasped by readers. And that irony builds on the ability to separate the sensibilities of author and narrator for ironic effect that Reed first established in his fiction. The theft of the village's property mirrors the deeds of the Spanish oppressors, who robbed Santa Maria del Oro of its gold and of its political self-determination. Reed clearly intends his readers to make that connection. Does he also understand that his own reporting project's complicity with interests only too ready to exploit the Mexican people might brand him a related species of "apparently amiable stranger"? It is as Reed had written of his narrator George in the short story "Seeing Is Believing": "He seemed to look into a world whose existence he had never dreamed of—a world from which he was externally excluded because he knew too much." In that story, the girl responds to George with the deeper insight: "It's because you know too little" (145).

Rosenstone and Duke address *Insurgent Mexico*'s Santa Maria del Oro scene briefly, but do not interpret it in detail. Duke suggests that it represents the "vitality and symbiosis of Mexican village life" (90); Rosenstone concludes that the scene is meant to evoke "the lingering romance" of peaceful, sleepy towns drowsing in the sun (168). "Here," Rosenstone comments—wrongly, to my mind—"beyond the reach of government, peons live without politics in a world where no such word as war or revolution is spoken" (168). Similarly, Christopher P. Wilson finds the scene "a shift away from geopolitics" (353). Yet the audience *does* discuss geopolitical war and celebrate revolution, even as the play unfolds. Moreover, the interruptions of revolutionary news and the Lucifer character dressed in the costume of Spanish *conquistadors* seems to prove that the Mexican peasants are never beyond the reach of government, and that Reed knows it, especially if he recognizes at some level that he is one of the unacknowledged emissaries of colonialism: the "Lucifer in their midst."

The book ends with Reed's drawing that possibility into a larger social question, one that has plagued many foreign reporters who return to tell the tale of some compelling out-of-the-way spot that without doubt will be altered—even ruined—by the very words that celebrate its existence. And beyond that concern, Reed seems to hint at deeper dilemmas, ones that he faced in varying degrees throughout the book: his recognition that the deaths of his friends helped spur the dramatic narrative that will build his own growing capital as a war reporter as well as his recognition that the U.S. banking and business interests that he had criticized around the Tropa campfire were the very ones that had made his reporting possible. The correspondent thus seems reluctantly to shift in his seat so as to directly address his modern readers as he and we contemplate our own complicity in the real-life drama of history amid the nightingales under the white, burning moonlight. He ends with an allusion to Sophocles and to Matthew Arnold's "Dover Beach"—to the turbid ebb and flow of human misery where sea meets moon-blanched land.

"But already around the narrow shores of the Mexican Middle Ages beat the great seas of modern life—machinery, scientific thought, and political theory," Reed concludes. "Mexico will have to skip for a time her Golden Age of Drama" (266). The reporter is lamenting the loss of Mexican medieval life, as represented by the medieval miracle play that might have given rise to a Mexican Renaissance. As Christopher P. Wilson observes: "Reed presents the land . . . as a lost precious object peons deserve to recover—a desire which provokes a combination of sporadic violence, sadness, despair, and even rebellion" (352). In this final episode of *Insurgent Mexico*, Reed laments that the economic disparities occasioning war are interrupting what could have been a flowering of a culture. Moreover, Reed seems to recognize that he might be despoiling that culture as well by hastening its commodification.

Considered in retrospect, Reed's closing words in *Insurgent Mexico* seem prophetic, not only for the fate of Mexico's revolution but for his own life. For his own golden age as a rising media star and one of the highest-paid reporters in the United States was soon to be over. The outbreak of World War I was to beat great seas of change around the narrow shores of his own artistry and reportage. After the success of *Insurgent Mexico*, Reed had his pick of the major magazine and newspaper markets. *Metropolitan Magazine* hailed him as its star of stars, featuring him in full-page ads and photographs; Walter Lippmann hailed him publicly as the eyes and pen "where reporting begins" (15). Yet within little more than two years, stunning changes ensued both in the political climate of the United States and in Reed's career. In that span, Reed was to see more than three hundred of his friends in the IWW jailed on some ten thousand federal charges, was to stand by as virtually all of his normal outlets for publication either refused to print his work or were forced out of business by U.S. postal regulators or federal indictments, and would face his own federal charges of sedition and espionage for conspiracy to obstruct the military draft.

Reed against the Great War

The Politics of Marketplace Journalism

IF EVERY WRITER may be said to have moments that define the stakes of his or her writing life, for Reed such a moment came when he sailed from New York to Naples in August 1914 to cover the rapidly escalating Great War in Europe. Fresh from riding with Pancho Villa in the Mexican Revolution and emerging as one of the nation's highest-paid, if sometimes impulsive, international correspondents, Reed traveled first class on a *Metropolitan Magazine* expense account, uneasily sharing quarters with barons, marquises, counts, and industrialists. Below, in the steerage, were three thousand working-class U.S. immigrants, full-sail back to their homelands where they were to provide the warring nations with trench fodder to fight that most bloody of wars. Caught in the contradiction of class and principles, Reed contemplated the working people from his vantage point of reporter's privilege:

> From the spaciousness and cleanliness of the first-class deck, we could lean our pongee and silken breasts on the rail and look down upon the seething life of the steerage. It must have infuriated them to look up from their filth and discomfort and see us smiling and pointing them out to each other as if they were strange phenomena; but outside of sullen, hateful looks, they watched us silently, curiously, and said nothing. And mind you, these were not bewildered peasants, coming for the first time to an appalling, strange land; they were men who had worked and lived in America, had conquered it, and possessed assurance. (15)

The article that grew out of his experience, "The Approach to War," was published in the November 1914 edition of the mass-circulation monthly *Metropolitan Magazine*, but has not been circulated since that time. It serves as a pathway, however, into the issues governing the middle section of Reed's writing career. In "The Approach to War," Reed combines his brilliant descriptive powers and his knack for graceful narrative with growing alarm at a world careening toward all-out war. Less obvious in the narrative, but essential to a deep reading of it, are the conscious and unconscious contradictions Reed betrays about the relationship of a reporter to his subjects, particularly that of a Harvard-trained writer of the upper-middle class.

In the narrative, Reed listens as his first-class neighbors on the Italian steamer, many of whom would command armies on opposite sides of World War I, fraternize on the top deck and argue about which of the "vermin" on the deck below would make better foot soldiers for their respective nations. Uncomfortable with his top-deck peers, Reed is alternately fascinated and alarmed by the masses of working people packed into the steerage. One night, as Reed plays cards with his upper-deck companions, they hear a frightful screaming and cursing from the steerage. It turns out to be an old man rudely awakened by a cruel prank. Reed picks up the story with his customary detail:

> The sailors with the hose had gruffly ordered the steerage down, at the same time starting the water in the powerful hoses. But one old man had fallen asleep against a coil of rope, and didn't wake up when the word was given, so the sailors calmly turned the hose on him. He had sprung up screaming and shivering, shocked in all his old bones; he had no other clothes and was drenched. For a moment even his shrill wailing denunciation, as he shook his fist at the sailors, was drowned in the roar of laughter from the first-class passengers looking down on the scene. But the steerage didn't laugh. It was a harmless enough joke, but the steerage realized suddenly that it typified how they were regarded. The sailors with the hose silently swept it along, the old man blasting them with curses, and giving way step by step as the water rushed about his feet. Behind him clustered others, muttering among themselves, undecided. But they, too, gave way, and slowly filed down the ladder. (15)

With the steerage passengers safely back in the ship's hold, Reed's upper-crust neighbors return to their cards, still chuckling at the sight of the old man staggering in the spray. "Well, that was an amusing break in the monotony," says one of Reed's companions.

A privileged topsider who particularly riled Reed that night was an Italian silk manufacturer from Paterson, New Jersey, whose striking workers Reed had covered a year earlier in articles for *Metropolitan* and the radical journal *The Masses;* from that time on, Reed's writing consistently confers symbolic weight to the production and wearing of silk. "Why didn't they throw the old fool overboard!" the silk manufacturer snaps as Reed observes the melee on the lower deck. "The beasts! They ought to be shot or starved to death!" Later that night, no doubt aware of the irony of his sharing quarters with a silk manufacturer, Reed tosses and turns in the first-class cabin booked on *Metropolitan* money as he listens to the sounds of the steerage passengers below: "That roar of voices, so powerful, yet so easily directed," he writes of the humans warehoused on the ship's first deck. "For hours afterward it seemed, the subterranean murmur and the screaming voice continued. I dreamed about it that night."

Between July 1913 and January 1917, Reed wrote twenty-seven articles and six short stories for *Metropolitan Magazine,* the New York monthly that at its peak had more than a million readers. With a heady brew of socialist politics and literary pretensions, during the three-plus years that Reed was a regular contributor *Metropolitan* also published essays and fiction by George Bernard Shaw, Havelock Ellis, Rudyard Kipling, H. G. Wells, Walter Lippmann, Joseph Conrad, D. H. Lawrence, Richard Harding Davis, Theodore Roosevelt, Ring Lardner, and Susan Glaspell. In those years, none of these writers was a greater star than Reed, whom the *Metropolitan* editors described as "a man of extraordinary gifts, a brilliant writer, a man who has imagination and feeling—a genuine observer [with] priceless insight" (April 1914, p. 10). Reed's articles for *Metropolitan* thus grew from a mutually beneficial, if somewhat short-lived, alliance between the young writer and the self-styled socialist monthly. Both Reed and the magazine managed to gloss some rather intriguing inner contradictions to make the relationship work as long as it did. *Metropolitan's* brand of socialism thrived amid a profit-seeking business plan whose investors included some of the most famous names of capitalism. Accordingly, *Metropolitan Magazine* expended its economic and cultural capital to make Reed the superstar of a reading public eager to consume tales of war along with its Lucky Strikes and Butter-Kist popcorn. Meanwhile, the young journalist choked back some of his own rather deeply held cultural and political principles because he knew the bounce that *Metropolitan* could bring to his expense account and to his literary exposure.

This chapter thus attempts to reckon the period of John Reed's greatest fame and sharpest fall against the cultural and political framework that made Reed a star and robbed him of that stardom. Although both Reed and his magazine were at first able to suppress their internal contradictions and differences, the outbreak of World War I tore the lid off that alliance. Reed broke both with his nation and with mainstream U.S. socialists, refusing to support either military preparedness or U.S. involvement in World War I. Meanwhile, *Metropolitan* soon was sketching cartoons of a sleeping America while German soldiers dug trenches in the sand traps of Long Island golf courses. Long-time rivals like Theodore Roosevelt and Richard Harding Davis gained the magazine's editorial blessing, while Reed skidded precipitously to the back of the book. Ultimately, his sharp break with *Metropolitan* would coax Reed to descend from the top deck of reporter's privilege and wade into the steerage of revolutionary journalism. How he got there is the subject of this chapter's examination of the varying ideologies and practices of Reed and of *Metropolitan Magazine*.

"What We Mean by Socialism": The Cultural Politics of a Literary Monthly

As it turns out, *Metropolitan* publisher H. J. Whigham wrote an exacting description of his magazine's particular brand of socialism during the same month that Reed was drinking his way toward Pancho Villa's Mexico for *Metropolitan*. Published in January 1914, as Reed joined forces with Mac, of "Mac-American," to find the Tropa, Whigham's editorial "What We Mean by Socialism" takes some pains to explain why a magazine operating with an editorial and business hierarchy would argue for a classless future. "The ideals of Socialism may be very far from accomplishment," Whigham argues, "but the community prospers best which advances steadily toward those ideals" (6). That advancement, however, does not preclude Whigham's magazine from carrying advertisements for Western Electric or the Pennsylvania Railroad. "If we were to attempt to run the magazine on ideally Socialist lines, each man working directly or indirectly for the *Metropolitan* getting an equal reward, we should quickly ruin the magazine[,] and you, dear readers, would be deprived of *The Metropolitan*," Whigham reasons. "And what we cannot do ourselves we should not expect any other business to do" (6). Under Whigham's leadership, therefore, *Metropolitan* rather neatly exempted itself and others from the practical application of socialism while continuing to editorialize for its universal acceptance.

While Whigham took care of the editorial policy of the self-styled "liveliest magazine in America," the task of soliciting writers, encouraging their projects, and nursing their prose fell to Carl Hovey, a visionary editor who was forging some of the principles that would guide literary journalism for the next century. Hovey, who had written biographies of J. Pierpont Morgan and Stonewall Jackson, believed in what he liked to call "pen pictures," a sturdy literary realism grounded in fact that focused on individual scenes and characterizations to tell a larger story. In September 1913, the same month that Reed wrote about the Paterson jail in his first big feature for *Metropolitan,* Hovey singled out an article by Frederic C. Howe about politics in Belgium as ideal for the magazine: "wise, temperate, picturesque, human; giving in a most attractive style the essential information concerning a country much in the news, but little understood over here." His magazine's signature, Hovey promised, would be "to present the real and the vitally interesting"—and its nonfiction would be as compellingly written as its fiction (3).[1] The magazine's large pages (eleven inches by seventeen) ensured that such articles would be surrounded by illustrations drawn by such popular contemporary artists as Boardman Robinson, Art Young, Everett Shinn, George Bellows, and D. C. Hutchison or by photographs from one of the many news services springing up to take advantage of the developing halftone reproduction technology. The advertising base of *Metropolitan*—in addition to national slicks from the American Tobacco Company, Pennsylvania Railroad, Western Electric, Borden's, and Ford—featured all the accouterments for a modern urban sophisticate: Riz La rolling papers, Old Town canoes, *Vogue* magazines, Cunard cruises, Collier's books, Velvet Grip hose supporters, BVD underwear, Ranger bicycles, Hamilton watches, Parker pens, and Colt automatic firearms ("under your pillow, it's safe when cocked") (September 1913, p. 59).

Ironically, only a year before his first articles were published in *Metropolitan,* Reed had written a sneering assessment of the magazine's transformation to use of large pages in an unpublished essay entitled "From the Inside Looking Out: Thoughts Inspired by a Slant at the New Magazine." Reed wrote: "In the popular magazine possessed of a conscience, truly delicate must be the adjustment between things of *quality* and things primarily intended to be *popular.* . . . Even more so in the extraordinary case where the magazine desires to make money" (bMS Am 1091:1138; Reed's emphases). Reed then shifts into high-gear imagery that recalls a session at Mabel Dodge's salon where young writers for *Metropolitan* and the more radical *The Masses* had nearly duked it out (Rosenstone, "Mabel Dodge," 144). He recalls his first look at a dummy for the larger-sized *Metropolitan:* "looking like a seed catalogue and hefting like a *Sears-Roebuck Monthly Bulletin,*" with room for "fiction galore [and] a column among advertisements where poets can moan." When a colleague tells him "People will buy it! People will read it! We will be wealthy!" Reed remains unconvinced and concludes with a rhetorical flourish: "The *Metropolitan* makes a wonderful show. But, alas! It is mostly Dead Sea apples. . . . If this dummy is indicative, the new magazine will have lost all our flavor, compactness, and dignity. . . . It is like a small, muscular man in a large, flowered-silk kimono" (bMS Am 1091:1138; Reed's emphases). Reed's metaphorical aversion to cross-dressing notwithstanding, he landed his first article in *Metropolitan* less than a year later: "From Omaha to Broadway: A Sad True Tale of a New Yorker," above the byline, "Torn from Life by John S. Reed." With sketches by well-known cartoonist Art Young, Reed follows greenhorn out-of-towners as they arrive on the Great White Way to consume the season's big shows. "You are a Business Man. Don't deny it!!!" Reed at one point addresses his subjects directly. "Art Young and I went around with a sketch pad and notebook the other night and got you dead to rights" (14).

A manifesto that Reed wrote for *The Masses*, the Greenwich Village monthly edited by Max Eastman, provides a deeper view into Reed's divided mind. If Reed was aware of the advantages and exposure that *Metropolitan* could give him, his spirited written defense of *The Masses* clearly shows he preferred their alternative editorial philosophy. Eastman already had published several of Reed's articles in *The Masses* when Reed presented the editor with something of a mission statement for the radical magazine. Typed neatly, folded into eighths, and titled "Statement of Purpose for *The Masses*," Reed's 1913 credo survives in the John Reed papers at Harvard:

> The broad purpose of *The Masses* is a social one; to everlastingly attack old systems, old morals, old prejudices—the whole weight of outworn thought that dead men have saddled upon us; and to set up many new ones in their places. So, standing on the common sidewalk, we intend to lunge at spectres, —with a rapier rather than a broad-axe, with frankness rather than innuendo. We intend to be arrogant, impertinent, in bad taste, but not vulgar. We will be bound by no one creed or theory of social reform, but will express them all, providing they be radical. . . . Poems, stories and drawings, rejected by the capitalist press on account of their excellence, will find a welcome in this magazine. (bMS Am 1091:1145)

Reed therefore found himself in a situation not unusual for a young artist with big ideas newly arrived in New York and eager to make his fame while retaining his independent principles. How much arrogance, impertinence, and bad taste could be ladled into the pieces for which he coveted a mass readership? How much rejection by the "capitalist press" on account of "excellence" could he afford and still gain the sort of funding and editorial support he needed for choice assignments such as Pancho Villa's Mexico?

Those questions were answered when Hovey, acting on a recommendation by Lincoln Steffens, assigned Reed to cover the Mexican insurgency. A close reading of Reed's Mexican journalism within the context of his Mexican notebooks was accomplished in the preceding chapter; here, I want to examine how

Whigham, Hovey, and *Metropolitan* marketed Reed's early journalism, how they created value around Reed's writing flair and dramatic rebelliousness, and how the young radical journalist responded to the creation of this myth. "[I]t was impossible to miss the presence of an untrammeled spirit ever so happily engaged," Hovey recalled, decades later, of his first meeting with Reed:

> The bursting energy, the continuous flow, the straight look at his material— such qualities were new.... I clutched the manuscript and spoke for the future work of the author, all on a breath, knowing that what this boy had to offer was as far from being a pale copy of that past master in the field, Stephen Crane, as it was from bearing the slightest resemblance to the "picturesque" reporting then in vogue. Such writing was like the sweep of a sudden wind come to shake the closed windows of the literary scene out of their frames. (Tamara Hovey, 78)

Metropolitan and the Construction of John Reed Superstar

If Carl Hovey had chosen the occasion of Reed's first "sweep of sudden wind" in *Metropolitan Magazine* to credit Howe's piece on Belgium as the magazine's "ideal article," it was not long before Hovey was won over to what he began to describe publicly as Reed's brilliance. Reed's initial articles on the summer Broadway season and the Paterson jail had appeared without fanfare or cover blurbs, although they were nicely illustrated by the magazine's artists. But with Reed in Mexico and with news of his having wrangled an interview with Pancho Villa, Hovey by January 1914 was telling his readers: "We have commissioned John Reed, the brilliant fiction writer and poet, to represent the *Metropolitan* at the front during the terrible fighting in Mexico."[2]

While Reed had yet to file an article from Mexico, Hovey took the liberty of publishing a portion of a letter from Reed, adding, by way of explanation: "Although not intended for publication, these pen pictures are too vivid to be lost" (72). Reed's letter contains some effective descriptive writing drawn from his Mexican notebooks, but Hovey chooses to foreground for his readers the access Reed had gained to Villa—without, of course, disclosing the price (a rifle and silencer) for which it was purchased. "I had a long talk with Villa today and he promised me that I was to go with him wherever he went, day or night," Reed assures his editor in the published part of the letter. "He is the most natural human being I ever saw—natural in the sense of being nearest a wild animal" (72). *Metropolitan* thus promises its readers exoticism and access: the enduring twin staples of reality narrative that still rule the mass-media market.

Reed's articles from Mexico had not yet arrived when the March 1914 issue of *Metropolitan* came out with stories and poems by Rudyard Kipling, Richard Harding Davis, Rupert Hughes, and H. G. Wells. But by the next month, Reed began a string of five consecutive months in which he dominated the magazine. In April, Hovey's note from the editor was even more enthusiastic, offering "priceless insights" for the price of a subscription: "John Reed is in Mexico with General Villa and the Army of the North. He is the only American correspondent at the front," Hovey told the magazine's readers. "The *Metropolitan* sent him in order to have a man on the spot who could tell the true story of the war. Reed is a man of extraordinary gifts; a brilliant writer, a man who has imagination and feeling—a genuine observer. His articles give us priceless insights into the Mexican struggle" (10). By May—when Reed reported the massacre that killed his friends Gino Guereca and Luis Martinez—his name was the largest on a cover he shared with Booth Tarkington, Richard Harding Davis, and Lincoln Steffens; and Hovey was touting "the first genuine pen picture of the Mexican soldier in flight" (9). For the June issue in which his profile of Villa appeared, Reed was given top billing on the cover of *Metropolitan* as well as his own full-page editorial to argue against U.S. intervention in Mexican affairs. "We do not realize that the Latin temperament is far different from our own—and that their ideal of liberty is broader than ours," Reed writes. "We want to debauch the Mexican people and turn them into little brown copies of American businessmen and laborers" (4).

Reed's apogee at the magazine undoubtedly was reached during late summer 1914 as the last of his Mexican articles was published. In July, Reed had long feature articles from Mexico and from Colorado (where, having left Mexico, he was covering a massacre of mineworkers). He also was making celebrity endorsements, as witness the magazine's ad picturing Reed writing a letter to Hovey on a Corona Folding Typewriter; the tag line states: "The men behind the men behind the guns—the men who hazard their lives in order to get the 'News'" (67). In August, Reed culminated his Mexican coverage with his account of the Battle of Torreon wrapped around an eleven-by-fourteen-inch portrait of Reed.[3] The brief biography in the portrait's caption called Reed "a gifted and fearless writer." And although his piece on the Paterson jail had appeared nine months earlier without much fanfare, the caption's revisionist narrative now termed it, "[a] remarkable article on jail life printed in the *Metropolitan* under the title of 'Sheriff Radcliff's Hotel'" (10). In fact, the magazine's praise of Reed was so glowing that the reporter a month later issued two disclaimers: the statement that he had developed "a remarkable friendship" with Villa was overdone, Reed said. And he also corrected the magazine's misimpression that he had been given the commission of brigadier general by the Mexican rebels (49).

April 29, on the train

Dear Hovey:
Gee this typewriter is certainly a
marvelous invention! It has absolutely
changed railway travel for me. I can
actually do a lot now on the train. The
bloody thing only weighs seven pounds,
and is about as big to carry as a large camera. Great, and standard keyboard too.
Here's the rest of the Battle stuff.
Good story altogether I think. If you

The War News You Read is
First Written on Corona Typewriters

The men behind the men behind the guns—the men who
hazard their lives in order to get the "News"—and who, when
they get that news—forward it with all possible haste to the
public, use Corona Folding Typewriters.

John Reed, Mexican War Correspondent of the Metropolitan Magazine,
is pictured above. We also reproduce excerpt from a letter he wrote his
Managing Editor just after he had first used a ——

CORONA
Folding Typewriter

He but voices the opinion held by all men and
women who have experienced the convenience and
reliability of this remarkable invention.

In the thick of the fray this little machine can be
easily carried—it weighs but 6 lbs. and folds up so
that it occupies a space of only 4¾ in. x 10½ in. x
9 in. You hardly know you have it with you—yet
when the time comes to use it—it's ready to go into
immediate action.

But, because of its lightness and compactness, do
not confuse the Corona with imitation typewriters
and toys for children to play with.

The Corona is a Standard typewriter in every particular—it has a universal keyboard, front stroke
type bar, back spacer, visible writing, two color ribbon—in fact, all the features of the heavier and more
cumbersome machines.

It's only in weight, size and price that the Corona
is different. Besides War Correspondents, the Corona
is used extensively by Authors, Teachers, Clergymen,
Salesmen, Actors, Doctors, Druggists, Business Men,
etc. Such firms as the Standard Oil Co., Singer Sewing
Machine Co., National Biscuit Co., Curtis Publishing
Co., General Electric Co., and many others have
purchased hundreds of Coronas.

The United States and Foreign Governments are
big users.

Wherever the Corona is known intimately it is
used. Many business houses and thousands of individuals would immediately purchase it they did
know, and so we say—Learn!

Send for free Booklet No. 44

It tells all about this wonderful typewriter—and
describes it thoroughly and completely. Write us now.

Corona Typewriter Co., Inc., Groton, N. Y.
Formerly the Standard Typewriter Co.

141 West 42nd Street, at Broadway, New York City   Agencies in principal Cities of the World

While his monthly reports from Pancho Villa's Mexico were enthralling *Metropolitan*'s
readers and earning him the highest pay of any U.S. journalist at the time, Reed had
occasion to pose for an advertisement for Corona's new seven-pound folding typewriter. In the ad, Reed's purported letter to his editor Carl Hovey extols the laptop
convenience of Corona's latest model—just the thing for "the men who hazard their
lives in order to get the 'News.'" *(Reprinted from the July 1914* Metropolitan Magazine,
courtesy of the Cleveland Public Library.)

Metropolitan's star machine was undeterred. "Word pictures of war by an American Kipling . . . What Stephen Crane and Richard Harding Davis did for the Spanish American War in 1898, John Reed, 26, has done for Mexico," the magazine trumpeted in newspaper ads accompanied by a drawing of Reed outfitted in sombrero, revolver, and gun belts (Rosenstone, 166). Elsewhere, the magazine's ads quoted Rudyard Kipling as saying Reed's writing had made him "see" Mexico for the first time (Rosenstone, 172).[4] And no less than H. J. Whigham himself revealed in an editorial that the magazine had rushed Reed to Colorado to cover the bloodshed surrounding the United Mine Workers strikes against Rockefeller mining companies at Ludlow and elsewhere. "When there is war," Whigham said, "John Reed is the writer to describe it. That is why the *Metropolitan* sent him straight from Mexico to Colorado" (3). Actually, Reed had returned to New York for at least two weeks before taking the train to Colorado after the April 19–20, 1914, massacre at Ludlow (Rosenstone, 172), but Reed's publisher was not about to be bothered with that minor detail in his marketing of the magazine's star reporter.

What Whigham got from Reed for his pains was a trenchant class analysis of the Colorado strike in terms so vivid that no news dealer in Colorado would carry the magazine. "The Colorado War" turned out to be a piece that jarred the business interests who backed the magazine as well as some of the industrialists who provided its advertising base. Perhaps because he traveled to the mining region with *The Masses* editor Max Eastman (Rosenstone, 172), Reed sent *Metropolitan* a 12,500-word article that reads more like a piece for *The Masses* than a comfortable fit with Whigham's brand of incremental socialism.

In the article, Reed discloses that John D. Rockefeller owned 40 percent of the stock in the Colorado Fuel and Iron Company, which—along with the Rocky Mountain Fuel Company and the Victor American Fuel Company—produced 68 percent of the coal in Colorado. Reed breaks down the amount the miners reputedly are paid—five dollars a day—and demonstrates how actual wages were barely two dollars a day, and how that was eaten up by virtually feudal living arrangements in company towns. Reed documents the inordinate numbers of fatal accidents in the Colorado mines and shows how the Rockefeller interests engage the Baldwin-Felts Detective Agency and state militiamen to break the United Mine Workers. He tells how the mineworkers were ordered out of the company towns after they went on strike, how they built massive tent cities off company property, and how Mother Jones and other radicals were jailed for their support of strikers.

Reed paints a portrait of peaceful workers, many of them Eastern European immigrants, living in the tent colonies during the strike, sharing food, song, and games. "Americans began to find out that Slavs and Italians and Poles were as kind-hearted, as cheerful, as loving and as brave as they were," Reed reports of tent-colony life. "The women called upon one another, boasting about their babies and their men, bringing one another little delicacies when they were sick. The men played cards and baseball together" (96). The mine guards and detectives, Reed insists, soon put an end to that peace. "And orders were that the Ludlow colony must be wiped out. It stood in the way of Mr. Rockefeller's profits. When workingmen began to understand one another as well as that, the end of exploitation and blood-money forever was in sight" (97). While Reed's article betrays a relatively simplistic "good guy/bad guy" cast of characters, he takes pains to show how nonstriking Coloradans in the mining towns supported the strikers against what they considered outside agitators and strike breakers.

The growing tension in the piece culminates in the burning of the Ludlow tent colony on April 19–20, an event that began on the Greek Orthodox Easter Sunday before Reed arrived in Colorado but that he presents in scenic detail.

> It was a fine day, the ground was dry, and the sun shone. At dawn the Ludlow people were up, larking around among the tents. The Greeks started to dance at sunrise. They refused to go into the big tent, but on a sun-swept square of beaten earth they set flags in the ground; and dragging their national costumes from the bottom of their trunks, they danced all morning the Greek dances. Over on the baseball diamond two games were in progress, one for the women and one for the men. Two women's teams had decided to play; and the Greeks presented the women players with bloomers as an Easter gift. So, with laughter and shouting, the whole camp took a holiday. Children were everywhere, playing in the new grass on the plain. Right in the middle of the baseball games, four militiamen came across the railroad track with rifles in their hands. Now, it had been customary for the soldiers to come over and watch the strikers play; but they had never before brought their arms. They slouched up to the men's diamond and took up a position between first base and the home plate, leveling their rifles insolently on the crowd. (113)

The night of that day produces a showdown between strikers and the militia when a union leader carrying a white flag is ambushed by company forces near the Ludlow railroad cut. "[S]uddenly, without warning, both machine guns pounded stab-stab-stab full on the tents," Reed reports. "It was premeditated and merciless" (115). Without naming names, Reed insists that he was told personally by militiamen that their orders on April 19–20 were "to destroy the tent colony and everything living in it" (115).

By April 20, a train carrying 126 members of the militia had steamed in from Trinidad, Colorado. Reed reveals all of the militia commanders by rank and by last name and reports their orders: "to shoot every God damned thing that moves" (116). As darkness falls, Reed takes up the story again: "At about 7:30, a militiaman with a bucket of kerosene and a broom ran up to the first tent, wet it thoroughly, and touched a match to it." Reed reports. "The flame roared up, illuminating the whole countryside. Other soldiers fell upon the other tents; and in a minute the whole northwest corner of the colony was aflame." The strike breakers "poured among the tents, shouting with the fury of destruction, smashing open trunks and looting" (116–17). Reed quotes a Lieutenant Linderfelt of the state militia: "We will kill every damned red-neck striker and we'll get every damned union sympathizer in this district before we finish" (118). Reed reports that "dead wagons sent out by the union from Trinidad to get the bodies of the women and children were attacked so furiously that they had to turn back. On the still burning ruins of the tents, militiamen were seen to throw bodies" (118–19). When the smoke had cleared, twenty-one strikers—mostly women and children—had died in the attack (Homberger, 73).

Finally, Reed reports that the Colorado legislature, house and senate, with coal-company support, had passed a bill authorizing $1 million in bond money to pay militia expenses "for their splendid work in shooting workingmen down and burning women and children to death" (121). Reed ends his piece by attacking John D. Rockefeller by name for what he calls "a significant fact" after the Colorado legislative session: "Mrs. Welborn, wife of the president of the Colorado Fuel and Iron Company, told her friends of the 'lovely telegram' her husband had received from John D. Rockefeller, Jr. It read, according to Mrs. Welborn [Reed probably could not have hoped for a better name]: 'Hearty congratulations on the winning of the strike. I sincerely approve of all your actions, and commend the splendid work of the legislature'" (121).

While Reed's piece romanticizes the same brand of spirited peasant life that had fueled his reporting from Mexico, and while it sets up the same sort of dramatically inevitable clash between the forces of people and of government, "The Colorado War" differs significantly from the Mexican reporting in ways that must have given his *Metropolitan* superiors pause. As a domestic story, its government villains are Americans; Reed names those responsible for the violence and links ruling economic interests with an armed attack of Americans. Gone is the Robin Hood romanticism of the Mexican coverage; nothing in Reed's reporting for either *Metropolitan* or *The Masses* had been so carefully researched or so polemical. With articles from both Mexico and Colorado on deadline, Reed had hired his friend Fred Boyd as a research assistant. A British socialist, whom Reed had met in Paterson when Boyd was arrested for reading the free-speech clause of the New Jersey constitution, Boyd had an informed Marxist analysis of social and economic issues that Reed admired (Rosenstone, 127, 146, 174). The article's resulting mixture of effective scene reporting and solid background research was to foreshadow the type of article that Reed would write about the economic underpinnings of the Billy Sunday campaign or the preparedness for World War I—a trend that would culminate in Reed's reporting of the Bolshevik Revolution.

"The Colorado War" drew strong reaction: by July 6, Hovey forwarded Reed a letter from the Kendrick-Bellamy book dealers in Denver sending back all their copies of the July edition of *Metropolitan* and discontinuing future orders. "Practically every news dealer in Colorado is taking this action in regard to your publication," wrote book dealer H. F. Bellamy. "Of all the vile unwarranted sensational lies that have been published about our state labor troubles, your article in the July number entitled 'The Colorado War' excels them all. The writer of that article is evidently an irresponsible person without any sense of right or wrong and any magazine who will publish such untruthful filth is not fit to go into the hands of decent people" (bMS Am 1091:494). While Whigham may have blanched at such high-placed vitriol, the magazine's circulation did not, after all, depend on its Colorado sales. The dramatic flair that Reed could lend to *Metropolitan* more than made up for his notoriety. Hovey's accompanying letter to Reed calls the news dealer Bellamy "an absurd object" and holds out hope that the magazine may be able to send Reed to China to cover revolutionary developments there, as Reed had proposed (bMS Am 1091:494).

Still, although Reed was to continue to publish regularly in *Metropolitan* for the next seventeen months, the magazine's enthusiasm never was quite as strong as it was during the late summer of 1914. Soon, Whigham and Reed were to face off over a much deeper and ultimately irreconcilable difference: the outbreak of war in Europe and the proper response to that war both by United States radicals and their government.

Where John Reed Stood: Class and Opposition to The Great War

An unpublished manuscript among Harvard University's John Reed papers entitled "The Collapse of the II Socialist International" (bMS Am 1091:1166) reveals Reed's deep disagreement with mainstream U.S. socialists during the years following the outbreak of war in Europe. Although the essay is not dated, Reed's bibliographers have placed its composition in late 1916 or early 1917. It most likely was written after Reed's thinking crystallized during extended reporting trips to Europe to cover World War I and after his relationship with *Metropolitan Magazine* and the more cautious American socialists had begun to sour. Though it is not literary reporting, the essay does offer a way to measure Reed's midcareer ideology in the context of his reporting of the world war.

More polemical than most of Reed's writing of the period, "The Collapse of the II Socialist International" sets out Reed's analysis of the failure of world socialism to oppose World War I and to be ready for world revolution. The manuscript attempts a specific analysis of Karl Marx's *Das Kapital* and *The Communist Manifesto*. It provides first-rate insight into Reed's thinking as the U.S. considered entry into World War I—why Reed opposed the war and why he broke with U.S. socialists such as Whigham and Walter Lippmann.

Reed contends that the death of Karl Marx in 1883 brought on stagnation among socialist theorists worldwide: "[B]ecause Marx knew profoundly well that the capitalist system had still a considerable lease of life during which the working class should be trained in revolutionary action by compelling concessions from the capitalists, his followers stepped blindly in the course he had pursued," Reed argues. Hence, instead of working toward the "total destruction" of capitalism, the Socialist International "persisted in devising various 'Transitory Programs,' 'Immediate Demands,' and so forth." In part, Reed says, the strategy was blind allegiance to Marx. And in part, the strategy made socialism more palatable to "the tribe of professionals—doctors, lawyers, social workers—that had flocked to the movement in droves as it began to manifest real power" and thereby made Marx "respectable and acceptable to liberal bourgeois sentiment by castrating him." Reed believes that the watering down of socialism, specifically its waning desire to capture the state, caused it to lose power and to miss the opportunity represented by the outbreak of World War I.

"Marx, in a series of monumental works, had traced the origin and development of the capitalist system, had disclosed the nature of its machinery and methods, and forecast with surprising accuracy its main lines of development," Reed contends. "He showed that the capitalist method of production and distribution contained within itself those forces which must eventually destroy the whole capitalist structure." To Reed's way of thinking, those forces were never more apparent than at the outbreak of World War I. Although capitalism had been able periodically to relieve its economic contradictions with the outbreak of more localized wars, thus "diverting the attention of the workers from the class struggle," for Reed a "great, final clash of the capitalist powers" is inevitable. "Hence," he argues, "all socialist propaganda could only have been committed to an uncompromising hostility toward all wars except the class war."

Reed was bitterly disappointed by the failure of international socialism to take advantage of the crisis posed by World War I. Had workers across Europe simply refused to fight, their ultimate victory over a decaying international economic system would have been inevitable, he contends. "And yet, what actually happened in July 1914? Almost without a struggle the most powerful single political party in the world [to his mind, international socialism] went down in ruins —the most spectacular political failure in history," Reed writes. "The working class, deserted by its leaders, divided and bewildered, was caught up in the whirlwind of patriotism and flung headlong into war." Its power to oppose the war had been sold out by its capitulation to "reformist parliamentary tactics" and, as such, it became a tacit supporter of the capitalist system. "On that account," Reed concludes, "the socialist movement was able to resist the war no better than the pacifist liberals who also opposed war, and were also part of the capitalist system" (bMS Am 1091:1166).

Reed's political analysis in "The Collapse of the II Socialist International" will strike many post-Soviet readers as relatively simplistic and doctrinaire, but a careful reading of how Reed's ideology had developed by 1917 is essential to understanding what his journalism attempts to accomplish at *Metropolitan* between 1914 and 1917. As early as "The Colorado War," Reed built scenes around the way that workers might unite across national and racial lines by playing baseball or sharing ethnic traditions. He attempted to show that a fundamentally inequitable system can be propped up only by violence and militia terror. And by examining Rockefeller's influence over the Colorado legislature, Reed tried to demonstrate that workers' interests fundamentally differ from those of their bosses and of the economic institutions—such as the mainstream press —controlled by their bosses.

Reed perhaps had not yet arrived at this systematic ideology when he wrote "The Colorado War" for *Metropolitan*, but something that he saw in Colorado, as well as the influence of Fred Boyd, seems to have begun to prepare him for those conclusions. Late in the summer of 1914, Reed wrote a brief essay for *The Masses*, "The Traders' War," in which he began to articulate his position on World War I. "The situation in short is this," he wrote. "German capitalists want more profits. English and French capitalists want it all. This war of commerce has gone on for years." Bismarck's "blood and iron" Germany, to Reed's way of thinking, would be pitted against "the raw hypocrisy" of Britain and France, "who shout for a peace which their greed has rendered impossible." Railing at editorial writers in the United States who "would have us believe that the White and Spotless Knight of Modern Democracy is marching against the Unspeakably Vile Monster of Medieval Militarism," Reed states: "No one can have a more utter abhorrence of militarism than I. No one can wish more heartily that the shame of it may be erased from our century" (76). His conclusion is a ringing call to U.S. radicals who read *The Masses:* "We, who are Socialists, must hope—we may even expect—that out of the horror of bloodshed and dire destruction will come far-reaching social changes—and a long step forward towards our goal of peace among men. But we must not be duped by this editorial buncombe about Liberalism going forth to Holy War against Tyranny. This is not Our War" (77).

Meanwhile, on August 15, 1914, Hovey offered Reed a $1,500 advance for exclusive coverage of the European war, and Reed sailed for Europe late that month. Reed used some of his advance to pay for a passage for Fred Boyd, who was eager to return to England because he believed war would spark a great social upheaval (Rosenstone, 182–83). It was on this trip that Reed found himself on the top deck of the ocean liner, symbolically and literally looking down on its working-class steerage. In the resulting article, "The Approach to War," the first of his European pieces for *Metropolitan Magazine,* Reed subtly reveals the contradictions within his professional and working life. His financial arrangements to cover war in Europe for both *Metropolitan* and for the *World,* the New York daily, had made him one of the highest-paid reporters in America, yet his political philosophy was developing in ways that threatened this privilege. The grinding dichotomy between his own upper deck and his steerage was enough to keep him awake at night.

Although *Metropolitan* would continue to publish his dispatches from Europe, Reed was sailing toward an inevitable collision with Whigham, who the month after Reed's "The Approach to War" published an editorial that Reed would certainly have described as dupery. Whigham wrote in December 1914 that the magazine would dissent from the doctrine of class war, preferring instead to abolish class itself. "For the Socialist party has at last begun to realize the absurdity of denouncing war and at the same time declaring that most disastrous kind of war, the struggle between men of different classes speaking the same language and owing loyalty to the same flag," Whigham contended. To the publisher of *Metropolitan,* the Great War, as it was known, already had begun to teach important practical lessons to socialists falsely enamored of worldwide revolution. "The leaders of the party have been obliged to recognize patriotism and racial loyalty as great human factors" (2), he said. In another six months, after the sinking of the *Lusitania, Metropolitan* would be depicting Germans crawling out of the sand traps of Long Island.

From Seduction to Sedition: Reed's World War I Coverage

The four Western Europe articles that Reed gave *Metropolitan* for its $1,500 advance were published between November 1914 and April 1915: "The Approach to War," "With the Allies," "German France," and "In the German Trenches." Of these, only "With the Allies" has since been reprinted; the other three are available only in rare copies of the original magazines.[5] Ironically, since Reed clearly was devoted to the concept of class war, *Metropolitan* published "With the Allies" the same month that Whigham's editorial denounced such social upheaval. Throughout his article, Reed builds a central motif of gathering darkness and explores the tragic effects that war wreaks on the men who fight it as well as essential similarities between German and French foot soldiers who must carry out the commands of their respective nations.

In retrospect, Reed's greatest challenge as a reporter was a lack of access to the fighting itself; French censors proved especially effective at keeping reporters from seeing events they did not wish them to see. "Richard Harding Davis, Morgan, and all the other correspondents got arrested yesterday at Rheims and the field here is definitely closed to newspapermen," Reed wrote to Hovey a month after his arrival in Paris. "You get two years in a French prison if you're caught within ten miles of the battle without a pass" (bMS Am 1091:129).

Frustrated by his inability to report from the front lines ("we had the beginning of a fine story—which needed actual battle to complete it," he complained to Hovey), Reed writes extended descriptions of new recruits arriving for duty, contrasting them with other descriptions of men who have tasted war. At Cernedon, Reed's train for Paris pulled in beside a troop train whose third-class carriages "rocked with singing and cheering . . . hundreds of young faces and waving arms." The young French soldiers boast of cutting the Kaiser's mustaches and chalk "lascivious caricatures" in the train car aisles of Prussian soldiers in humiliating postures before conquering French soldiers. "They were the youth and the young blood of France, the class of 1914," Reed observes, "bound for the military centers to undergo a training that should stamp out all their impulses and ideas, and turn them into infinitesimal parts of an obedient machine to hurl against the youth of Germany, who had been treated the same way" (78). Reed builds another sketch of veteran regiments returning from Algeria and Belgium. To Reed, the soldiers are exploited labor rather than patriotic heroes. "Their cars were not decorated," Reed writes. "They neither cheered nor sang, although they were going to the front. *They went with that curious, detached professional air of a man going to work in a silk mill in the morning.*

Beasts, they wisely spent their spare time eating, drinking, and sleeping, and for the rest obeyed their officers. That was what the Class of 1914 would become. It was not a pleasant thought" (78–79, emphasis added).

If the machinery of war can extinguish human exuberance, Reed seems to reason, how will it affect civilization? The metaphor he chooses is Paris, the eternal city of light now shrouded in literal and symbolic darkness. On a beautiful September morning, the kind of day during which the great city normally sparkles, "we emerged from the station into a city of the dead," Reed writes. The normal thunder of omnibuses, the roar of motor horns, shouting of street venders, and tramping of horses' hoofs are all quiet. To Reed, "it was as if the city had decked itself out for some vast rejoicing, and then had sickened. For a deathlike silence was over everything, in which the hoofs of my cab-horse echoed loudly" (80–81). At night the change is even more dramatic, and Reed exploits the scene for all its visual and aural detail, locking in the symbolic association of a lost city and its doomed troops:

> The cafes closed at eight o'clock and the restaurants at nine. There were no theaters except an occasional moving-picture show. The brilliant flood of lights from the cafes, the great golden arcs in the boulevards, the graceful necklace of lamps that traced the curves of the river and the bridges, the white brilliance of the Champs-Elysees—all were dark. At half-past nine the streets were absolutely deserted. But the great white beams of five searchlights played above the roofs of Paris, sweeping the sky for the long-expected airship attack. And through the dark streets the swinging tramp of regiments under my window, coming from unknown posts, and bound no one, not even themselves, knew whither. (82)

For the first time in its history, Reed concludes, once-glorious Paris is unable to excite any emotion: to his mind, the city and its people are "tranquil, ignorant, apathetic" (82).

Standard criticism of Reed's reporting from Western Europe terms it flat and unexciting because Reed could not get close enough to the battles to write with the sort of flair and vividness that marked his best work from Mexico. David C. Duke contends that Reed "failed to develop any real feeling for what was happening. He could never describe as forcefully the war of the trenches as he had his adventures with the Villastas or capture the flavor of conflict as he had during the battle for Gomez Palacio" (96). Similarly, James C. Wilson finds Reed's Western European writing to be "forced, labored" (118). Finally, in a much more deeply researched analysis, Reed's biographer Robert Rosenstone relies on a letter Reed wrote to Hovey on September 25 in which the reporter says, "I have never done such awful work. . . . I haven't seen anything worth writing" (bMS Am 1091:130) and two subsequent letters in which Reed describes his writing as "ghastly" and "horrible" (Rosenstone, 193). Although Reed was talking about specific unpublished manuscripts in these letters, Rosenstone generalizes their self-criticism. Rightly noting that, in Europe, Reed found that "culture, learning and civilization were taking a back seat to the business of death," Rosenstone suggests that the Western Front exposed Reed's "limitations" as a writer and reporter. Reed's biographer concentrates on documenting the reporter's anxiety and depression and concludes: "Emotionally constricted by lack of sympathy for a cause, he was unable to depict battle as a glorious pageant, to cover death with the romantic glow that had lit his descriptions of Mexico. Moved toward analysis of the war's origins, he had found little audience for his angry, radical viewpoint" (199–200).

While Rosenstone's position is extensively researched and has a certain merit, all three writers underestimate how Reed deliberately undercut the "glorious pageantry" and "romantic glow" of death in Mexico. Two brief reminders: Both at the Battle of La Cadena and in Gomez Palacio at the Battle of Torreon, Reed had concluded that war is "the most boring thing in the world if it lasts any length of time . . . all that slaughter for nothing" (*Insurgent Mexico*, 211). And if the deaths of his friends Martinez and Guereca had satisfied a reading public more than ready to consume exotic Mexican tragedy for the price of a picture magazine, Reed knew better: "I felt sick. Sick to think of so many useless deaths in such a petty fight. Blithe, beautiful Martinez; Gino Guereca whom I learned to love so much" (82).

A competing interpretation of Reed's writing from Western Europe in 1914 and 1915 finds Reed less anxious to glamorize war, more ready to see it in a larger political context, more able to focus on its mechanism and death. If those tactics fail to excite the romantic expectations of his consumers or critics, perhaps that is precisely Reed's point. In "The Worst Thing in Europe," an essay that *The Masses* published early in 1915, Reed says: "I hate soldiers. . . . I hate to belong to an organization that is proud of obeying a caste of superior beings, that is proud of killing free ideas, so that it may the more efficiently kill human beings in cold blood. They will tell you that a conscript army is Democratic, because everybody has to serve; but they won't tell you that military service plants in your blood the germ of blind obedience, of blind irresponsibility" (137).

Even in his *Metropolitan* stories, Reed takes every opportunity to explore the horrific impact of war on both French and German soldiers. "With the Allies" ends with Reed skimming along the white road to Sezanne in an army convoy. In the forest by the road, French soldiers hunt "a few miserable half-starved Germans" hidden in the aftermath of a recent battle. "[A]nd from the heart of the forest we heard, indeed, two rifle shots," Reed reports. "All the time, immeasurably distant in the north, sounded the troubling thunder of the cannon, where sleepless, wretched men mechanically killed each other near Rheims" (87). The reporter stands on the yellow, rolling plains of Champigny, where Attila the Hun had invaded more than a thousand years earlier, and surveys "long flat mounds of yellow earth—traces of quicklime about their edges— where the dead had been dragged by the leg and buried; Germans and French together." The dead lie there under a yellow mound, covered by "a wooden cross hung with flowers" (87). As in his best writing, Reed depends on close, lyrical description to make his point: the dead are victims of tribal fervor little changed since Attila the Hun. They are wrenched into the earth; their suffering is effaced by the very tribal symbols that make their deaths possible.

Although Reed may have complained about his "ghastly" writing, the evidence at the Harvard archives is that Reed's editors at *Metropolitan* made few, if any, stylistic changes. Reed's typescripts are extraordinarily clean of editing marks other than the dollar signs and ampersands, $$$$$$ and &&&&&&, that the author himself used to pound out corrections. In fact, from the evidence of these typescripts, *Metropolitan* was far more interested in editing Reed's Western European dispatches for ideological rather than stylistic reasons. In Reed's "With the Allies" dispatch, for example, a section was removed from the galleys in which Reed had written—with an inescapably ironic reference to alarmist pro-war editorials—that he expected at the French frontier to see something "special" because "we were entering a country at war for its very life." Instead, the reporter sees that "little villages of France lay quiet and undisturbed" (bMS Am 1091:1154, p. 3). Later in the piece, the editing is even more transparent. Struck from Reed's galleys, near the section about the dead lying buried under the cross, is the following: "Unstirred, unemotional, clear-sighted France acquiesced to the blind stupidity of militarism . . . the socialists forsook their primary proposition that war is always made by the capitalist class and cried: 'To arms'" (bMS Am 1091:1154, p. 12). While Reed's political opinion admittedly is unalloyed in the passage, its tone does not differ greatly from similarly strong opinions that survived *Metropolitan* editors in the heralded Mexican journalism; for example: "Carranza's political program . . . carefully avoids any promise of settlement of the land question, except a vague endorsement of Madero's plan of San Luis Potosi, and it is evident that he does not intend to advocate any radical restoration of land to the people" (*Insurgent Mexico*, 116).

By March 1915, Reed's dispatch to *Metropolitan* that was given the title "German France" was accompanied by an editor's note decidedly devoid of the breathless praise for Reed's earlier reporting: "Mr. Reed has just returned from the War. He found conditions in Northern France worse than in Belgium. This article tells what he saw and is the most recent description that has come from the front" (3). Reed opens his account of the German occupation of the countryside around Lille with the vignette of a "wonderful story of the Christmas Truce," during which French and German soldiers visited each other's trenches and exchanged gifts. "The Saxons were in trenches somewhere not far from Rheims; on Christmas Eve, the French *soldiers* opposite, against the commands of their officers, sent an envoy under a white flag to ask for a truce on Christmas Day," Reed recounts. "But on Christmas morning, the Saxon *soldiers* declared the truce in spite of the officers; and the two enemies kept it up in brotherly love and increasing friendliness for six days, until finally the mutinous regiments had to be withdrawn from both sides" (13; Reed's emphases). Reed claims to have spoken personally to one German enlistee who defied his officer's orders and met a British foot soldier. "The German carried a little Christmas tree with flickering candles on it, and the Englishman a plumb pudding. They sat there almost all Christmas night, in the open field between the two armies, with the Christmas tree between them, and ten yards on either side, the firing went on just as fiercely" (13–14).

Reed also concentrates in "German France" on the way war deprives civilians, remarking with obvious self-irony: "In the cafe where I took my *aperitif,* men and women crawled about under the tables like animals, picking up scraps of food. A coal wagon passed along the street, a throng of women crouching underneath with outstretched aprons to catch the dust that filtered down—for it was January and cold" (14). In the slums along the road to Ghent, Reed sees the poor amid "smokeless factories . . . a world only just now pulsing with furious life, and in an instant stricken dead" (81). Riding in a German troop convoy through the slums, Reed relies on close detail to contrast the army's power to the poor along the roads: "[I]n the doorways stand a slatternly woman or so, ragged, pale children, and here and there a man with his hands hanging loosely by his sides. They look after us with dull sullenness, and the women spit. The bugler on our first automobile blows the royal fanfare, which means, 'Get out of the way of the Kaiser's automobiles!' and old women, with their aprons full of stolen coal, squeeze back against the houses to avoid the fan of muddy water from our wheels" (82).

In the Trenches at *Metropolitan*

Reed's next piece, "In the German Trenches," appeared in the April 1915 edition of *Metropolitan:* a pivotal issue for the reporter's deteriorating relationship with the magazine. The magazine had previewed Reed's coming piece in the March issue with the flat statement "In our April issue we will print his description of a night in the trenches with the Germans" (3). When the April issue appeared, it touted a section of Richard Harding Davis's new book, printing a full-page photograph of the dashing war correspondent—an honor that *Metropolitan* had once accorded Reed. Somewhat ironically, Davis's new Scribner's book *With the Allies* took a title that was the same as that used for Reed's second dispatch from Europe. The resemblance, however, ends there: the two reporters had very different slants on the war. Davis saw himself as *with the allies* in a partisan sense that never applied to Reed.

A brilliant stylist well-known for his sometimes jingoistic coverage of the Spanish-American and Mexican wars, in *With the Allies* Davis coined the famous "river of steel" metaphor to describe the German troops and to urge reluctant Americans toward preparedness. "All through the night like the tumult of a river when it races between the cliffs of a canyon, in my sleep I could hear the steady roar of the passing army," Davis wrote. And then, like "giant pile-drivers," the army advances like "a Cataract of molten lead. The infantry marched singing with their iron-shod boots beating out the time. They sang, 'Fatherland, My Fatherland.'" In the preface to his book, written in December 1914 for a release by Scribner's, Davis makes no secret of his allegiance in the European war. His writing is as opinionated as any that marked Reed's competing position, but seems to have earned Davis a full-page endorsement, not an editor's red pen:

> Were the conflict in Europe a fair fight, the duty of every American would be to keep on the side-lines and preserve an open mind. But it is not a fair fight. To devastate a country you have sworn to protect, to drop bombs upon unfortified cities, to lay sunken mines, to levy blackmail by threatening hostages with death, to destroy cathedrals is not a fair fight. That is the way Germany is fighting. She is defying the rules of war and the rules of humanity. And if public opinion is to help in preventing further outrages, and in hastening this unspeakable conflict to an end, it should be directed against the one who offends. If we are convinced that one opponent is fighting honestly and that his adversary is striking below the belt, then for us to maintain a neutral attitude of mind is unworthy and the attitude of a coward. When a mad dog runs amuck in a village it is the duty of every farmer to get his gun and destroy it, not to

lock himself indoors and toward the dog and the men who face him preserve a neutral mind. (xiii–xiv)[6]

Reed's simultaneous reporting from Germany is sharply different. Although he was no friend of the German cause, Reed concentrates on the wastefulness of the war and its effect on those who fill its trenches. In one vignette from "In the German Trenches," Reed follows a general through a sick bay as he awards the Iron Cross to three foot soldiers. The first to receive the Iron Cross for bravery and sacrifice is a red-haired youth whose arm has been torn from its socket; the second is a man, too weak to speak, who has been shot through the lungs while he carried food to the men trapped in the trenches. Reed allows precise diction and understatement to speak for him as the general approaches the third recipient of the Iron Cross:

> The third man's skin looked like ivory, so tightly was it drawn over his wasted face. I noticed his great eyes fixed steadily on the general as he spoke—he had had one leg carried away by a shell and the other wounded. Gangrene had set in and both legs had been amputated at the thigh. He was a famous long-distance runner. The general dangled the Iron Cross before him, and he slowly reached out his hand for it and held it for a moment in front of his eyes, twisting it this way and that. Then, without a word, he deliberately held it out at arm's-length and dropped it on the floor. . . . The general went on as if nothing had happened. (8; Reed's ellipsis)

The writing here reveals Reed at the top of his form; in the bleak sentence "He was a famous long-distance runner," he lets the reader's understanding of the verb *was* resonate. Filled with strong verbs and precise observation, the scene compares with the best Reed had written in Mexico and combines with several other vignettes in "In the German Trenches" to build a war dispatch as effective as any Reed ever wrote.

In Reed's article, Davis's river of spit-and-polish steel empties into a swamp as trench warriors sink steadily in the muck of living graves. The occasion is a visit by Reed and another reporter, Robert Dunn, to a German trench that stretches from the North Sea to the Swiss frontier. For Reed, the trenches hide life, and ultimately they reveal death. "[A]bove ground there was not the least sign of human life—although we knew that within three hundred yards of us a thousand Germans were eating, drinking, sleeping and shooting, and two hundred yards from them a thousand French" (7), Reed reports. Building his extended metaphor, Reed opens the article with the portrait of "two spotless German officers in beautifully polished boots and the martial elegance of

Prussian long coats" (7), but that elegance devolves through scenes where it becomes too muddy to snap heels and culminates on a shell-shocked German soldier, bound and gagged by fellow soldiers to squelch his screams, "wild, staring eyes snapped wide like a savage beast's . . . wrench[ing] his muddy shoulders convulsively to and fro. He was quite mad" (71).

In the article, Reed examines how mechanical war affects the men who fight it and how modern public relations skews public perception of war's ideology. The Germans of "In the German Trenches" seem anxious to put on a little show for their American visitors and arrange the bombardment of French troops so the reporters can see how it is done. "'So you have come to see the guns,' said the captain of the battery politely, trying to click his heels in the mud. . . . He blew his nose in his handkerchief and nodded carelessly to the gunners. 'All right,' he said. They jumped back and clapped their fingers to their ears. *Crash!* A flat roar, flame and gray haze belched—and the whistling scream of the soaring shell rose and dwindled" (8). The Germans then make meticulous adjustments to their guns, twisting screws and turning cranks to calibrate the proper range. "He telephones back here the range, elevation, and trajectory, and the effect of the fire," the battery captain tells Reed. "We have been here for two months now and we have never yet seen the enemy" (9). As Reed listens to the German guns and to the responding French fire, a picture comes to him of "that great switchboard singing and humming" in brigade headquarters, of "quivering miles of telephone wire," of men speaking things "into a little metal tube strapped on the chest," of the "calm deliberate judgment" of far-off officers who bark the orders along telephone wires that will train the guns of one army on another.

While it is certainly true that Reed was put off by the mechanization of European warfare in 1914 and 1915, it does not follow that he was unable to report it effectively. It is precisely Reed's point that the battles of World War I are devoid of passionate human interaction. His vision draws its strength from his ideology: the working-class men who fight World War I, to his mind, are nothing more than interchangeable parts in some vast engine of death. "We were near the central nervous spot upon which all these elaborate telephones, transports, hospitals, barracks, starred uniforms, decorations, Iron Crosses, kings and emperors—the social, political and economic forces of a great Empire— were concentrated: a single line of men four hundred miles long" (10), Reed writes. And in that spot, foot soldiers are buried alive in the war's futility. The trenches they must dig to survive the modern war become their very graves.

Reed's battle reporting in "In the German Trenches" equals any that he wrote from Mexico, even (or especially) if it refuses to make heroes of either side. All those mathematical calculations, all those phone calls, all that concentrated power of kings and emperors and Iron Crosses produces for Reed an extended description in which he tries to capture the deafening cadence of modern weaponry in overheated prose:

> One-two-three-four!—One-two-three-four! They leaped along the French line in great bounds, without reverberations, smashing the doors of sound. Diabolical whistlings laced the sky, and shrapnel cracked suddenly near, back over our heads, and past, showering their screaming bullets, cracking and splitting into the mud. Far down the trench a man yelled, the rifles cracked into a steady roll. Excited men pumped their hot breach-blocks spouting empty shells, firing madly into the dark, for the rockets had ceased for the moment. One-two-three-four! Then, immeasurably deeper, whacking the air, the great guns opened. Far away a mighty lightning split the night, and the roaring, accumulated thunder of a bursting big shell smote our ears and sent us reeling. Behind us the German howitzers began again, and we could see the blasting flame leap from their *Granaten* half a mile behind the French trench. The ground shook, and we were conscious of no rifle fire, so deafening was the heavy roar of the cannon. Shrapnel were bursting quite near us now. We found ourselves floundering along in a staggering run toward the secondary trench, our one confused idea to get back into the lieutenant's dugout. A heavy thing hurtled into the earth two hundred meters ahead and blew up like a world exploding. For minutes, it seemed, the air was full of hissing mud and singing steel. (70)

Reed's metaphors here are orgasmic, if ultimately impotent: Men pump their hot breach-blocks, spouting empty shells. The ground shakes. After the gunfire, soldiers lie in the trenches, "smoking in the hot moistness" (70).

Reed is ever alert for war's absurdities. With a lull in the battle, a German major who had met Reed and Dunn telephones their trench. Would the American correspondents like to hear a little Chopin? He has arranged a telephone hook-up to the cellar of his chateau. "'Well, I'm giving a concert, and I thought you'd like to listen.' We took turns, Dunn and I, with the receiver," Reed reports, "while for half an hour the major played Chopin waltzes on the grand piano, and the bullets swished overhead, and men stood to their thighs in muddy water shooting one another" (80). Another offer comes from the ever-accommodating hosts. Would the American correspondents like to see some evidence of casualties? The lieutenant can arrange two or three rockets so the Americans can observe the trenches on the French line. Reed sees French bodies, only eighty meters distant, felled by the big guns:

For a minute it was as bright as day. Up a gentle hill straggled the French trench, a black gash pricked with rifle flame. Between lay flat ooze, glistening like the slime of a seabed uncovered by an earthquake. Only a little way off lay the huddled, blue-coated bodies of the French in three thick, regular rows, just as they fell a week and a half ago, for there had been no cessation of the firing.

"Look," cried the lieutenant, "how they have been slowly sinking into the mud! Three days ago you could see more. See that hand, and that foot, sticking up out of the ground; the rest of the bodies have sunk."

We saw them, the hand stiff, five fingers spread wide like a drowning man's. "No need of graves there. They are burying themselves!" (70)

The strong antiwar theme of "In the German Trenches" isolated Reed at the magazine. Years later, in a letter to his daughter, Carl Hovey would praise "In the German Trenches," saying it revealed "the actual ordeal of the soldier—the endurance of mud, monotony, desperate fatigue, the nerve strain of apocalyptic lighting and earth-shaking guns . . . the peculiar awfulness of a new kind of war" (Hovey, 128). But at the time, Reed's acceptance seemed far less secure. In addition to the full-page notice for Davis's pro-war book in that month's issue, former President Theodore Roosevelt wrote a guest opinion piece on "Preparedness." An acquaintance of Reed's and a Progressive Party ally of Reed's father, Roosevelt called for the United States to reconsider its neutrality stance and rejected views on the war such as those held by Reed. The magazine also provided a forum for John Kenneth Turner's ironically titled essay "Villa as Statesman," which attacked the Mexican as a ruthless murderer and argued: "The Villa theory is that the state exists for Villa and his friends" (25).[7] In his editorial, Whigham was content to report that, for the first time, the circulation of *Metropolitan* exceeded one million readers. By the next month, Reed was back in the United States and, at Hovey's suggestion, was writing domestic reports. The magazine's editorials meanwhile had become increasingly pro-war as Theodore Roosevelt analyzed the ramifications of the sinking of the *Lusitania*.

Reed, having returned to New York, was mired in an increasingly bitter feud with Roosevelt. He also was at odds with Davis, whose exclusive war dispatch in the July issue of *Metropolitan* accompanied the infamous "Germans-in-the-golf-course" illustration. It turned out that on the trip made by Reed and Dunn to the German trenches, the ever-accommodating Germans had offered the U.S. reporters a chance to fire a weapon in the general direction of the French lines. Rosenstone, Reed's biographer, takes up the story: "In a quiet moment their guide took a Mauser from a rifleman and, half jokingly, handed it to Jack. Without thinking, Reed took the weapon, pushed it through a slit and pulled the trigger twice. A moment later Dunn did the same" (198).[8] Dunn was moved to report the incident in an article for the *New York Post,* and Davis, among others, branded Reed as little short of treasonous. To his chagrin, Reed was compelled to ask Teddy Roosevelt for a letter of reference in an attempt to mollify the French, which Roosevelt provided with an addendum: "If I were Marshal Joffre and Reed fell into my hands, I should have him court-martialed and shot" (quoted in Rosenstone, 211).

Meanwhile, in August 1915, Roosevelt's next article for *Metropolitan,* "Peace Insurance by Preparedness," appeared, and two months later the cover of the magazine announced that Roosevelt from then on would write exclusively for *Metropolitan.* In November 1915—little more than a year after Reed's star had reached its peak at the magazine, with full-page photo, fawning caption, and two world exclusives—Whigham wrote the editorial "Let Radicals Face Reality." The publisher reasoned: "And until all men on an equal footing undergo military service to make themselves efficient patriotic citizens, we are far from realizing democracy and still further from the ideals of Socialism" (3).

The War in Eastern Europe

With relations deteriorating in New York and no chance to return to the Western Front, between April and October 1915 Reed made a long trip to the Balkans and Russia, filing eight reports that *Metropolitan* published between August 1915 and July 1916 and illustrated with evocative sketches by Boardman Robinson. Later collected in Reed's *The War in Eastern Europe,* published by Scribner's, the dispatches from the Eastern Front begin and end in the Balkans and feature a lengthy central narrative concerning Reed's and Robinson's travels and travails in Russia and Russian-occupied Poland. Scribner's titled the book *The War in Eastern Europe,* to fit the publishing company's "War on All Fronts" series that matches Reed's work with war dispatches from Germany, Britain, France, and Italy written by Davis, Mary Humphrey Ward, Edith Wharton, and E. Alexander Powell. (For a fuller analysis of how Scribner's marketing strategy affected the reception of Reed's writing, see chapter 6.) Because he had actually seen almost no combat during his seven months in Eastern Europe, Reed surely knew that the publishing company had misnamed his book. He therefore wrote a sarcastic preface specifically for the Scribner's edition that critiques the manner by which editors build marketing capital from the voyeuristic impulse to witness human beings at war.

"It was to be a three-months' flying journey," Reed writes. "We were going to see Italy enter the war, Venice destroyed by the Austrians; be in Serbia in time for the last stand of the Serbs; watch Rumania plunge into the conflict; stand by at the fall of Constantinople; accompany the Russian steam-roller to Berlin; and spend a month in the Caucasus reporting barbarically colored battles between the Cossacks and Turks." Instead, it seems that the damnable war refused to appear on schedule: "We were gone seven months and didn't see any of these grand dramatic climaxes" (269), Reed confesses. During his and Robinson's visit, Italy exhibited a "most disappointing calm" (269); Turkey was "disappointingly placid" (270). Learning that Rumania might be mobilizing for war, the two journalists "made for Bucharest hotfoot—to find much smoke but little fire" (270). And so it went: Constantinople was "calmer and safer than ever" (270); "nothing was doing in Salonika" (271). In fact, to read Reed's preface, Reed and Robinson themselves came closer to getting shot than anyone else during their visit to Eastern Europe: arrested in Cholm, Poland, by Cossack soldiers, they were booked on suspicion of being German spies and expelled from the country on pain of death.

That Reed wrote such a preface for *The War in Eastern Europe* shows how he reacted not only to a war that he had long since concluded was a colossal mistake but also to his growing recognition that the business of journalism was anchored on the commodification of widespread misfortune. In his preface, Reed stops just short of directly contesting the entire premise of the Scribner's series. Witness his somewhat rueful closing: "Of course we left [for home] at exactly the moment when the German and Austrian armies invaded Serbia, Bulgaria attacked her from the rear, and the English and French troops were only six hours' sail from Salonika. But we abandoned the warring nations to their respective fates" (271).

Therefore, rather than produce the guns-a-blazing book that his editors wished him to write, Reed turns his attention to the indirect impact of war: the epidemic of typhus in Serbia, the breakdown of the social structure in European cities, the rise of ethnic factionalism in many Eastern European nations, and the brooding revolutionary impulse that was beginning to surface in Russia and elsewhere as the war dragged on. To Reed, the chronic militarization of Europe had become as important a theme as the success or failure of any particular battle. "In the excitement of sudden invasion, desperate resistance, capture and the destruction of cities, men seem to lose their distinctive personal or racial flavor, and become alike in the mad democracy of battle" (269), Reed says. But as warfare becomes chronic, citizens settle down to "war as a business" and adjust to it as a "new way of life" (269). Therefore, Reed will examine the ideological impact of warfare and the ways it affects people of varying classes and ethnic origins. "As I look back on it all," Reed concludes in his preface, "it seems to me that the most important thing to know about the war is how the different peoples live; their environment, tradition, and the revealing things they do and say" (271–72).

The War in Eastern Europe, therefore, seems to concentrate on the manner by which the regulation of warfare is ruptured to expose the violence at its core—particularly that waged on and by peasants and working-class soldiers. Additionally, at the heart of the book, Reed explores the passion of the Russian people and their desire for autonomy in a repressive czarist system. Reed is entranced by the exoticism of Eastern Europe's many ethnic groups, particularly the Jews of Novo Sielitza, the Muslims of Constantinople, and the many colorful factions in regions such as Serbia, Bosnia, and Macedonia. Boardman Robinson's pencil sketches support Reed's writing strategy. Only a handful of Robinson's fifty sketches depict fighting itself. The vast majority capture the details of everyday life in Serbia, Poland, and Russia: peasant carts, oxen and wagons, a fully armed Serbian woman toting a violin and a rifle, the squalor of the typhus hospitals.

As with *Insurgent Mexico,* Reed varied the order of his episodes in transferring the original *Metropolitan* dispatches to *The War in Eastern Europe.* Unlike his earlier book, however, Reed wrote no new material (other than the preface) nor drew from other publication sources such as *The Masses.* The chief variation between the sequence of the original articles and the structure of Reed's book lies in his decision to reposition his scenes from Poland and Russia in the center of the volume and to open and end the book with reporting from the Balkans. While it may be tempting to draw deeper conclusions from these alterations, the fact is that Reed merely restored the account of Eastern Europe to his trip's original chronology. Reed had begun and ended his journey in Salonika, Greece, and had traveled in the Balkans on his way to and from Russia. *Metropolitan's* editors, not Reed, had decided to place all the material from the Balkans into four initial articles because the four-to-nine-month lapse between his itinerary and the magazine's publication schedule allowed them to do so. Still, Reed's restoring the trip to Russia to the center of *The War in Eastern Europe* adds a measure of impact to the Russian material and unifies the overall work —as does his decision to open and end the book with devastating scenes of trench warfare, the typhus epidemic, and ethnic conflict in the Balkans.

Without doubt, the most compelling descriptive writing in *The War in Eastern Europe* is drawn from Reed's journey to the mountaintop trenches that separate Serbian and Austrian combatants at such locations as Goutchevo. Reed's "Goutchevo and the Valley of Corpses" story already has been discussed in chapter 1, in my initial analysis of Reed's writing style, but here it is worth demonstrating how the Goutchevo piece builds on Reed's war-long metaphors. In the mass graves at the top of the mountain, Reed again sees the half-buried bodies that he had seen in the trenches of northern France. On this occasion, the combatants are Serbians and Austrians, "most of the bodies covered only with a film of earth, partly washed away by the rain" (368). As on the earlier occasion, the soldiers' nationalities matter little in their death; indeed, it is difficult to determine whose decaying body belongs to which army. All are destroyed, and the gore flows to the river, hence to the flat lands, where it will pollute the fields of the living.

The thin veneer that separates publicly accepted war ideology and the grim realities of the killing machine for Reed is represented by the thin crust of earth that ineffectually attempts to contain the soldiers' bodies in their shallow graves. The covering is ruptured even as Reed ruptures war's patriotic ideology to expose the brutality at its heart. Elsewhere in his dispatches, Reed explores that thin line between heroism and horror by visiting typhus clinics or the hospitals in which maimed soldiers have been sent to die. Given Reed's eventual death from a related disease, the reporter's descriptions of the typhus hospitals in Chere Kula, Serbia, are now eerily effective. Chere Kula (Chere Kula is Turkish for "Mound of Skulls") is a fetid barracks filled to overflowing. "The wind set our way," Reed reports, "carrying the stench of bodies sweating with fever, of sick men eating, of the rotting of flesh." In the feeble light of the shelter, Reed sees patients writhing in dirty blankets, five or six crowded in only a bed or two. These are the common soldiers who always interest the reporter and who suffer the direct effects of war while their bosses insulate themselves. Ruefully, Reed notes that later at the hospital he shared good wine with military officers, "forgetting for a moment the poor devils lying on the other side of the wall," as a Serbian general boasts of an important victory over the Austrians (322). Similarly, at Valievo, Reed is given a tour of a whitewashed, gleaming hospital by a proud medical officer, but spies "a horrible room" nearby that is not on the official tour. The men there suffer from posttyphus gangrene. "The only hope of stopping it is by amputating the afflicted part—and this room was full of men without arms and legs, of men with rotting faces and breasts. They moaned and screamed, crying '*Kuku Mayka!* Holy Mother, help me!' For most of them there was nothing to be done. Their flesh would slough away until it reached their hearts or brains, and death would come in dreadful agony" (375).

Considered in their parts, particularly in the reporting from Serbia and Russia, the episodes of *The War in Eastern Europe* build on Reed's enduring World War I theme: the gulf between the officers who prosecute the war and the common men who fight it. The techniques of literary journalism—artfully constructed scenes, dialogue, evocative description—allow Reed to make his

Illustrator Boardman Robinson, Reed's companion on a reporting trip to the Eastern Front of World War I, drew a haunting image for one of Reed's most widely reprinted stories from the war, "Goutchevo and the Valley of Corpses." The drawing depicts dogs feeding on half-buried bodies in the trenches on Goutchevo Mountain in Serbia. The image of the soldier's half-buried body became a frequently repeated motif in Reed's World War I journalism. *(From the original Scribner's edition of Reed's* The War in Eastern Europe, *1916.)*

case. Everywhere, Reed emphasizes the unity of common soldiers, not their national differences. The effects of war, inevitably, are decay and mass death, particularly for those who have the fewest resources to survive it. Occasionally, Reed constructs an ironic narrator eating in a polished mess hall while common soldiers suffer nearby. Ultimately, human bodies regulated by war's machinery break down in Reed's vision. The spit and polish of military life masks the disease at its core. Because Reed is so interested in the way that the war affected the workers and peasants, his journalism tends to cover the rhythms of everyday life, not those of generals and military tactics. In this way, Reed's strategy seems well suited, even influential, for the sort of literary journalism that was to develop during the remainder of the century. From smaller and more intimate portraits of life, Reed will build explanations of the political and social macrocosm.

Set against the Balkans' horror, Robinson's and Reed's trip to Russia at the heart of the book achieves the sort of effective local reporting that Reed had produced in Mexico's gold region and builds some quiet hope for a way out of the European traders' war. Published between March and July 1916 as *Metropolitan* articles, Reed's Russian reporting ("Behind the Russian Retreat," "Pinched in Poland," and "Holy Russia") foreshadows the themes that would dominate the final third of his reporting career. In Russia, Reed found a people who fascinated him for their love of philosophy and political argument. And as detainees of the Cossack army at Cholm, he and Robinson tasted the sort of incarceration that would nearly end Reed's life at the hands of White Russians in Finland a little more than three years later.[9]

Clearly fascinated by the Russian people, even if they eschew the sort of internationalism that intrigues him, Reed is moved by their distaste for imperialism and their fierce defense of their land. It's something about their romance with ideas that entrances him: "In Russia every one talks about his soul. Almost any conversation might have been taken from the pages of a Dostoievsky novel," Reed reports of his first encounter with Russians. In this people who would so intrigue him in the years to come, he glimpses a passion that might break the back of institutional, impersonal violence. "The Russians get drunk on their talk; voices ring, eyes flash, they are exalted with a passion of self-revelation. In Petrograd I have seen a crowded cafe at two o'clock in the morning—of course no liquor was to be had—shouting and singing and pounding on the tables, quite intoxicated with ideas" (468). Added to that passion is the significant gulf Reed sees between the common people and their leaders—a gulf he believes might be pried open to allow common people to break free. "The government itself—the bureaucracy—commands no loyalty from the masses; it is like a separate nation imposed upon the Russian people," he notes with obvious satisfaction. "As a rule they do not know what their flag looks like, and if they do, it is not the symbol of Russia. And the Russian national hymn is a hymn, a half-mystical great song; but no one feels it necessary to rise and remove his hat when it is played" (469).

Filled with resentment toward Germans who have effectively made their nation "a German commercial colony" (482), the Russians with whom Reed spoke expressed a strong determination for autonomy. Reed presents a vignette with a Cossack military commander—personally decorated by the czar—who is smugly certain that the peasants will join the czar in defending the motherland against the Germans. "So the peasants think that by beating the Germans they will get rid of poverty and oppression?" Reed asks the commander. "He nodded good-humoredly. Robinson and I both had the same thought: if the peasants were going to beat anyone, why didn't they begin at home?" (415). Later, in reporting on the czar's refusal to negotiate with liberal reformers in the city councils across Russia, Reed detects "some powerful, quiet menace as yet vaguely defined," and he asks the rhetorical question that would consume his reporting in coming years: "Is there a powerful and destructive fire working in the bowels of Russia, or is it quenched?" (487).

Reed believes that a powerful and destructive fire might portend great things. On his trip to Moscow, the reporter takes a river steamer one Sunday up to Sparrow Hills, where Napoleon had stood to watch Moscow burn. He sees groups of men and women bathing along the banks of the river. "They sprawled on the grass, ran races, moved in big singing droves under the trees; and in little hollows and flat places accordions jiggled, while the wild stamping dances went on" (496). Reed sees drunks harangue huge audiences. He sees senseless men asleep. He sees an old woman in rags, hobbling down a hill shouting hysterically, and a man and a girl pounding each other with their fists and weeping. Reed clearly is moved by a people who can express such passion and sees it as the first necessary condition of effective rebellion. "On a high point of land stood a soberly dressed man with his hands clasped behind his back, evidently making a speech to the restless flowing crowds beneath him. There was in the air a feeling of recklessness and gloom, as if anything might happen" (496).

Against this potential of the Russian people, Reed discovers a senseless repression that is symbolized by his and Robinson's incarceration at the hands of the Russian Cossacks in Poland. The American reporters are detained on suspicion of espionage for more than two weeks in "a malodorous chamber under a hot tin roof . . . four strides wide by five across" (449). In captivity, Reed and Robinson are hounded by a brutish Cossack named Ivan, whom they throw forcefully from their room to the delight of the other Cossack officers. Although he chafes at his incarceration, Reed does not waste his time. From the windows of the room, he can observe the teeming life of Cholm, which he captures in his customary detail: the gay lozenges and grotesque onion domes of the buildings, fanatic-faced priests with beards and long curly hair, girls in the lovely white headdress of the Russian Red Cross, and, as always, the wounded of the war.

As in his best reporting of the early fighting in World War I, Reed explores the gulf between depersonalized regulation (symbolized by his incarceration) and the suffering that such regulation seems to hide. From his room, Reed spies an ambulance, "in which the body of a huge man writhed in the grip of four nurses who were trying to hold him down. Where his stomach had been was a raw mass of blood and rags, and he screamed awfully all the way up the hill, until the trees swallowed the automobile and his screams simultaneously" (454). Ultimately, the manner of the journalists' release is as absurd as many other aspects of World War I. For two weeks, Reed had alternated between observing life outside his room and cabling and badgering anyone and everyone that he believed might sway the Cossacks to grant the reporters' freedom. Suddenly, the two American correspondents are released as mysteriously as they had been incarcerated and are given a pass out of Cholm. "We didn't wait," Reed reports, "but took the next fast train south, fearing that perhaps some one might change his mind" (467).

A third aspect of Reed's reporting from Eastern Europe concerns his ability to capture the domestic life of the many ethnic factions that bustled in the cities of Poland, Serbia, Russia, Turkey, Rumania, and Bulgaria. In his vivid description of the Jews of Novo Sielitza that remind him so much of his Lower East Side of Manhattan, Reed mixes stereotype and sympathy: "bowed, thin men in rusty derbies and greasy long coats, with stringy beards and crafty, desperate eyes, cringing from police, soldiers and priests, and snarling at the peasants—a hunted people, made hateful by extortion and abuse, by murderous competition in the foul, overcrowded cities of the Pale," he writes. Reed sees "venerable *ravs* and great scholars bent under the weight of virtuous years, with leather-bound tomes under their arms; sensitive-faced boys who passed repeating their lessons, on the way to *heder*—a race inbred and poisoned with its narrow learning, because it has been 'persecuted for righteousness sake,' and butchered in the streets by men whose banner was the Cross" (397).

In Constantinople, which Reed calls ancient Istamboul, the reporter awakens "to an immense lazy roar, woven of incredibly varied noises—the indistinct shuffling of a million slippers, shouts, bellows, high, raucous peddler voices, the nasal wail of a *muezzin* strangely calling to prayer at this unusual hour, dogs howling, a donkey braying, and, I suppose, a thousand schools in mosque courtyards droning the Koran" (507). Always, Reed is on the lookout for the incongruous detail that will capture life as it is, not as it is expected to be: the word-picture that will craft journalism as literature. "Veiled women in whose faces no man looked, hurrying along in little groups, robed in *tcharchafs* of black and gray and light brown, wearing extravagantly high-heeled French slippers too big for their feet, and followed by an old black female slave; Arabs from the Syrian desert in floating white cloaks; a saint from the country, bearded to the eyes, with squares of flesh showing through his colored rags, striding along, muttering prayers, with turban all agog, while a little crowd of disciples pressed after to kiss his hand and whine a blessing" (512). At the booth of Youssof Effendi in Constantinople's Bazaar of Egypt, Reed revels in the orientalism of alien commerce. He sees "dervish beggar-bowls made from the brittle skin of sea animals, ostrich eggs, tortoise-shells, two human skulls, and what was evidently the lower jaw of a horse. On the counter and the shelves behind were crowded glass bottles and earthen pots full of crude amber, lumps of camphor, hashish in powder and in the block, Indian and Chinese opium and the weak opium of Anatolia, bunches of dried herbs to cure the plague, black powders for love philters, crystals of oil for aphrodisiacs, charms to avert the evil eye and to confound your enemies" (517–18).

These descriptive vignettes clearly satisfy Reed's love of local color and Byzantine variation, but on a deeper level they strike him as a powerful resistance to the sort of gray-hued capitalistic regimentation that he sees sweeping Europe and contributing to the Great War. On the legendary Orient Express, Reed discovers that regimentation: "the ancient habit of cosmopolitan existence tak[ing] possession" of upper-class passengers from a half-dozen warring nations, who set aside their differences to join in bridge parties and gossip, safe in their insulation from the masses who will fill the trenches for their battles. For Reed, until those masses recognize their common economic interest, the passions of regional identity stand as good a chance as anything to ignite some measure of defiance to the sort of chronic militarism that he explores throughout *The War in Eastern Europe*. And for a reader at the beginning of the twenty-first century, the reporter's evocation of regional ethnic identity provides one of the book's enduring values, particularly in the post-Soviet age when outsiders once more struggle to understand why so many races and religions vie for some of the same Eastern European territories.

One example among many is Reed's description of Macedonia's ancient dispute whereby a half-dozen neighboring nations wish to carve a slice of the land for themselves. His political analysis remains as fresh as today's news. "The Macedonian question," says Reed, "has been the cause of every great European war for the last fifty years, and until that is settled there will be no more peace either in the Balkans or out of them. Macedonia is the most frightful mix-up of races ever imagined. Turks, Albanians, Serbs, Rumanians, Greeks, and Bulgarians live there side by side without mingling—and have so lived since the days of St. Paul. In the space of five square miles you will find six villages of six different nationalities, each with its own customs, language, and traditions" (551). Of the many factions struggling for domination of the region, Reed most compellingly describes the Serbs, "from the ruins of a whole people, imperial ambitions . . . already springing" (310). At his birth, each peasant child will be greeted by its mother: "Hail, little avenger of Kossovo"—an infant one day destined to free that region from the Turks (329).

Ultimately, Reed's *The War in Eastern Europe* is as sprawling and undisciplined as its subject, a war book in which war rarely appears yet is everywhere apparent. Harry Henderson terms *The War in Eastern Europe* "a dismal failure" because "history has played an ironic joke on Reed by realizing his favorite metaphor [war] in its ugliest form" (428). Yet surely Henderson fails to see that that theme is precisely Reed's point. As with his earlier reporting from the

Western Front of World War I, the reporter is scrupulous not to glorify a war he cannot abide. From his sarcastic preface to his ironic ending (whereby a departing Reed sees twelve British troop ships steaming toward Salonika to commence the invasion and the reporting opportunity he will miss [567]), Reed's book strives to reveal the "ugliest form" of war: not its battles, but its unceasing attack on the dreams of the people who must fight those battles. At its most compelling, says Eric Homberger, Reed's second book is "a journey into the darkest heart of darkness of the European continent, through a diseased land" (*John Reed*, 94). Homberger doubts, however, that Reed possessed "an inwardness and psychological depth" to pull off a masterpiece in the style of Joseph Conrad's *Heart of Darkness* (94). On many of its pages—the decomposing bodies in the half-covered trenches atop Goutchevo Mountain, the fetid typhus wards in Nish, the quarreling Russian peasants bending elbows and ears in Moscow, the ghettos of Novo Sielitza and bazaars of Istamboul—Reed gets to that depth. Still, for the sustained passion for his topic and the psychological and political instinct to pull it off, Reed, no doubt, would have to wait for November 1917 and for his ten great days in Petrograd.

Finally, although *Metropolitan* gave adequate positioning to Reed's articles from Eastern Europe, and although Robinson's sketches improved their exposure, the magazine no longer devoted its promotional efforts to Reed's work. Retrospectively, it is not difficult to understand why. Reed's set pieces on the futility of war no longer squared with the magazine's larger political mission. By 1916, each issue of *Metropolitan Magazine* was featuring another article urging U.S. war preparedness. And while Reed was reporting in the February 1916 issue on the soul of the Russian peasant, the magazine that once counted him as its brightest star was depicting in its editorial cartoons a sleeping Lady Liberty holding a glum-looking eagle in a neck choker and chain. "Awake and prepare," Theodore Roosevelt booms in that issue, while a Whigham editorial asks, "Are We a Nation of Slackers?" It would not be long before Whigham would answer that question in the affirmative—at least as he applied his judgment to the fallen star of his reporter John Reed.

"You can shoot me if you want and try to draft me to fight"

A year after his publisher at *Metropolitan* openly condemned slackers and drummed for the draft, a defiant Reed traveled to Washington, D.C., on April 14, 1917, to testify at hearings before the House Committee on Military Affairs. At issue was a bill authorizing the president to increase temporarily the "military establishment" of the United States. "Is it democratic to force men who do not believe in this war to go to war?" Reed thundered at the committee hearings. "I do not believe in this war. I am not a peace-at-any-price man or a thorough pacifist, but I would not serve in it. You can shoot me if you want and try to draft me to fight—and I know that there are 10,000 other people—" At this point a U.S. congressman cut off the fiery young reporter. "I do not think that we need to hear this gentleman any further," he said, according to the official transcript of the hearing held in the Reed archives. Another congressman snapped: "This kind of man is found in every country, but we should be thankful that the country does not depend on them." Finally Reed was asked if he had a personal objection to fighting. "No, I have no personal objection to fighting," Reed replied. "I just think it is unjust on both sides, that Europe is mad, and that we should keep out of it" (bMS Am 1091:1560, pp. 31–33).

Comments like these ended Reed's relationship with Charles Townsend Copeland, his old English professor. "Copeland was all for the conflict," recalls Heywood Broun in a *New Yorker* profile on the professor. "His boys were on every front, in the waters, under the earth and the heavens above. Here was the test of gallantry which was the shibboleth of Copey. They wrote to him, scores of them, and brought the lilt of battle to the little man from Maine up in his room in Hollis. Jack was not one of them. Jack was against the war. Out of the whole Copeland fraternity he was the one who stood out and faced trial for obstruction. . . . Nobody spoke of John Reed. He had been dropped from the Harvard Club" (22).

By 1917, it had become not only deeply unpopular but potentially criminal to utter opposition to conscription. Reed would be indicted that year by a federal court for sedition against the U.S. government for counseling against the draft; his publishing opportunities would be effectively suppressed as the government banned periodicals like *The Masses* from the mails and indicted its editors. And Reed no longer was welcomed at *Metropolitan*—the magazine that had once called him the most brilliant writer in America. Julian Street, a New York writer, reports the growing tension at the magazine. "H. J. Whigham, who was editor of the *Metropolitan Magazine,* tells me that in 1916 he gave Jack up for lost," Street recalled in a later article in *Saturday Evening Post.* "'You and I call ourselves dear friends,' Jack said to [Whigham], 'but we are not really friends because we don't believe in the same things, and the time will come when we won't speak to each other. You are going to see great things happen in this country pretty soon. It may kill me and it may kill you and all your friends, but it's going to be great!'" (67).

Throughout 1916, these tensions had been building. At the magazine's suggestion, Reed had concentrated on such domestic pieces as his short stories and profiles of Henry Ford and the like.[10] Meanwhile, the magazine's editors had broken with President Woodrow Wilson over the issue of war and hoped their star columnist Theodore Roosevelt and the Progressive Party might mount an effective opposition to Wilson's policies. For his part, Reed thought Wilson represented the best chance for peace and, therefore, had to turn to *The Masses* to publish his article "Roosevelt Sold Them Out," about the collapse of Roosevelt's Progressive Party during the political conventions of 1916. "I had the most terrific time since last night," Reed wrote to Louise Bryant of that collapse. "Roosevelt sold out his party and the delegates wept and went to pieces—many of them broken men, men without anything left. . . . I wouldn't have missed this for the world! But, oh, I wish you were with me. It's an awful story and a magnificent one" (bMS Am 1091:30).[11]

A review of correspondence between Reed and his *Metropolitan* editors during late 1916 and early 1917 discloses the painful deterioration in their relationship. In June 1916, Carl Hovey still held out hope that Reed might write more stories from the Great War: that is, if he could manage to capture how young Americans "taken out of their offices and away from their jobs without warning" would fare as they "go to make a big incident." Hovey wrote: "If we have a war you ought to get the story" (bMS Am 1091:496). But within three months, Hovey no longer would encourage any writing by Reed on the war and could suggest only more "Grampus Bill" stories, escapist fiction that Reed wrote for profit, perhaps "with a terrible female in it" (bMS Am 1091:497). By a month later, Hovey had refused an advance for a Reed story, and before the end of the year he would reject two more out of hand.

Finally, the period also marked the dashing of Reed's long-cherished hope that *Metropolitan* would finance a trip to cover revolutionary developments in China. Hovey and Whigham earlier had agreed to the plan, but thought Reed should delay it in favor of European war coverage. By September 1916, their enthusiasm had cooled. Hovey reported to Reed that the magazine still might publish stories from China, but would pay only on a per-article basis. In January 1917, the magazine announced the trip to its readers. But by February 1917, Hovey dashed the idea permanently. "The break with Germany has thrown us up in the air as far as our immediate plans are concerned," Hovey wrote to Reed. "It seems rather absurd for us to be planning to spend a large sum on articles on China in view of the possibility of the country going into the war. Whigham and I think that we had best put off consideration of your trip to China until we can see more clearly ahead" (bMS Am 1091:500).

Reed's last article for *Metropolitan* was "Industrial Frightfulness in Bayonne," his reporting of a wildcat strike at the Standard Oil plant in New Jersey.

Reed's strategy was to convince his liberal Eastern readers that workers' conditions on their doorstep were as desperate as those in more remote or exotic locations. In the piece, Reed seeks to lay the blame directly at the feet of John D. Rockefeller, his old Colorado nemesis, and the press institutions that Reed believes support capitalist power. "New Yorkers have a hazy idea that these things happen in distant, half-civilized countries—the Michigan peninsula, the mountains of Colorado and Minnesota; and the metropolitan press is indignant at capitalist injustice. But this same injustice goes on in Bayonne, a city visible from the Battery and almost within the city limits of Greater New York, and most of the newspapers will not, or cannot, tell the truth about it" (12).

As he had in "The Colorado War," Reed attempts to replay the key moments of the contentious labor dispute, showing how the mainstream press had gotten the story wrong because of its unwillingness to talk to working-class people. Much of the best scene writing in the article concerns Polish tenement dwellers, contemptuously called "Hunkies" by better-off neighbors. Reed enters their homes and their schools to report what he sees: "the tenements grow flimsier and closer packed, the saloons thicken, the sky darkens with acrid black smoke from the refineries; squat, flat-faced women, who all seem to be pregnant, shuffle along the sidewalks or look dully from the windows, and swarms of filthy, pale children boil up from the littered pavement" (12). In one house that Reed visits, a Polish family of seven children and nine boarders take their turns sleeping on piles of dirty rags, rising, in turn, for round-the-clock shifts at the refineries. By article's end, the strike has been broken, mostly because—as Reed meticulously tries to prove—of the misreporting of the mainstream press, and the conditions have not improved.

Reed ends "Industrial Frightfulness in Bayonne" with a deeply ironic scene that seems to sum up his increasing bitterness at his own nation. The strike broken, Reed accompanies the Polish children to Public School 5, where he overhears teachers in their lounge saying, "Those dirty hunkies ought to be shot down." In the classroom itself, the Polish children, "with blank, enthusiastic, uncomprehending faces," were being made into U.S. citizens. "My heart sank," Reed reports. "As we were going out, one teacher followed us into the classroom and pointed proudly to the blackboard. 'This is our exercise for the week,' she said. I looked. Upon the blackboard was drawn an American flag in colored chalk; above it was inscribed, in uncertain childish letters, 'America, I Love You'" (68).

These words were the last that Reed ever was to write for *Metropolitan*

Magazine, closing out a chapter in his career that marked some of his most stylistically ambitious writing and by far his closest and most careful reporting to date. Although many of the articles have not been collected and remain virtually unread today, Reed's profiles of Billy Sunday and Henry Ford, his exposé of the Paterson jail, his labor reporting from Colorado and New Jersey, as well as his relatively better-known reporting from Mexico and Europe, stand out in the history of U.S. literary journalism. But they also stand out as a testament to the ways in which cultural and ideological tides, both on the part of the reporter and his magazine, affect writing markets and publishing opportunities in ways that often are not documented. Hovey sums up that point precisely in a subsequent letter to his daughter:

> Reed had become what he wished to be, the embodiment of rebellion against the course his country had chosen to follow. The vision that hovered before his eyes—the poet's instinctive dream of a world entirely better—could not be shared . . . by a publication widely read and with its feet on the ground of native soil. It was fine for Reed to hate war and say so. But the magazine could no longer be his platform; even if its editors saw with his eyes, which was not the case, it would merely mean the end. *The Metropolitan* would have been instantly, cheerfully, squelched. (153–54; Hovey's ellipsis)

Ironically, "Industrial Frightfulness in Bayonne"—as defiant of John D. Rockefeller as *Metropolitan* would allow him to be—lies side by side with a half-page house advertisement for the annual supplement of "Automobile and Accessory Manufacturers." The advertising copy supplied by the magazine contains a revealing, and almost certainly inadvertent, pun: "More *striking* [emphasis added] editorial features, announcements of more automobile and accessory manufacturers and specifications of more models than ever before. The *Metropolitan* carries more automobile and accessory advertising than any other general monthly magazine" (65). Across the river in New Jersey lay the oil refineries and their striking Polish workers who would fuel those automobiles and create profits for the Rockefellers and other industrialists. The resulting contradictions between reporter and magazine—striking in all senses of the term—finally became too great to reconcile.[12]

And so, Reed's final article on World War I, "This Unpopular War," was not published in *Metropolitan.* In retrospect, it seems to follow the suggestion that Hovey had made to report what happens to young Americans as they prepare for world conflict. But it was not quite the article that Hovey would have envisioned, and it was published in the August 1917 edition of *Seven Arts,* not *Metropolitan.*[13] Reed opens the article on a stifling summer night in Washington,

D.C., listening to a group of young college graduates think up "talking points" to sell the war as drummers might sell cheap clothes. One young man suggests that the nation should just send several thousand Americans to slaughter to "wake the country up" (166–67). Reed muses on this interchange and confesses to his readers that he went over to Europe with "the fixed socialist idea that the capitalistic ruling classes had cynically and with malice tricked their people into this war," but that what he found were young troops "not even reasonable enough to make trickery necessary" (168). Reed again writes about troops "the color of mud, their teeth chattering incessantly" (171), sinking into the mud, going mad, firing at anything that moved. "I asked those mud-colored men, leaning against the wet mud bank in the rain, behind their little steel shields, and firing at whatever moved—who were their enemies?" Reed recalls in what would be the defining imagery of his war coverage. "They stared at me uncomprehendingly. I explained that I wanted to know who lay opposite them, in those pits eighty yards away. They didn't know—whether English, French, or Belgians, they had not the slightest idea. And they didn't care. It was Something that Moved—that was enough" (172).

The United States now has its taste for the war, and the only thing to follow will be war fever, suppression, the beating of pacifists by soldiers and sailors, Reed warns. "It's getting to be as much as a man's liberty's worth to say that this is not a popular war, and that we are not going democratically about 'making the world safe for democracy'" (173–74). The article's culminating vignette takes the reader to an exclusive club on the eve of Woodrow Wilson's war message to Congress. The papers are reporting that the Germans have torpedoed another U.S. ship, drowning several American citizens. In the club, a war-hungry youth drawls, in terms that recall Mac's commitment to freedom in "Mac-American," "I must confess that my ardor was somewhat dampened when I read that one of the victims was a Negro" (175).

Reed was correct in predicting the suppression of articles such as these. *Seven Arts* ceased publication the next month when a major patron withdrew subsidy directly because of Reed's "This Unpopular War." Seventy-five publications, including several for which Reed wrote, were banned by the postmaster-general under the Espionage Act, although the ban on the *Nation* was lifted when its editor refused to print any more articles by Reed. *The Masses,* one of his most reliable sources of publication, was banned from the mails in August 1917, then denied regular publication mail status for September because it had not mailed copies in August. Its five editors, Reed included, were indicted for conspiracy to obstruct the draft, primarily for an article Reed had written that had questioned the sanity of enlistees (Rosenstone, 321–24).

John Reed Descending: From Top Deck to Steerage

By August 1917, Reed was back on board an ocean vessel, again sailing to Europe. This time, he was on his way to Russia, where the March revolution had succeeded in toppling the czar and the Bolshevik Revolution was waiting in the wings. Carrying credentials for *The Masses* and the *Call,* the New York daily, Reed had financed the trip with $2,000 raised by Max Eastman from an anonymous donor (Rosenstone, 282). Only three years earlier, Reed had shifted uneasily in the upper deck, on a *Metropolitan* expense account, as he watched the teeming steerage passengers gather on the lower decks, ready to fight what Reed believed to be a "traders' war." On that occasion, Reed's fellow passenger was a silk-mill boss, who along with the steerage passengers had troubled Reed's thoughts and cost him a night of sleep. But on this occasion, captured in a unpublished manuscript called "Across the War World," the reporter stands on the lower cargo deck shoulder to shoulder with returning Russian workers, "precisely the kind of people one sees in the garment-workers' strikes . . . They gathered on the cargo deck, dirty, unlovely people, a little ridiculous to look at and listen to—but familiar and busy with the most sublime dream men have ever dreamed. . . . One little black-haired baby couldn't say a word except 'Socialism'" (bMS Am 1091:1179).

The comparisons and contrasts between Reed's initial *Metropolitan* piece on the European conflict, "The Approach to War," and the unpublished "Across the War World" are too startling to miss: two ships, a pair of upper and lower decks, two brands of returning workers, two direct references to the silk strikes that earned Reed his first notoriety as a reporter. Two resulting articles, three years apart: one guaranteed by an expense account while Reed was one of the highest-paid reporters in the United States, but ultimately disappointing to its publishers; the second, likely written from the heart, unpublished because by then the markets were gone. This time, Reed surveys from a different angle the gulf between the upper deck and the cargo hold: "Up in first class," he now observes, "a charmingly cultivated Russian, once officer in the czar's army, erratic and fascinating, claiming to have fully accepted the revolution, stood at the window looking down on the steerage" (bMS Am 1091:1179). On this occasion, Reed was one of those in the steerage upon whom the cultivated Russian could gaze. Reed no longer had the place of the cultivated Russian on the top deck— the Russian who claimed to have accepted a revolution, but was still traveling first class.

It was in this mood of recommitment to the struggle for justice that Reed, recovering from the removal of a kidney, wrote his brief autobiography "Almost

Thirty" (the title refers not only to his age in 1917 but also to the then-common journalistic practice of signaling on copy the end of an article: -30-). "The War has been a terrible shatterer of faith in economic and political idealism," he confesses. "And yet I cannot give up the idea that out of democracy will be born the new world—richer, braver, freer, more beautiful" (142). Stripped of his writing markets, scorned by the clubmates who once toasted the brash writer as one of the nation's best, Reed had symbolically stepped off the top deck of his life as a writer and dropped down into the steerage. And there, to his mind, he would find and write the story of that new world.

Ten Days That Shook the World

The Rising Tide of Revolution

> So. Lenin and the Petrograd workers had decided on insurrec-
> tion, the Petrograd Soviet had overthrown the Provisional
> Government, and thrust the *coup d'etat* upon the Congress of
> the Soviets. Now there was all great Russia to win—and then
> the world! Would Russia follow and rise? And the world—what
> of it? Would the peoples answer and rise, a red world-tide?
>
> —John Reed, *Ten Days That Shook the World*

Ten Days That Shook the World is John Reed's attempt to measure the rising
tide of class revolution in what he believed was to be a transformed universe.
Within that universe, "human society flowed molten in primal heat, and from
the tossing sea of flame was emerging the class struggle, stark and pitiless—and
the slowly cooling crust of a new planet" (717–18). Subsequent events in the Soviet Union and the eventual collapse of the Soviet system by necessity inject a
certain measure of irony to any contemporary reading of *Ten Days*. Yet the author of *Ten Days*, as in all of his best writing, renders it impossible for the
reader to separate his politics from his poetics. Assessing the achievement of
Ten Days That Shook the World—the book that built Reed's lasting reputation
and in many ways still defines his contemporary reception—therefore requires
that we judge the book's reporting and writing achievements against the personal and political transformation forged in its author by the events of November 6–15, 1917.[1]

Although he had lost all but the most marginal of his writing markets and faced federal indictments for sedition, the Reed who climbed to the second floor above the Greenwich Village Inn during the last two months of 1918 to write his account of the Bolshevik Revolution was far more sure of his own identity than the younger Reed who had written *Insurgent Mexico*. As detailed in chapter 4, Reed, before the end of 1918, already was disinherited from the ruling interests of the United States and had been abandoned by most of his countrymen. By the time he wrote *Ten Days*, Reed seems to be past worrying about his acceptance by his nation and instead looks with hope toward world-wide revolution. A year earlier, in "Almost Thirty," Reed had declared: "I have not any God and don't want one; faith is only another word for finding oneself" (143–44). Now he seems sure of his citizenship on the new earth he believed was being formed in Soviet Russia, a significant change from his status in Mexico, where he was always the outsider looking in, unable to shed the privilege of race and nationality, no matter how deeply he buried it in his fictions.

Reed therefore constructs interlinking metaphors—the figures of rising tide and revolutionary fire—in *Ten Days That Shook the World* to foreground that personal and political transformation. Together, these metaphors produce the steam that powers the turbines of change. When Russian reformers are overwhelmed by revolutionary workers at Tsarskoye Selo, "hordes of the people, gathering in the darkness around the battle, rose like a tide and poured over the enemy" (776–77). On the streets of Petrograd, the Russian people fight for newspapers with the latest political information, "pouring in slow voluble tides up and down the Nevsky" (625). Before the storming of the Winter Palace, "the tides of people flowed endlessly" (640–41). When Reed joins the revolutionaries in overwhelming the palace, he is "carried along by the eager wave of men" (675). Later, at revolutionary headquarters, "[t]he hall of meetings was crowded with people roaring like the sea" (681). The morning after the Winter Palace is taken, "[d]ay broke on a city in the wildest excitement and confusion, a whole nation heaving up in long hissing swells of storm" (685). And of the end of the ten days, when Moscow's Kremlin falls to the Bolsheviks, Reed wrote "This was the Day of the People, the rumor of whose coming was thunderous as surf. . . . Already through the Iberian Gate a human river was flowing [into] the vast Red Square" (806; Reed's ellipsis). Finally, Reed summons "a river of red banners, bearing words of hope and brotherhood and stupendous prophesies . . . the proletarian tide" (808).

Reed's many water images are kindled to a revolutionary boil by the fires of insurrection: "molten primal heat"; "tossing seas of flame" (717–18). Elsewhere, the engine of revolution "buzzed and hummed all day and all night . . . hummed like a gigantic hive" (653). And at the Bolsheviks' headquarters, "the

Military Revolutionary Committee flashed baleful fire, pounding like an over-loaded dynamo" (735). Like Henry Adams, Reed seems to see this dynamo as "wholly new," a "symbol of infinity," a "moral force," "humming an audible warning" (H. Adams, 380).[2] And as with Adams and his patron Samuel Pier-pont Langley a generation earlier, Reed is intrigued by the transformational or "anarchical" forces he discovers in the dynamo of revolution: "Always the me-thodical muffled boom of cannon through the windows, and the delegates, screaming at each other," Reed observes. "So, with the crash of artillery, in the dark, with hatred, and fear, and reckless daring, new Russia was being born" (667).

Reed's belief that he may have found a new world in Bolshevik insurgency developed almost immediately after he arrived in Petrograd in September 1917. Carrying credentials from the New York *Call* and *The Masses*, Reed met Albert Rhys Williams, a reporter for the New York *Post*, who was an old acquaintance of Reed's from labor coverage in New Jersey and Massachusetts and from vari-ous meetings around Greenwich Village. Williams's memories of that exciting fall in Petrograd (published in 1969 in his *Journey into Revolution: Petrograd, 1917–1918*) provide a first-rate perspective on Reed's romance with the Bol-sheviks. Williams recalls that Reed "viewed me as almost a veteran on the scene, and he immediately proceeded, like the good reporter he was, to sound me out on all I had seen and heard and much that I had not" (22). According to Williams, the two reporters made a good team because "Reed always came to grips with the meanest part of the problem; I always saw the glowing overall picture" (39). Williams says he and Reed were the only American reporters in Petrograd who put socialism before patriotism—that is, before the United States' need to prosecute its role in World War I successfully (35). Having al-ready studied the speeches of Lenin and Trotsky, Williams communicated his enthusiasm to Reed, who told Williams: "You sound like a full-blown Bolshe-vik" (34). Somewhat nettled, Williams retorted, as best as he can recall: "No, I was not a Bolshevik, I said, if he wanted to be literal about it. And then, before I knew it, I had made a decision and found myself saying, almost belligerently, for some reason: 'I expect to be working with them, just the same, when they find something for me to do, because as I see it, the Bolsheviks want the sort of social justice you and I want. They want it more passionately than any other group here. They want it *now*'" (35; Williams's emphasis).

The two reporters' support of the Bolsheviks seemed to galvanize around two issues: their program to seize the means of production and their refusal to fight World War I under the terms set by the allied armies. As the two men mulled the issues over in their minds, Williams recalls, they became more and more convinced that Lenin's boldness might pay off in what they believed would be a far-reaching revolution. "[T]he Bolsheviki were the only party in Russia with a constructive program and the power to impose it on the country," Reed would write in his preface to *Ten Days*. "If they had not succeeded to the Government when they did, there is little doubt in my mind that the armies of imperial Germany would have been in Petrograd and Moscow in December, and Russia would again be ridden by a Czar" (579).

Williams remembers a key moment when one door seemed to open in Reed's mind and another door closed: "Reed burst into a guffaw, slapped me on the back, and wanted to know: 'Do you think we'll ever make the grade? Or are we tagged for life—the humanitarians, the dilettantes?'" Reed then grew moody, according to Williams: "'What counts is what we do when we go home,' he said somberly. 'It's easy to be fired by things here. We'll wind up thinking we're great revolutionaries. And at home?' He laughed bitterly. 'Oh, I can always put on another pageant'" (41).

The most interesting point in Williams's assessment of Reed is how anxious the latter was to prove his worthiness to some greater cause. As in Mexico, Reed expended a great deal of emotional capital in earning his stripes among the insurgents he covered. Although he does not make quite so direct an issue of his agenda in *Ten Days That Shook the World* as in *Insurgent Mexico*, that underlying urge—as well as Reed's genuine belief that a new world was at hand—explains much about how Reed the reporter and writer covered the Russian Revolution. Williams recalls an anecdote that makes Reed's impulse clear. The two reporters met a worker who, like them, was less than impressed by a Menshevik speech he had just heard at the Duma (the Petrograd council controlled by reformers). According to Williams, Reed decided to test the worker: "Ask him if you're right. If no one but the Bolsheviks wants the job now." Williams recalls the worker regarding the two Western reporters suspiciously. He "spat out a sunflower seed or two, shook his head, and said slowly, 'I don't know why you ask. This is not my government. This may be *your* war, but it's not mine. You are bourgeois'—he called it *burzhuy*—'and I am a worker.' And he stalked away. Reed was delighted" (29–30). In retrospect, it is easy to see that Reed spent the fall and winter of 1917–18 trying to earn acceptance from men like the Bolshevik worker. "It was Reed's curse," Williams observed, "to have this contradiction in his personality—a buoyant, lighthearted spirit, a creative talent, and at the same time a mocking self-judge within him. It had driven him into many unexplored channels in which he found success too easily; the judge was not satisfied" (41–42). Building on this biographical context, this chapter makes a fresh reading of *Ten Days That Shook the World*. I examine Reed's attempt to make good with his impulse for Bolshevism—to write a unified narrative adequate to what he believed was the rising tide of world insurgency and the fire of revolutionary possibility.

Structurally, the book is built around the swell, ebb, and inevitable triumph of revolutionary events: beginning with the Bolshevik uprising in Petrograd on November 6, 1917, and culminating with the White Guards' surrender of Moscow's Kremlin to the Bolsheviks ten days later, on November 15. Artistically, Reed weaves his ten days of drama from extraordinarily careful reporting, evidenced by hundreds of pages of handwritten notes and boxes of speeches, flyers, and handbills that the journalist took home with him from Russia. That strength of evidence provides the backbone for Reed's skillful narrative effect; he foregrounds the inevitability of history by constructing a dramatic immediacy in the narrative within a background of historical determinacy. That is, the book achieves genuine present-moment suspense even though most of its readers know that the Bolsheviks already had prevailed. Finally, Reed manages these techniques from his own gently ironic narrative persona: a persona that completes the political and artistic transformation that Reed began in *Insurgent Mexico* and that had altered significantly in his political opposition to the war in Europe.

Smolny and the Duma: The Structure of Revolutionary Inevitability

Ten Days That Shook the World is the only one of Reed's three books that was conceived and designed as a volume from the moment the author began its writing. Unlike *Insurgent Mexico* and *The War in Eastern Europe*, which Reed later arranged from the monthly dispatches he had published in *Metropolitan* magazine, *Ten Days That Shook the World* took shape in Reed's mind virtually in a single sitting—the two months he spent above the Greenwich Village Inn during November and December 1918. Surrounded by pamphlets, newspapers, notes, and memories, Reed wrote chapter after chapter whose titles reawaken the real-life drama of what he called the "pageant of the rising of the Russian masses" (604): "The Coming Storm," "On the Eve," "The Fall of the Provisional Government," "Plunging Ahead," "The Committee for Salvation," "The Revolutionary Front," "Counter-Revolution," "Victory." Reed's overall narrative effect is one of present suspense (the revolutionary struggle) within a web of past-tense historical inevitability, and the book's title reflects this strategy: *Ten Days That . . . Shook the World*. *Ten Days* gains from having a clearer structural plan than those of Reed's other books. As in all of his best writing, Reed strives in *Ten Days* to weave his narrative drama within a larger fabric of historical background and research—even as he had built the sawdust trail drama of his Billy Sunday profile atop the systematic examination of the evangelist's economic and political construction.

The Reed who wrote *Ten Days* expects quite a bit from his readers. He imagines that readers will wade through page after page of "Notes and Explanations" about the byzantine inner workings of Russian politics before they arrive at two background chapters outlining the events between the overthrow of the Russian czar in March 1917 and the developing political crisis that by early November had begun to overwhelm Russia. "I am aware that these two chapters make difficult reading," he admits, "but they are essential to an understanding of what follows" (575). Perhaps Reed imagines that his readers will make this commitment to history because he knows that the inner core of his drama will succeed: ten days and nights filled with the march of boots in the streets, the fall of the Winter Palace, the great orations and heated arguments in the municipal halls of Petrograd, the massing of loyalist troops against the Bolsheviks on the outskirts of the city, and the eventual flight of reformist Alexander Kerensky as the Bolsheviks consolidate power in Petrograd and spread out across Russia. That *Ten Days That Shook the World*—despite its exacting "notes and explanations" and some eighty-four pages of historical minutia in its sprawling appendix—has remained in public circulation since its publication in 1919 appears to vindicate Reed's confidence in his story and his readers. "No matter what one thinks of Bolshevism," he writes in the book's preface, "it is undeniable that the Russian Revolution is one of the great events of human history. . . . In the struggle my sympathies were not neutral. But in telling the story of those great days I have tried to see events with the eye of a conscientious reporter, interested in setting down the truth" (580).

Reed's belief in his project is further underscored by his assertion that *Ten Days* will be but the first of several volumes about the Russian Revolution and will be continued in *Kornilov to Brest-Litovsk*, a second history whose scope was to carry to the German armistice (575). Reed's zest for the arcana of Russian politics seems to contradict the conclusion of his biographer that "it would be a serious mistake to see him basically as a political animal. The regular activities of that normally practical process—elections, campaigns, coalitions, compromises—never held his attention long" (Rosenstone, "Reform and Radicalism," 144). In Russia, at least, Reed had found that commitment.

Within the core ten days of the finished book, Reed orchestrates two competing motifs that swell, ebb, and swell again until the central movement of *Ten*

Days—the rising tide of revolutionary transformation—becomes inevitable. At the center of the competing motifs are the Duma (the municipal council of Petrograd that at the beginning of the book is under the control of the Mensheviks, the constitutional democrats, and other reformers loyal to Kerensky [587]) and Smolny Institute (the former women's college on the banks of the Neva River, where the Soviets of Workers' and Soldiers' Deputies and the Petrograd Soviet are plotting the Bolshevik takeover of Russia [618]). Although each of these coalitions is formed from a bewildering array of smaller and somewhat fluid factions, Reed employs metonymy for clarity and often refers to the competing factions simply as the Duma and Smolny. The Duma remained committed to the political transformation of Russian society following the March overthrow of the czar, Reed concludes, while the Bolshevik factions at Smolny became increasingly committed to its economic transformation. In Reed's most concrete terms, the Duma's "only reason for failure to hold the masses during the Bolshevik Revolution was the general decline in influence of all purely *political* representation in the face of the growing power of organizations based on *economic* groups" (587; Reed's emphases).

Ten Days That Shook the World thus gains its structural momentum from the shifting political fortunes of the Duma and Smolny during the ten days of November 6–15. Early in this central chronology, Smolny-backed Bolshevik revolutionaries wrest control of the Winter Palace in Petrograd from pro-Duma Kerensky reformers. At its midpoint, this more extreme form of revolution seems almost certain to be quashed as Duma forces align with parties loyal to the czar so as to counter the Bolsheviks. Finally, however, the Smolny forces prevail: Kerensky is sent packing, while the Kremlin in Moscow falls to the Reds amid all-night funerals for revolutionary workers and soldiers. Throughout the core scenes of his narrative, Reed employs an "I was there" eyewitness strategy as he hurries through the darkening Petrograd streets—first to the Duma and then to "great Smolny" (653). He frequently addresses his readers directly in the text, presents political arguments as virtually Socratic dialogues, and reprints texts and speeches verbatim to present a pastiche of revolution.

The ten days of Reed's book begin in the "On the Eve" chapter (November 6). Reed witnesses Kerensky's "passionate and almost incoherent" (643) speech at the Marinsky Palace in which the reformist leader states his "firm conviction that the Provisional Government, which defends at this moment our new liberty, that the new Russian state, destined to a brilliant future, will find unanimous support except among those who have never dared to face the truth" (645–46). Against Kerensky's assertion, Reed pits Leon Trotsky, with whom he had gained an exclusive interview some days earlier. "The Provisional Government [Kerensky loyalists] is absolutely powerless," Reed quotes Trotsky as saying. "The bourgeoisie is in control, but this control is masked by a fictitious coalition. . . . [O]ne sees revolts of peasants who are tired of waiting for their promised land; and all over the country, in all the toiling classes, the same disgust is evident" (633). The reporter thus scrambles from Smolny, where the Petrograd Soviet is meeting continuously (649), to the headquarters of the provisional government, where he discovers that the Duma, for all intents and purposes, has made a "declaration of war against the Bolsheviki" (655).

Reed slept very late on the morning of November 7, perhaps because he sensed that the day and the following night were to be among the most important in Russian history. His chapter "The Fall of the Provisional Government" becomes the book's second day and contains some of his more compelling eyewitness reporting, as in my next section I demonstrate by a detailed comparison of Reed's finished text with the original notebooks that he wrote in Petrograd. Structurally, "The Fall of the Provisional Government" accomplishes the first direct clash between Reed's metonymic Duma and Smolny, thereby rendering inevitable their fight to the finish. Reed runs with the Red Guards through downtown Petrograd and is with them when they burst into the Winter Palace, taking control of it from the provisional government. The Bolsheviks' battle inevitably will be joined. Later the same night, the reporter walks into the City Duma Building to discover that the Kerensky loyalists have formed the Committee for Salvation of Country and Revolution, its strongest anti-Bolshevik coalition to date. An eyewitness, Reed reaches for a symbolic detail that will foreground the coming clash. Outside the Duma "were Red Guards and soldiers squatting around fires," while inside, "the City Duma Building was all illuminated. We mounted to the galleried Alexander Hall hung with its great *gold-framed red-shrouded Imperial* portraits" (680; emphasis added); it is around these portraits that the constitutional democrats plot their revenge on the Bolsheviks. With his imagery, Reed attempts to ally the moderates with the despised imperial monarchy and suggest that the "red" Bolsheviks will serve as their funeral shroud. Meanwhile, an hour later, across town, Reed sees that "the windows of Smolny were still ablaze, motors came and went, and around the still-leaping fires the sentries huddled close" (681). Inside, Trotsky declaims: "[T]he whole task of defending and saving the Revolution rests on our shoulders, it is particularly necessary to work—work—work! We have decided to die rather than give up" (682).

The third of Reed's ten days brings V. I. Lenin out of hiding to address the Second Session of the All-Russian Congress of Soviets. Meanwhile, Kerensky is said "to be leading a great army against the capital," and Reed reprints a fiery

Kerensky speech published in the loyalist *Volia Naroda:* "The disorders caused by the insane attempt of the Bolsheviki place the country on the verge of a precipice," Kerensky charges, "and demand the effort of our entire will, our courage, and the devotion of every one of us, to win through the terrible trial which the fatherland is now undergoing" (685). Kerensky's rhetoric is matched thematically and structurally by Lenin's historic speech at the Congress of Soviets, a scene that again will provide the opportunity for a comparison between Reed's notes and his finished draft. For the purposes of the present discussion of Reed's vision for *Ten Days That Shook the World,* it is sufficient to note that the first wave of Bolshevik ascendancy reaches its pitch in the "Plunging Ahead" chapter's account of day three. Reed finds himself shoulder to shoulder with other revolutionary delegates at the chapter's climax, singing the "Internationale" and the "Funeral March" and listening to Lenin read the proclamation that effectively ends Russian participation in World War I.

Were *Ten Days That Shook the World* a single-voiced celebration of Soviet victory, Reed most likely would not have launched the second movement of the book, wherein the anti-Bolshevik Committee for Salvation of Revolution and Country amasses its forces (Reed labels the three subsequent chapters "The Committee for Salvation," "The Revolutionary Front," and "Counter-Revolution"). The reporter spends most of the fourth of his ten days at the Duma building, where Reed builds a narrative primarily about the reaction of middle-class political insurgents to the Bolshevik takeover. Although his sympathies lie on the opposite side, Reed is physically with the Duma in the dramatic centerpiece of day four as the hall is surrounded by Red Guards and the rumor flies that it will be stormed by Bolshevik sympathizers (723). Reed asks a Duma leader if the council will be disbanded. The man responds, "My God, no! . . . It is all a mistake" (724). In these sections, Reed develops the contrast between the varying approaches to revolution at the level of more common Russians, observing: "Everywhere the same thing happened. The common soldiers and the industrial workers supported the Soviets by a vast majority; the officers, *yunkers,* and middle class generally were on the side of the Government—as were the bourgeois Cadets and the 'moderate' Socialist parties. In all these towns sprang up Committees for Salvation of Country and Revolution, arming for civil war" (717). Meanwhile, the Smolny revolutionary headquarters "flashed baleful fire, pounding like an overloaded dynamo" (735).

On day five, Reed travels to the outlying Petrograd suburb of Tsarskoye Selo to see for himself whether the Kerensky forces will, as is rumored, join with White Russian Cossacks loyal to the czar and counterattack the Bolsheviks (736). Here, at the center of the book, Reed hears everywhere that the Bolsheviks' time is numbered: the Social Revolutionary Party has voted to expel all Bolshevik sympathizers, key provincial leaders are declaring against the Bolsheviks, the garrison at Luga has remained loyal to the provisional government, the railway workers are putting on pressure, and the Bolsheviks are rumored to be interested in compromise. "'If they last that long!' laughed the City Engineer, a stout ruddy man" (740). Western and Russian journalists who had been barred from the Bolshevik-controlled Smolny are delighted by the rumors. "One confided to me, in the strictest secrecy, that the counter-revolution would begin at midnight" (752), Reed reports.

Thus, at the midpoint of *Ten Days*, Reed's dramatic strategy—which his literary journalism borrows from fictional plotting—makes it appear that the world won't be shaken so much after all. Yet the reporter's careful readers are treated to inside information; Reed's surreptitious trip to Tsarskoye Selo, accomplished under a pseudonym, reveals that many regular soldiers are siding with the Red Guard. At the book's center, Reed presents an extraordinary three-page dialogue between one such revolutionary soldier and a moderate student. The dialogue provides a microcosm of his book's structural argument and deftly echoes the challenge from a worker that Reed himself faced soon after arriving in Russia in the incident recalled by Williams: "There are two classes, don't you see?" says the soldier, "the proletariat and the bourgeoisie. We—" The student bursts out in response: "Oh, I know that silly talk! . . . A bunch of ignorant peasants like you hear somebody bawling a few catchwords. You don't understand what they mean." The student assures the soldier that Lenin is a German collaborator and declares his opposition to the Bolsheviks, "who are destroying our Russia, our free revolution" (748). The soldier can only respond: "I'm not well educated. It seems like there are only two classes, the proletariat and the bourgeoisie. . . . And whoever isn't on one side is on the other" (748–49).[3] Back in Petrograd, Reed discovers "Smolny—not abandoned, but busier than ever, throngs of workers and soldiers running in and out, and doubled guards everywhere" (740).

On day six, Kerensky enters Tsarskoye Selo in command of loyalist Cossack troops. Reed can't resist adding two symbolic details that might resonate ironically for his North American audience: "Kerensky himself *riding a white horse* and *all the church-bells clamoring*" (754; emphasis added). This white knight, showered as he is by the approvals of state religion, is doomed to failure in Reed's narrative universe if not in the dominant symbolism of Reed's home country. By Reed's way of thinking, Kerensky has made the fatal mistake of assuming that the regular army will not oppose him—that the regulars will lay down their arms and will remain neutral before the Cossack invasion. As

Reed had predicted one chapter earlier, many Russian soldiers instead choose to fight on the side of the Red Guards. In this chapter, Reed relies on critical eyewitness reports from his wife Louise and from his reporting colleague Albert Rhys Williams for proof that Kerensky's provisional government no longer is able to control any but the most pro-czarist soldiers.

With the aborted counterrevolution clearly stalled, Reed's day seven remains mostly a stalemate. "The eyes of all Russia were fixed on the gray plain beyond the gates of Petrograd, where all the available strength of the old order faced the unorganized power of the new, the unknown" (765), Reed reports. He travels to the Petrograd Soviet for a progress report from Trotsky, who tells the Bolshevik delegates that the Cossacks are falling back on one side of Petrograd, though he admits that from Moscow the news is not so good for the Bolsheviks. "The Kremlin is in the hands of the [loyalist] *yunkers,* and the workers have only a few arms," Trotsky reports. "The result depends upon Petrograd" (772). As the book enters its final third, therefore, Reed has set up his ten days of narrative to his structural advantage. Reed's swell of revolution has first given way to burgeoning counterrevolution, but a second wave is coming that will overwhelm Russia with what Reed believes will be the irresistible rising tide of revolt. And the arena for the final battles will be Petrograd and Moscow —two cities that the reporter will witness firsthand.

Writing a year after the events, Reed of course knew how the final act of his ten days would play out, so it is not surprising that Kerensky's forces are rebuffed at Tsarskoye Selo on the eighth day of Reed's narrative. Again, as the reporter had predicted from insider knowledge gained during the preceding two days, an army of the proletariat, "gathering in the darkness around the battle, rose like a tide and poured over the enemy (776–77). From Moscow, the news is similar: although loyalist White Guards and Yunkers still hold the Kremlin, they are surrounded by forces from the Military Revolutionary Committee, and an attack by Bolshevik troops appears imminent. With momentum now firmly on the revolutionary side, Reed again visits Smolny: "I noticed that everywhere on the floor, along the walls, men were sleeping. Rough, dirty men, workers and soldiers, spattered and caked with mud, sprawled alone or in heaps, in the careless attitudes of death. Some wore ragged bandages marked with blood. Guns and cartridge-belts were scattered about. . . . The victorious proletarian army!" (778; Reed's ellipsis). Ironically, just as the Red Army appears to be in control of Russia's important urban centers, Reed himself must survive a potentially fatal challenge to his legitimacy, as this study will detail in a subsequent description of the echoes between *Insurgent Mexico* and *Ten Days That Shook the World.* In the present discussion of the book's structure, it is enough to note that the Bolsheviks and their sympathizers have gained a dramatic momentum that now seems impossible to stop.

Sure enough, on Reed's ninth day (November 14), Kerensky is forced to flee from Gatchina in the disguise of a Russian sailor, after first agreeing to travel to Petrograd for surrender negotiations. "I ought to commit suicide," an overthrown Cossack general quotes Kerensky as saying in a deposition that Reed secured among the papers he later brought back from Russia. When the former head of the provisional government instead adopts a disguise and disappears, Reed reports with some scorn, "[B]y that act [Kerensky] lost whatever popularity he had retained among the Russian masses" (794). An elated Reed returns from Tsarskoye Selo to Petrograd on the front seat of an "autotruck" filled to the brim with Red Guards. The scene reveals Reed's eyewitness reporting at its most personal. "Immense trucks like ours, columns of artillery wagons, loomed up in the night, without lights as we were. We hurtled furiously on, wrenched right and left to avoid collisions that seemed inevitable, scraping wheels" (794). "Across the horizon spread the glittering lights of the capital, immeasurably more splendid by night than by day, like a dike of jewels on the barren plain," Reed reports. An old workman drives the troop truck with one hand, "while with the other he swept the far-gleaming capital in an exultant gesture. 'Mine,' he cried, his face all alight. 'All mine now! My Petrograd!'" (794).

The structure of *Ten Days That Shook the World* can be completed after Reed chronicles November 15, when news spreads that the Bolsheviks have bombarded the Kremlin as well as other political and religious landmarks in Moscow. The reporter understands quite clearly that the political stakes have been raised. "Nothing that the Bolsheviki had done could compare with this fearful blasphemy in the heart of Holy Russia," Reed reports with some irony. "To the ears of the devout sounded the shock of guns crashing in the face of the Holy Orthodox Church, and pounding to dust the sanctuary of the Russian nation" (797). Not content with secondhand reports and rumors, Reed sets off with the *Post*'s Williams to witness in person the changing of Moscow's governmental guard. What he finds in the central Russian capital provides some of his most vivid reporting and extends the personal contrasts between Reed's projects in Mexico and Russia in ways that will be explored more deeply later in this chapter. At the funerals in Moscow's Red Square for those who have died for the revolution, the street chapels are now locked and dark, their candles out for the first time since Napoleon occupied the city. "Dark and silent and cold were the churches; the priests had disappeared," Reed reports. "There were no popes to officiate at the Red Burial, there had been no sacrament for the dead, nor were any prayers to be said over the grave of the blasphemers" (806). Yet the sun rises as the last mourners cross Red Square, and the scales drop from Reed's eyes. "I suddenly realized that the devout Russian people no longer needed priests to pray them into heaven. On earth they were building a kingdom more bright than any heaven had to offer, and for which it was a glory to die. . . ." (808; Reed's ellipsis).

With his "ten days that shook the world" structure now in place, Reed has only to supply two summary chapters to bookend the twin background chapters at the book's opening. Reed's "Notes and Explanations" section is balanced by a copious appendix at book's end, resembling a steamer trunk stuffed with handbills tumbling out on Reed's printed page. From the book's beginning to its close, therefore, the reporter has managed the ebb and flow of the competing interests represented by the Duma and Smolny over ten days of narrative bracketed by a documentary frame. He has managed the complementary metaphors of revolutionary fire and rising tide to explain the creation of his new universe. Here, at the book's end, Reed envisions those revolutionary fires burning brightly—"the lasting accomplishment of a just peace and the victory of Socialism" (852).

Reed's Russian Notebooks and the Construction of a Dramatic Present

An examination of the more than seven hundred pages of Reed's Russian notebooks and the boxes of handbills, speeches, pamphlets, and newspapers he carried back with him from Petrograd proves that the reporter labored hard to deliver structural and dramatic power to his *Ten Days* manuscript. Some of the book's most memorable scenes—Lenin's return from hiding on day three to join the presidium of the Congress of Soviets, the moving funeral dirge as the new Soviet government votes to end its participation in World War I, the trip to Tsarskoye Selo on day five, Reed's near shooting by zealous revolutionary soldiers on day eight, and the culminating, somber funeral in Moscow's Red Square on day ten—are painstakingly crafted from Reed's three-by-five-inch notebooks or from quarter-folded stationery he borrowed from the J. Negley Farson Company on Gogol Street in Petrograd. The notes provide an eyewitness historical foundation for Reed's reporting, the theme on which Reed can work out his narrative variations of dialogue, details, and controlling metaphor. "For Reed himself," says Abel Startsev, "these notes were a kind of shorthand which he, of course, could decipher without difficulty the next day [when he wrote up his reports], being still under the impression of what he had just seen" (165).

As in Mexico, the notes formed the foundation of Reed's literary journalism. But while the Mexican notebooks mostly are made up of diary-like impressions of the people and events he saw directly, Reed deepens his Russian notebooks to include more ambitious background reporting as well as the personal impressions that always serve his writing well. Reed follows debates point by point, placing a straight line in his notes between comments. He includes little attribution unless the words come from a well-known speaker, but he has a sure sense of all the parties and where they stand on Russia's political spectrum. Whole notebooks (e.g., bMS Am 1091:1322) are devoted to determining the background positions of the many factions of Russian politics and to learning all he can about the role of the church in Russia and the variations of faith and practices among religious and social groups. In some sections, when he could take a moment to reflect, Reed's handwriting grows smaller and his writing is more polished, lending to his notes the appearance of a journal. By contrast, in interviews or at the many tumultuous meetings during his ten dramatic days in Petrograd, Reed's handwriting blooms into a rounded scrawl as he dashes from page to page, scribbling quotes as quickly as he can and adding background impressions as he has time. In those interviews and meetings, Reed seems to give priority to the words of soldiers who are aching for peace and often quotes these soldiers verbatim for whole pages. Ever the reporter, Reed, presumably having asked people how to spell their names, carefully writes them out. Sometimes a person Reed is interviewing will scribble an address in the notebook in his own hand, probably to set up a later meeting. The notebooks also include rough phonetic transliterations of the Cyrillic alphabet and a translation from the Julian to Gregorian calendars.

Reed inserts scores of documents into the text of *Ten Days*—handbills he had ripped from the walls in Petrograd, texts of speeches cranked from the printing presses each night by supporters of the various political factions, and broadsides from the Kerensky and Trotsky/Lenin factions. "Much of the material in this book is from my own notes," Reed writes in "Notes and Explanations." He says he relied on "a heterogeneous file" of Russian, French, and English-language newspapers, the daily reports of the French *Bulletin de la Pressê*, the official publication of all Russian government decrees and orders, and the secret treaties and documents discovered when the Bolsheviks took over the Ministry of Foreign Affairs. Finally, he says, "I have in my possession almost every proclamation, decree and announcement posted on the walls of Petrograd from the middle of September 1917 to the end of January 1918" (590).

The relationship between Reed's notes and his finished text can be shown by a close reading of scenes from days two and three, beginning when the workers storm the Winter Palace on November 7 and culminating the following day at the Second Session of the All-Russian Congress of Soviets. An examination of the notebooks against the book's version of these central scenes shows how Reed's notes lay the foundation for the narrative strategy of the completed book. Reed was in Williams's hotel room when the two heard, across from the Winter Palace, the commotion of soldiers massing at the Telephone Exchange, on a square known as Admiralty Quay. Reed's notes sketch the square: "covered with soldiers in front of the telephone office . . . police great bunch of sailors and soldiers. Across middle of square a cordon thrown. Nobody allowed to pass, either Palace or down streets at sides for two blocks palace side of square blocked both sides. On fortress side thousand or so troops and sailors—more coming as fast as can see. At both ends sweeping square a big armored car . . . At one end great boxes barrels and old bed springs . . . piles of lumber. Before palace all across from building barricades logs" (bMS Am 1091:1328, p. 135–37).

Writing from the immediacy of these notes a year later, Reed adds the descriptive grace of accomplished sentences to the initial impressions he scrawled on his notepad. First, the "great bunch of sailors and soldiers" of his notes becomes a finished sentence, continuing his use of water metaphors: "Like a black river, filling the street, without song or cheer we poured through the Red Arch" (675). Then Reed adds direct, dramatic dialogue: "Look out, comrades! Don't trust them. They will fire, surely!" (675). Next he introduces the immediate scene: "In the open we began to run, stooping low and bunching together, and jammed up suddenly behind the pedestal of the Alexander Column" (675). Unidentified soldiers in Reed's notes are separated into the loyalist *yunkers* and the Bolshevik Red Guards, in keeping with Reed's book-long structural strategy: "By this time, in the light that streamed out of all the Winter Palace windows, I could see that the first two or three hundred men were Red Guards, with only a few scattered soldiers," Reed reports. "Over the barricade of firewood we clambered, and leaping down inside gave a triumphant shout as we stumbled on a heap of rifles thrown down by the *yunkers* who had stood there. On both sides of the main gateway the doors stood wide open, light streamed out, and from the huge pile [of firewood] came not the slightest sound" (675).

Reed's finished text thus establishes an "I was there" tone of personal reporting that is anchored by the documentary facticity of his notes. From his memory and his ear for language, he adds scraps of dialogue and adopts a controlling metaphor that contrasts darkness and light. The essentials of Reed's finished passage build from his notes: the mass of advancing soldiers and Red Guardsmen, the roadblocks of scrap wood, the retreating loyalists. The finished passage moves the scene from the "black river" of repression toward the "streaming light" of human liberation, from the regulating piles of scrap wood toward the "wide open" doors of political self-determination.

With the Winter Palace taken, the stage is now set for a Bolshevik-controlled Second All-Russian Congress of Soviets. Reed sets up the suspense of day three at the opening of his "Plunging Ahead" chapter: "Day broke on a city in the wildest excitement and confusion, a whole nation heaving up in long hissing swells of storm" (685). Although all is superficially quiet, a war of leaflets already has begun, and Reed can document it because he has the tracts in hand. Kerensky blames the Winter Palace disorders on "the insane attempt of the Bolsheviki," while the revolutionaries post their own handbills calling for their followers "to take every measure for the immediate arrest of Kerensky and his conveyance to Petrograd" (685–86). The central drama of November 8 forms around the arrival of Lenin from his hiding place and the successful resolution at the Congress of Soviets to end Russian participation in World War I.

Of Lenin's appearance, Reed mixes quick visual impressions of the man with dashed notes of his remarks. His notes read: "8.40—Entrance Hall. Lenin. Bald-headed man with snub nose, strong chin . . . Lenin practical measures to realize peace—great mouth—to offer peace Soviet formula. Soviet treaties to be repudiated: Anglia, Francia, Germaine (Why not America?). Little winking eyes, hoarse voice, faces looked up adoringly" (bMS Am 1091:1328, pp. 152–55). In his finished prose, Reed's amplification of his notes retains the same blend of visual impression and political content. An extended description that strays into hagiography, it is an example both of Reed's gift for the brief word-sketch and his lack of objectivity. It stays in the present, clocking time as it passes from the evidence in Reed's notes, but it also shifts from the certainty of the past to the inevitability of the future as it suits Reed's needs: "It was just 8.40 when a thundering wave of cheers announced the entrance of the presidium, with Lenin—great Lenin—among them," Reed reports. "A short, stocky figure, with a big head set down on his shoulders, bald and bulging. Little eyes, a snubbish nose, wide generous mouth, and heavy chin: clean-shaven now but already beginning to bristle with the well-known beard of his past and future. Dressed in shabby clothes, his trousers much too long for him. Unimpressive, to be the idol of a mob, loved and revered as perhaps few leaders in history have been" (697).

Over the outcry of Bund and Mensheviki objections, Lev Borisovich Kameniev, Lenin's supporter and the chair of the congress, declares the abolition of capital punishment, the restoration of the rights of propaganda, the release of dissident prisoners, and the nationalization of food supplies. As Lenin stands to speak, Reed revels in the scene he is about to present, signaling his engagement and forcing the reader into the present by using the adverb *now* and describing the response of the crowd: "Again that overwhelming human roar." It is as if Reed has been preparing for this moment since that day on Billy Sunday's sawdust trail when he found himself swayed by a religious zeal he could not endorse. Here, Reed seems to have found his political and spiritual home:

> Now Lenin, gripping the edge of the reading stand, letting his little winking eyes travel over the crowd as he stood there waiting, apparently oblivious to the long-rolling ovation, which lasted several minutes. When it finished, he said simply: "We shall now proceed to construct the Socialist order![4] Again that overwhelming human roar. . . . "We shall offer peace to the peoples of all the belligerent countries upon the basis of the Soviet terms—no annexations, no indemnities, and the right of self-determination of peoples. . . ." His great mouth, seeming to smile, opened wide as he spoke; his voice was hoarse—not unpleasantly so, but as if it had hardened that way after years and years of speaking—and went on monotonously, with the effect of being able to go on for ever. . . . For emphasis he bent forward slightly. No gestures. And before him, a thousand faces looking up in intent adoration. (698; first two ellipses added; the final ellipsis is Reed's)

The initial visual impressions in Reed's original notes (bald, snub-nose, strong chin, great mouth, winking eyes, hoarse voice, adoring crowd) thus are pressed into the service of his scene, which Reed presents as immediate history although he interjects a reference ("well-known beard of his past and future") that reminds the reader that Reed can foretell the future. In *Ten Days,* Reed then amplifies the historic moment of Russia's withdrawal from World War I with a printed version of the peace declaration that he brought back with him from Russia and inserts verbatim into his book.

After Lenin's speech, the delegates of the second congress vote on the peace resolution, an action for which Reed has been waiting. Because he had sacrificed his mainstream journalism career to his opposition to World War I and had argued unsuccessfully with his socialist friends in the United States that the "traders' war" did not deserve leftist support, Reed seems thrilled to bear witness as the first socialist nation declares its separate peace. He remembers to jot down the historic time in his notes: "10.35 Kameniev, All in favor of immediate peace say aye! Lift cards. Against? [indecipherable] tumult, laughter, cheers, lots of tears, sing Internationale." Listing the names of the notables at the table toward the front of the hall (Lenin and Trotsky among them), Reed then notes that he hears, "voice from rear: 'Let us remember those who have died for liberty' all stand immense singing 'Death March.' Kollontai winking. Emotion. Lenin now going to abolish private property and land" (bMS Am 1091:1331, pp. 1–2).

Reed's notes, anchored by his recall of the exact time of the historic vote, the songs, and the personal details of Alexandra Kollontai's tears and the voices from the crowd, form one of the more compelling eyewitness scenes of *Ten Days That Shook the World,* worth quoting at some length:

> It was exactly 10.35 when Kameniev asked all in favour of the proclamation to hold up their cards. One delegate dared to raise his hand against, but the sudden outburst around him brought it swiftly down. . . . Unanimous. Suddenly, by common impulse, we found ourselves on our feet, mumbling together into the smooth lifting unison of the *Internationale.* A grizzled old soldier was sobbing like a child. Alexandra Kollontai rapidly winked the tears back. The immense sound rolled through the hall, burst windows and doors and soared into the quiet sky, "The war is ended! The war is ended!" said a young workman near me, his face shining. And when it was over, as we stood there in a kind of awkward hush, someone in the back of the room shouted, "Comrades! Let us remember those who have died for liberty!" So we began to sing the Funeral March, that slow, melancholy, and yet triumphant chant, so Russian and so moving. (702–3)

Reed quotes the "Funeral March" words: "[B]ecause you believed that justice is stronger than the sword . . . The time will come when your surrendered life will count. That time is near; when tyranny falls, the people will rise, great and free!" (703; Reed's ellipsis). The reporter, his objectivity long since burned at the altar of partisanship ('By common impulse, we found ourselves on our feet"), allows himself the summative rhetoric: "For this did they lie there, the martyrs of March, in their cold Brotherhood Grave on Mars Field; for this thousands and tens of thousands had died in the prisons, in exile, in Siberian mines. It had not come as they expected it would come, nor as the *intelligentsia* desired it; but it had come—rough, strong, impatient of formulas, contemptuous of sentimentalism; *real*" (703; Reed's emphases). The passage culminates with a line that brings full circle the Kerensky-Trotsky contrast that anchors Reed's motifs of the Duma and Smolny, a line whose power to implicate at least some readers still results in its suppression from Communist Party–sponsored anthologies (*Education of John Reed,* 206–7): "Then up rose Trotsky, calm and venomous, conscious of power, greeted with a roar" (705). Ironically, Reed pulls the powerful line from an innocuous, far less dramatic jotting in his notes: "Trotsky (ovation) Those arrested ministers not our comrades because they arrested our comrades" (bMS Am 1091:1331, p. 5).

A close reading of the Russian notebooks, therefore, shows that, from raw notes, Reed was able to add polished sentences, dialogue, evocative details, controlling metaphors, and graphic descriptions of scene. Reed's overall strategy

—buttressed by the raw material of his notes and by the hundreds of tracts, pamphlets, and handbills he carted back from Russia—clearly seeks to build a narrative immediacy to his reporting that makes the reader a vicarious participant in the historic event. Such is the enduring project of literary journalism, and Reed's was one of the early U.S. nonfiction books to have practiced it in detail.

Narrative Form in *Ten Days:* Across the Dramatic Present to the Inevitability of History

As long ago as Horace, critics of the historical epic have recognized the subtle interplay between the received historical text to which an author must remain more or less faithful and the author's being invited to write compellingly and dramatically. "[L]iterary property that belongs to everybody is the hardest to invent well," Horace says in *The Art of Poetry.* "Poets who carve up songs of ancient Troy, constructing the well-shaped plays, work harder than poets that make it all up as it falls on the page." Then Horace slips in a warning beneath the overt invitation of the passage: "Old stories are yours for the working—*if* you walk somewhere off the beaten path and *never* use the names without the substance and spirit" (70; emphasis added). Horace's point is that the historical epic offers plenty of opportunity for compelling storytelling and dramatic tension within a matrix of larger historical inevitability; that is, the dramatic wandering that a skillful writer can summon in the "substance and spirit" of received tradition. Agreement on that "substance and spirit," of course, is more easily suggested than accomplished because both writer and readers share deeply held and sometimes conflicting ideas about the events and traditions that underlie the historical narrative. Those underlying ideas may trigger the sorts of deeper social implications that derive from the best and most compelling historical epics.[5]

In *Ten Days That Shook the World,* Reed uses a writing strategy common to the epic form. He holds his readers in a "present action" of the narrative (the ten days of November 1917) to generate suspense even as he sweeps toward a conclusion that many readers outside the written text already know to be inevitable (the triumph of Bolshevism that, by the time of the book's publication in 1919, was well known). And in *Ten Days,* the triumph of Bolshevism is a conclusion that many of the book's readers, particularly in the United States, will despise—both in Reed's time and in ours.[6] Therefore, Reed's fusion of narrative immediacy, historical context, and political implication at its best moments achieves great power. "[A]n artillery shell, a peal of thunder, or ocean surf does not possess the power of the book that is lying on that desk," Reed told a visitor shortly after *Ten Days* was published by Boni & Liveright in 1919 (quoted in Duke, 54).

Reed's first big scoop as a reporter in Russia provides an extended occasion to observe his intertwining of present scene and prophetic future. When, in *Ten Days That Shook the World,* a week before the Bolshevik Revolution he interviews Alexander Kerensky, the reform prime minister, Reed notes that it is "the last time [Kerensky] received journalists"—a comment that throws the reader outside the immediacy of the narrative into a wider context, one that can foretell that the interview will be the last one Kerensky will give as prime minister: "The world thinks that the Russian Revolution is at an end," Reed quotes Kerensky as saying during the interview. "Do not be mistaken. The Russian Revolution is just beginning." Reed cannot resist interjecting, with some irony, "Words more prophetic, perhaps, than he knew" (624).

At the time of the interview, Kerensky meant that the March revolution, the one he had led and the one to which he remained deeply committed, had not yet run its course, and that the Bolshevik threat, which Kerensky never considered a true revolution, would be denied. But in 1918, when Reed wrote *Ten Days,* as well as the following year when it was published, both Reed and his readers knew otherwise: they see that the Bolshevik version of the Russian Revolution is "just beginning" and that Kerensky will be deposed. Reed, as he sat in his room above the Greenwich Village Inn a year after the Bolsheviks took power, knew Kerensky would be proved wrong. His choice of the word *perhaps* is therefore deliberately rhetorical: meant to pull his readers back into the moment when he sat in Kerensky's study and the future seemed uncertain. Reed thus exploits the drama of present action (Kerensky's discounting the Bolshevik threat) to build the suspense and inevitability of the future (the successful Bolshevik Revolution). A brief contrast of that rhetorical strategy to a version of the Kerensky interview that Reed wrote six days after their meeting for the radical periodical *Liberator* (Homberger and Biggart, 64) shows that Reed was not then sure of the unintended irony of Kerensky's remarks and thus did not make a comment like "words more prophetic, perhaps, than he knew." In this earlier version, Reed quotes Kerensky at length as the Russian leader compares his nation's political situation to that of the French Revolution. "Remember that the French revolution took five years," Kerensky says, and he elaborates on this. Then he concludes: "No, the Russian revolution is not over—it is just beginning" (66). With no undercutting aside available in the original article, Reed moves directly to another subject; no subtle narrative strategy, such as the one Reed used in *Ten Days,* is to be found.

Reed's intertwining of present-tense drama and historical inevitability is perhaps most readily seen in cliff-hanger passages he sprinkles throughout *Ten Days*. In his initial "Background" chapter, Reed paints a picture of increasingly unstable political and social life in Russia under the Kerensky government. Speculation and food shortages are endemic as merchant families hoard scarce supplies: "And so, while the masses of the people got a quarter pound of black bread on their bread cards, [a chocolate merchant] had an abundance of white bread, sugar, tea, candy, cake, and butter" (598), Reed reports. The ill-equipped Russian army is growing sick of World War I, and political tensions are rising. Then comes Reed's foreshadowing final sentence: "It was against this backdrop of a whole nation in ferment and disintegration that the pageant of the Rising of the Russian Masses unrolled" (604). Two strategies are worth noting in Reed's sentence: his belief that the future already is tangible and needs only to be unrolled or revealed; and his idea that this inevitable revolution will resemble some great "pageant"—perhaps like the one Reed had staged five years earlier at Madison Square Garden for the Industrial Workers of the World.

Reed's narrative strategy deepens in the chapter "The Coming Storm." Here, as we have seen, he has begun to alternate between meetings called by the Kerensky loyalists at the Winter Palace and those at the Bolshevik center on the east side of Petrograd at the Smolny Institute. The social ferment he had spotted in the earlier chapter is now deepening. "On the streets the crowds thickened towards gloomy evening, pouring in slow voluble tides up and down the Nevsky, fighting for the newspapers," he writes. "Hold-ups increased to such an extent that it was dangerous to walk down side streets. On the Sadovaya one afternoon I saw a crowd of several hundred people beat and trample to death a soldier caught stealing" (625–26). Reed presents living history here, characteristically examining the larger political picture through a close-up of the daily lives of people. This technique of literary journalism draws most readers into the time of action, while the author controls the larger narrative project. Reed thus ends "The Coming Storm" chapter by extending the metaphor of its title: "And in the rain, the bitter chill, the great throbbing city under gray skies rushing faster and faster towards—what?" (626). The answer to Reed's rhetorical question is "revolution," of course, though he won't say it here. At the time of action, therefore, Reed means to project genuine suspense, but at the time of composition, the author has predetermined the answer to his own question.

Reed's narrative persona manages other subtle rhetorical shifts between past, present, and future in subsequent passages. For example, on the night of November 5, Reed is hurrying from his interview with Trotsky, held in a small bare room of the Smolny revolutionary headquarters of the Bolsheviks, toward the Winter Palace, which houses the reform Council of the Russian Republic.

For almost thirty pages, Reed has carefully tightened the circle of revolution and counterrevolution, first interviewing the reformer Kerensky, then the revolutionary Trotsky—pitting the two in inevitable conflict, now traveling to the Winter Palace, now to Smolny. Outside the Winter Palace, Reed reports, "an armoured automobile went slowly up and down, siren screaming. On every corner, in every open space, thick groups were clustered: arguing soldiers and students. Night came swiftly down, the wide-spaced street-lights flickered on, the tides of people flowed endlessly. . . . It is always like that in Petrograd just before trouble" (640–41).

The dramatic description of this passage provides further evidence of Reed's rhetorical strategy. He uses the present tense ("It is always like that in Petrograd just before trouble") to drag the reader into the immediacy of the scene as the sky darkens and lights flicker on. Reed's present-tense drama thereby tempts the reader, willingly or unwillingly, to suspend knowledge of how soon or in what manner the "gathering storm" will break. Later, Reed will use the same strategy to report the mood of Petrograd on November 7 just before the storming of the Winter Palace. "Always the methodical muffled boom of cannon through the windows, and the delegates, screaming at each other," writes Reed, with a quality of description that draws the reader into the immediacy of the scene. And then the prophetic edge that herds the reader toward historic inevitability: "So, with the crash of artillery, in the dark, with hatred, and fear, and reckless daring, new Russia was being born" (667).

At the center of *Ten Days That Shook the World*, when Kerensky's provisional government falls and the Bolsheviks plunge ahead to construct the socialist state, Reed combines his most dramatic scene writing with his most rhetorically ambitious foreshadowing. He strives to capture a dramatic present while revealing his strategy of historical inevitability at its most audacious. Although Reed's notes include Trotsky's most famous words of the revolution only as an afterthought ("Last night said 'refuse will be swept into the garbage heap of history'—Trotsky" [bMS Am 1091:1328, p. 151]), the final *Ten Days* version delivers their power in scenic immediacy. An extended passage shows the building animosity between Trotsky and Rafael Abramovich, a member of the social democratic Bund, who accuses the Bolsheviks of armed attack on the Winter Palace. The passage thus builds a critical contrast between Trotsky partisans and Kerensky partisans: "Unarmed," says Abramovich, "we expose our breasts to the machine guns of the Terrorists." Abramovich, says Reed, is shouted down in "a storm of hoots, menaces and curses which rose to a hellish pitch." Then Trotsky rises, like some chief demon in the Pandemonium of revolution: "And Trotsky, standing up with a pale, cruel face, letting out his rich voice in cool contempt, 'All these so-called Socialist compromisers, these frightened

Mensheviki, Socialist Revolutionaries, *Bund*—let them go! They are just so much refuse which will be swept away into the garbage-heap of history'" (671).

In the scene, the Winter Palace in Petrograd has fallen to the rebels, Lenin is ready to come out of hiding to address the assembled Soviets, and Krylenko, "staggering with fatigue," has begun to read a telegram from the Twelfth Army on the Northern Front, declaring that the army is under the command of a Military Revolutionary Committee. "Pandemonium, men weeping, embracing each other," Reed observes of Krylenko's news, then continues:

> So, Lenin and the Petrograd workers had decided on insurrection, the Petrograd Soviet had overthrown the Provisional Government, and thrust the *coup d'etat* upon the Congress of Soviets. Now there was all great Russia to win— and then the world! Would Russia follow and rise? And the world—what of it? Would the peoples answer and rise, a red world-tide? Although it was six in the morning, night was yet heavy and chill. There was only a faint unearthly pallor stealing over the silent streets, dimming the watch-fires, the shadow of a terrible dawn gray-rising over Russia. (684)

In this passage, Reed's series of rhetorical questions crosses the line from those answers he knows to those answers he believes he knows. In 1918, writing the book, Reed and his potential readers already knew the answer to the question "Would Russia . . . rise?" The accompanying queries: " . . . the world, what of it? Would the peoples answer and rise, a red world-tide?" are considerably less certain—both to the Reed writing in 1918 and most certainly to present-day readers after the fall of the Soviet bloc. Writing near the end of the second decade of the twentieth century, Reed hoped that the historic inevitability of his narrative would sweep his readers into an affirmation of his global rhetoric. That Reed is able to construct the dramatic core of *Ten Days That Shook the World* compellingly enough to coax readers toward its revolutionary inevitability is what drives the book rhetorically and what made it so controversial as to be effectively suppressed at various times both in the Cold War West and in Stalinist Russia.

From Insurgence to Revolution: The Political and Artistic Transformation of John Reed

A close reading of the notes and the narrative strategy of the final text reveals fascinating echoes of *Insurgent Mexico* in *Ten Days That Shook the World*: in Mexico there are scenes of Reed's acceptance or rejection by the subjects he is covering; in Russia there are moments when he and Williams attempt to distribute gifts to the rebels to buy their acceptance. In both books, Reed rides at some personal risk in a battered conveyance that is carrying bombs; in both he is challenged by hotheaded revolutionaries who contest his identity and threaten to take his life. In both narratives, Reed contrasts a reformer (Carranza/Kerensky) with a revolutionary (Villa/Trotsky and Lenin). And in both books, the rebels question him closely about U.S. embarrassments such as Tammany or the Mooney scandal. But in *Ten Days That Shook the World*, Reed has traded in a compromised personal identity for a fresh one; thus, although his descriptive style remains consistently polished in both books, his writing is more triumphant and assured in *Ten Days*.

An exchange of letters between Reed and his long-time mentor Lincoln Steffens during June 1918 offers insight into the manner in which Reed had changed between his stint in Mexico and his reporting from Russia. On his return to Manhattan on April 28, 1918, after being detained in Oslo for two months without a visa, Reed was interrogated and searched. His trunks of notes, Russian handbills, newspapers, and speeches were seized by the U.S. Department of State. "With Louise Bryant I waited at the pier for hours, while a swarm of Department of Justice men stripped him, went over every inch of his clothes and baggage, and put him through the usual inquisition," recalls Michael Gold, an eyewitness to Reed's arrival.[7] "Reed had been sick with ptomaine on the boat. The inquisition had also been painful. But I like to remember how he kissed his girl again and again as our old-fashioned open carriage rolled through the New York streets and how hungrily he stared at the houses, the people on the sidewalk, the New York sky, with his large honest eyes" (9–10).

Burning to write what he believed to be the greatest story of his life, Reed asked for advice from Steffens, who for years was his role model as a progressive journalist, muckraker, and the closest political associate to Reed's late father. As the man who had arranged Reed's assignment to the Mexican Revolution, Steffens was an important link to his early success. Reed tells his mentor that no newspaper will touch his syndicated events in Russia:

> Collier's took a story, put it in type, and sent it back. Oswald Villard told me he would be suppressed if he published John Reed! I have a contract with Macmillan to publish a book, but the State Department took away all my papers when I came home, and up to date has absolutely refused to return any of them. . . . I am therefore unable to write a word of the greatest story of my life, and one of the greatest in the world. (Quoted in Rosenstone, 319)

Steffens's reply counsels patience. Publishing the story of the events in Russia, even if truthful, might be undemocratic while the United States is at war: "Jack, you do wrong to buck this thing. . . . It is wrong to try to tell the truth now. We must wait. You must wait. I know it's hard, but you can't carry conviction. You can't plant ideas. Only feelings exist, and the feelings are bewildered. I think it is undemocratic to try to do much now. Write, but don't publish" (bMS Am 1091:854). Reed's response to his mentor is brusque: "I am not of your opinion that it is undemocratic to buck this thing. If there were not the ghost of a chance, if everybody were utterly for it, even then I don't see why it shouldn't be bucked. All movements have to have somebody to start them and, if necessary, to go under for them" (Rosenstone, 320).

Steffens remained unconvinced. "Convictions were what I was afraid of," he wrote later. "I wanted to steer him away from convictions, that he might play, that he might play with life, and see it all, love it all, live it all, tell it all; that he might be it all; but all, not any one thing. And why not? A poet is more revolutionary than any radical." Reed's longtime mentor believed that Reed had become single-minded and doctrinaire in Bolshevik Russia. "He became a fighter; out for a cause; a revolutionist at home here, and in Russia a communist. He didn't smile any more" (Steffens, n.p.).

Reed was undeterred. If Steffens represented Reed's entrance pass into insurgent Mexico, a pass underwritten by the inherited fortunes of *Metropolitan Magazine*, Reed's chronicle of revolutionary Russia seemed destined to evoke significant echoes between his first book, *Insurgent Mexico*, and his last, *Ten Days That Shook the World*. An early draft of *Ten Days*—written for the *Liberator* while Reed still waited for his notes to be released (published as "A Visit to the Russian Army" in April/May 1918)—reworks the image of a Western journalist trying to buy acceptance from revolutionaries with the price of a gift. In Mexico, Reed had bragged of buying the friendship of Antonio Montoya with the gift of a watch and buying Pancho Villa's favor with a pistol and silencer. But in "A Visit to the Russian Army," Reed and his companion, Williams, decide that "we might as well give away our superfluous cigarettes. Accordingly we sat down on a trunk and held out a big box making generous sounds" (56). Several hundred soldiers are milling about, and only a few take the gifts that Williams is offering them. "Williams sat alone in the midst of an ever-widening circle. The soldiers were gathered in groups talking in low tones," Reed reports. "Suddenly he saw them coming toward him, a committee of three privates, carrying rifles with fixed bayonets, and looking dangerous. 'Who are you[?]' the leader asked. 'Why are you giving away cigarettes? Are you a German spy, trying to bribe the Russian revolutionary army?' All over the platform the crowd followed, slowly packing itself around Williams and the committee muttering angrily— ready to tear him to pieces" (56).

Reed's notes of his and Williams's trip survive in the Harvard archives and present a fine example of how the reporter builds quality journal description into an article with deeply developed images. This aspect of Reed's Russian writing builds on the compelling antiwar reporting Reed had done in Mexico and Europe—particularly at the Battle of Torreon and in the trenches of France —and the way that reporting had broken with the tradition of Stephen Crane and Richard Harding Davis. In Russia, a more secure vision allows Reed to stand out of the way and train his journalistic eyes on the emotions of others. During their visit to the Russian army, Reed and Williams attend the funeral of three Latvian soldiers. "First come the carts full of fir boughs and cedar, with two soldiers tossing out on the road," read the reporter's notes. "Before cemetery carts stop. One of the soldiers brushes hands off, pulls out cigarette, lights it, and cries (bMS Am 1091:1322, p. 65). In the final article, Reed considerably strengthens the verbs and rhythms of his sentences and adds details: "They were burying three Lettish sharpshooters, killed in action yesterday. First came two carts, each with a soldier who strewed the road with evergreen boughs. At the gate of the cemetery one of the soldiers brushed off his hands, heaved a sigh, took out a cigarette, lighted it, and began to weep" (54). In his notes we find: "an aeroplane drifting down the sky, anti-aircraft guns begin"; and, after noting nine volleys of honorary gunfire during a funeral hymn against the backdrop of applause from a distant meeting: "here death, there life" (bMS Am 1091:1322, pp. 62, 67). These notes are compressed into near-omniscience and sharpened imagery in the final version:

> No funeral has the poignant solemnity of a funeral at the front. Almost all these men and women have lost some men in the war; they know what it means, death. And these hundreds of soldiers, with stiff, drawn faces; they know these three dead—perhaps some of them even spoke with them, heard them laugh, joke, before the unseen warning shell fell out of the sky and tore them to bloody pieces. They realize well that perhaps next time it will be their turn. To the quiet deepness of the pastor's voice and muffled sobbing everywhere, the coffins are lowered down, and thud, thud, drops the heavy wet earth, with a sound like cannon far away. The chairman of the Iskostrel is making a revolutionary speech over the graves. The band plays, and a quavering hymn goes up. Nine times the rifles of the firing squad crash on the still air. . . . Overhead is the venomous buzz of an aeroplane. From the woods comes a faint roar of applause. Here death—there life. (54–55)

Reed had cause to remember the principled and brave Latvian men and women when he returned to Petrograd, and—as evidence of the way that his material was shaping his life even as he was shaping his material—soon had reason to cast one such Latvian soldier in a starring role. In *Ten Days*, in the most pivotal scene of the most pivotal day (November 7, at the Congress of the Soviets of Workers' and Soldiers' Deputies) Reed sets up a confrontation that symbolically passes the torch from the Cadets (constitutional democrats) to the Bolsheviks. In his exhaustive catalog of Russian factions in the "Background" section of the book, Reed identifies the Cadets as the Russian equivalent of the (U.S.) Progressive Party, Reed's boyhood heroes and the party of his father's and Lincoln Steffens's reform politics. As the argument at the congress ebbs and wanes, and as rumors spread that counterattack is on its way to Petrograd, a lean-faced Latvian soldier stands amid the clamor and cuts the Russian reformers to the heart:

> "No more resolutions! No more talk! We want deeds—the Power must be in our hands!" . . . The hall rocked with cheering. In the first moments of the session, stunned by the rapidity of events, startled by the sound of cannon, the delegates had hesitated. For an hour hammer-blow after hammer-blow had fallen from that tribune, welding them together but beating them down. Did they stand then alone? Was Russia rising against them? Was it true that the Army was marching on Petrograd? Then this clear-eyed young soldier had spoken and in a flash they knew it for the truth. . . . *This* was the voice of the soldiers—the stirring millions of uniformed workers and peasants were men like them, and their thoughts and feelings were the same. (670; Reed's ellipses and emphasis)

Reed thus symbolically disassociates himself from the reform politics of his father and the fatherland. In the writing of *Ten Days*, he resolutely will break Steffens's advice not to "buck this thing." "It is wrong to try to tell the truth now," Steffens had counseled. "[Y]ou can't carry conviction. You can't plant ideas. . . . I think it is undemocratic to try to do too much now. Write, but don't publish" (bMS Am 1091:854). Reed's articles on the Russian front for the *Liberator* and on the Latvian soldier in *Ten Days That Shook the World* were his answers to such counsel.

In fact, "A Visit to the Russian Army," stylistically as effective a piece of artistic reportage as any Reed wrote, identifies Reed straightaway in the article's lead as the bearer of a note proving him to be a member of the American Socialist Party "authorized to proceed to the active army to gather information for the North American Press" (28). The access to material that Reed had hidden or purchased in *Insurgent Mexico* is here laid bare for his reader. Similarly, the two trips that Reed made to Tsarskoye Selo on November 10 and 13 replay key identity moments that Reed had traced in *Insurgent Mexico*, wherein the reporter had been challenged to make clear his mission and allegiance. In the first trip, Reed accompanies the Bolsheviks as they attempt to respond to a counterattack planned by Kerensky forces three days after the taking of the Winter Palace. As in his journey to the Mexican front with Mac of "Mac-American," Reed is less than candid with his readers about his access, but in an intriguingly different way. This time, instead of hiding his conduit out of shame for Mac's xenophobia or burying his disappointment in near-comic intrigues as in "Shot at Sunrise," Reed hides his own identity to save the Bolshevik officers who are granting him and Williams access to the front without official authorization. Lenin, himself, had turned down Williams's request for a pass (Williams, 139), and the reporters were anxious not to embarrass him or get his soldiers into trouble. Reed calls himself Trusishka (what an American might now call a "wimp," or "nerd") and reports that Trusishka "got in [the officers' car] and sat down and nothing could dislodge him" (745).[8] Diffidently asserting that he sees no reason to doubt Trusishka's version of the trip, Reed weaves one of the few really comic tales in *Ten Days* as the Peoples' Commissars for War and Marine first try unsuccessfully to borrow a military vehicle from the troops they now command, then must hail a battered taxicab flying the Italian flag. The Bolsheviks eventually must borrow a notebook and finally a pencil from the ever-accommodating Trusishka, so they can write a requisition for ammunition for the Red troops at the front. The significance of the scene is that Reed has such firm access to the material he wants that he is able to withhold evidence of his solidarity with Russian insurgents for their sake, rather than withhold evidence of his complicity with North American business interests for his own sake as he had in *Insurgent Mexico* by burying the gunrunner Mac in his fictions.

Even more importantly, on a second trip to Tsarskoye Selo on November 13, Reed—without in any way acknowledging it—replays the scene he had drawn in Mexico on the way to the front with Urbina's troops. On both journeys, Reed is packed into a conveyance with a load of incendiary bombs. In both cases the bombs bump and jounce on the rutted roads as the good-natured Reed hangs on for dear life. The Russian journey even features the same sort of close questioning of Reed about U.S. embarrassments like Tammany or the Mooney case with which the Mexican rebels had challenged him in Mexico. Finally, on the road to Tsarskoye Selo, Reed is forced out of the Sixth Reserve Engineers truck and is interrogated by Red soldiers as a suspected spy. Reed's first account of the incident is in a notebook: "As we rush along bombs bang around the floor between legs. . . . Further on stopped passes asked for. I am arrested R.G. [Red Guard] protests, I submit. Sentries see only that my pass not like others, though can't read. Around corner are going to lynch. I persuade take me to soldier

who can read. Then to barracks where almost lynched again. Dinner at officer's mess."

From that abstract, Reed builds the following dramatic scene in *Ten Days*.
For an irrepressible reporter who often overestimated his own importance, the
scene is notable for its relative understatement, yet it clearly makes the point
that Reed wishes it to make. "The soldiers consulted in low tones for a moment," Reed writes in *Ten Days*, "and then led me to a wall, against which they
placed me. It flashed upon me suddenly; they were going to shoot me" (789).
At the point of a gun in Mexico, Reed had bought off his accuser Montoya with
a two-dollar watch, then shared a private joke with his North American audience as the childlike Montoya marveled at the movement of the watch's hands
and pledged his undying fealty to Reed. Here in the new Soviet Russia, Reed—
who a few days earlier had donated his reporter's pad and his pencil to the
cause under the pseudonym of Trusishka—finally finds a local committeeman
who can read his pass from Smolny: "The bearer of this pass, John Reed, is a
representative of American Social-Democracy, an internationalist." The committeeman is convinced. "Comrades," he says, "this is an American comrade. I
am chairman of the committee and I welcome you to the regiment." Reed reports "a sudden general buzz grew into a roar of greeting, and they pressed
forward to shake my hand" (790–91). As his original notes attest, Reed has dinner as a guest in the Red Army mess hall. Reed has been personally accepted by
the revolutionaries—closing the gap that Williams remembered when Reed
had been brushed aside as bourgeois, *burzhuy,* by the Russian worker. As in so
many other scenes in *Ten Days*, the story bridges the gap between Reed and the
subjects of his reporting, but opens the gap between the author and a majority
of his Western readers, both then and, subsequently, throughout the cold war.
Reed makes no pretense of objectivity in the scene; the Bolsheviks are his comrades and his story of their revolution will be impassioned and partisan.[9]

After *Ten Days:* Reed as Citizen of a New World?

In the article "A New Appeal" that he wrote for *Revolutionary Age* within a few
weeks of completing the typescript of *Ten Days That Shook the World,* Reed explains why he clearly preferred the Bolsheviks' revolutionary socialism over the
more cautious reform tactics of Kerensky and the Mensheviks. Socialist reformers, Reed believed, "give an impression that Socialism is really Jeffersonian
democracy," that all workers want are "reasonable reforms, labor legislation,
the full dinner pail." Instead, Reed insisted, the Bolsheviks "found out from the

working people what they wanted most. Then they made those wants into an immediate program and explained how they were related to the other demands of the complete Socialist Revolution" (1–2).

Reed wrote *Ten Days* to re-create in prose the rising tide of revolution he believed he saw in the Bolshevik program. He wanted to write a book that would connect with his readers in visceral ways, that would draw readers into the details and scenes and personalities that would make revolution sympathetic and palatable. And, certainly, Reed believed that the historical destiny of such a process was inescapable. "Comrades who call themselves 'members of the Left Wing' have an immediate job to do," Reed concludes in "A New Appeal," "and they must explain this in terms of the whole Labor movement, and they must make the workers want more—make them want the whole Revolution" (2).

Such were the beliefs that prompted Steffens to conclude ruefully that Reed "got a conviction and so, the revolutionary spirit got him" (Steffens, n.p.). Reed had written the birth pangs of a nation—the Soviet Union—that would, later, become his own country's greatest enemy, and he had presented it as truth, as living history, with the power to attract and repel its readers both inside the book and in the larger political sphere. The price Reed paid for that ambition was that for more than half a century after his death his nonfiction deeply alienated both the West and the Stalinist Soviet Union. Trotsky had been banished to his own refuse heap, Lenin was dead, and Reed had committed the unpardonable sin of ignoring Stalin. The Soviet writer Anatoli Rybakov summarizes the case for the Stalinist prosecution: "The main task was to build a mighty socialist state. For that, mighty power was needed. Stalin was at the head of that power, which meant that he stood at its source with Lenin. Together with Lenin he had led the October Revolution. John Reed had presented the history of October differently. That wasn't the John Reed we needed" (quoted in Homberger, *John Reed*, 1).

Meanwhile, Reed's crime against the United States, if it was a crime, was that he believed in Petrograd that a red tide was rising to sweep the world. And in his fervor to be the chronicler of that story he obliterated any opportunity he had to come back inside his nation's fold. By 1919, Reed's only U.S. publishing outlet in addition to the *Liberator* was the *Revolutionary Age,* edited by Louis C. Fraina from Socialist Party headquarters in Boston. Reed was listed as a contributing editor to the journal, and he sent a series of articles in which he laid the groundwork for a social revolution in America. What he has to say is unflinchingly polemical; he does not attempt the graceful scenes and descriptions that represent his best writing over the years. For example, compare the immediate dramatic writing from *Ten Days* that evokes V. I. Lenin's entrance at

the second congress ("Now Lenin, gripping the edge of the reading stand, letting his little winking eyes travel over the crowd" [698]) with his account of the
same historical event in the *Revolutionary Age* of July 12, 1919, in an article entitled "Aspects of the Russian Revolution": "On November 7th, 1917, the Soviets
—which in the meanwhile had developed a Bolshevik majority—took over the
government," Reed says flatly. "And the Provisional Government, supported by
the 'moderate' Socialists, was unable in all Russia to rally to its aid more than a
handful of Cossacks, junkers, and White Guards!" (8). This sort of summary
writing was to mark most of Reed's articles that year; in his rush to defend
the Bolshevik insurgency amid a generally hostile America, rarely does Reed
pause to build a scene or capture an immediate moment. The Constituent
Assembly, Reed says in "Aspects of the Russian Revolution," refused to ratify
either the People's Government of Soviets or the popular demands: "So the
people dissolved it—and the dissolution provoked not a ripple of protest
among the Russian masses; only the Soviet intellectuals and the *New York
Times* objected" (8).

The foregoing is the sort of writing that causes at least one reader, Robert
Humphrey in *A Sourcebook of American Literary Journalism,* to conclude that
Reed "became an apologist of the [Bolshevik] regime and a political activist,
thereby ending his career as a literary journalist" (159). Humphrey's assessment
seems to ring true when applied to articles like "A New Appeal" or "Why Political Democracy Must Go," published in the *Revolutionary Age* and the *New York
Communist,* respectively. In the former article, Reed flatly rejects the thinking
of what he describes as American Mensheviks in favor of what he terms practical, programmatic socialism. Yet even here, while Reed is declaiming rather
than describing, one senses the searching rhythm of words that marks Reed's
best writing. "My idea is to make Socialists, and there is only one way of doing
that—by teaching Socialism, straight Socialism, revolutionary Socialism, international Socialism." Building his repetitive cadence to a revival pitch, he
continues: "This is what the Russian Bolsheviki did; this is what the German
Spartacus group did. They approached not Socialists, but people: workers,
peasants, soldiers, who did not know what Socialism was. First they found out
from working people what they wanted most. Then they made those wants
into an immediate program. . . . They explained, explained, eternally explained" (10). And in "Why Political Democracy Must Go"—a title (and forum:
the *New York Communist*) that was calculated to alienate even his most ardent
non-Bolshevik supporters—Reed contends that even the capitalist class in the
United States now understands "that government is not carried on in legis-
latures, but in banks and Chambers of Commerce" (4). Still, Reed contends,

American workers believe against all the evidence that political democracy can solve the problems of wage earners. Pressed to a new service, Reed's writing can ring crisp and clear during this period, but it is unfailingly declamatory, fueled by a sense of injustice that "makes me write propaganda when I would rather play" ("Almost Thirty," 142).

Reed's best writing of the postrevolution period appears in the *Liberator*, which published the compelling profile of Eugene V. Debs and the gracefully written coverage of the IWW trial before Judge Kenesaw Mountain Landis. As I attempted to show in chapter 1, the *Liberator* articles prove that Reed's writing had not diminished by the end of his life. In fact, the evidence of his typescripts at Harvard is that at that time Reed was making more pencil corrections, polishing his prose for rhythm and precision, than at any other time of his career. Thematically, what comes through both the Debs and IWW articles is a Reed reluctantly saying goodby to his homeland as he prepares for the new world he believes to be at hand. When Reed visited Gene Debs in Terre Haute on July 4, both were under indictment for sedition, and the long sun lingered across the Indiana prairie as the two shook hands on the porch and clapped each other on the shoulder. "I have a picture of Gene Debs," Reed writes, "his long bony head and shining face against a backdrop of bright petunias in a box on the rail, his lean hand lifted with the long, artist's fingers giving emphasis to what he said: 'Say, isn't it great the way most of the boys have stood up? Fine! If this can't break them down, why then I know nothing can. Socialism's on the way'" (191). And in the courtroom of Judge Landis (as we saw in chapter 1), Reed deliberately allows his eyes to swim into a new vision in which the IWW defendants were trying the judge for counterrevolution. "These hundred and one are outdoor men, hard-rock blasters, tree-fellers, wheat-binders, longshoremen, the boys who do the strong work of the world." Reed is comfortable in an imaginary nation that accepts them. "They are scarred all over with the wounds of the industry—and the wounds of society's hatred. They aren't afraid of anything" (177).

A third post–Bolshevik Revolution piece that displays Reed's still-robust descriptive and poetic style is "America, 1918," his long poem that I discussed earlier (also in chapter 1). On that occasion I cited it for its rhythms, for its quick sketches of working people, for its Whitmanesque enumerations. Here I note it for its preamble—twelve lines over which Reed labored, crossing them out on one typescript and then reasserting them in another (bMS Am 1091:1277). The preamble reveals the lengths to which Reed had gone in surrendering his lease on his native country for a citizenship in a new world. His pain is apparent as he waits for his native land to live up to its ideals:

Across the sea my country, my America,
Girt with steel, hard-glittering with power,
As a champion, with great voice trumpeting
High words, "for liberty ... democracy ...
Deep within me something stirs, answers—
(My country, My America!)

(bMS Am 1091:1277)

Only two years earlier, in "Almost Thirty," Reed still had the hope that the United States might be redeemed through the ideals of liberty and democracy that stir in the hearts of the writer and his nation. "I cannot give up the idea that out of democracy will be born the new world—richer, braver, freer, more beautiful. As for me, I don't know what I can do to help—I don't know yet. All I know is that my happiness is built on the misery of other people, so that I eat because others go hungry, that I am clothed when other people go almost naked through the frozen cities in winter; and that fact poisons me, disturbs my serenity" (142).

After the November revolution in Petrograd, Reed thought he knew what he could do. And it required saying farewell to his lost one, to his first lover.

Deep within me something stirs, answers—
(My country, My America!)
As if alone in the high and empty night
She called me—my lost one, my first lover
I love no more, love no more, love no more ...

(bMS Am 1091:1277)

Reed's Literary Legacy

WHAT WOULD BE John Reed's literary reputation if we knew nothing of his notorious life? Would today's readers recognize his talent? Or does Reed's fame depend on his living fast and dying young—a literary James Dean or Jim Morrison in a pop-culture nation that worships youth and markets doomed insurgency? Jim Finnegan, on balance an admirer of Reed's work who argues Reed's ability to "unleash . . . revolutionary writing as a form of communal, dialogic chaos" (9), frames the problem in an intriguing manner. Noting the way Reed still lives in the margins of popular culture, even among those who have never read his work, Finnegan concludes: "John Reed has been more alive, and in some ways more interesting, since his death, popping up in strange places and mysterious forms" (135).

Given an opportunity, Reed's work still evidences a remarkable power to capture new audiences and to draw admirers from across the political spectrum. When Robert D. Kaplan, author of *Balkan Ghosts: A Journey through History,* planned a trip to the former Yugoslavia in order to understand its brewing ethnic conflict, he made an exhaustive search for Reed's *The War in Eastern Europe.* Kaplan considered Reed's reports so essential that he paid $389.11 for an out-of-print edition. He couldn't put the book down. "It never remained back in my hotel room," Kaplan recalls, writing of his trip to Serbia in *Balkan Ghosts,* which itself was a *New York Times* best book of 1993. More recently, an issue of *River Teeth: A Journal of Nonfiction Narrative* paired Reed's reporting from Serbia in 1915 with Philip Smucker's reporting on the war in Kosovo during the spring of 1999 (Smucker was reporting for the *Pittsburgh Post-Gazette, U.S. News and World Report,* and the *London Daily Telegraph*). Even though that issue of *River Teeth* featured the work of three Pulitzer Prize winners and other decorated journalists and essayists, the narrative that produced the greatest reader response and praise was the one Reed wrote eighty-four years earlier about the battle above the clouds in Goutchevo, Serbia. Jon Franklin, a two-time Pulitzer winner for literary reporting, has cited the "insightful pairing of the pieces on Serbia": "As a professional journalist I have surely read hundreds of thousands of words on the subject, but I never really got it until now," he told me.[1]

Christine Stansell, a first-rate historian, disagrees with the assessments of Kaplan and Franklin, however, contending in her *American Moderns: Bohemian New York and the Creation of a New Century* that Reed's reporting from Serbia "was incapable of grasping more complex divisions and antagonisms," such as those in the Balkans, because "Reed's model of meaningful political conflict required a tension between the people and their overlords" (195). Although her study considers a substantially broader topic than the writings of John Reed, her arguments are engaging because they represent an intriguing counterbalance to the conclusions of this study and because hers is the first careful assessment of Reed's writing to be published in the twenty-first century. Of particular value in Stansell's work is her examination of the cultural relationship between Reed and his subjects—an aspect of nonfictional discourse that is critically important. Stansell writes:

> John Reed—the paradigmatic writer friend of revolution—tried to invigorate realist genres with a lyricism born of fellowship, imagined and actual, with his plebeian subjects. . . . As a writer Reed was good, but as a master of cultural politics he was extraordinary. Ever the journalist on the make, he used radical politics to bolster his limited talents; ever the Harvard man, he used his literary talents to generate inordinate intellectual authority. His trail of friendships, hearty if superficial, ran from the Lower East Side to Mexico to Petersburg. It was not that his political commitments were spurious. But he did usually manage to use lessons learned in lower Manhattan to turn an outsider's luck to an insider's advantage. (185–86)

Specifically, Stansell finds *Insurgent Mexico* to be an exercise in self-generated literary heroism—to be more imperial travel literature than about either insurgency or Mexico. "The effect," she says, "as in other travel writing, is to enhance the writer's incantatory power over a mysterious countryside that seems like his personal possession, a Mexico according to John Reed" (188).

Of Reed's coverage of World War I, Stansell joins Reed's other critics in finding his writing from the Western Front to be flat and uninspired. She determines *The War in Eastern Europe* to be "a more interesting book to read now than *Insurgent Mexico*" (195), but ultimately finds that Reed never really understood the societies he was covering despite a desire "to shape their material within the tropes of human interest" (195). Finally, Stansell recognizes that Reed's *Ten Days That Shook the World* "would make him, in the years to come, an icon of the writer friend in a greatly altered world" (197). Yet she appears to conclude that *Ten Days* mostly reworks the fashion of Reed's self-persona from "romantic adventurer and man of the people—so successful in Mexico—into a more powerful personage, the revolutionary citizen of the world" (197).

Critics such as Stansell who see Reed as "ever the journalist on the make" seem unable to account for the way that the last three years of his life move in exactly the opposite direction. The evidence seems far more compelling that Reed was transformed by two factors: the bitter personal cost that resulted from his bucking the U.S. tidal wave of war-preparedness and his belief that the war would kindle international revolution. When he stepped outside the master narrative of these events, he seemed to forge a new role for the revolutionary writer of political nonfiction. If Reed had been "on the make," he could have put his career back together after his break with U.S. political hegemony. After all, Reed's friend and fellow defendant against sedition charges Max Eastman was able to move from helping to form the nonaligned American Trotskyist Movement during the 1920s ("Memoir," xiv) to become a sort of grand old man of American letters, a staunch anti-Communist and the author of *Enjoyment of Living*. Other writers as diverse as Walter Lippmann and Lincoln Steffens in the United States—or, most certainly, George Orwell a few years later in the United Kingdom—managed an about-face from their earlier radicalism that helped to enshrine them squarely within the respective canons of political commentary, journalism, and literature. Whatever his motivations, Reed refused that alternative—perhaps stemming from his almost pathological inability to compromise and his eagerness always to stake out the more extreme stance available to him.

At first glance, many such stances were self-indulgent. No careful reader can overlook the literary preening that marks Reed's self-portrait in *Insurgent Mexico*. At twenty-six, Reed was ill-suited to resist the promotional frenzy that Carl Hovey and H. J. Whigham built around his Mexican exploits. In large part, he capitulated to the reportorial myth constructed for him, even if he was quick to reveal in several passages of *Insurgent Mexico* how mythmaking lies at the heart of all U.S. coverage of Mexico. We have seen how Reed banishes Mac-American to the margins of his fiction and lies about Antonio Montoya to mask the exploitative relationship that Mac and he enforced on the Mexican peasants. The truth of that relationship strikes too close to home for Reed to admit; far better to construct scenes of friendship: quaffing the fiery *sotol,* tearing *carne crudo* in one's teeth, and sleeping around the campfire, singing rousing songs of revolution. Still, within that context, Stansell seems to overlook substantial elements of Reed's reporting—particularly his challenge to the ideology of warfare. "For Reed," Stansell says, "the story is always with the stomping, shooting, riding, drinking men. The effects of war go unimagined, even if pressures from background characters sometimes intrude" (191). A rare exception Stansell finds is when Reed paints a mass of men and animals fighting for water around a troop train. "But such powerful passages are exceptions; mostly, he was 'sick with boredom,' and he escaped as soon as he could" (193).

Stansell seems to misplace Reed's "sick with boredom" line and overlooks some of the book's strongest passages about war's effects on civilians. Reed's boredom comes not when he observes the civilians fighting for water, but at the end of Villa's successful night attack on Gomez Palacio some sixty-three pages later. Reed's point is that war's *killing* ultimately becomes banal and boring. He quotes an anonymous foot soldier who understands that most battles are fought in the interests of other, highly placed partisans. "'How brave we Mexicans are,' he said drolly. 'Killing each other like this!'" As Reed listens to the man and contemplates the wounded about him, he finds himself not elated by victory, but "sick with boredom. A battle is the most boring thing in the world if it lasts any length of time," he says. "It is all the same" (211).

In addition to Reed's change of heart in this scene, two women he meets, in a passage he terms "On the Cannon Car," and the peon he quotes at the Battle of Torreon also seem to argue against Stansell's thesis. In "On the Cannon Car," Reed presents a girl who has been forced to accompany her soldier to battle to cook his tortillas. "I was sick," she says, "and the baby was born in a desert just like this place, and died there because we could not get water." Her older female companion responds: "When we go so far and suffer so much for our men, we are cruelly treated by the stupid animals of Generals" (165). Near Torreon, Reed pesters an old man, "stooped with age and dressed in rags," for directions to "get in close and see the fighting." The old man stares down the young reporter. "If you had been here as long as I have you wouldn't care about seeing the fighting," he says. To Reed's claims of partisanship, the man rejoins: "I am very old, and I have not long to live; but this war—it seems to me that all it accomplishes is to let us go hungry" (186). Reed thus brackets his most traditionally effective war scenes with portraits of disheartened soldiers, exploited women, and scornful peons. In battle, then, Reed finally understands war's terrible boredom. Together with his genuine mourning at the death of his friends and his recognition that he traded on that death for his literary reputation, Reed— despite his preening self-construction—would not seem to be a writer to whom "the effects of war go unimagined" (Stansell, 191).

Given her call for Reed to focus more on the devastation of war and less on its romantic "fellow feeling" (189), it is surprising that Stansell is so disappointed by Reed's World War I reporting. "When brought to bear on the actualities of trench warfare," Stansell writes, "Reed's techniques of rendering 'experience' were useless" (193–94). Stansell here echoes conventional criticism of Reed's Western Front writing: Robert Rosenstone misses the glorious pageantry of Mexican battles, the "death with the romantic glow" (199); David C. Duke misses "the flavor of conflict" (96) that Reed captured south of the border. Stansell's valuable critique of exactly that romantic mythology would seem to prepare her for a narrative like "In the German Trenches," which, as I argued in chapter 4, is perhaps the most effective war dispatch that Reed ever wrote. As do the best literary journalists, Reed makes extensive use of specific experience to build a wider context for his reporting. His understated depiction of the medal-presentation ceremony is clear-eyed; in Reed's vision, the German army trades a miniature Iron Cross for a famous runner's legs and expects the soldier to console himself by substituting their notions of heroism and patriotism for his mobility. Perhaps uncharacteristically, Reed manages to produce that effect without ever stating it directly. The soldier's horrible wounds result from a new sort of war. In Reed's German trenches, mud-drenched soldiers fire big guns at an unseen enemy; crackling telephones order minute calibrations to make the killing more efficient; German and French casualties bury themselves in the muck. No doubt Reed also missed the rowdy charm of a romantic infantry charge; after all, he had grown up worshiping the writers who created that genre. But in World War I, precisely at the place where traditional criticism finds him most wanting, Reed fashions a new style of reporting for a new physics of war.

In her assessment of *The War in Eastern Europe*, Stansell comes close to recognizing that reporting breakthrough, noting that Reed almost turns to advantage his inability to get to the front lines. Reed's tour of the war-ravaged countryside, the typhus zones, and the refugee camps draws attention to war's secondary terror, but Stansell correctly detects a flavor of "listlessness" (195) in Reed's reporting from the Balkans, without quite naming its cause. Notoriously insecure and still not yet thirty, Reed was emotionally ill-prepared for the listless response his own work generated, and he allowed self doubts to blunt his writing instincts. Rosenstone's careful citations from Reed's letters of the period make this case, as I do in this study's close reading of the way *Metropolitan* manipulated Reed's rising and fading public stock in the pages of their magazine. Unlike diarists or even novelists, most writers of nonfiction, especially working reporters, labor in a system regulated by their editors and subjected to the whims of advertising and marketing. Reed was only a year or two removed from the sort of publicity hype of which any writer dreams. Although he was prepared to break politically with the editorial philosophy of *Metropolitan,* Reed seemed unable to sustain the emotional cost brought on by that break. Therefore, the best scenes of *The War in Eastern Europe*—particularly the way in which Serbia's Goutchevo Mountain extends the themes of the German trenches—all are built on decay, devastation, and loss, the tangible correlatives of Reed's inner turmoil.

Secondarily, in partial evidence of the book's flatness, Stansell correctly notes that sales of *The War in Eastern Europe* were "minuscule" (195). A closer look reveals why that was so. Like nonfiction scholar John J. Pauly, I believe that journalistic narrative demands a combination of close textual and social analysis, and I agree with Pauly's call to study the "institutional sites at which the story was written, printed, disseminated, and discussed" (112). Such an analysis of *The War in Eastern Europe* is enlightening. The book appeared in Scribner's "The War on All Fronts" series, alongside Richard Harding Davis's *With the Allies,* Mary Humphrey Ward's *England's Effort,* Edith Wharton's *Fighting France,* and E. Alexander Powell's *Italy at War.* Scribner's marketed the series as "a single authoritative treatment, reasonably small in compass and in price, from which to derive strong and vivid impressions of the character of each of our Allies" ("Publisher's Note," vii). Scribner's leaves little doubt as to the purpose of the series: it was not only to describe the part each allied nation would play in fighting Germany but also to evoke the worldwide threat that, it was believed, that country was presenting.

Davis, assigned to cover Germany, "saw the blue-gray rivers of German troops flow into the gallant country [France] and inundate it" (vii); Powell draws Italy, "reveal[ing] this most spectacular and romantic warfare, often among the clouds on the snow-covered mountain tops . . . [and] the great advances in man and machine power developed in recent months" (ix). Wharton's beat is France, "and when war broke upon the country she gave all her strength and talent—not only in writing, but in organizing—to serve the nation's cause" (viii). The "Publisher's Note" saves its greatest hyperbole for Mary Humphrey Ward, the antisuffragette grandniece of Matthew Arnold, the aunt of Julian and Aldous Huxley, and the author of the popular novel *Robert Elsmere.* With a plug from Theodore Roosevelt, Scribner's sets the stage for her coverage of England's glorious war:

> The question was, could this great democracy [England], holding individual liberty supreme, so chasten herself as to develop the huge organization, military and industrial, by which only could the Entente be saved. For months people asked, "What is England Doing?" Her part in the war is described by a writer who, to use Theodore Roosevelt's characterization, "has influenced all who speak and read English more profoundly than any woman now alive." Mrs. Humphrey Ward in the second volume, "England's Effort," presents the operations of England not only on the fronts and on the sea, but especially in the vast factories and shops which fill the storehouses of herself and largely of her allies. (viii)[2]

That all-fronts patriotic appeal contrasts strongly to Scribner's promotional effort for Reed's *The War in Eastern Europe*. Of his contribution to the series, the publisher's note says only that Reed writes in "simple, flowing text" and brings "a singular reality" to the events that he covers. Given his stiff criticism of the very nations that the "War on All Fronts" series was celebrating, Reed had no chance for success. Although Rosenstone notes that the outside reviews of *The War in Eastern Europe* were better than any Reed had enjoyed to that time (232n), Scribner's lackluster promotion of Reed's book doomed sales to about a thousand copies.

I take some pains to illustrate the reception of *The War in Eastern Europe* within its wider publishing context because of the way that nonfictional stories of political and other public disputes tend to ignite passionate response. While readers might also react strongly to fictional narratives, stories that claim to be true (as in Scribner's promise to deliver "a single authoritative treatment, reasonably small in price") draw their characters and conflict from the public domain and almost automatically set off competing claims of interpretation. By the middle of 1916, Reed had become largely isolated from the central interpretive communities that were forming around the Great War in Europe. No longer did Reed fit comfortably within the role set out for him—the heroic American sent forth to exotic locations to conquer narrative meaning for his homeland. Therefore, if it is true that Reed was "ever the journalist on the make" (Stansell, 186), one would expect the reporter to have adjusted the ideology of his nonfiction so that he could reinvigorate the successful role that employers like *Metropolitan Magazine* and Scribner's had carved out for him. That Reed failed to do so becomes one of the enduring mysteries of his life, and Stansell's assertion that his "romantic adventurer and man of the people" persona retooled rather seamlessly into a "revolutionary citizen of the world" does not account for it.

Adjoining passages in Stansell's study of Reed illustrate the conundrum. At one moment she writes: "To pay the rent, the American Kipling now took on boilerplate assignments—slice-of-life human-interest and celebrity interviews" (196), while in the next she asserts: "Reed's vision of his authority in American society had long been bound up in his writerly ambitions, his politics inseparable from his search for literary eminence" (196). These two manifestations of Reed's ambition would appear to be as contradictory as the competing tropes of "boilerplate" and "literary eminence." For example, the pieces that Reed wrote about Billy Sunday and William Jennings Bryan are anything but boilerplate; instead, they disclose the very terms of their mythmaking to the reader and reveal how Reed and the subjects of his profiles engage in a struggle for meaning. Moreover, Reed's reporting of the oil workers' strike in Bayonne, New Jersey, during the period Stansell is discussing—given his understanding of *Metropolitan*'s changing political climate and its power largely to control his domestic literary reception—would not appear to satisfy the strategy of a writer motivated solely by fame and eminence.

Although Georg Lukacs would not write his essay "Reification and the Consciousness of the Proletariat" until two years after Reed's death, I believe that Reed recognized something of the same problem that Lukacs later identified: the manner by which standard nonfiction stands ready to market meaning as commodity. Writing in 1922, Lukacs said that modern administration and law had assumed the characteristics of a factory, producing dominant culture in the way that a factory produces a commodity. "This phenomenon can be seen at its most grotesque in journalism," Lukacs said. "Here it is precisely subjectivity itself, knowledge, temperament and powers of expression that are reduced to an abstract mechanism functioning autonomously and divorced both from the personality of their 'owner' and from the material and concrete nature of the subject matter at hand" (100). Similarly, Scribner's had claimed to produce, for a small price, the "single authoritative treatment" of World War I, but had deliberately sidelined competing accounts such as Reed's from that authority. *Metropolitan Magazine* and Reed's other standard market outlets had done precisely the same thing. It stands to reason that Reed would understand by this bitter experience the power of capitalism to control meaning in the marketplace; certainly his reporting after 1915—especially the domestic profiles that Stansell describes as boilerplate—always takes pains to reveal its subjective construction.

Therefore, Reed's contribution to nonfictional narrative in general and to literary journalism in particular is somewhat more complex than the role that Stansell traces for him. As this book has argued, Reed's value derives partly from his formal initiatives—his ability to write vivid description with precise, active verbs and sensory detail. Reed also displays an excellent ear for language and writes convincing dialogue, though a study of his notes shows that he probably constructed dialogue as much from memory or from imagination as from precise records. When Reed takes the time to edit his work carefully, he creates an effective rhythm of language; his best descriptive scenes are the work of a writer with a poet's ear.

Reed's most enduring contribution to the writing of history as literature may be his effort to free his writing from the "abstract mechanism" of journalistic commodity—a marketplace of meaning that Lukacs says depends on "the journalist's 'lack of convictions,' [and] the prostitution of his experiences and beliefs" (100). Reed always had been capable of fine irony in the narrative persona he created for himself. He constructed that persona artfully, if not always honestly, and worked intriguing variations on his self-construction from text to text. Studying how Reed the writer plays his variations on Reed the character provides the critical perspective to understand how he broke out of the sort of writerly contradictions that Stansell cites. The arguments of chapters 4 and 5, if persuasive, have demonstrated that Reed began to face up to his responsibilities in a new way. Where he had hidden his relationship to U.S. power in *Insurgent Mexico* and played at being a revolutionary while marketing his stories of revolution, the Reed of *Ten Days That Shook the World*, for better or worse, was more candidly disclosing his role in the events he was covering. In Lukacs's terms, he had rejected the role that standard journalism prepared for him; from now on he would champion his convictions, his experiences, and his beliefs. That he did so against the grain of what journalism historian John C. Hartsock identifies as a period during which the ideology of "objective news" began to supplant subjective/literary reporting (154–55) shows that Reed was less a self-serving careerist than a writerly iconoclast.

Reed's literary deceptions perpetrated by *Ten Days That Shook the World*, therefore, become part of his playful self-parody—Trusishka, the nerd—by which Reed undercuts his otherwise self-important role of John Reed, emissary of international socialism, and reveals how both his text and the new world are created. That transformation puts to new use the sort of deliberate self-construction that always had marked Reed's writing. Where, in Mexico, Reed had created his literary persona from the master narratives of romantic self-fulfillment, by the time he is in Russia he fashions a self who will be present in the rising tide of a new world and will return to tell its story.[3]

Still young at the time of his death, Reed had not yet developed the discipline to get the best out of his own writing. At the time of its publication, *Ten Days* represented his best effort yet at constructing a book with an overall structural plan, yet Reed still rushed manuscripts into print and, from the evidence of his typescripts, often ignored the rewriting stage. Had he done more self-editing, Reed might have improved his books and articles. As I showed in chapter 1, Reed's ear for the rhythm of language always produces marked improvements when he takes the time for revisions. At the time of his death, Reed had not yet met an editor who really understood his work and who took the time to help him envision its larger terms. Carl Hovey came close to that standard, but because of marketplace politics Hovey had to withdraw. Had Reed met an exacting editor who would have recognized his unique fusion of the artistic and the political, and had Reed lived longer, he might have produced far more mature work. Despite its brilliance, much of Reed's work remains episodic, flashes of compelling description and dialogue strewn among more pedestrian passages.

Reed's ability to research facts and to weave those facts into his text had improved greatly by the end of his career, but he still was caught in the critical paradigm that was to rule the century. He believed, as do most of his critics, that journalistic narrative represents an innately inferior alternative to "artistic" prose. Therefore, he often described his best work as propaganda, rather than art, even if he had the instincts to know that the writing of history as literature could produce powerful returns. By 1917 and 1918, however, Reed seems to begin to understand the real possibilities that derive from merging literary and journalistic narrative. Had he taken more than a few weeks to write *Ten Days That Shook the World*, Reed might have found even more skillful ways to intertwine that book's political background with its dramatic scenes. Still, the range of reporting and artistry that Reed manages in that book and several shorter pieces remains fresh in a contemporary age when writers of literary nonfiction still struggle to meet the challenge of factual significance. Perhaps one of the more interesting compliments ever paid to John Reed stems from that recognition. Writing in 1973, Tom Wolfe concludes that Reed—whose politics he detested—was one of only a few writers capable of producing "nonfiction written by reporters, and not autobiographers or literary gentlemen in the grandstand, showing many of the characteristics of the New Journalism" (45). What struck Wolfe was Reed's ability—such as in the *Ten Days* scene where a group of workers challenges the authority of a naval officer—to capture the essence of life through dialogue and description and to report that life with background research.

Reed was still young, four days short of his thirty-third birthday, when he died, and no one can say with certainty how the changes evident in his writing between 1916 and 1920 would have played out over a greater number of years. I will not join what has become something of a parlor game in the closing chapters of Reed biographies: speculation about whether Reed would have stayed in the Communist Party or would have denounced Stalinism. Certainly, Reed would have become deeply alienated from a Soviet state system that condemned Leon Trotsky and executed many of V. I. Lenin's political allies. And it seems impossible to imagine his enthusiasm for a nation that would not allow its own citizens to read *Ten Days That Shook the World* because Reed's account of the revolution no longer squared with the state version of events. I join Reed's most recent biographer, Eric Homberger, in believing that, later, as the Soviet empire toppled, Reed would certainly have been a dissident, a supporter of a Dubcek or a Gorbachev, not of Soviet hardliners (5).[4]

Far better to explore Reed's potential future from the immediate plans that remained. We know that Reed planned *Ten Days That Shook the World* to be the first of a trilogy; a second part, *Kornilov to Brest-Litovsk,* was to cover events between the November revolution and the Soviet-German peace (*Ten Days,* 575; Williams, 43n). No doubt he would have grown in his confidence and in his ability to produce a finished text. The final reports of Reed's career, though often polemical, show he still retained the ability to write convincing scene and dialogue and that he was not too serious to marshal first-rate irony for effect.

In addition to his journalism plans, Reed left three partial outlines for books under two working names, "The Ever-Victorious" and "The Tides of Man," which survive in the Harvard archives. Taking its title from a legendary fighter of Reed's imagination, "Ever-Victorious" is derivatively romantic, hardly an improvement on Reed's schoolboy writing, but the manuscript does contain an insight into Reed's thinking during the spring of 1920 while he was jailed in Finland. In Reed's notes, an old king lies rigid, his body so weighted by robes of silver that he cannot move. He is spirited away by ten black-clad warriors toward the edge of Earth, where dawn burns in the east (bMS Am 1091:1226). The notes thus reveal Reed's continuing belief that a new dawn would rise to overtake a decaying economic system made rigid by its devotion to wealth. From the evidence of the notes Reed made in prison in Finland, it does not seem likely, however, that "The Ever-Victorious" could have sustained its allegorical weight.

Far more promising are two sets of notes written under the title "The Tides of Men." While the first treatment, concerning the adventures of a young writer named Robin, appears to be hastily written with handwriting often too sloppy to decipher, the second set of notes is far more coherent. Written on large pages (leaves fourteen by eighteen inches) under the heading "Novel No. II" (bMS Am 1091:1230), the second draft contains fascinating variations on the themes of Reed's own life. Changing his protagonist's name from Robin to Harvey, Reed tells of a young man whose father lost his life in an attempt to provide a better financial future for his sons. Moving to New York, Harvey covers a Tammany benefit obviously based on "The Dinner Guests of Big Tim," but—in a radical departure from Reed's own life—signs on as a mainstream newspaper reporter with the Tammany politician's patronage. For a time, life is good for Harvey. He doesn't have to work hard at the newspaper since the Tammany boss is secretly paying off its editor to have Harvey write favorable publicity for him. Each time that Harvey gets into a scrape, he finds himself secretly protected by his Tammany godfather. But soon bored and restless, he begins to cover more meaningful events—an execution at Sing Sing, a labor riot on Union Square, a colorful evangelist with secret business connections, a Long Island murder case with political overtones, free-speech rallies. The better and more compelling are Harvey's stories, the more likely they are to be cut by his city editor. His Tammany boss finally sends for Harvey, and the young reporter asks to be released from his obligations to his godfather. Harvey now seems to understand at what cost his success in the world of commercial journalism has been purchased.

The portions of "Tides" wherein Reed outlines the young reporter's relationship with the Tammany boss are replete with enigmatic and underscored references to "Steff," as if Reed believes that his relationship with his father's long-time reformer friend also carries the makings of a restricting patronage. From this point in the narrative, Reed's notes grow more sporadic, but to the reader versed on the details of his life they are quite meaningful. A sampling of Reed's notes: "Meeting with Bill, Gurley, Tresca. Echoes of the great Lawrence strike. The salon. Collapse of the I.W.W. . . . Bayonne. The break with his paper. Freelancing. Poverty. Marriage. The War. Against star-spangle. Collapse of salary, etc. Conscientious objection but registers. Not called" (bMS Am 1091:1230). The notes Reed wrote in the Finnish prison for "The Tides of Men" then imagine Harvey as an increasingly politicized reporter, covering "clearly sharpened class lines" through general strikes. "The Reform Administration being over, the town is open," Reed writes. "Harvey sees the beginning" (bMS Am 1091:1230).

Whether Reed could have produced a novel worthy of his journalism is far from established. Certainly there are hints within "Tides" that it either would have become an intriguing novel after the best of John Steinbeck or that it would have been the sort of proletarian novel fashionable during the decades following Reed's death and forgotten soon after. Regardless, it is doubtful that a nation ready for the narrative experiments of the great modernist writers would have been satisfied for very long by Reed's fiction. Far more likely that Reed would have continued to write compelling nonfiction, that he would have continued to challenge the boundaries of what it means to write truth through imaginatively presented reporting. It is certain that his experiments—especially if not ruled by the predispositions of genre—would have been interesting, indeed. What is far less certain is whether they could have convinced a literary establishment that fiction writers can find their ultimate form in nonfiction.

"Whenever I have tried to become some one thing, I have failed; it is only by drifting with the wind that I have found myself, and plunged joyously into a new role," Reed admitted in "Almost Thirty," his brief autobiography. "I have discovered that I am only happy when I'm working hard at something I like" (126). Near the end of his life, Reed seems to have drifted into that one thing he had sought—the writing of revolution. How long it would have lasted is far less clear. But for a time—in fact for a very long time—John Reed had found a way to write the literature of life in words that seem startlingly new.

Appendix

Two *Metropolitan Magazine* Articles by John Reed

In the German Trenches

(April 1915)

"Now you shall see the trenches," said our staff officer complacently. "But I warn you it is dangerous."

The rain, which had drenched us since dawn, ceased suddenly. We got out of our automobiles and stood in the muddy road, where two spotless German officers in beautifully polished boots and the martial elegance of Prussian long coats bowed stiffly, clicking their heels and murmuring their names—"Von Langen, Roediger!" To the left lay the considerably demolished farmhouse which served as regimental headquarters. The wide French road on which we had been traveling climbed to a gentle hill, and then descended again between rows of poplars straight as an arrow into Arras, six kilometers away. It was on the other side of this rise that the trenches lay. An occasional spent bullet whined wearily overhead, and except for the lazy thunder of distant cannon, the only other sound in all the still country was a rifle shot perhaps every half minute.

Part way up the hill we abandoned the road, crossed a potato field, and descended suddenly into the laufgraben, or approach-trench, which was seven feet deep, two wide, and held about a foot of water. The laufgraben zigzagged through the field and brought up against the wall of a house just where a great shell had torn a hole. There the path emerged to the surface, crossed the kitchen, passed diagonally through a rude door hacked with pickaxes, out through the window, straight as a railroad track through other houses and across little gardens, plunged deep into the earth again to cross the Arras road, then through a church just beyond the hill's crest—where, through a rent made by bursting shrapnel above the high altar, one could look out over the vast plain—the red roofs of Arras glistening; gaunt, tattered, abandoned windmills full of holes still whirling their broken arms; a sky rent and torn as if with shell fire, mighty masses of white cloud driving across the pale blue, and a watery sun steaming the soaked earth in traveling golden blotches. Way to the north a black rainstorm blurred the horizon, and under it slow great guns spoke like flashing swords; one could see the black pillars of smoke where heavy shells burst, and the dark mass of trees dotted with white shrapnel explosions, vivid when the sun struck them.

"See, there are the French trenches," said an officer, pointing. A little heap of thrown-up mud, such as comes out of a draining-ditch, marched across the field, over a little hill, reappeared, was lost, dwindled away north, until it could not be distinguished from the ground. One could see all around for a radius of about four kilometers; and above ground there was not the least sign of human life—although we knew that within three hundred yards of us a thousand Germans were eating, drinking, sleeping, and shooting, and two hundred yards from them a thousand French.

Beyond, the laufgraben came again into the open field, and we splashed along laughing and joking in a queer mixture of French, German and English, the officers with their monocles and "swagger sticks" still jaunty, but their smart uniforms muddied to the waist, until we came into a broad, sunken footway, drained, hard-packed by ceaseless labor, where an imitation of a Berlin street sign announced that this was the Unter den Linden. About fifty yards to the left another trench zigzagged forward in the direction of the enemy, and this was labeled the Wilhelmstrasse—a jocular reference to the German Foreign Office's zigzag methods of leading toward the enemy. At its end, perhaps fifty yards nearer the enemy, there was a series of little individual pits where the advance guard stood, and a couple of machine guns. Every two hundred yards or so one of these advance trenches pushed out a nervous tentacle from the main passage.

Along the Unter den Linden little alleys led forward to open spaces where two soldiers generally had their stand, and from which subterranean chambers opened where the soldiers slept and rested. Some had beds and chairs, a few even doors and windows, all looted from the ruined village behind. To enter the dugout of the commanding officer you descended a flight of ten steps, and found yourself in a room quite ten feet by fifteen feet and seven feet high, furnished with a large Empire looking glass, a handsome old brocaded chair, a Louis Quinze bedstead carved with cupids, a table and a stove—and draped with exquisite Flemish tapestries taken out of the battered chateau there on the hill. Here the soldiers were in the trenches three days and out three, so that two sets of men occupied the same chambers. There was a healthy rivalry in ornamentation and elaboration of the common dugout. There were also deep subterranean rooms where the men dined in common, played cards, and gathered around a stove on cold nights; these all bore placards with the names of splendid Berlin hostels and cafes, like the "Hotel Adlon" and the "Tauenzienpalast"— and I remember one which flaunted an elaborately painted advertisement, "At the Sign of the Wild Bedbug."

"How long is this trench?" I asked idly.

"It extends from the North Sea to the Swiss frontier," answered the captain. "You can land somewhere south of Nieuport, climb over a dune or so, get into this trench, and walk along below the surface of the ground to Mulhausen in Alsace. And you can eat in the trench dining room, and sleep in a spare dugout, and never see anything except two mud walls, unless you want to climb and look over————"

"Now are you satisfied?" asked our staff officer when we got back to the autos. "You have seen a trench, haven't you?"

"No, we're not satisfied!" came a chorus; and my partner, who was more fluent than I, went on: "We've seen a few muddy-legged soldiers strolling around and every now and then taking a shot from their little openings; and we've looked into the dugouts and admired the engineering skill of the Prussian soldier. But we want to see the machine in action. We want to see a battle in the trenches. We want to be there daytime and nighttime, and smoke with the men, and talk with them, and eat with them. We want to see war, and this"— he searched about for a comparison—"this is the Harlem of war!"

Some of the officers laughed, and one or two frowned, and all of them remarked:

"Oh, impossible! Quite impossible!"

"Very well, then," we said. "We want to go back to Berlin, so that we can leave the country and go where there is some real fighting to be seen."

So, largely because of the influence borne by Senator Beveridge, who happened to be along, good Captain Kliever did some telephoning, and came out grinning all over.

"It's all right," he said. "The general in command of the Second Bavarian Army Corps says 'Sure! Send them along and we'll show them something!'"

At noon we were having lunch with a Bavarian general and his staff in the house of a wealthy manufacturer who had fled the country. This was in Comines, a great industrial city black with the ceaseless smoke of fifty years. If you had not seen the factories, you would know that Comines was a great industrial city because of the magnificent hospital supported by private charity, where five hundred free beds had once been at the disposal of the fortunate workers. Now, of course, it was a German military hospital.

The officer in charge, a genial Bavarian surgeon, with an immense pride in his equipment and a childish joy in having so much raw material to work with, led us through ward after ward where men lay white and still, or tossed feverishly mumbling incomprehensible words; with the eye of a connoisseur he ripped the bedclothes from them one by one to show where a leg or arm had been, or perhaps the place where a jagged piece of the melinite shell had ripped a man's stomach to pieces, so that nourishment would have to be injected into his wrist with a hypodermic syringe all his life. In the middle ward a bed was screened off from the other beds, and from it streamed a continuous shrill groaning, like a pig with its throat cut. The doctor hesitated at the foot of this bed, rubbed his hands, and then looked disappointed.

"Ah, well," he said, humanely, "we'll not trouble the poor fellow. He'll be dead in three hours."

There was a Frenchman, too, who had been blinded by twin fragments of a bursting shell. We condoled with him, and he smiled a happy smile. "Don't waste your pity on me, messieurs," he grinned, turning up the bandage over what were once his eyes. "Think of the other poor fellows! Why, some of them are only slightly wounded! I won't have to go back to the trenches!"

"Come here! Come here!" said the doctor suddenly. "The general is going to give the Iron Cross to three heroes."

We stood in the middle of the room as the general passed among the beds, and stopped at one where a grinning red-haired youth lay with an arm gone.

"For having brought your wounded captain off the field under fire, with the loss of your right arm," said the general simply. The boy whispered something, and they raised him up in bed. Again he whispered, and the general leaned forward and tied the little black-and-white ribbon through the button-hole of his nightshirt.

The next man was still too weak to speak.

"Shot through both lungs," went on the general, "while bringing food from the camp kitchen to the men in the trenches." He laid the cross on the bed-clothes.

The third man's skin looked like ivory, so tightly was it drawn over his wasted face. I noticed his great eyes fixed steadily on the general as he spoke—he had had one leg carried away by a shell and the other wounded. Gangrene had set in and both legs had been amputated at the thigh. He was a famous long distance runner. The general dangled the Iron Cross before him, and he slowly reached out his hand for it and held it for a moment in front of his eyes, twisting it this way and that. Then, without a word, he deliberately held it out at arm's length and dropped it on the floor.

The general went on as if nothing had happened.

Thousands of soldiers in the field gray and the heavy boots of the German army and the little flat caps bearing the red and black buttons, drifted in and out of the cafes, where flowed inexhaustible kegs of the ever-present Munchener beer. There were girls, too—French girls and German girls.

Comines was the place of rest for the men relieved from the trenches. Three days they stayed on the firing line, and anywhere from three to six they lay around and smoked and drank and slept and made love—the number of days of repose depended on the nature of the trenches and the strain of duty. A great French dynamo factory had been roughly made over into a sort of tremendous barracks that held five thousand men. First came the canteen, where soldiers could buy beer and schnapps and cigars for a few pfennigs. Then the long machine rooms, stripped of their equipment, where each man had a twelve-foot box of clean straw in which he slept, played cards, and wrote letters. The machinery of the factory was gone, but the furnaces glowed, and black smoke poured from the chimneys; for the Germans had installed an elaborate system of hot-water heating, laundries, bright lights over the bunks, and in the glass-roofed laboratory a system of seven galvanized steel troughs, each one a hundred feet long, filled with running hot and cold water for bathing—a hot and cold water tank for their heads, one for their feet, and so on. A squad of twenty free barbers worked eight hours a day, and in the big machine shop fifty cooks kept a thousand meals going all the time.

In the French army the men who come off duty often have no adequate place to rest, no arrangements for washing, and no change of dry clothes; for months they are covered and caked in mud, and the smell from them as they march past in the streets of Paris is dreadful. But the Germans are clothed and fed and warmed and rested. The difference is tremendous.

Our good Bavarian friends insisted that we have one more glass of Munchener before we left, and the young officers clung to the running-boards of our automobiles to tell us the end of the last funny story. They dropped off skylarking like boys and waving us goodby. Our four machines crossed the Lys and immediately the booming of far guns, that never ceases in that land, became the dominating note. In Comines, men thought of their families and their girls and their food; beyond it, you felt that battle was the only business of the human race. We caught up to and passed column after column of motor and horse trucks heavily laden, covered with rubber tarpaulins; long files of slouchy, thick-set soldiers—their hands, faces, shoes, clothes, rifles, the monotonous color of mud.

"Hep!" and three hundred dirty figures clicked into soldiers. "Hep!" Their eyes concentrated on our officers, knees stiffened, great feet smote the ground with a blow that shook their bodies, and they goose-stepped past in the mud. Little squads of Uhlans, horses muddied to the eyes, lances awry, jogged along.

A flag post and a battered customs house marked where the French frontier had been. Now we were in Belgium.

The roads and fields were pitted with clean round holes full of water where shells had hit them; for we were now within range of the French heavy guns. One saw no more civilians. Houses smashed with shells; houses with doors hanging by a hinge and windows punched out; houses intact, but blank and empty—fields with the rotting crops half gathered, trees blasted as if with lightning. The country might have been swept by a gust of deadly gas. Everything was concentrated on that shocking jumble of sound that filled the whole north. We overtook five immense motor vans lumbering frontward with two thousand bottles of Munchener on board.

The village of Houthem—or what was left of it—grasped a knot of roads. Long transport trains going to the front, empty trucks coming back, fresh soldiers and those returning from the trenches, cannon, ambulances, and field kitchens laboring along like grotesque steam rollers, met in the little place as in a heart, and poured out again along the pulsating arteries of roads north and south. Only here and there a house stood arbitrarily untouched by a shell. There was the little country hotel and cafe—a sentry before its door—where a General of Brigade had his headquarters. On the front show window were pasted the latest official photographs of the war sent each week to the soldiers at the front, copies of the daily newspapers hurried from Berlin by fast trains every night and distributed in the trenches, Chancellor von Bethmann-Hollweg's last speech in the Reichstag, a circular beginning "Comrades!" and signed by the Central Council of the Social Democratic Party, explaining the causes of the war. The village was full of soldiers, too, standing in little knots and looking down the roads. They were largely members of the Class of 1914 who had not yet been sent into the trenches, but who had been brought here, as an officer told me, to complete their training under artillery fire so that they would get used to it.

"Almost every afternoon," he said, "the French bombard Houthem. They have taken to firing back of our lines in order to smash up our transport service; so now, of course, the transports do not go beyond Houthem except at night."

In the Church of the Annunciation of the Holy Virgin, four hundred young recruits were learning how to salute. A hole in the roof made by a French shell the evening before let in a shaft of light on the great altar riddled with shrapnel, and a great plaster crucifix dangled in two halves. A drill sergeant with his legs crossed sat on the altar steps shouting: "Next two!" Then a couple of rigid young fellows marched stiffly up the center aisle, stiffened, and jerked their eyes to meet his as they wheeled left into the nave, and came back past him goose-stepping, jerking their stubby hands to the rigid German salute.

"Schweinhunde!" he yelled. "Didn't I tell you ———— animals to look at me as if I was your superior? Stiffen your necks, there! You are nothing, you pig-dogs! Remember that! Next two. . . ."

"Now," said our officer, as we climbed into our automobile again, "we are going to see a battery in action. But only two automobiles at a time, and they must travel three hundred yards apart. If the French saw four automobiles, they would drop a shell on us."

We were held up on a bridge across a canal by two Landsturm men with crossed bayonets—grizzled old men of threescore, straight and soldierly, though they had not been training for over thirty years. They saluted with the smart precision of Prussian Guardsmen, and we rolled on into a country where nothing seemed alive except shrapnel bursting miles ahead, and jerky columns of black smoke from a village to the left which was being shelled. Miles ahead the gently rolling land culminated in a long low crest, where there were trees and the smashed roof of a big chateau. No house or shed in all our vista around had escaped shellfire; and yet a beam of sun breaking through the clouds glittered on a long greenhouse where evidently not a pane of glass was broken. Not even soldiers were to be seen—not even transports; only a long parallel row of dainty motor-ambulances on their regular trip back from the Verbandplatz. There was nothing whatever spectacular in the desolation here—or perhaps it was that we had become calloused. It seemed a cheerful country enough, but dedicated entirely to the business of war. The smashed houses and neglected fields were old; so thoroughly were they cleared of anything but war that a peaceful civilization might never have flourished there. The officer who was riding beside me said:

"I don't understand why the French don't fire on us; they have seen us now for half an hour. This is the first time I ever came along this road without dodging Granaten. You see where a piece came through here only the day before yesterday," and he put his finger in a jagged hole in the limousine.

Here an animated discussion arose as to whether we should go any farther in the machines. The older officers said that we were just passing the dead line of the French artillery, beyond which no vehicle and no body of men could move without being fired on. One of the younger officers remarked that it was great fun, and that it was an experience a war correspondent ought to have. I cleared my throat and said that I didn't think it was necessary for my story at all. So we disembarked just as a roaring shell burst behind a railroad embankment two hundred yards ahead.

"That's the battery you're going to see," remarked our staff officer. We straggled along the road under the railroad culvert, crossed a little canal and emerged on a muddy flat. Three short field howitzers, ten feet apart, rested on little platforms of brick taken from a ruined house. They were daubed with the mud of the field, no steel showed, and limbs of trees stuck in the ground around them met overhead like clumps of brush, so that they should be completely invisible to aeroplanes. Four muddy men, smoking cigars and chatting, were loading a cannon in a leisurely manner; two took the shell out of the caisson and, shouting "boom," pretended to throw it at the third, who put up his hands, laughing; the fourth was fiddling with a sighting apparatus. They suspended operations to look curiously at us. To right and left in front were scattered farmhouses, all demolished, and trees with the tops blown off. Straight ahead a sugar-beet field sloped gently up for two miles, and about three-quarters of a mile across it a big shell spouted a roaring geyser of mud from time to time. Beyond lay a greenhouse, and farther still a broken chateau and trees, which marked the crest of the hill and position of the German trenches. One could hear continuous spitting rifles, but, of course, nothing could be seen, except occasional shrapnel smokes poking around in the open field, and the Granaten whistling down into the mud from unseen guns.

Some bedraggled chickens, evidently quite accustomed to the noise, were pecking about in a discouraged way under the cannon. An irritated artilleryman kicked at one—it fled squawking. Crows wheeled and alighted, cawing.

"So you have come to see the guns," said the captain of the battery politely, trying to click his heels in the mud. "Well, it's very quiet here, you know. They almost never find us. Last week we lost a gun and twelve men, but that was just a happy accident on the part of the French. Still, you can't tell—a wild shell is liable to bluster down here any time."

He blew his nose in his handkerchief and nodded carelessly to the gunners. "All right," he said. They jumped back and clapped their fingers to their ears. *Crash!* A flat roar, flame and gray haze belched—and the whistling scream of the soaring shell rose and dwindled. Almost immediately an eager voice cried from the bank of the canal behind:

"*Kolossal!* In the trench! Two and three guns a point down, six left, elevation five-sixths!"

The gunners turned little cranks and twisted screws.

In the side of a steep canal bank behind the guns there was a doorway hollowed out which led into a subterranean chamber. On a battered but fine old Flemish oak bedstead covered with straw lay a young man with his knees crossed. An electric light dangled from a peg driven into a dirt wall. He had a telephone receiver strapped to his ears, a novel lay open against his legs, and he was munching a veal sandwich and reading.

"Can't hear you!" he shouted into the mouthpiece on his breast, and then laughed. "Oh! The same to you. I tried to see you Christmas night. He's gone, eh? Poor fellow!" He listened. "Yes, sir." And then bellowed: "Gun No. 3: half right, three-sixteenths!" A voice outside repeated: "Gun No. 3, half right, three-sixteenths!" The little chamber shook as the two guns fired and flakes of earth came tumbling down.

"The fellow at the other end of the wire is in the trenches beyond that hill," said the battery captain. "He telephones back here the range, elevation and trajectory, and the effect of the fire. We have been here for two months now and we have never yet seen the enemy."

"Cease firing!" cried the young fellow on the bed, and something in rapid German. The captain explained:

"You see," he said, "we have just got news that a French battery of big guns is wheeling into position just outside our range to get after us. If we keep on firing they will find us and we'll wiped out sooner or later. This battery is just cancelled, that's all. Come on outside and I'll show you the French aeroplane coming up to look for us."

The young man with the novel closed it and yawned, unstrapped the telephone from his ears and chest, and preceded us into the open air. Above the chateau roof a black, thin wafer was zigzagging slowly up against the clouds.

"Oh! That's too bad. He won't come," said the captain. "Look." The strumming of motors struck our ears and to our left about half a mile two silvery monoplanes ran jumping out across the uneven ground like ungainly cranes running to take the air. They rose slowly, laboriously, and then seemed to leap forward up a long slanting plane toward the far crest of the hill. The Frenchman hung motionless for a moment, and then went sliding down the air out of sight again, and the two Taubes wheeled and came back.

"Cease firing!" The gunners slowly shut their breach-blocks, slammed the steel covers of the caissons and locked them with a key, put their hands in their pockets and strolled off down the road under the railroad culvert, laughing and talking. We followed behind with the young telephonist and the captain of the battery.

"I think it only fair to tell you fellows," said our officer, when we got back to Houthem, "that you are running a terrible danger in going to that trench. The laufgraben has been shot all to pieces and is full of water, so that in order to reach the trench you will have to go after dark across an open field for about a kilometer—the French fire on that field all night with rifles, machine guns and artillery on the chance of hitting our men, and the mortality is pretty heavy. Of course, there are lulls; but the chances are small of your ever getting to the trenches—about one in five. Then you'll have to stand all night in water up to your waist, and in the place where you are going, we lose six or seven men a day by ordinary rifle fire, not to speak of the artillery."

Another officer nodded. "A shell dropped in the trench today and got six men," he said.

"Well, I am not going to commit suicide," I remarked. "If it is anything like that I don't want to do it." The rest agreed.

"So I think it is better all around," went on Captain Kliever smoothly, "if we start for Lille now." And he prepared to get into the automobile.

We thought about it for a moment; it seemed terribly disappointing to have to return without having seen the real fighting.

"Hold on!" cried my partner. "I'll tell you what. Let us see what we have to do, and if it seems too dangerous we'll go back with you."

The captain couldn't do that, he said, because it would then be too late to reach Lille, for we had to do a mile or so on foot.

"Well, then, take us to field headquarters and let us stay the night there."

"But there is no place to sleep."

"Never mind. We'll sleep on the floor."

And so it was arranged.

At Infantry Brigade headquarters, in a big farmhouse, we drank a farewell glass of Munchener with the general, a dapper little Bavarian with twinkling eyes, who painted sentimental mottoes on cards and hung them around the room. "Gruss Gott tritt ein Bring Gluck berein," we read over the door. In the kitchen an entire wall was one huge telephone switchboard, with twelve operators connecting miles and miles of trenches and headquarters to Lille and even Brussels. Then we were outside in the twilight and falling rain, our blankets under our arms, and our officer waving us goodby from the open door.

"Have a good time!" he laughed. "Not for me!"

Two soldiers with rifles walked in front, and we followed. Ahead, great guns boomed like bells and rifles spluttered.

"It is better here," said the soldiers, "to walk two by two; space sixty paces."

The darkness deepened; the drizzling rain fell. Something went whi-i-i-t! And we suddenly became conscious of a droning in many keys, like the wind in telegraph wires. *Snap!* A bullet hit the fence quite near. *Plopp!* Little stinging pellets of mud showered up from the road.

"Yes," said one of the soldiers. "We lose four or five a day along here. But you get so you don't think about it at all."

Those correspondents who had wives and children began to think of them with a peculiar tenderness.

"It's easy to tell the difference between the spent bullets and the ones that are meant for us," explained the soldier. "The spent bullets sound tired, but the ones with the vicious whine—they've got the stings in their tails. This part of the road from now on the French can't see, even in the daytime; but they tell off a squad to keep up a fire on it day and night."

The road turned at right angles, flanking the shattered walls of what had been a great church, and for half a mile we kept up along a gentle grade where the air was never quiet of whispering and whining and whistling steel. Against the massed black of a wood lay a low solid Flemish farmhouse with two generous wings of stables, which enclosed a big farmyard. Half the roof had been blown off, and there was no light except what came through the cracks of the door.

"This way!" cried the soldier, turning toward the stable. Under a rough shed at the end a flight of wooden steps led underground to a long, low room, whose ceiling was the barn floor and whose sides and floor were the solid earth. At one end half a dozen soldiers lounged on a pile of blankets and coats and sacks of potatoes. A telephone switchboard hummed and buzzed and clicked with faint musical sounds, and a young sergeant with a receiver to his ear shouted continually and took shorthand notes, which another man read aloud. At the other end sat three or four officers bending over a table covered with maps. The oldest, a tell, grizzled, kind-faced man with the stars of a colonel, gave us both his hands.

"Hello!" he said. "They telephoned you were coming. I can't tell you how glad we are to see company out here. It gets devilish lonely when you spend six days in a dugout, and then have to drill recruits all the time you're relieved. Will you have cognac or beer?"

We sat there talking, our coats off and our sleeves rolled up, for the damp heat was awful.

"I spend most of my time down here," explained the colonel, "because the farmhouse up there became untenable. But come on; let's go to dinner, and I'll show you."

We climbed up into the rain again and walked across to the house.

Strange, lurid, blue lights flamed suddenly in the dark behind the trees, intensely illuminating for a second the whole drizzling arc of sky.

"Rockets," explained one of the officers, "so they can see what they're shooting at. That mass of trees there is the park of the Chateau of V———, which King Leopold gave to one of his mistresses. The trenches where you are going lie beyond. We used to go through the Park, which was very convenient; but there have been three battles here, and the ground is torn to pieces with shells, so we have to go around by the road."

Overhead the bullets droned, far cannon bellowed, the rain fell steadily. In the stable soldiers of the reserve were singing to a jerky mouth organ.

We dined in the old kitchen of the farmhouse, a great square room with an enormous curved fireplace and heavy-beamed ceiling black with smoke. In one corner a jagged shell-hole was stuffed with rags, and an opening in the north wall like a door had been covered with planks.

"That's what I mean," said the colonel, pointing to it. "About a week ago I was dictating to an orderly when a shell exploded into the room. You can't tell *when* they're liable to come."

The menu consisted of soup from the field kitchens, canned ox-tails, cheese, bread, white wine and exhaustless bottles of Munchener.

"We Bavarians can't do without our beer. If the beer failed us a day, I think Germany would be beaten," laughed an officer.

There was a duplicate telephone switchboard, and as we dined and chatted the news came from miles and miles of trenches how the battle was going, and was passed on to other headquarters.

Always the telephonist repeated aloud the messages; the colonel didn't seem to pay much attention, but he heard everything, and sometimes broke off in the middle of his gentle talk with a crisp order. He was telling us the story of the Bavarian soldier who fell asleep in the trench, and woke up to find that his company had abandoned it and that a body of French were approaching.

"Shell dropped in B Company trench," sang out the telephone operator. "Three men hurt."

"Telephone for the ambulance, Comines," snapped the colonel. "Schurz! Tell Schmidt to take six men to B Company trench."

Schurz saluted and went out.

"As I was saying," went on the colonel, "he woke up in the trench all alone and saw a company of Frenchmen coming over the field. And as he says, in the Bavarian dialect: 'Well, I kind of thought to myself I'd better make an attack in force,' and he did, and captured forty Frenchmen!"

"They tell another one," said one of the officers, "about an English soldier in the field hospital. The nurse gave him a bath, and after he was back in bed she said: 'I beg your pardon, but I didn't see your wound. Where were you wounded?' 'Oh, I'm not wounded,' he said. 'It is the captain who is wounded; I'm his orderly.'"

"You people drink like real Bavarians," laughed another. "Schwartz! Go get half a dozen bottles." Just then the door opened and in came a young officer covered with mud.

"I've come to escort these gentlemen into the trench!"

We stumbled along the road in the pitch black night, Dunn and I and the officer, chattering fragmentary French and still more fragmentary German. The rain fell steadily. On our right the stumps of trees broken by shell fire pricked sharply up against the hellish illumination of the rockets. The whistle of bullets over our heads blended into an almost steady sound and lashed tree trunks like whips. Half a mile ahead on the left three big howitzers smote the air one after another with deep sound. Footsteps crunched the muddy road.

"*Rechts!*" cried deep voices.

"*Ober!*" responded our lieutenant.

We filed single to the right, flashing our pocket lamps on the ground. Four muddy giants staggered by with a stretcher on which something moaned. Another followed, and another.

"What is the password?" I asked.

"There is no password," said the lieutenant.

"But spies?"

"There are no spies inside the German lines."

We trudged on in the rain, hushed at the splendor of the great sounding guns and the whining network of steel overhead. Horses stamped by, drawing a heavy thing that rumbled like a truck on steel rails. It had a chimney belching smoke and sparks, and left a trail of glowing cinders hissing in the mud. The two men upon it were singing. "*Gruss Gott!*" they cried, "God's greetings!" like the simple Bavarian peasants that they were. "*Gruss Gott!*" responded our companion.

"That's the *feldkuchen*—the field kitchen. Big pots hang inside over the fire. Twice a night they drive as near the trenches as they can go and feed the men from there."

The big guns fell suddenly silent, and away across the fields another battery began. We could see the blinding flash from their muzzles and the pale flicker of flaming gas that whirled around them for half a second after.

"You see," he went on, "they get the range of the trenches in the daytime, and then fire at the same range at night."

The others stopped suddenly. I wondered why the big guns fired and stopped for no apparent reason, and there flashed to my mind the picture of that great switchboard singing and humming in the kitchen of the Brigade headquarters, and the quivering miles of telephone wire from the trenches where muddy men with night glasses watched the French lines under the blinding glare of the rockets, and spoke things into a little metal tube strapped on the chest; of question and answer and calm deliberate judgment, from trench to gun again, to Houthem, to Comines, Lille, Brussels—

"*Ober!*" said many voices, and I bumped into men stumbling along in the dark.

"Artillery relieved," said the lieutenant shortly.

A Meldendienster on a horse, another stretcher with its four carriers, two feldkuchen, stragglers—life poured along that road. We were near the central nervous spot upon which all these elaborate telephones, transports, hospitals, barracks, starred uniforms, decorations, Iron Crosses, kings and emperors— the social, political and economic forces of a great Empire—were concentrated: a single line of men four hundred miles long.

The road emerged into a great highway turning sharply to the right.

"The road to Ypres," said the lieutenant.

"How far is Ypres from the trenches?"

"About six kilometers."

To our right hand the western wall of the park still paralleled the road. On the left the flat sugar beet fields stretched over gently rolling country, vast stretches of rain-soaked mud, broken by little clumps of trees and small farms. Strange lights flickered here and there where lay knots of men, or guns, or patrols. The gutters beside the road poured heavy water. The rain fell steadily. Bullets whizzed all around us now. Up and down the road were little mysterious flashes of light where men snapped on their pocket lights to see where they were going. A sharp cracking snapped about our ears, the light caliber revolvers.

"Explosive bullets?" asked Dunn.

"No," answered our guide. "Just bullets, hitting the wet mud. This stretch of road is in full sight of the French, and they keep up a steady fire on it til morning on general principles. We lose at least twenty men a night here. We had better string out, I guess."

A dazzling, bluish-white fireball sprang into the sky, smoking, hung there in an unearthly blaze, showering sparks, lighting vividly every rotting beet plant, trees, houses, miles of country, checkering the road with the sharp shadows of tall trees—and snuffed out in a vicious burst of rifle fire.

"French light rocket," explained the lieutenant, as a gust of bullets swept the mud around us like a handful of dried peas. "They can't see us on this road. Light's bad. Too many shadows."

"*Ober—Rechts!*" Another stretcher passed. A man stumbled against me in the pitch black and cursed. Rearward, a great gun suddenly bellowed and ceased. A shrill, gigantic tap—tap—tapping began, halted, began again, syncopated with another. The air was suddenly alive with whistling steel. In less than a second it had ceased.

"That's luck," said the lieutenant calmly. "French machine guns. They swept us twice. Now we are right back of the trenches, and all these bullets you hear come from the French firing at our men. They always fire a little too high, and that's what makes it dangerous for us."

We turned abruptly to the right through high-pillared stone gateposts, and breathed a sigh of relief behind the solid walls of the chateau stables. Then came the chateau itself, a great square building which had once been three stories high and was now one and a half. We picked our way through piles of broken stone, brick and splintered doors.

"The English held this place," continued the lieutenant, "and hardly a man got out alive. Our guns did that about the first of November." He nodded toward the shattered house.

In one of the cellar windows a light gleamed.

"Come down and say hello to the major," invited the lieutenant. "He is in direct command of the trench we are going to. He was quite a pianist before the war—made a concert tour in your country, I believe."

We found the major installed deep in a roomy, stone-vaulted wine cellar, remnants of magnificent oak brocaded furniture around him, and tall gilt pier glasses. At one wall the usual soldier fronted the usual singing switchboard, monotonously repeating messages. The major sat at the chateau's grand piano, which he had found miraculously unscathed under a wreck of stone and plaster, running his fingers idly over the keyboard.

"I say," he cried, when we were introduced. "So you are Americans! Tell me, do you know the beautiful Miss Clark of Washington, D.C.? I can't get over that girl!" he said. "Ah, well, perhaps it's a good thing the war broke out, or I would be hanging about Washington still. She is simply too beautiful . . . and I have lots of time to practice here."

Need I say that we drank a bottle of Hoffbrau beer with him?

"There runs the laufgraben." The lieutenant pointed to what appeared to be a small canal. We passed through a great breach in the wall which encircles the park, and sank to our ankles in the sucking mud of the open sugar beet field. For miles a monstrous arch of blazing rockets linked the French and German trenches together.

"You see, they quite destroyed part of our laufgraben with shell fire, and then one lucky shot hit on us. That is the Ypres canal—that broad dark line that parallels the laufgraben. Wait for another rocket and you can see the bridges."

We staggered forward in the mud ten feet apart.

"There go our guns again," he went on. "The French guns aren't working tonight." Bullets snapped and crackled like a forest fire, slashing us with mud. The rockets shone reflected on the black waters of the canal, which marched northward straight as a Roman road. The laufgraben here turned away from the canal and zigzagged up a little hill. We scrambled down into it, plunging up to our knees in soft mud, and struggled on, staggering, falling, thrusting our arms to the shoulder in the wet slime of the trench side. The rain continued to fall. The trench mounted, became shallower, so that we had to stoop, and the ground was harder beneath our feet. A rocket burst into diabolical radiance straight above and settled slowly down on us, cascading sparks.

"Out of the way," grunted a voice, and we flattened ourselves against the muddy wall as a stooped man staggered past carrying a limp body on his back. Then, in the pitch black, we were among dark forms slouching about and talking guttural Bavarian; the secondary trench opened to right and left; to the right marching unbroken like the Great Wall of China to the North Sea; to the left joining the "Unter den Linden" thirty miles south, and thence three hundred miles to the Swiss frontier.

"Guten Abend mein Kinder!" greeted the lieutenant.

"Guten Abend!" answered a score of voices.

He plunged his hand down on the right as if into the solid earth, and a little square of light appeared, just large enough to crawl through. Inside it was quite four feet high and eight feet square. The ceiling was of tar building paper, glistening in the light of a candle with drops of hot sweat. Moisture oozed slowly down the mud walls, and the air was heavy with the smell of earth and with steam. Soggy curtains of gunny sacking hung across the door. A wooden floor showed occasionally through drying mud. Across a bench at one end slouched four soldiers; clothes, hands, face, and hair the color of mud; one with the invariable telephone on his ears and chest, and a portable steel switchboard hanging from a peg in the earth, humming and buzzing. Every minute or so the peg board fell off; he caught it dexterously, patiently drove the peg in a new place, and hung the switchboard back. A young lieutenant sat on a pile of straw in the corner talking familiarly with the soldiers and pulling on a pair of mud-caked riding boots. The other corner was occupied by three dozen bottles of Munchener.

"Come in and sit down," he cried in French with a grin, "and have a drink. We're rather crowded in here, but all the extra bedrooms are occupied by Belgian refugees, as the English say!"

He set himself to work pulling corks, served us, then the soldiers, then himself, and called out to the grinning faces in the doorway to know if they had enough out there. They replied that they had.

"Do you know why this trench is so dry?" said he. "This whole section is paved with beer bottles. Just wait a minute until I get these confounded boots on and I'll take you around. What do you want to see first?"

We said that we wanted to see everything. He led the way into the drizzling rain and along the trench. Thin lines of light showed in the black wall on either side—the dugouts of the soldiers.

"We have about a thousand men in my section," he explained, "a third of them on duty fighting all the time in the front trenches. They shoot for two hours and come back here for four."

"Do they sleep in these places?" I asked.

He laughed and, reaching down, lifted a ragged curtain. A candle burned inside. The floor was soggy mud, cluttered with straw. Water dripped steadily from the ceiling. On a bundle of rags and pieces of blanket lay a man exactly the color of the mud walls, from head to foot, reading a week-old copy of the Berliner Tageblatt. He looked up, grinned, nodded, and raised his hand in salute.

"Now we will go to the front trench," said the lieutenant, turning sharply to the right.

We plunged again into deep, sucking mud, struggling forward, sinking suddenly up to the thighs, and being pulled out by those ahead and behind. This cut was narrow, and we scraped continuously against the legs of mysterious men lining both sides who were three feet apart. The lieutenant plowed ahead, bawling:

"Inspection! Attention for the American reporters!" And we could feel the stiff muscles of their bodies as we brushed them, standing rigid, knee-deep in mud.

"We just keep these fellows here on Guard," said the lieutenant. "Don't use them much. Damned rotten trenches, these. Dug by the French. We took them just three weeks ago. If it were not for the boards under your feet you would sink completely out of sight in this muck. We put in fresh flooring every day, and in three hours the damned boards have disappeared."

And now, suddenly, we were in the front trench. Leaning against its front wall men stood shoulder to shoulder, shielded by thin plates of steel, each pierced with a loophole through which the rifle lay. Sodden with the drenching rain, their bodies crushed into the oozy mud, they stood thigh-deep in thick brown water and shot eight hours of the twenty-four—nor slept the rest of the time. For three days they kept this up—and these men had been there three days, for they were to be relieved at four o'clock. The shooters paid no attention to us. Through their loopholes they stared absorbed, alert, into the blackness, waiting until the next rocket should show the least movement above the edge of the French trenches. By its light they got the range and took a sight on a few meters of heaped-up earth, and when it went out they kept on firing in the dark. The lieutenant ordered one of the soldiers to stand aside and invited us to look through the loophole.

"We are going to send up two or three rockets for you so you can see the French trenches. They are only eighty meters away, and if you will look about twenty yards from here you will see the bodies of the French who fell in their last attack. They came on in columns, four abreast, as the Prussians did at Liege, and our machine guns got every one."

The rocket-pistol cracked. A twinkling point of light spiraled up, became a blinding, ghastly sun, and fell slowly. Before it was out another followed, and then another. For a minute it was as bright as day. Up a gentle hill straggled the French trench, a black gash pricked with rifle flame. Between lay flat ooze, glistening like the slime of a seabed uncovered by an earthquake. Only a little way off lay the huddled, blue-coated bodies of the French in three thick, regular rows, just as they fell a week and a half ago, for there had been no cessation in the firing.

"Look," cried the lieutenant, "how they have been slowly sinking into the mud! Three days ago you could see more. See that hand, and that foot, sticking up out of the ground; the rest of the bodies have sunk."

We saw them, the hand stiff, five fingers spread wide like a drowning man's.

"No need of graves there. They are burying themselves!"

All at once, far down the line, the sharp, flat roar of cannon—one-two-three-four! began.

"Tiens!" said our friend. "The French."

The squealing of shells in flight grew on us, and the shrill explosions of shrapnel.

"After the trenches!"

One-two-three-four!—One-two-three-four!

They leaped along the French line in great bounds, without reverberation, smashing the doors of sound. Diabolical whistlings laced the sky, and shrapnel cracked suddenly near, back over our heads, and past, showering their scream-ing bullets, cracking and splitting into the mud. Far down the trench a man yelled, the rifles crackled into a steady roll. Excited men pumped their hot breach-blocks spouting empty shells, firing madly into the dark, for the rock-ets had ceased for the moment.

One-two-three-four!

Then, immeasurably deeper, whacking the air, the great guns opened. Far away a mighty lightning split the night, and the roaring, accumulated thunder of a bursting big shell smote our ears and sent us reeling. Behind us the Ger-man howitzers began again, and we could see the blasting flame leap from their Granaten half a mile behind the French trench. The ground shook, and we were conscious of no rifle fire, so deafening was the heavy roar of the cannon. Shrapnel were bursting quite near us now. We found ourselves floundering along in a staggering run toward the secondary trench, our one confused idea to get back into the lieutenant's dugout. A heavy thing hurtled into the earth two hundred meters ahead and blew up like a world exploding. For minutes, it seemed, the air was full of hissing mud and singing steel.

"No use in here," grinned the lieutenant when we were under cover, "if anything comes this way."

"What is the chance of getting out of here?" I asked.

"Oh, you had better wait until it is over."

He sat down with a grunt of relief and began pulling off his boots. "I do hate wet feet," he remarked, parenthetically. "No; when they are turning the ar-tillery on you, the safest place in the world is a trench. It's narrow, you see, and almost impossible to drop a shell in—they can't get the range by night, and the recoil of the gun shifts it a little eventually. They don't keep it up long."

Almost as he spoke the tremendous noise chopped suddenly off. Such a si-lence rushed down!—a silence in which the never-ceasing rifle fire sounded like crickets in a pasture.

A little while later, as we lay about smoking in the hot moistness, the tele-phone operator beckoned to us.

"Somebody wants to speak to the two Americans in the trenches," he said. I put the receiver to my ear.

"Hello. It's Major F———; you know you met me in the cellar of the chateau. Well, I'm giving a concert, and I thought you'd like to listen."

"We took turns, Dunn and I, with the receiver—while for half an hour the major played Chopin waltzes on the grand piano, and bullets swished over-head, and men stood to their thighs in muddy water shooting each other.

When it was over, he spoke again. "Wait a minute! I'm switching you on so you can hear the applause." Click! A confused buzzing, incoherent words of thanks, "Sehr schoen!" in many voices, and the clapping of hands.

We hung up.

"That's to show you how delicate our instrument is," said the lieutenant. "I could connect you with a trench three miles away, and ask them to hold up the mouthpiece, and you could hear rifle shots. Perhaps twelve regimental and brigade headquarters listening to that concert, and all the officers on trench duty for fifteen kilometers. He plays for us every night."

It grew on toward morning, and already the reserves just off duty were splashing in single file down the laufgraben on their way to Comines.

We said goodby to the lieutenant on duty and followed them; down the hill through the deep mud of the approach trench, up the slippery bank and across the clinging field whipped still by snapping bullets. But the firing was less intense, and only an occasional rocket glared. It was as if both sides were exhausted by the long strain and the excitement of the plunging shells.

Along the road we caught up with the soldiers, straggling along with rifles carried under their arms, and drooping shoulders; silent, for the most part, with the silence of desperately weary men. A stretcher went along unnoticed in their midst, and one man leaned on two companions. "Rheumatism," he replied to our officer's questioning.

"That is terrible in this part of the line." He shook his head. "Almost a third of the regiment has it."

Suddenly a man immediately ahead began to scream. We could not see him in the dark, but we could hear moans and unintelligible yells, and the scuffle of struggling feet. A moment later the lieutenant flashed his pocket lamp on, and we saw him. A gag had been forced into his mouth; ropes bound his arms tightly to his sides; two comrades held him firmly by the elbows, forcing him forward. His wild, staring eyes snapped wide like a savage beast's at the sudden light— he wrenched his muddy shoulders convulsively to and fro. He was quite mad.

"Another one," muttered the lieutenant. "They have to gag him because his shouting would attract the French fire."

We walked briskly ahead, passing the last shuffling man, and were alone again, on the road that led to the farmhouse. None of us talked much—we had a good deal to think about.

The lieutenant took hold of my arm and halted us. "Hark!" he said. "Here comes the relief! This is the real spirit of the Bavarian army."

A humming deep chorus of hushed voices grew upon us. It grew nearer, gained in volume, swing, power, but still subdued; ranks of marching blackness grew from the deeper black and the thud of myriad heavy feet in perfect time. And so, singing "Grosses Gott, wir lieben dich!" the thousand men from Comines, washed, dried, fed and rested, swept past us to take the places of those who had been as irresistible and strong as they, and would in turn come up the road a resurrected race, also singing hymns as they swept into battle.

Back of Billy Sunday

(May 1915)

Billy Sunday, the sweat pouring from his red face, his trembling tense left leg thrust out behind, both arms stretched wide, as he leaned out over the vast crowd like a diver, shouted hoarsely:

"Say, it would milk any bishop dry to stand here and preach eight or nine weeks! If you don't believe me, try it."

And twenty thousand people, worked up to the point of hysterics by loathsome descriptions, funny stories, and the uncanny, long-drawn "O-o-o-oh, come to Jesus!" broke the tension in a mighty shout of laughter.

So Billy, and "Ma" Sunday, his wife, and George, his son and business agent, and *his* wife and baby, motored to John Wanamaker's country house for a day of rest.

Billy had preached sixteen sermons in six days, they said. Homer W. Rodeheaver, his choirmaster and chairman, was also visiting out of town. Jack Cardiff, his ex-prizefighter trainer and bodyguard, was holding evangelistic meetings on his own account in Reading. Bentley D. Ackley, his secretary, pianist, and the composer of his gospel hymns, was playing golf at Whitemarsh. Joe Steice, his mechanical inventor and tabernacle constructor, who insists on non-union labor for the glory of the Lord, was at the Central Trades Council, they said with a grin, showing organized labor the wickedness of being organized. Mrs. Ascher and Miss Saxe, subsidiary preachers, alone did not alter their schedule. They were organizing workingmen and working girls in the factories into Bible classes.

At the white-faced house on Spring Garden Street, which was rented for Sunday, other less important members of the party were about—large, determined-looking women with glasses and a breezy middle-western twang, running up and down stairs and talking loudly about household affairs. A big, raw-boned Swedish woman, with the light of Salvation in her eyes, opened the door for us and let us into the parlor—which was the most screamingly hideous example in the world of what bad taste and much money can do. There were heavy gilt moldings, a "satin-finish" wallpaper of violent green leaves and purple morning glories, mirrors from ceiling to floor, fearful oil paintings in shadow boxes, bunches of artificial lilacs in vases with red electric lights concealed in them. There were enormous wreaths and bunches of flowers standing everywhere, presents to Billy Sunday; pictures in heavy gilt frames; a two-hundred-dollar Victrola; and a railway engine made entirely out of baby-blue wicker, four feet high and seven feet long—presented, full of flowers, by the railroad men of the Reading. A white-haired stout old lady, with the exultant look of a village social leader who has ruined her worst enemy, loomed upon us in the corner. Without any preface she said:

"You're the newspaper folks, ain't you? Well, we've jarred this town loose! We've stirred 'em up some! Huh! Conservative Philadelphia! Conservative indeed!"

Two male members of the party chewing toothpicks were reading the stock reports in the evening papers. One said:

"I tell you what, Jim; with wheat going the way it is now, those fellows that got in on wheat shorts are certainly the lucky guys!"

He rose abstractedly from his seat, slipped in a record, and the Victrola produced dismal strains of "Way Down Upon the Suwanee River." The violent smell of continuous cooking drifted from the dining room, the clatter of dishes; lady members of the party in aprons shouted to one another, "Jane, haven't them beans come yet?"

A STEADY STREAM of clergymen in chokers, and Y.M.C.A. officials with the hard eye of an efficiency expert, and pale, undernourished converted stenographers and clerks, and fat, emotional women in furs, drifted in and out. The entrance of Mr. Rodeheaver, and the loud voice of the servant girl saying, "Homer, there's a couple of magazine men in there," caused us to rise.

"What do they want?" said Mr. Rodeheaver, suspiciously.

"They want to see Mr. Sunday."

Mr. Rodeheaver came in, a short, stocky man with a deep, sanctimonious voice, suspicious eyes, and the kind of a clammy hand that won't let yours go.

"No boys, I can't help you. You'll have to see Mrs. Sunday. She runs everything around here. If she tells you that you can see Billy, you can see him. Yes, I'm a convert. All the party are converts of Mr. Sunday's. You come back tomorrow morning."

So it occurred to us that we might pass the time interestingly if we looked up members of the Sunday Campaign Committee who had invited Billy Sunday to regenerate Philadelphia.

Now the Campaign Committee is composed of forty-four of the most prominent businessmen of Philadelphia, and about an equal number of clergymen. For the clergymen, we went to the Reverend George H. Bickley, vice chairman of the entire committee, a hard-eyed individual with a slack, enthusiastic mouth.

"The reason for getting Billy Sunday here is quite simple," he said smoothly. "It is moral regeneration—the saving of souls—the first step in the regeneration of the city, the state, and the country. Reform is in the air. A number of the most prominent businessmen in Philadelphia, realizing the futility of materialistic reforms—you know, that kind of reform doesn't last, while conversion to Christ does—determined to invite Billy Sunday here to preach. The bringing of men to Christ is the first prime fundamental reform; and, of course, after that is accomplished no other reform is necessary. If all men were converted the world would be good."

"What is it that determines Sunday to come to a city?" I asked.

He misunderstood the spiritual nature of my question.

"The Citizens' Committee secured pledges to the amount of $50,000 to underwrite the cost of the campaign," he said glibly. "We took the pledges to the banks as collateral, and borrowed cash to float the enterprise. In that is included the cost of the tabernacle, rent of offices, employment of staff, literature and rent of halls for meetings, rent of house for the Sunday party, and all other expenses while in town, and payment of two-thirds of the salaries of Mr. Sunday's assistants, which run from $25 to $100 a week. There are eighteen in the party, and most of them are on the payroll. Mr. Sunday himself pays the other third *out of his own pocket*." He paused and fixed us with his cold eye. "Mr. Sunday doesn't get a cent of that," he said.

"What does he get?" we asked.

"Well, on the last day a thank offering is collected for him. In Wilkes-Barre it amounted to $19,000; in Scranton, $21,000; and in Pittsburgh, $29,000. Philadelphia will probably give him anywhere from $30,000 to $50,000."

"Not bad wages," we said to ourselves, "for ten weeks of work." "And now, Mr. Bickley, does Sunday's preaching have any particular effect on social and political conditions?"

"Just what do you mean?"

"I mean, will it help make politics any better in Philadelphia? Will it help workingmen to get a living wage? Will it help clean up the Third Ward, where 130,000 people live packed in one-room tenements in the worst square mile of slums in the world?"

"It will!" said the Reverend Bickley enthusiastically. "It will redeem men from the improvidence that comes from drinking. Slums, you know, are largely the fault of those who live there—dirty, disreputable, vicious people. I can give you two examples. Only two weeks ago, a manufacturing man from Riverton, N.J., came to hear Sunday and 'hit the trail.' He had been accustomed to carousing with his associates in a club, and spending his nights in cards and liquor. He returned to Riverton a new man, and went ceaselessly among his vicious associates preaching Jesus Christ. The following week he set down five hundred of his employees, and more than a hundred were converted. The other was the son of a millionaire, who was fast dissipating the wealth left him in sacred trust by his father among vile women and viler amusements in the low places of Philadelphia. He owns a woolen mill. One night he went to the tabernacle to scoff at Sunday, and was filled with the vision of Jesus Christ; the next day that man stopped work at his mill at ten o'clock in the morning and had Billy Sunday preach to his workingmen, and he also testified to his own conversion."

"Did he raise wages after being converted?"

"N-o," admitted the Reverend Bickley. "You see, he has only been converted a week. You don't seem to understand; raising wages is a question of economics, not of religion. It would be utterly impossible anyway to raise wages in the textile industry with conditions as they are. What we need is the Republican Party in power before we can hope to do that."

"So the logical result of Billy Sunday's sermons would be the election of the Republican Party?"

"Well," he agreed, "we hope it will help." We burst out laughing, and he had the grace to blush as he hurriedly said: "But that is not the important thing, you understand."

The list of the Citizens' Committee reads like a compendium of Philadelphia's rich, respectable and socially great. One encounters such names as Bonsall, McQuilken, Drexel Biddle, Stotesbury, John Wanamaker, Ball. Of the forty-five, twelve are captains of industry, twelve bankers, at least four eminent corporation lawyers, three city officials, the president of the Union League Club, the provost of the University of Pennsylvania, the president of a Wanamaker newspaper, the presidents of Girard College and Temple University, the general secretary of the Y.M.C.A., and the vice-president of the Chamber of Commerce.

Directly or indirectly, all the great industrial corporations in and around the city helped to bring Billy Sunday to Philadelphia; the Baldwin Locomotive Works, Cramp's shipyards, the Midvale Steel Company, the Pennsylvania Railroad, the Reading Railroad, Wanamaker's store.

I was curious to know why they had done it, so I went to see Mr. Alba B. Johnson, president of the Baldwin Locomotive Works.

He is a large, well-fed man of slow, deliberate movements, a ruthless mouth, and the coldest, most businesslike eyes behind his spectacles that I ever saw. I did not take stenographic notes, but as he talked directly at an open window, behind which his stenographer was concealed, these remarks can doubtless be verified. He said, in answer to my question of why the businessmen of Philadelphia had invited Billy Sunday to their city:

"I had long decided that what the country needed was a moral awakening. Purity, modesty, contentment and thrift—the virtues which made the American people what they are—have been crumbling before our growing ostentation and extravagance. Saloons and dance halls and low theaters are corrupting our laboring classes, just as the fashionable whirl is corrupting society. The universal craze for riches is sapping the moral strength of the race. Why, a poor man mortgages his house to buy his wife silk dresses and himself an automobile. There are immoral plays on the stage, sensual and licentious dances in private houses, and women and young girls go about the streets in disgusting and immoral clothing which reveals every line of their bodies. People's minds are obsessed with material things. Some way we must turn their thoughts and their hearts to things of the spirit. What we need in this country is a Moral Influence."

"By material things, Mr. Johnson," I said, "I suppose you mean labor agitation and such phenomena?"

"Yes," he answered, "among other things. You know the widespread Social Unrest is largely due to the workingman's envy of those who make a little more money than he does. Now Billy Sunday makes people look to the salvation of their own souls; and when a man is looking after his soul's good, he forgets his selfish desire to become rich. Instead of agitating for a raise in wages, he turns and helps some poorer brother who's down and out."

"But," I objected, "when you people, who employ thousands of laborers, are converted, doesn't it also cause you to turn your own thoughts to your soul's salvation and make you forget the terrible slums where your workingmen live?"

"It has entirely the opposite effect," returned Mr. Johnson, with a smile. "When men are converted to true Christianity, they are always inspired by its noble and high ideals, which make them love their brothers better. The first step in civic reform is to reform men's souls. The Christian desires beauty and goodness naturally. Men must be converted individually, by personal appeal and not in the mass."

I thought to myself that this was exactly the way Mr. Johnson talked about organized labor—that it was better to hire men "individually" and not "in the mass."

"What is the effect of Billy Sunday's campaign upon practical political and economic questions? Does it help to solve the unemployment problem, for example?"

"The unemployment problem," said Mr. Johnson with some asperity, "cannot be solved that way. That is due entirely to too much Democratic administration. If the Republicans were in power, the problem of the unemployed would settle itself."

What does conversion do to a man? What were the conditions in the mills and factories administered by these gentlemen inspired by "noble and high ideals"? I went to the labor unions and asked the workmen employed in the Baldwin Locomotive Works, of which Mr. Johnson is president, and they told me a bitter and terrible story.

In Baldwin's they use the infamous piece work contract system, by which a man with a family sometimes makes $13 a week; laborers work ten hours for $1.50 a day; there is a compulsory Sick Benefit Association, which does away with damage suits for injury or death. The plant is congested and so few are the safeguards that the Garretson Hospital is kept busy with the great number of injured workers that are constantly taken there from the Baldwin Works. Strike after strike, broken with private detectives, armed guards, the blacklist, testify to the workers' hopeless fight for the right to organize. I heard the tragic story of the great sympathetic strike of 1910, when the city police stood in the middle of the street and shot into the factory windows. The strikers won; pledges were solemnly given by the Baldwin Locomotive Company, and most of the other large plants around the city, that the men should be allowed to form unions in the shops, that they should deal with their employees collectively through elected committees, and that no one should be discharged because he belonged to an union. In 1911 business depression hit the Baldwin Company; thousands of men were laid off, and among the first to be discharged were the members of the men's committees, who were cynically told that this was the chance their employers had been waiting for.

Today in Baldwin's the men dare not admit belonging to a union. And that is true in the other big industrial concerns of Philadelphia. In Cramp's, where the last strike, in 1901, was so bloodily and thoroughly suppressed, the workers have never dared to strike since; they are paid comparatively low wages and they work nine hours a day. Conditions in the textile mills are like Lawrence. I asked a textile union officer about the mill owned by the young millionaire convert that the Reverend Bickley had told us about; he grew sarcastic and profane. In most of these plants the Blacklist and the Bible class march hand in hand.

The list of the Citizens' Committee reads almost like a roster of the

Penrose-Vare-McNicholl machine, for a description of which I must refer you to Lincoln Steffens's "Philadelphia, Corrupt and Contented," published in 1903. What is Billy Sunday doing in that *galere*—Billy Sunday who, from the pulpit of the tabernacle thunders day after day against graft, corruption, and the misuse of great wealth, and says: "Philadelphia is one of the most religious cities in the country and the rottenest politically"? He shakes his fist in the faces of 20,000 people and cries: "Christ is in this city! He has seen every stone laid in Philadelphia. He has heard every lie; seen every false vote; known every vicious thought; every sneer at high and holy things; every yielding to low ideals; every corrupt practice, every oath, every theft." How can he accept as converts the 130 members of the Thirtieth Ward Republican Club who hit the Sawdust Trail under the leadership of City Treasurer William McCoach, a prominent member of the Penrose gang? How can he allow Treasurer McCoach to say, "The Republican organization in Philadelphia stands for all the principles of Christianity laid down by Billy Sunday in his teachings. Look at Jim McNicholl: he is one of the greatest churchmen in Philadelphia. Same way with the Vare boys."

How is it that Billy Sunday, who pledges 40,000 men to vote against liquor in the next election, can receive a eulogy from Mr. Walter H. Finley, the Camden saloon-keeper and vice president of the New Jersey Liquor Dealers' Association? Why is it that the members of the Penrose machine, who are tied up with the liquor interests of the state of Pennsylvania, support Billy Sunday when he preaches his blasting sermon on "Booze"? "Too many men in Congress owe their election to the liquor interests," cries Billy. "Wherever I can I shall fight every man who wears the brewery collar."

But Billy Sunday is tactful. When he preaches against booze, he preaches against drinking, and not against politicians. He advises the people to vote for local option, which is just what the Penrose machine advises them to do. When he inveighs against graft, corruption, and the evils of enormous wealth, he nullifies the lesson by something like this:

"I have nothing to say against the rich man. Solomon was worth about three billions of dollars if you reckon his wealth according to our standard of gold and silver. He could have hired Andrew Carnegie to black his boots, or Rockefeller to hitch up his horses, or J. Pierpont Morgan to dust his clothes and cut his lawn.

"But there's a lot of good-for-nothing lobsters think they are called by God to go up and down the country harping for a limitation of wealth and cussing and damning the rich man for every dollar he has, while they sit around and cuss and damn and never work.

"If you want to use your genius and ability to get all you can, and use the surplus over your own needs for the good of humanity, I hope you all will be millionaires."

In the same breath he curses child labor and striking workingmen, the greed of rich men and the envy of poor men. But he mentions no names.

When the Philadelphia *Public Ledger* challenged Sunday openly to tell the truth about the men who were backing his campaign, Sunday consulted his wife and answered as follows:

"If that editorial is aimed at the men who serve on my Campaign Committee in this city, why doesn't the *Public Ledger* go after them directly? I never introduce personalities into my sermons. I attack corruption in politics itself, not particular men. I would not for any consideration whatever endanger the work I am doing for God by injecting personalities into it at this stage."

Day after day from his pulpit in the tabernacle he denounces "the cocktail drinking, gambling, indecently dressed, automobile-riding, degenerate God-forsaken gang you call Society. You put Society first," shouts Billy. "If you put God at all, He has to come tagging along after some beer, wine or champagne-soaked Society leader, and God has to play second fiddle and be a trailer to every jackrabbit proposition that comes along."

Hence it is with some surprise that we see Billy suddenly breaking into Philadelphia Society. He visits John Wanamaker's country house, rides to meeting in his automobile, and accepts Mr. Wanamaker's invitation to address the Lincoln dinner of a Friendly Association composed largely of Mr. Wanamaker's employees, where he is egged on by Mr. Wanamaker to convert 68 of the employees. Mrs. E. T. Stotesbury holds a reception for him. Mrs. Anthony Drexel Biddle holds another. He is the Smart Set's newest sensation. A newspaper account of Sunday's visit to the Drexel Biddles said that the audience was "one of the most distinguished assembled in Philadelphia for years. Every set and clique of fashionable society was represented. Leaders in finance, law, the church, medicine, the big mercantile interests of the city, were among those present. It would be easier to print the Social Register and be done with it than to give a complete list of those present."

And to these people Billy Sunday spoke not of cocktail drinking, degenerate, or "indecent" dressing. No. He said, with an admiring smile, "Philadelphia society folk take their religion seriously."

Mr. Kraft, of the Central Labor Council, informed me half-heartedly that organized labor had put the Billy Sunday tabernacle on the Unfair List, because it had been built with non-union workmen. He answered my question about what he thought of Billy Sunday with a laugh. "I haven't heard of any of the boys being converted yet," he said, "but they may be. You see, it is not the workingmen who go to hear him. It is the clerks and stenographers and little business people." I remembered that Mr. Alba B. Johnson had told me the same thing, and then he had said that these were the people that it was the most important to convert, because they governed the city and the state.

"But look here," I objected to Mr. Kraft, "what about the Bible classes that Sunday and his assistants go around forming in the factories? What about the five or six delegations from the big factories which are given reserved seats at every meeting in the tabernacle? What about the eight thousand Pennsylvania Railroad men who are coming to hear Sunday preach Wednesday evening?"

"Well," he said, doubtfully, "you see, most of those places are not organized, and besides, I think Billy Sunday is doing a fine work. I believe in God myself, you see."

Then Mr. Kraft went on to explain that the streetcar men were being treated so well that they *didn't need a Union!*

It needed only that last touch to convince me that union labor in Philadelphia is as dead as the Church, and that, if it doesn't actively aid Billy Sunday, Alba B. Johnson, and Boies Penrose, at any rate it doesn't oppose them.

Why should it? Billy attacks Labor no more than he attacks anything else. Occasionally he refers in accents of sorrow to "the strike-maddened crowd." He says:

"Sometimes people say to me, 'What will be the outcome of the labor question?' I don't know. Sometimes they ask me how the problems of capital are to be solved. I don't know. But I do know that there will be a judgment, and that it won't be a class judgment. Capital and labor, rich and poor, idler and toiler, all will stand alike in Judgment." And he is continually preaching contentment to the workingman, the detachment of his mind from material things—"To serve God in the place where He has called him." He says: "The stone that lies deep at the foundation of a building has a bigger job than the flagstaff on top."

What about the Church? Some three hundred ministers joined in the invitation to Billy Sunday to come to Philadelphia. Philadelphia is notoriously religious; and the old rich congregations, with their pastors, have been Boies Penrose's sturdiest support. Then don't forget that every convert who "hits the Sawdust Trail" in Billy Sunday's tabernacle—and at this writing there are more than 25,000 of them—writes the name of the church and pastor he prefers on the little card under the printed words, "I now accept Jesus Christ as my personal Savior." That means 25,000 new church members—for a while, anyway.

So the clergy can afford to put up with Sunday's bitter denunciation of them as "ossified, petrified, dyed-in-the-wool, blown-in-the-bottle, stiff-as-apoker, cold-as-a-dog's nose Pharisees! The church, in her endeavors to serve God and Mammon, is growing cross-eyed," he cries. "You preach a kind of religion detached from civic and daily social life." And then, characteristically reversing himself: "The church needs more of God and less of strife, money and politics."

According to his custom, Billy Sunday attacked the Unitarians as "infidels" when he first came to Philadelphia, but the Unitarians, who are powerful, returned his fire with such good effect that Billy abandoned the attack immediately.

Some criticize him because he is vulgar and undignified; others praise him because he produces "a healthy, emotional disturbance in the community." Neither of these opinions is of the least importance in discussing Billy Sunday.

But the Rev. David M. Steele points out that Sunday's methods are the methods of the Negro camp-meeting exhorter, and hotly denounces the debauchery of little children, 2,400 of whom hit the trail. And the Rev. George Chalmers Richmond has emphasized the deadly parallel between Billy Sunday's exhortations to Christianity and the corrupt political affiliations of his Citizens' Committee.

In the morning we went back to the house on Spring Garden Street, and Ma Sunday came down to where we sat in the parlor. She looked at us suspiciously.

"You're the magazine boys, aren't you?" she said. "Well, what do you want?"

We said we wanted to see Billy.

"What did you want to see him about?"

We wanted to get acquainted with him and ask him a few questions.

"What kind of questions?"

"Well, I don't know; about himself; about his work."

"Well, you can't see him today," said Ma. "He's busy all morning with delegations of ministers from Buffalo and Richmond, Va., and Boston, and other places—all those cities want to get him there. And then this afternoon, after the sermon, he goes to bed and rests until the evening talk."

"Well, can't we talk with you, then, for a little while?"

She hesitated, scrutinizing us sharply with her alert brown eyes—a good-looking woman of middle age, handsomely dressed, of quick, certain movements, and an air of thorough practicality.

"I can give you boys five minutes," she said suddenly. "Come on into the dining room, where we can talk alone. Now fire them at me. What do you want to know?" She nodded, seating herself.

As we talked she made nervous swift movements with her hands, picking up things and slamming them down.

"I am very curious," I said, "to know what it is that induces Mr. Sunday to come to a city."

"Well, in the first place, the Citizens' Campaign Committee must guarantee the expenses of the campaign—in Philadelphia $50,000—"

"I mean the spiritual reason," I said.

She picked up my hat, crushed it, and dropped it.

"Are you a Christian man?" she asked suddenly.

"I am not," I responded.

"Then," she said firmly, "I can't discuss those things with you. All I can say is that every one of Mr. Sunday's movements—and mine—are directed by God."

We digested this.

"The Reverend Dr. Bickley told me," I said, "of the moral value of converting men individually. What I want to find out is, from your long experience, if you have noted any immediate practical good to come out of Billy Sunday's campaigns. Do they purify the social and political life of the city?"

"Every soul saved," she answered, "votes straight and acts straight. There are twenty-five thousand new people in Philadelphia today living according to the dictates of Jesus Christ—"

At this moment a woman came in. "Chicago's calling you on the 'phone, Mrs. Sunday," she said. Ma excused herself and flew into the telephone booth, the door of which she left opened.

"Hello!" we heard her say. "Who is this? Oh, yes, the agents. No, I tell you I wouldn't sell for less than twelve thousand. That's the fourth time in two weeks you've called me up to offer a low figure. What are they all nibbling after that lot for? Are you holding something back on me? Is there a boom on in Chicago? No, I told you before I won't sell for less than twelve thousand. You can tell those fellows they haven't got a chance with ten thousand five hundred. You tell them I won't consider it. Say, just make 'em understand—not from me, you know— that if they want to offer eleven thousand five hundred I'll listen to 'em. But I won't sell for less than twelve thousand."

She hung up the receiver and came back. "I've got a lot out in Chicago," she said, laughing, "that there's been nothing doing on for a long time. Now they're all after it. I think somebody's trying to put one over on me."

"Reverting to Billy Sunday," I said, "what is the effect of a Sunday campaign on the industrial conditions of a city? Does it help to solve the question of unemployment, for example?"

She fixed me with a steely eye. "The poor you always have with you, the

Old Testament says. And you can't go against the Old Testament. I haven't got any patience for a man that can't find a job. He has usually wasted his strength and his brain through drink, or cigarettes, or women."

"But how about the textile workers in Lawrence, for example? There a man gets wages that do not enable him to support his family. If he gets converted, does he get any better wages?"

"If he gets converted," said Mrs. Sunday, impressively, "and shows by his actions that he is trying to do good and live cleanly, the well-off Christians in that town will help him."

"But suppose there are twenty-five thousand or more underpaid workmen."

She disregarded this. "I say that a Christian can always buy his own shirt, no matter how poor he has been. I've seen thousands and thousands of people get converted and begin to make good money right away. A good Christian is always successful, and when a man gets converted and accepts Jesus Christ as his personal Savior, he quits drinking and gives his money to his wife. Then there's lots of men who are perfectly good men, but who indulge themselves with light literature and tobacco. When those men get to be good Christians they take that money they have spent on books and cigarettes and buy loaves of bread for their families."

She hastily quitted us, for there was a delegation of ministers from Richmond, Va., waiting to be led upstairs to see Billy. As we passed out, the ministers were filing up. Mrs. Sunday leaned over the top of the stairs and shouted down to them:

"Say, don't you gentlemen speak a word to those two reporters. They're slick."

One of the Sunday party later told us that Billy had been invited to Washington as well as to Richmond. "But you see," he said, "we don't know what to do about the color line. We've all been in conference several days seeking spiritual guidance. We don't know whether to have a Jim Crow tabernacle, or to alternate meetings of blacks and whites. It's very difficult."

One of the Richmond ministers later on told me that they were seriously considering whether or not Billy Sunday should preach a Jim Crow heaven. Billy, of course, put himself on record in a sermon to the effect that "A black man is just the same as a white man in the eyes of God." But it won't bother him to reverse himself.

Mr. Ackley informed me that a Citizens' Committee, consisting of silk manufacturers and the reputable clergy of Paterson, N.J., was inviting Mr. Sunday there. "You see," he said, "Paterson has always had the name of being a turbulent and unchristian city; and they think that Mr. Sunday will turn the thoughts of the working population to the salvation of their own souls, and regenerate Paterson." He was talking this way after the afternoon service, when we had returned to the house in the forlorn hope of getting past Ma Sunday and seeing Billy. The secretary sat at his desk in what had evidently been the library, a room quite as hideously furnished, upholstered and decorated as the front parlor. Telephones rang unceasingly at his elbow, typewriters clicked, ten or twelve newspapermen hung around joshing familiarly with him. In front of the desk was the bed where he slept—indeed, beds were set up everywhere in the halls and on the stair landings—and at the other end of the library a screen marked off the temporary chamber of Jack Cardiff, ex-prizefighter, ex-actor, and now physical trainer and rubber-down to the evangelist. A cord was stretched from the bedpost to a tack near the window, upon which hung the shirt and underclothes of Billy Sunday, wringing wet from the afternoon sermon. Jack himself was in his undershirt after rubbing Billy down. He had the face of a pleased child, entirely simple—and he blushed when my companion asked to sketch him.

"I was well on my way to be the welterweight champion of the world," said Jack. "When I converted I was getting $800 a week to fight in theaters. It's been three years ago now since I heard Billy Sunday and saw the Light." His face glowed with satisfaction and real happiness. "Yes, I sure gave up something for my Savior, but it was worth it. I've been with Billy now about a year, sparring with him and rubbing him down. He's a great man!

"Most people can't see why I got converted at all, because I never smoked, and I never went with women, and I never drank a drop of liquor in my life. I used to go around with the boys all the time, and I used to see them drink and smoke and all that, but I just kept out of it. I've been in Europe, too," he went on with naive vanity, "fought twice in London. I got offers to go to Paris, France, and Berlin, Germany, but I says to myself, 'Jack, if you go across there and get down among them cafes and beer gardens, God knows whether you've got strength enough to resist.' So I passed them up."

"What country did your people come from?" we asked him.

"Well, I've got a little Welsh and English and Irish in me; but my old man was born in this country." He chuckled. "He's about seventy-five years old, as hale and hearty an old man as you ever see. He can go six fast rounds, and he's smoked continuously ever since he was a kid, and drunk enough whisky to swim to Ireland and back." Mr. Cardiff chuckled admiringly.

We suggested that he might take us in to see Billy Sunday as he lay in bed, and he answered: "Sure. Just wait till I get my shirt on." So we gathered by Mr. Ackley and went into a front room, where, robed in white pajamas, in the midst of an enormous bed, Billy Sunday lay reading a book by the light of an electric lamp over his shoulder.

"Here's a couple of fellows from a New York magazine," said Ackley. "They wanted to shake hands with you."

Billy lifted his head with the swift movement of an animal and looked at us with eyes in which cordiality, appraisal, doubt and fear of ridicule chased themselves like wind on water. The upper part of his face was extraordinarily alive and expressive; his mouth was strong, mobile, enthusiastic—trembling into a kind of embarrassed grin. He looked at us as if he thought that perhaps we had come to persecute him. He looked at Cardiff, and then at Ackley, for an explanation. The gray thin hair on top of his head was almost invisible, making his face seem incredibly boyish—for Billy Sunday is fifty-two. Since the sermon a gray stubble of beard had sprouted on his cheeks and chin, and there were sagging pouches of flesh and tired lines at the corners of his mouth.

"I'm glad to see you, boys," he said, smiling a little doubtfully. "What can I do for you?"

"We sat next to you in the tabernacle today, Mr. Sunday," we told him, "and heard you speak. But we just thought we would come in and shake hands with you. We wanted to see what kind of guy you really were."

With a delighted smile he dropped the book and thrust out both hands.

"Well, now," he said heartily. "I like that. I'm real glad you came. Sit right down."

We asked him what book he was reading. It was entitled "All's Love, All's Life," by Rev. James L. Gordon of Toronto, Canada, and Billy was studying a chapter called "The Theory of Vibrations," liberally sprinkled with religious poetry. "I've read a doggone good deal," said Billy, tapping the book, "and I tell you this is one of the best books I ever enjoyed. This man Gordon, he's a real fine writer."

His eyes and face were full of easy, childlike enthusiasm. He discovered that I had just come back from Europe.

"Say," he said in wide-eyed admiration, "there's too many bullets flying around over there for me. A fellow's got to have a good deal of courage to go over there now, hasn't he?"

We asked him what he thought of the war, and his eyes suddenly filled with tears.

"I think it's the most horrible, awful thing in the whole world," he said earnestly. He was proceeding, but there was a swift rustle of skirts behind us, and the nervous voice of Ma Sunday snapped:

"You villains! Didn't I tell you you couldn't see Billy? What have they been doing, Billy—pumping you?"

She went over to him, pulled up the covers, lifted his head, and turned over the pillow for him.

"Not a pump," laughed Billy. "They're just good-natured human beings come to shake hands with me."

Is Billy Sunday sincere? I think he is. I have seen him absolutely dominate two audiences of twenty thousand people in one day, and I do not believe he could put the fire and passion and enthusiasm into his words and actions if he were not sincere. He is generous, even reckless, with his money—he seems to have no idea of its value. Everyone who talks with him loves him. As to the social, economic, and political relations of the world about him, I think he is just ignorant, that's all.

On Logan Square, about a block from the magnificent home of McNicholl, the Boss of Philadelphia, is the Billy Sunday tabernacle, holding twenty thousand people and built out of wood and tarpaper, to serve the ten weeks' revivalist campaign. Flanking it is the temporary fire-engine house with its equipment and sleeping quarters for a full crew; the temporary police station; the immense temporary restaurant and literature store, and the baby-checking nursery furnished with every toy that money can buy, and served by ten volunteer nurses. The emergency hospital, handling sometimes a hundred cases a day of hysterics, emotional fainting, and accidents from the enormous crowds, is inside the tabernacle itself. Next door is the newspaper room, with its chairs and desks and twenty telephones for the use of the men crowded in the two great press boxes which flank the platform.

We started for the tabernacle early that evening, yet already street cars in uninterrupted lines disgorged their crowds on Logan Square, and a slowly moving mass of automobiles crammed every approaching street. Two blocks from the immense building we passed the first barrier of street hawkers selling hymnbooks.

Rodeheaver and Ackley, who write respectively the words and music of the new hymns, have a monopoly on the hymnbooks, and sometimes they sell a thousand a day at $1 apiece. A slowly moving mass of thousands of people was packed before the many tabernacle entrances. Great yellow arc-lights shone on them. The hawkers shouted: "Git yer hymnbook here! Git yer only authorized life of Billy Sunday!" All was laughter, excitement—like a circus. Although none of the Sunday party had arrived, ten thousand people in the tabernacle were already singing hymns by themselves. One voice began, and at the end of the first line a thousand joined in; then somebody would start another hymn; three or four different songs were running counter to one another in immense choruses like the shock of a cross-sea.

We sat staring out across that limitless waste of faces, our faces on the level of the platform from which Billy spoke. It stood about ten feet from the ground. In its center was a small wooden pulpit raised and strengthened with steel rods, so that Billy could climb on it. A trapdoor to the right of the pulpit gave into a little pit in which Billy sat when he shook hands with the converts. A great space in front of the platform like a half a circus ring, was left empty and covered with fresh sawdust; eight wide aisles led into it. Those were the "Sawdust Trails" down which the faithful stumbled to seal their conversion by shaking hands with Billy. Immediately behind the platform, on the same level, was the grand piano, at which Mr. Ackley, industriously chewing gum, presently took his seat. Beyond that, sloping up gradually, fan-shaped, to two immense red and black signs reading: *Get Right With God!* and *Saved for Service! Christ in Philadelphia! Philadelphia for Christ!* were the reserved seats for the visiting delegations of ministers and for the choirs of eighteen hundred trained voices, three of which alternated with one another during the week.

This choir, by the way, was of immense service to Billy in getting his effects. Right in the middle of his sermon on "Booze," when he had painted in furious words the fate of a drinker rotted by disease, forsaken by his family, going down into the very flames of a burning hell, the choir burst into "The Brewers' Big Horses," all provided with Klaxon horns and automobile whistles —which jerked the frayed nerves of twenty thousand people into laughter. And then one time Billy told of the return of the Prodigal Son, his mother on her deathbed with a broken heart, his father sodden with drink because he had lost his only son, the home sounds and the home memories and the home smells that came so poignantly to that youth across his years of wasted life . . . until in the audience forlorn and starving men, who had been unable to get work, trembled and began to sob. All at once these eighteen hundred voices began to sing very softly, "Home, Sweet Home," and Billy, stretching out his arms over the auditorium cried, sharply: "Come home to Jesus! Come home now! Jesus is holding out his arms to you." More than a thousand were converted that time.

WHEN EVERY SEAT in the house was crowded, and the window-like apertures around the immense hall were thronged with the heads of those standing in the outside aisle, choirmaster Rodeheaver mounted to the platform with a trombone which he laid on the pulpit. Above his head extended the scalloped sounding board with the legend, "Patent Applied For," which was invented for Billy by his chief mechanic, Joe Steice, and which enables his voice to reach the farthest corner of the auditorium. Rodeheaver's job was to work up the congregation by getting them singing.

"Well, folks," he shouted, "let's have the 'Ninety and Nine.'" Ackley beat upon the piano, and it and every other sound was lost in the roar of twenty thousand voices singing a song they knew and loved. Erect at the pulpit, Rodeheaver led with the trombone, waving it up and down as he played. He tried to stop them at the end of the first verse, but could not be heard, because the twenty thousand had started the second on their own account.

"And now," he said at the end. "I understand there's a delegation here from the Lawton Machine Works. Will the delegation from the Lawton Machine Works please stand up?"

They did so, two hundred of them, to a roar of applause.

"That certainly is a fine-looking bunch," he shouted. "What hymn do you like best?"

"Two hundred and forty!" came the roar.

"We'll sing it," said Rodeheaver, and they did.

"And now the delegation from the Franklin National Bank." The same performance was gone through. Rodeheaver glanced at his slip of paper and muttered an aside to the press boxes. "Say, fellows, how to you pronounce V-i-a-v-i? There's a delegation here from a company of that name." We told him.

"Let's see the folks from the Viavi Company," he shouted. They stood up. "I was afraid to try and pronounce that name," he continued to great laughter. "Glad to see you tonight, folks." And then, in another aside to the press box: "What do they manufacture over there? Some kind of dope?" And then aloud: "Yes. We're very glad to see such a fine-looking bunch of folks."

Then they sang "Brighten the Corner Where You Are," one of those good old revival hymns with an almost Negro swing to it. The crowd refused to stop singing "Brighten the Corner" until they had gone through four verses. "Now we'll cross the house with it," shouted Rodeheaver. "You on the left sing the first line; you on the right the second; the last twenty rows the third, and the policemen and firemen standing around at the doors will sing the fourth line." It was done, and so effectively did the police and firemen render the fourth line that the crowd delightedly insisted on the performance again and again. "Those police and firemen have certainly got religion since we've been here," shouted Rodeheaver amid laughter. "Now we'll try the visiting ministers and see if they've got religion too. You clergymen, take the fourth line."

During the singing Billy Sunday himself came down the steps to the back of the platform, followed by his bodyguard, Jack Cardiff, and by Ma. He threw off his fur overcoat with a quick, nervous movement and stood looking over the house with glowing eyes and a delighted smile, singing. Mrs. Sunday beckoned to him and spoke to him. He leaned down to hear her, never stopping the song. As he stood there he grew visibly more exalted. Violent emotions passed over his face—sometimes almost imbecile with exultation, sometimes twisted and tortured; the muscles of his wiry body jerked beneath his clothes; he twisted and wrenched his clasped hands behind him. Then the music ceased and he bounded to the platform like an athlete and stood beside Rodeheaver. A string of men came up the central aisle, bearing gifts. The first was a large canvas bag of money.

"This money is the gift to Mr. Sunday from the Germantown Bible classes," said Rodeheaver. "Will the Germantown Bible classes please stand up?" They did, filling the whole end of the auditorium—a thousand or more.

Billy grinned and hefted the bag. "Huh," he chuckled, "that's certainly very generous of you folks, huh. I've certainly got a lot of good friends. Glory to God. I'll use this money to help along the good work. I always bank a tenth of what I get in the Lord's name—give it to charity. I get lots of letters for money, but I don't sit down and write a check to some fool I don't know anything more about than a Fiji Islander—huh—no, sir, I don't consider that good charity nor good sense either. I give to folks that are investigated—needy folks that are worthy."

This was an echo from Billy Sunday's speech when he took up a collection for the Organized Charities of Philadelphia, in which he absolutely reversed his speech of a week before when he fiercely denounced organized charity for letting people starve to death while they investigated. But then the Citizens' Committee was heavily interested in the Organized Charities.

The next gift was a religious picture framed in heavy gilt from the Franklin National Bank employees. Neither the money nor the picture seemed to make a great impression on him; but when the Lawton Machine Works men handed up a beautifully finished, sixteen-bore shotgun, with a letter stating that it was to defend his home and kill the devil, Billy's delight knew no bounds. He chuckled continuously, turning it over in his hands, looking down the barrel, testing the trigger.

"Why now," he said, "that's *wonderful!* That's a dandy! Will's been teasing me for a shotgun for the longest time. I'm going to take this gun out to my ranch in Oregon. Say, that takes me right back to the old Iowa log cabin where I was born, when I used to go out through the autumn woods, through leaves dyed red in the October sunshine, after turkeys with my gun and my dog." He paused and put the shotgun down.

"The women have requested me to preach tomorrow the sermon on Booze. Don't like to do it particularly, but I'll just do it for the women."

He strode up and down the platform for a minute, walking quickly and more quickly. Suddenly he wheeled and shot his arm out at the people.

"My text tonight," he cried, in a high, harsh, tense voice, "is 'Woman, is it well with thee? Is it well with thy husband? Is it well with the child?'" He snapped off his voice, but held his arm extended like a menace.

There was not a sound in the huge auditorium. "Could it be well with you if the police were hunting for you?" He let his voice drop, then suddenly shook both fists above his head, and lifted his right knee almost up to his chin, roaring: "Then how could it be well with thee if the powers of Heaven are against you. I tell you, it don't make any difference whether you're ignorant or not if you don't repent! You'll go down to flaming hell to fry on the coals forever.

"Do you hear me? This is the last chance for Philadelphia! This is the last chance for Philadelphia! Repent or you are lost!" He kneeled on top of the pulpit and lifted his hands above them. "If you want your sin"—his voice dropped again—"well, you can just take your devil and go to the devil with him!

"Huh," he said, grinning; and then shouted: "O-o-o-o-oh men and women, don't let God go! Just let me tell you, you be good and scared of God! I'm going to tell you a story to show you how Jesus Christ punishes unbelievers." He told of a young Scotchman, strong, intelligent and healthy, who had come to Chicago when Billy was doing gospel work among the immigrants. The Scotchman was born of strict Covenanters, and had turned out to be a thorough atheist. Billy prayed with him to repent, but the Scotchman only said: "You can't convince me. There is no God."

Then Billy went on to tell how many years later he had been called to a charity hospital to see a dying man. "I won't tell you what I saw," said Billy. "That man was dying of a loathsome disease. His body was a mass of putrefaction. His nose had rotted away. Diseased matter was oozing from his eyes." A shudder of disgust ran through the crowd. "He recognized me, and he said: 'Billy, you were right. I want you to introduce me to Christ.'"

Sunday suddenly flung himself across the platform like a baseball player sliding for second. "It's too late, Philadelphia!" he bawled. "It's too late. Come to Jesus!" He turned to the clergymen's bench. "Come o-on Church! Come on! In the name of God, let's rescue the perishing!" He threatened the clergymen. "Why do you swell up like poisoned pups?" he snarled, stamping his feet. "Where did you Methodists come from if not from the blessing of God on Charles Wesley? Where did you Lutherans come from if not from the blessing of God on Luther? Where did you Presbyterians come from if not from the blessing of God on John Calvin? And you sneer at a revival!" He squatted and leered at them. "Don't you know that when you sneer at revivals you spit in the face of God, that you jab your hands in the bloody palms and feet and side of Jesus Christ—that you laugh at him on the way to Golgotha—that you laugh—ha-ha-ha-ha!"

He staggered across the stage like a drunken man, howling like a Negro evangelist. "Don't you dare sneer at a revival," he said, solemnly, "you infinitesimal, miserable, puny, pigmy intellects! There's lots of these highbrow churches where the elders have taken so many pills that their joints are all ball-bearings." He grinned: "And before they get a book of gospel hymns they have to wait for the consent of the official board. Why, if you had to wait until that bunch did things, you'd be dead and buried and the devil would have had you forty years before anybody noticed it. Religion is a music-maker huh—glory to God! Hallelujah!"

"Amen!" shouted voices, and "Hallelujah!"

"Sing!" cried Sunday, thrusting his left leg out behind him. "I don't care if you don't know a note from a horsefly. Sing 'Ring the Bells of Heaven for There's Joy Today,' and you'll start the heavenly harmonies a-jangling." He was red in the face now, and the sweat was pouring from him—climbing on the pulpit, sliding from one end of the platform to the other, crouching like a runner, leaping, crouching, every movement as graceful as a wolf's. His lithe, springy body beneath his clothes was as beautiful as a Greek runner's. When he wrenched himself into a contortion twenty thousand heads and shoulders involuntarily followed.

He painted them vivid pictures from the Old Testament.

"The Bible is a great picture-book," he cried. "It is the most wonderful picture-book made—it never wears out." He switched suddenly to tell of the feast of Belshazzar. "Night was about to come down on the famous city of Babylon, and the shadows of her two hundred towers lengthened into lines, and the waters of the Euphrates rolled along, outlined by the splendor of the fiery setting sun; the hanging gardens of Babylon wet with the heavy dew, began to pour forth their fragrance. The haunts of pleasure invited the wealth and pomp and grandeur famous in that old city. A royal feast had been proclaimed by Belshazzar. Chariots drawn by fiery-eyed steeds stamped and reared and plunged, and their charioteers drove them furiously around corners, as thousands of lords and ladies, dressed in the glories of that Assyrian age, came to the banquet. I hear the rustle of their silks and the carols of the music, and I see the gorgeous banquet hall as they fill and quaff from the goblets. I tell you, it was no common sauerkraut, wienerwurst, pretzel, and lager beer crowd that was invited that night. It was the real goods." And he went on in his terse American way to tell them of the handwriting on the wall. "Belshazzar's countenance changed, his thoughts were troubled, the joints of his loins were loosed, his knees smote one upon the other, and I tell you old Bel was about all in that night."

From that he switched suddenly, inconsequentially, to the loathsome description of an unbeliever rotting from disease. Suddenly, he shook them by a long-drawn bestial howl: "It's too late, Philadelphia!" Then he pulled their excited nerves into laughter with a funny story; calmed them with another vivid picture; and jerked them into cold terror with a hideous prophecy of perdition.

He broke off in the middle, crying suddenly: "Do you know anybody you want to be saved? Stand up! Have you a husband, a wife, children, that you would like to see converted?" All over the tabernacle they rose by hundreds. "Brother!" they shouted; "Sister!" "My babies!" "My husband!" "God will take you all," cried Sunday. "I don't care if you have been made drunk with your mother's milk! As long as there's one sinner in the world, the world'll be bad.

"Huh," he grinned, "can't you see that? Turn a sinner loose in the world, and the world will stink. You can't cure the smallpox by crawling between clean sheets. Turn a polecat loose in the parlor, and see which'll change first. You make me sick," he bawled, "you give me a stomach ache, blaming the church for its shortcomings. No, you big mutt, go home and look in the looking glass and say to God, 'There's the sinner!' I could walk through this audience with blue and white ribbons and hang them on every person in this tabernacle; on one person would be the word 'Saved' and on the other 'Lost.' Come on. Who's coming to Jesus Christ!" He made one leap across the platform, jerked open the trapdoor, and dropped into the little pit. The sermon was over.

A dirty old man without a collar stumbled up the aisle with a dazed look of one hypnotized; a little boy about eleven years old followed him, weeping bitterly; a tall girl in white furs with a white drawn face staggered after him. Everywhere all over the tremendous hall you could see the Voluntary Church Workers hustling people into the aisle, turning them forward as they went toward the exit, climbing over the benches and plucking the shaken ones from their seats and leading them forward. An endless steady trickle of hysterical women, children and men of all conditions and ages poured along the Sawdust Trail. They flooded into the open space in front of the platform, weeping, hardly knowing what they did.

Billy leaned down from his pit, keeping up a steady stream of wild, incoherent talk, an exultant smile on his face, the sweat pouring from him. Guided by the church workers they filled up the Glory Benches up front, row after row, their eyes fixed steadily and glowingly upon Billy, moving unconsciously as he moved, bursting into shouts of "Hallelujah!" until there were more than six hundred of them. Among them circulated the church workers with the little cards which read: "I now accept Jesus Christ as my personal Savior," and giving the names and pastors of the churches to which they wished to be affiliated.

Billy Sunday, the tired lines on his face accentuated, the light dying from his eyes, put on his fur coat and went slowly up the aisle toward the door where John Wanamaker's automobile waited for him. The faithful Jack Cardiff followed him closely, warding off the mobs that tried to get to him, the hands that many stretched out to touch him as he passed.

We left yet unconverted; but there didn't seem to be anything else to do. Philadelphia was saved.

Notes

Introduction

1. There is no standard edition of Reed's writing. Of his three nonfiction books, only *Ten Days That Shook the World* is readily accessible as a single volume. More readily available is *The Collected Works of John Reed*, a Modern Library edition published in 1995 that contains the complete texts of *Insurgent Mexico, The War in Eastern Europe,* and *Ten Days That Shook the World.* For ease of reference, I cite page numbers for Reed's books from the Modern Library volume; e.g., the epigraph to this introduction is from *Ten Days That Shook the World,* pp. 575 and 580. For works contained in the John Reed papers at Harvard University's Houghton Library, I use the library's citation system for the Reed collection: bMS Am 1091, followed by the folder number; I cite page numbers for manuscripts and typescripts when they are given. In long quotations, paragraph breaks are frequently omitted.

2. Finnegan's intriguing project takes a quite different approach from this book. Finnegan says he is "not interested in recovering Reed's works as 'lost masterpieces'" (8) and wishes to study Reed as a cultural artifact capable of "unleashing . . . revolutionary writing as a form of communal dialogic chorus capable of 'naming the system' on a geopolitical, historical scale" (9). Finnegan is particularly interested in Reed's celebrated countercultural shenanigans such as his organizing industrial workers to sing revolutionary lyrics to Harvard fight songs, traveling to Mexico with Mabel Dodge in flaming orange corduroy, firing a shot in the general direction of the French army, briefly joining a Red Guard troop in Petrograd, and wrangling an ambassadorship from Leon Trotsky in the early days of the Bolshevik regime: "Such mass media exploits and interventions, traditionally relegated to the margins of Reed's criticism and modernist studies as anecdotal asides, are central to understanding Reed's texts" (128), Finnegan contends. He draws interesting conclusions by considering Reed's work in the light of contemporary queer theory—particularly in the broader sense of queer as "odd, irregular, and idiosyncratic," as well as in its narrower sense as sexually adventurous or ambiguous. Finally, Finnegan's work and my project join in the following goal: "If Reed's narratives are worth recovering at all, then they are so because the recovery of them, along with the recovery

of other elements of our forgotten/repressed past, will work to continue to open and dialogize the American canon" (161).

3. Of particular note among these critics are Phyllis Frus's *The Politics and Poetics of Journalistic Narrative;* Dorrit Cohn's *The Distinction of Fiction;* Shelley Fisher Fishkin's *From Fact to Fiction: Journalism and Imaginative Writing;* Lillian R. Furst's *All Is True: The Claims and Strategies of Realist Fiction;* John Hellmann's *Fables of Fact: The New Journalism as New Fiction;* Naomi Jacobs's *The Character of Truth: Historical Figures in Contemporary Fiction;* Barbara Lounsberry's *The Art of Fact: Contemporary Artists of Nonfiction;* and the collection of essays edited by Norman Sims, *Literary Journalism in the Twentieth Century.* See also essays by Eric Heyne and by Daniel W. Lehman in the October 2001 issue of the journal *Narrative.*

4. Unless otherwise noted, all text references to Rosenstone are to his *Romantic Revolutionary.*

5. The example of Reed's uncle apparently stuck with him; on two occasions Reed himself either nearly received commissions from foreign powers or perhaps spread the rumors that he had. While Reed was covering Pancho Villa in Mexico, word filtered back to New York that Villa had appointed Reed a brigadier general, and *Metropolitan* published a note about it. An embarrassed Reed had to prepare a clarification for the magazine's November 1914 edition. In 1917, Reed was appointed Soviet consul to New York by Leon Trotsky. Fellow reporter Albert Rhys Williams recalls that Reed said to him: "When I'm consul, I suppose I shall have to marry people. I hate the marriage ceremony. I shall simply say to them, 'Proletarians of the world, unite!'" (208). V. I. Lenin canceled the appointment when Alexander Gumberg, a U.S. citizen with ties to both the Bolsheviks and the U.S. government, managed to discredit Reed over a scheme to finance a prospective newspaper (Williams, 207–11; Rosenstone, 314).

6. One can easily recognize the way that Eliot's college-days criticism foreshadowed his classic essay "Tradition and the Individual Talent": "[I]t is not the 'greatness,' the intensity of the emotions, the components, but the intensity of the artistic process, the pressure, so to speak, under which the fusion takes place, that counts . . . the difference between art and event is always absolute" (469). Of necessity, the work of literary journalists like Reed directly challenges Eliot's rigid separation of art and event.

7. Reed's typescript in the Harvard archives contains an interesting exchange between Reed and the subject of this anecdote, identified only as W. T. Fisher. A handwritten note on the first page of the typescript: "For God's sake, cut this silly lie if it's about me.—Fisher." Reed's handwritten reply: "Now I begin to believe it. The Harvard radicals haven't any sense of humor" (bMS Am 1091:1139).

8. In her essay "The Paterson Strike Pageant of 1913," Linda Nochlin describes such pageants as "mass art par excellence" (90). She shows how the radicals co-opted the form from patriotic pageants and masques that celebrated civic achievement. Nochlin concludes: "Reed may be said to have turned the patriotic rhetoric, the well meaning melting pot psychology of the do-gooder civic theater leaders, back upon itself, revealing its idealistic vision . . . for the sentimental cant it was" (93).

9. If anecdotes from the Greenwich Village Bohemian community can be believed, Boyd was not always so wise or patient. Stories have it that Boyd twice pulled a gun in

the presence of friends—once at a drunken party on the week that World War I broke out in Europe (Homberger, *John Reed,* 80) and a second time when Boyd waved a revolver in the presence of Reed and Louise Bryant and offered to kill Eugene O'Neill on Reed's behalf as retribution for the playwright's affair with Bryant. Boyd "became enraged and determined that the only solution was to buy a gun and kill O'Neill," writes Bryant biographer Mary V. Dearborn:

> Lacking the money to buy a pistol, at around four in the morning he appeared drunkenly in the doorway of the bedroom Louise and Jack shared in the house on Commercial Street demanding forty dollars. "Jack asked him what he wanted it for," Louise wrote. "He said that he had to kill Eugene O'Neill because I was untrue to Jack and Gene was the culprit." In response, Jack leaned over and kissed Louise and told Boyd to go home and go to bed. (54)

10. Examples of this sort of criticism can be found in Harry Henderson's "John Reed's Urban Comedy of Revolution," which contends that "art is typically distinguished from journalism by its appeal to a unity based on probability rather than randomness of phenomenal detail" (423) and considers Reed's work to be "gropings toward major form" (424); and in John S. Bak's "Eugene O'Neill and John Reed: Recording the Body Politic," which concludes that "Reed's work never transcended their social message as O'Neill's did, and that's why he is remembered more as an historian than, like O'Neill, as a literary artist" (32).

Chapter 1

1. The turn of a new millennium has seen an explosion of interest in what is variously termed creative nonfiction or literary journalism. Scores of new creative-writing programs specializing in nonfiction have sprung up at universities. Three journals specializing in nonfiction—*Creative Nonfiction, River Teeth: A Journal of Nonfiction Narrative,* and *Fourth Genre*—began publication in the 1990s. Journalists working on texts with literary ambitions consulted each other regularly through online discussion groups like WriterL and gatherings such as the "Neiman Narrative Journalism Conference" at Harvard University and at the Poynter Institute in Saint Petersburg, Florida. Debate about what can and cannot be done under the aegis of literary reporting and creative nonfiction remains lively. See Neiman Foundation for Journalism, *Neiman Reports* 54, no. 3 (2000).

2. One of the few scholarly sources regarding Reed's work on Billy Sunday other than the Harvard archives and Reed's original *Collier's* article can be found at the Billy Graham Center Archives at Wheaton College, Illinois. The archives place Reed's reporting ("Hitting the Sawdust Trail with Billy Sunday") on Sunday in the context of hundreds of other contemporary reports. Reed's was one of the first articles on the evangelist, who at his prime commanded entire newspaper supplements and daily coverage in the cities where he appeared.

3. Reed's roster of names at the IWW trial may have been influenced by the

November 1, 1917, issue of the *New International* in his possession (bMS Am 1091:1561). Under the title "The I.W.W. Arrests and Trials," the article lists the names of eighty-two who were arrested. The names that Reed chose for his article lie near the top of the article, but Reed rearranged their order to make the sequence of names scan more poetically.

4. Reed's "Goutchevo and the Valley of the Corpses" passage from *The War in Eastern Europe* still retains its power to implicate readers. It produced significant reader response when it was reprinted in 1999 by *River Teeth: A Journal of Nonfiction Narrative*. An edition of Reed's reporting from the Balkans released in 1995 by a London publisher, Phoenix Press, also includes the famous passage.

5. Reed's coverage of the Paterson jail perhaps owes a debt to Charles Dickens's "A Visit to Newgate Prison" or to Henry Mayhew's *London Labour and the London Poor*. Reed's strategy of telling readers about the horrors and colorful personalities he found behind bars functions in a way that is similar to the narratives by Dickens and Mayhew. In all cases, the narratives deliver on journalism's promise to bring narratives of impact, conflict, and unusualness—factors that build news value in the budgets of newsroom editors—to the homes of news consumers (see Lehman, 121–30, 199–200n).

6. Rhetorically, Reed seems also to want the reader to understand that the power to control history hinges on the power to control narrative, thereby anticipating a claim made by historiographer Hayden White some seventy years later: "To acquiesce in the adequacy of a given way of representing 'reality' is already to acquiesce implicitly to a certain standard [or ideology] for determining the value, meaning, or worth of the 'reality' thus represented" (135). Reality and ideology, then, to both Reed and White, inescapably are intertwined.

7. "In Short," an unpublished piece that Reed wrote from El Paso in 1913, reveals Reed's notion of the way historical narrative responds to economic and cultural assumptions. Reed reports that he asked Americans in El Paso to summarize Mexican characteristics and found that it mattered much whether they thought him a journalist or a potential investor. Here I will give one example among a half-dozen that Reed cites in his manuscript. On enquiring about the Mexican character: "Information for journalists: He is treacherous, untruthful, lazy and cruel. Information for investors: He is gentle, patient, a good worker when he wants to be, happy on very little and honest. You never lock your door in Mexico" (bMS Am 1091:1148).

Chapter 2

1. Although considerations of genre are never exact, a writer's decision to use a real name in a text carries enormous weight. In most cases, the use of real names in a text labeled as nonfiction signifies the text's narrative operation on an actual body or bodies rather than on imaginary characters. Such an operation opens up legal claims of defamation and libel, among other textual and social ramifications. See Lehman, *Matters of Fact*, 7–15, for a more extended discussion.

2. Finnegan presents a fascinating "counterintuitive queer reading" (245) of "Another Case of Ingratitude": he explores the possibility that the protagonist's desire to

obtain a story from the bricklayer might also disguise a desire to solicit him for sex. Finnegan attaches significance to the narrator's placing "a box of cigarettes in front of the newly fed, 'transformed' hunk of a man . . . [then] offers him a match," which Finnegan calls "perhaps the most widely recognized camp pick-up line" (247). Finnegan also is intrigued by the bricklayer's response to the narrator's offer to help: "You just had to save somebody to-night. I understand. I got a appetite like that too. Only mine's women" (245). Finally, Finnegan notes that the narrator assures the reader that he will go home to wake up Drusilla, perhaps "a homophobic disclaimer reassuring his readers that he too has an appetite for women" (245). Finnegan says of this interpretation: "It's always possible that Reed himself remained completely oblivious to the possibility of any such queer subtexts operating in his own work, but these meanings would nevertheless remain available to those readers who knew more" (246). Finnegan also offers a second, and to my judgment less convincing, queer reading of Reed's story "A Taste of Justice" (250–51).

3. Reed owned a copy of *George's Mother,* a Crane collection that includes the sketch "An Experiment in Misery." Although the text is not marked, Reed wrote a list of his favorite authors on the book's back flyleaf—among them, Dickens, Thackeray, Conrad, H. G. Wells, Shaw, Hardy, and Shakespeare (bMS Am 1091.3:42).

4. Michael Robertson's *Stephen Crane, Journalism, and the Making of Modern American Literature* provides helpful background on how Crane's disguising himself as a tramp derived from a long tradition in U.S. journalism. Crane's initial publication of "An Experiment in Misery" included an introduction that made the reporter's identity even more clear. "Two men stood regarding a tramp. 'I wonder how he feels,' said one, reflectively" (Bowers, 862). From that opening, Crane reveals his experimental masquerade directly to the reader. When the piece was reprinted as an accompanying article in a Crane collection, the explanatory opening was dropped (Bowers, 863). Unless Reed had obtained a copy of the original newspaper account, published when he was only six years old, he would have been familiar with the latter opening of "An Experiment in Misery" —the version that I compare and contrast specifically with Reed's "The Capitalist."

5. The source of the confusion may be Reed's note, "Being Revised," handwritten at the top of the expanded typescript (bMS Am 1091:1152). The catalogers of the Reed archives may have believed the manuscript that they classified as bMS Am 1091:1153 was the revision to which Reed referred. A close reading of the two versions convinces me, however, that the expanded version (bMS Am 1091:1152) was written second because of the way it directly expands on the text (bMS Am 1091:1153) that Reed designated for *Metropolitan Magazine.* I believe that Reed's "Being Revised" note on the expanded version meant that he had originally planned to do even more work on it. The piece ends rather abruptly in its current form.

6. Philip Gerard asserts the following standard in *Creative Nonfiction: Researching and Crafting Stories of Real Life:* "The hardest part of writing creative nonfiction is that you're stuck with what really happened—you can't make it up. You can be as artful as you want in the presentation, draw profound meanings out of your subject matter. But you are stuck with real people and real events. You are stuck with stories that don't always turn out the way you wish they had turned out" (6).

7. The book was *The Shameless Diary of an Explorer,* which chronicled Dunn's exploits around the world and established his reputation as an adventurer. In his memoir *World Alive: A Personal Story,* Dunn says only this of the "Shot at Sunrise" incident: "[O]ur efforts to make the front, with or without official permission, by car, bike or afoot, were [in] vain" (210–11).

8. By using Dunn's name in "Shot at Sunrise," Reed gains the context that readers would associate with Dunn's name, but in turn opens new questions of historicity. If Reed subsequently had marketed the text as nonfiction, Dunn and other named characters in the piece would have been able to contest Reed's version. For example, had Dunn objected to Reed's depiction of epilepsy in his family history, he at least hypothetically might have had redress in the courts for imputing a disease falsely—a threshold standard of libel. Although that alternative would be highly unlikely, the incident does show how texts asserted to be nonfiction might trigger a contest between writers and subjects over facts and meaning.

9. E. Alexander Powell was an actual reporter; later, he enlisted in the U.S. Army, where he rose to the rank of captain. His book *Italy at War* was published by Scribner's as part of its "The War on All Fronts" series that included Reed's *The War in Eastern Europe* (Davis, "Publisher's Note," ix). For an expanded discussion of how Powell's views on the war differed from those of Reed, see chapter 6.

Chapter 3

1. Jim Tuck's careful reading of *Insurgent Mexico* and its source documents helps to untangle the complex chronology of Reed's book. Tuck correctly identifies events that happened at Villa Allegre and Santa Maria del Oro, with which Reed ends the book, as actually taking place before the events Reed placed at the book's opening. Tuck also traces Reed's pathway across Mexico and raises intriguing questions about how the journalist may have gotten from one place to another. "I do not charge Reed with conscious falsification," Tuck concludes. "He apparently had no maps, his knowledge of Mexico was limited, and there was a considerable language barrier" (107).

2. *Metropolitan Magazine* also relied on Mutual Film photographs of the Mexican War for illustrations in its magazine. Whether staged or not, photographs purporting to depict Villa's troops at war accompanied Reed's article "The Battle," about the fall of Gomez Palacio, in the August 1914 issue of *Metropolitan.* While other reporters covering the war tended to efface Villa's role in his self-construction, Christopher P. Wilson accurately notes that Reed "talks persuasively of how Villa was an active participant in the news narrative" (348) of the battles.

3. The decision not to publish a nonfictional narrative releases its writer from many of the implications that derive from making truth claims about people and events in a public forum. Hence, the publication status of nonfiction often plays a substantial role in its meaning. By declining to market his essay "The Mexican Lower Classes," Crane released himself from the Wheeler Syndicate's underlying ideology on Mexico and thus presumably was more free to tell the truth. Christine Stansell, in an assessment

of Reed that I address in chapter 6, unfavorably compares Reed's reporting of Mexico and Europe with the private diary written by Isaac Babel in 1920 about the Red Cavalry in the Russian Civil War. Stansell discounts the difference between public and private writing in assessing a writer's choice of subject matter (190). In doing so, she chooses to ignore the expectations that a reporter's employer brings to bear on a published text. The Wheeler Syndicate and *Metropolitan Magazine* paid Crane and Reed to deliver exotic stories of foreign society and conflict written in terms that would entice, but not substantially challenge, a North American audience. Writers of private diaries and journals face no such externally imposed mandates. In comparing and contrasting the impoverished people of Mexico and the United States, Crane apparently decided to keep his ideas to himself. When Reed stepped out of the role that *Metropolitan Magazine* preferred for his coverage of foreign conflict, Reed no longer received assignments from the magazine (see chapter 4).

4. Elizabetta, after losing her man, had already been picked up by a captain, who was treating her as his property. His protests when "the gringo," Reed, takes her into the house are essentially silenced by a senior officer, who says it is up to Reed and the woman. Tuck doubts this Elizabetta story: "This is the stuff of a French bedroom farce, not of the *machismo*-obsessed world of revolutionary Mexico. It is hardly believable that a tough ex-bandit who rose to a command position under Urbina would have let himself be cuckolded in front of the entire troop by an unarmed gringo" (113). Tuck's point is well taken, although he seems to overlook that the relationship was not consummated when he adds that "such a tale of battlefield seduction would make good reading among Jack's raffish cronies in the Village" (113). A lack of either notes or other more independent source documents renders it impossible to evaluate the truth of Reed's tale. If it is made up, Reed chooses a name—Elizabetta—that directly links the incident to the Elizabethan morality play with which Reed ends the book. In both cases, Reed finds himself entranced by the beauty and innocence of Mexico and seems to recognize the threat that unrestrained masculine aggression would pose to that innocence.

Chapter 4

1. In an August 1914 editorial in *Metropolitan,* Hovey called the sort of writing that he was promoting "fiction from an editorial viewpoint." The somewhat misleading phrase refers to writing that, though grounded in fact, resembles fiction in scene and character development. While the name he gave the genre would not stick, Hovey's editorial philosophy marks him as an important contributor to what has since come to be known as literary journalism.

2. Hovey was engaging in more than a little hyperbole by terming Reed a "brilliant fiction writer and poet." Reed had published eighteen poems of varying quality between college and the date that Hovey wrote the promotional blurb. During the same period, Reed had published only nine short stories. Most of them were derivative at best; the four with most promise—"Where the Heart Is," "A Taste of Justice," "Another Case of Ingratitude," and "Seeing Is Believing"—had appeared in *The Masses* (Hicks, 426–28).

3. Hovey had sent a telegram to Reed on February 14: "Rush us good picture of yourself. Local color stuff. Uniform if possible" (bMS Am 1091:492). Apparently that was not possible. The magazine's full-page portrait shows a relatively sober Reed in a business suit, boutonniere, and hat. Not to be deterred, the magazine's artists sketched Reed in sombrero and gun belts for subsequent advertisements.

4. Although Rosenstone can find no source for this quote (172n), Rudyard Kipling may have delivered his opinion directly in conversation with *Metropolitan* editors. A Kipling short story appeared in the magazine during the same weeks that Reed's first long dispatch from Mexico, "With *La Tropa*," would have appeared at the editorial offices.

5. During his lifetime, Reed published collections of his Mexican and Eastern European dispatches that had first appeared in *Metropolitan*. After his death, most collections of Reed's writing were sponsored either by the Communist Party, which had little interest in *Metropolitan Magazine*, or by editors interested in Greenwich Village radicalism. A recent such collection is *Shaking the World: John Reed's Revolutionary Journalism*. By contrast, Reed's *Metropolitan* articles from Western Europe and the United States mostly have not been collected.

6. By far the most popular and important war correspondent of his day, Davis made a distinction between Americans of German descent ("among our sanest, most industrious, and most responsible fellow countrymen") and "the military aristocracy in Germany." He called the latter "military mad. To our ideal of representative government their own idea is as far opposed as is martial law to the free speech of our town meetings" (xi).

7. John Kenneth Turner, the author of *Barbarous Mexico*, was another prominent figure of the American Left. He had close ties with the nascent labor movement in Mexico, and those relationships brought him in contact with opponents of Pancho Villa. "Turner's hostility to Villa was for similar reasons shared by many leaders and members of the IWW," writes Villa historian Friedrich Katz (321).

8. All of Reed's biographers with the exception of Eric Homberger accept Reed's firing in the general direction of the French lines as fact. Homberger interprets rather ambivalent language in Robert Dunn's *Five Fronts: On the Firing Lines with the English-French, Austrian, German, and Russian Troops* (1915) as "exempt[ing] Reed from this act" (89). In his 1956 memoirs, *World Alive: A Personal Story,* Dunn writes of the incident: "[O]ur lieutenant offered a Mauser for a trial shot through the eye hole of the steel trench rim. A flare went off, but you saw only the French mud banks 450 feet away. Jack fired, then I, high into the air. Back over our typewriters Jack was amazed to hear I'd written about the shots. 'It could get us in a jam,' he said" (216). Later Dunn adds: "Jack had been right; my story of the shot from the German trenches meant trouble—for him, too, though he never reproached me" (221).

9. In 1920, when Reed was in a Finnish prison, Hovey and Whigham were among many Americans with former ties to Reed who urged the U.S. government to intervene for Reed's release. Whatever hard feelings Reed carried toward the men seemed to be forgiven when he heard of their support. "Please thank all my friends for me, and I wish particularly that you would give my love to Carl Hovey, and tell him how much I was

touched by his actions. Also Mr. Whigham's," Reed wrote to Bryant on June 16, 1920, the day he was released from prison in Finland (bMS Am 1091:117).

10. Reed traveled to Detroit to interview Ford in June 1916 and produced articles about him both for *Metropolitan* and *The Masses*. Given Reed's politics, the articles are curiously laudatory. Reed believed Henry Ford's plants gave workers more rights than did more conventional industrialists; he wrote "Why They Hate Ford" in *The Masses* to explore how Ford deviated from standard capitalism. In *Metropolitan*, Reed wrote: "The Ford car is a wonderful thing, but the Ford plant is a miracle. Hundreds of parts, made in vast quantities at incredible speed, flow toward one point. The final assembly is the most miraculous thing of all" (10). Reed approved of the company's profit-sharing plan for its thirty thousand employees, but later in the article he captured the following interchange: "'Do you believe in Democracy?' 'Democracy?' he queried. 'The right of the people to govern themselves,' I explained. 'A Republican form of government.' 'I don't know,' he answered simply. . . . 'I have noticed that an efficient business organization is almost always built up around one man'" (67). Reed did not disclose to his readers that he hoped Ford would bankroll a daily newspaper devoted to the antiwar movement (Rosenstone, 247). "I have had two glorious interviews with Ford and am putting up to him the most magnificent scheme ever conceived," Reed wrote to Bryant on June 14, 1916. "I haven't time to tell you about it now, but if it goes through, you and I may come to live in Detroit for a while" (bMS Am 1091:32). Four days later, Reed wrote to Bryant again: "Damn my luck at having had to come back here—and for the purposes I was secretly after, all for nothing, too, I'm afraid. But anyway, I shall have a better article on Ford now. It is going to be a world-beater" (bMS Am 1091:34).

11. The always contentious relationship between Reed and Roosevelt was further exacerbated by a quote that Reed had attributed to Roosevelt: "By war alone can we acquire those virile qualities necessary to win in the storm strife of actual life." When Roosevelt claimed never to have said such a thing, Reed produced a printed copy of a Roosevelt speech that contained the line. "By the colonel's own definition of the term, he is the liar and not you or I" (bMS Am 1091:1338), Reed wrote to the man who had supplied the clipping.

12. Ironically, the third chapter of Reed's serial, "Dynamite," had appeared on a jump page in *Collier's* next to a Standard Oil Company advertisement for Nujol, a laxative. "[I]f the life you lived was the healthful active life Nature intended—you wouldn't suffer from constipation" (38), the ad declares. Standard Oil claimed that its petroleum-based medication would get rid of the "headaches, nervousness, and depression which constipation causes" (38).

13. Founded by Waldo Frank, Van Wyck Brooks, and James Oppenheim, *Seven Arts* published the best of an emerging class of American writers that included Sherwood Anderson, Theodore Dreiser, John Dos Passos, Eugene O'Neill, Carl Sandburg, and Robert Frost. The magazine had always rejected Reed's short stories (Hicks, 245), so Reed was thrilled when it accepted "This Unpopular War." He wrote to Louise Bryant: "To my real delight, the *Seven Arts* has accepted an article of mine—a short one. I'm beginning to feel as if I could do something again—at long intervals" (bMS Am 1091:75).

Chapter 5

1. Prior to February 1918, the Julian calendar was in use in Russia; thus the revolutionary events during the ten days between November 6 and 15 under the standard Gregorian calendar happened, in terms of the Julian, between October 23 and November 1. I have used Gregorian dates throughout this book; Russia itself changed to the Gregorian calendar after the Bolsheviks took control. In conformance with Reed's usage, I refer to the Russian city of Saint Petersburg as Petrograd; generally, I use Reed's spellings of Russian names.

2. The comparison of Reed's metaphors in *Ten Days That Shook the World* with Henry Adams's famous chapter 25 of *The Education of Henry Adams* is speculative but suggestive. Of his encounter with the dynamos at the Paris Exposition of 1900, Adams says in his essay: "Before the end, one began to pray to it; inherited instinct taught the natural expression of man before silent and infinite force. . . . No more relation could he discover between the steam and the electric current than between the Cross and the cathedral. The forces were interchangeable if not reversible, but he could see only an absolute *fiat* in electricity as in faith" (380–81). The revolutionary dynamo in *Ten Days* appears to incite something of the same measure of awe for Reed. Like Adams, he explicitly compares his dynamo with a religious transformation, most dramatically during the final scenes of *Ten Days* at a workers' funeral in Moscow's Red Square. "I suddenly realized that the devout Russian people no longer needed priests to pray them into heaven. On earth they were building a kingdom more bright than any heaven had to offer, and for which it was a glory to die" (808). Dramatist Eugene O'Neill, Reed's partner and sometimes rival at the Provincetown Players, also was fascinated by the dynamo's transformation of mechanical to electrical power and made it the metaphorical center of his 1929 play *Dynamo*.

3. In his comparison of the writing of Reed and O'Neill, John S. Bak is quite critical of Reed's dialogues in *Ten Days*, calling them "unintentional caricatures, voices of political ideologies, and not flesh and blood human beings who truly feel the impact of the words they utter" (25). In leveling this charge, Bak concludes that "Reed's works never transcended their social message as O'Neill's did, and that is why he is remembered more as an historian than, like O'Neill, as a literary artist" (32). For his part, Reed never intended his writing to transcend its social message; indeed, that social message lay at the heart of everything he wrote. His importance to the history of literary journalism is that Reed (unlike Bak) saw no inherent disconnection between history and literary artistry. Perhaps he was so attracted to Russian people because they also tended to see the political as intertwined with the personal. When Reed first traveled to Russia on the reporting trip for *Metropolitan*, he found that the Russians were able to engage in long discourses on politics and philosophy at all hours of the night. "I have seen a crowded cafe at two o'clock in the morning—of course no liquor was to be had—shouting and singing and pounding on the tables, quite intoxicated with ideas" (*The War in Eastern Europe*, 468).

4. Intriguingly, the seven hundred pages of Reed's Russian notebooks make no mention of what has been called the "red-letter sentence" (Williams, 125) of Russian

Communism: "We shall now proceed to construct the Socialist order." Reed's notes of November 8 move straight from the entrance of the Bolshevik leader to Lenin's "practical measures to realize peace" (bMS Am 1091:1328, pp. 152–53). Although Williams recalls Reed copying Williams's translation of the line during Lenin's speech, the paper on which Reed copied it apparently does not survive. In his memoir, Williams recalls Lenin's line as: " 'Comrades, we shall now take up the formation of the socialist state.' Mechanically, I repeated the words after Lenin—in English—and noted John Reed, sitting next to me, writing down the sentence," Williams writes. "Satisfied that he had it and I could get a fill-in later, I continued to stare at the man who had pronounced these words" (125). Reed's notes of the historic Second All-Russian Congress of Soviets primarily are contained in one of his longest notebooks (bMS Am 1091:1328). The notes on the peace resolution and the singing of the Russian "Death March" are in a small folder of loose pages (bMS Am 1091:1331). It seems likely that the loose pages originally were part of the long notebook and that other loose pages—including the "red-letter sentence" that Williams dictated to Reed—have been lost. Although their memories of the exact sentence differ and Williams sticks to his version, he graciously defers to Reed's "greater accuracy as a reporter." Noting that Trotsky had once said, "Reed could not have made it up," Williams concludes, "Either way it's a great sentence" (125).

5. In the margins of Reed's Harvard economics notebook there is a scrap of heretofore unnoticed poetry celebrating Milton's *Paradise Lost*. Penned by Reed when he was a college student during the 1908–9 session, it foreshadows Reed's project in *Ten Days That Shook the World* and also creates an intriguing link with the final passage of *Insurgent Mexico:*

> With sure unhampered vision that saw
> The dread avengers of the changeless law,
> And splendid Satan beating at the bars.
> To have that dream you stand
> Above the alter; rapt unscaling eyes
> Rending the awful veil of Paradise.

(bMS Am 1091:1291)

In the poem, Reed is entranced by the creative power represented by new worlds as well as by the figure of rebellion suggested by Satan or Lucifer. These motifs show up in Reed's best-known books as well as in a number of his shorter pieces. As I have shown in chapter 2, Reed ended his account of the Mexican Revolution by summoning the character of a remorseful Lucifer, perhaps to symbolize the threat that Western capitalism, and indeed his own reporting project, might represent for traditional Mexican life. Yet Reed's overriding concept of Lucifer, first glimpsed in his college-day ode to Milton, draws its inspiration from a more romantically rebellious source than that evoked in *Insurgent Mexico*. Following the tradition he would have inherited from Percy Bysshe Shelley, Reed's "John Milton" poem portrays Satan as a "splendid" figure "beating at the bars" with which an avenging God enslaves him. Reed, fascinated with Milton, suggests that the blind poet, like Satan, dares to rend the veil with which the deity separates humankind from Paradise. In so doing, Milton sheds the scales from his own eyes and stares at Paradise unveiled, thereby with Satan altering forever the heretofore "change-less law" of God's power. If Reed considered any link between *Ten Days That Shook the World* and Milton's story of the creation and fall, that link might suggest some of the reasons why Reed adopted a narrative of epic inevitability such as that outlined by Horace.

6. The collapse of Soviet power in Russia in 1989 and the subsequent dissolution of the Soviet bloc, of course, adds yet another layer of irony to Reed's narrative. Because the Bolshevik victory no longer is seen as permanent, Reed's foreshadowing strategy loses some of its bite, and many of his most compelling scenes now tend to be experienced at a second remove. That is, the reader not only is aware of what Reed knew in addition to his immediate dramatic scene, but now also understands subsequent events that Reed perhaps never dreamed. Such is the complicated and fascinating by-product of nonfiction reportage: the author never can quite count on containing his narrative inside the boundaries of a book.

7. Gold was a prime organizer of John Reed Clubs at colleges and universities across the United States during the early 1930s. He also was instrumental, along with other Communist Party members, in the founding of *The New Masses* in 1926 and the "Proletcult" movement that celebrated working-class aesthetics (see Homberger, "Proletarian Literature and the John Reed Clubs").

8. Although all of Reed's biographers conclude that Reed disguised his own identity as Trusishka, Williams—who was there—believed that the Trusishka role was played by Alexander Gumberg, an American with ties both to the Bolsheviks and the U.S. government. Williams believed that Reed meant the episode as an inside joke, dubbing Gumberg a nerd because he was angry that Gumberg had managed to overturn his appointment as Soviet consul in New York. In any event, Reed did accompany the Bolshevik leaders on the car trip to the front, but was so confident of his insider access that—contrary to his Mexican reporting—he was not compelled to boast about it in his text.

9. Reed may have done it primarily to tweak the noses of U.S. embassy personnel, but he was partisan enough to the Bolsheviks that he once hoisted a weapon and marched with the Red Guard. Williams recalls in *Journey into Revolution:*

> Jack took it in his head to go on patrol duty with the Red Guards in front of the foreign office building. It was pretty silly, for the C.A. [Constitutional Assembly] deputies who trailed away in the small hours from the Taurida had no forces, and represented nothing but the dying gasp of the socialists who had lost out. It was right for Jack, however, as it gave him a chance to work off his fury over the way the embassy had begun to set sleuths after his wife. (201)

Chapter 6

1. Jon Franklin, personal correspondence with the author. Recent political turmoil in the post-Soviet Balkans generally has built interest in historical documents about the region. Reed's war narratives, in particular, have received attention.

2. Mary Humphrey Ward expanded on her recollections of the Western Front in

her autobiography *A Writer's Recollections*. Ward recalls that her friend Henry James had died the same day. Her evocation of battle differs strikingly from Reed's:

> All through that wonderful day, when we watched a German counter-attack in the Ypres salient from one of the hills southeast of Poperinghe, the ruined tower of Ypres rising from the mists of the horizon, the news was intermittently with me as a dull pain, breaking in upon the excitement and novelty of the great spectacle around us. I was looking over ground where every inch was consecrated to the dead sons of England, dead for her; but even through their ghostly voices came the voice of Henry James, who spiritually had fought in their fight and suffered in their pain. (Quoted at http://www.spartacus.schoolnet.co.uk/wward.htm)

3. Although Reed remained relatively unknown in the United States, his grand-niece Susan Reed found a different story in Soviet Russia after Stalin fell out of favor, when Russians were permitted to regain access to *Ten Days That Shook the World*. Returning to the Soviet Union in 1987, Susan Reed visited schools where children were taught that "John Reed was the first foreign journalist who wrote the truth about the Revolution" (119). In an article for *People Weekly*, Susan Reed recalls the following interchange with a teacher: "'How many monuments to him [John Reed] are there in America?' asked Helen. 'None,' I answered with a twinge of regret, explaining that the U.S. government didn't make a habit of building monuments to people it had once indicted for sedition" (119).

4. Reed's most recent biographer, Eric Homberger, is a strong proponent of the view that Reed was deeply disillusioned by Soviet factionalism by the time of his death. Citing documents released since the publication of Rosenstone's biography, Homberger quotes a recently declassified document authored by Col. Matthew C. Smith of the U.S. Military Intelligence Division that purports to quote Louise Bryant from a June 10, 1921, interview after Reed's death: "He was so imbued with the idea of communism, but when he really got in touch with the Russian situation, he found so few communists and so many who used communism as a means to get comfortable positions, extra food, homes, etc., that he was disappointed." Citing Theodore Draper's *The Roots of American Communism*, Rosenstone, too, believes that Reed was disappointed by what he found in the new Soviet Russia. But Rosenstone concludes that "it certainly would have taken much more than some disagreements with individuals like Zinoviev to turn him onto a different path" (379n). Of Reed's earlier biographers, Granville Hicks was strongly supportive of the Communist Party and believed that Reed stayed true to its ideals, while Max Eastman, the former editor of *The Masses*, led the faction that believed Reed to be anything but a committed Communist. Although he knew Reed well, the normally affable Eastman refused to be interviewed by Hicks and instead wrote his own memoirs of Reed. "Anyone . . . who knew John Reed could have predicted that where the Bolsheviks abandoned fundamental reality and truth-speaking, and the impetuous honesty that he loved in Lenin, he would abandon the Bolsheviks. He hated priests; he could not endure the smell of the casuist. He hated hypocrisy and jesuitry, and the smug complacence of those who think they represent the purposes of the universe" (79).

Works Cited

Works by John Reed

"Across the War World." John Reed Papers (hereafter, JRP), bMS Am 1091:1179.

Adventures of a Young Man: Short Stories from Life. Berlin: Seven Seas, 1963; San Francisco: City Lights, 1975.

"Almost Thirty." In *Adventures of a Young Man,* 125–44.

"America 1918." JRP, bMS Am 1091:1277.

"Another Case of Ingratitude." In *Daughter of the Revolution and Other Stories,* 149–52.

"Approach to War, The." *Metropolitan Magazine,* Nov. 1914, 15+.

"Article on New York City." JRP, bMS Am 1091:1137.

"Aspects of the Russian Revolution." *Revolutionary Age* 12 (July 1919): 8–10.

"Back of Billy Sunday." *Metropolitan Magazine,* May 1915, 10+.

"Bryan on Tour." *Collier's,* 20 May 1916, 11+.

"Bryan on Tour." JRP, bMS Am 1091:1161.

"Capitalist, The." In *Daughter of the Revolution and Other Stories,* 105–13.

"Carranza Warns U.S. of Hatred in Latin America." *New York World,* 4 Mar. 1914, 1.

"Collapse of the II Socialist International, The." JRP, bMS Am 1091:1166.

Collected Works of John Reed, The. New York: Modern Library, 1995.

"Colorado War, The." In *The Education of John Reed,* 88–121.

"Daughter of the Revolution." In *Daughter of the Revolution and Other Stories,* 3–19.

Daughter of the Revolution and Other Stories. Ed. Floyd Dell. Freeport: Books for Libraries Press, 1927.

"Dinner Guests of Big Tim, The." *American Magazine,* Dec. 1912, 101–4.

"Dynamite." *Collier's,* 26 Aug. 1914, 18+; 2 Sept. 1914, 18+; 9 Sept. 1914, 18+; 16 Sept. 1914, 18+.

Education of John Reed, The. Ed. John Stuart. New York: International Publishers, 1955.

"El Paso." JRP, bMS Am 1091:1147.

"Essay on Chinese Servant." JRP, bMS Am 1091:1101.

"Ever-victorious, The." JRP, bMS Am 1091:1226.

"Foreign Affairs." In Homberger and Biggart, 144–51.

"From Omaha to Broadway: A Sad True Tale of a New Yorker." *Metropolitan Magazine*, July 1913, 14+.

"From the Inside Looking Out: Thoughts Inspired by a Slant at the New Magazine." JRP, bMS Am 1091:1138.

"German France." *Metropolitan Magazine*, Mar. 1915, 13+.

"Harvard Renaissance, The." JRP, bMS Am 1091:1139.

"I.W.W. in Court, The." In *The Education of John Reed*, 175–85.

"I.W.W. on Trial, The." JRP, bMS Am 1091:1199.

"I.W.W. on Trial at Chicago, The." In *Daughter of the Revolution and Other Stories*, 162–64.

"Industrial Frightfulness in Bayonne." *Metropolitan Magazine*, Jan. 1917, 12+.

"Industry's Miracle Maker." *Metropolitan Magazine*, Oct. 1916, 10+.

"Insurgent Mexico." In *The Collected Works of John Reed*, 1–266.

"In the German Trenches." *Metropolitan Magazine*, Apr. 1915, 7+.

"Involuntary Ethics of Big Business, The: A Fable for Pessimists." *Trend*, June 1911, 288–96.

"John Milton." JRP, bMS Am 1091:1291.

John Reed Papers, bMS Am 1091–1091.3. Houghton Library, Cambridge, Mass. (elsewhere cited as JRP).

Letter to Boardman Robinson. 17 Sept. 1917. JRP, bMS Am 1091:136.

———. 16 Oct. 1917. JRP, bMS Am 1091:137.

Letter to Carl Hovey. 25 Sept. 1914. JRP, bMS Am 1091:129.

"Letter to Louise, A" [poem]. In *The Education of John Reed*, 223.

Letter to Louise Bryant. 10 Feb. 1916. JRP, bMS Am 1091:24.

———. N.d. JRP, bMS Am 1091:25.

———. 11 June 1916. JRP, bMS Am 1091:30.

———. 18 June 1916. JRP, bMS Am 1091:34.

———. 5 July 1917. JRP, bMS Am 1091:72.

———. 10 July 1917. JRP, bMS Am 1091:75.

———. 16 June 1920. JRP, bMS Am 1091:117.

Letter to Sally Robinson. N.d. JRP, bMS Am 1091:140.

"Margaret Sanger." JRP, bMS Am 1091:1156.

"Mexican Notebooks." JRP, bMS Am 1091:1316.

"New Appeal, A." JRP, bMS Am 1091:1234.

"Peripatetic Prince, The." *Trend*, June 1913, 45–52.

"Red Russia: Kerensky, I." In Homberger and Biggart, 63–68.

"Roosevelt Notes, The." JRP, bMS Am 1091:1338.

"Roosevelt Sold Them Out." In James C. Wilson, 149–55.

"Russian Notebooks." JRP, bMS Am 1091:1322–33.

"Seeing Is Believing." In *Daughter of the Revolution and Other Stories,* 133–46.

"Serbia: The Country of Death." *River Teeth: A Journal of Nonfiction Narrative* 1, no. 1 (1999): 108–21.

Shaking the World: John Reed's Revolutionary Journalism. Ed. John Newsinger. London: Bookmarks, 1998.

"Sheriff Radcliff's Hotel." *Metropolitan Magazine,* Sept. 1913, 14+.

"Shot at Sunrise." JRP, bMS Am 1091:1152–53.

"Soviet Russia Now." In Homberger and Biggart, 268–80.

"Statement of Purpose for *The Masses.*" JRP, bMS Am 1091:1145.

"Taste of Justice, A." In *Daughter of the Revolution and Other Stories,* 127–30.

"Ten Days That Shook the World." In *The Collected Works of John Reed,* 569–937.

"This Unpopular War." In *The Education of John Reed,* 166–75.

"Tides of Men, The." JRP, bMS Am 1091:1230.

"Traders' War, The." In *The Education of John Reed,* 74–77.

"Villa Is Brutal, Yet He Has Ideals, World Man Finds." *New York World,* 1 Mar. 1914, 1+.

"Visit to the Russian Army, A." In Homberger and Biggart, 28–58.

"War in Eastern Europe, The." *The Collected Works of John Reed,* 267–567.

War in Eastern Europe, The: Travels through the Balkans in 1915. London: Phoenix, 1995.

"War in Paterson." In *The Education of John Reed,* 39–47.

"What Mr. Bryan Said." JRP, bMS Am 1091:1162.

"Why Political Democracy Must Go." *New York Communist,* 24 May 1919, 4–5.

"Why They Hate Ford." In James C. Wilson, 156–63.

"With Gene Debs on the Fourth." In *The Education of John Reed,* 186–91.

"With Gene Debs on the Fourth" [typescript]. JRP, bMS Am 1091:1137.

"With the Allies." In *The Education of John Reed,* 77–87.

"With the Allies" [typescript and galleys]. JRP, bMS Am 1091:1154.

"Worst Thing in Europe, The." *The Masses,* Mar. 1915, 17–18.

Other Works

Adams, Henry. *The Education of Henry Adams.* Boston: Houghton Mifflin, 1974.

Adams, J. Donald. *Copey of Harvard: A Biography of Charles Townsend Copeland.* Westport: Greenwood, 1960.

Atkin, Ronald. *Revolution! Mexico, 1910–1920.* New York: John Day, 1970.

Bak, John S. "Eugene O'Neill and John Reed: Recording the Body Politic, 1913–1922." *Eugene O'Neill Review* 20, nos. 1–2 (1996): 17–35.

Bowers, Fredson, ed. *Stephen Crane Reports of War.* Charlottesville: University Press of Virginia, 1971.

———. *Stephen Crane Tales, Sketches, and Reports.* Charlottesville: University Press of Virginia, 1973.

Brenner, Amila, and George R. Leighton. *The Wind that Swept Mexico.* New York: Harper, 1943.

Broun, Heywood. "The Passionate Professor." *New Yorker,* 21 Jan. 1928, 19–22.

Bryan, William Jennings. Letter to John Reed, 18 Feb. 1916. JRP, bMS Am 1091:234.

———. Letter to John Reed, 26 Feb. 1916. JRP, bMS Am 1091:236.

Cheuse, Alan. *The Bohemians, John Reed, and His Friends That Shook the World.* Cambridge: Apple-Wood, 1982.

Crane, Stephen. "An Experiment in Misery." In Bowers, *Tales,* 283–92.

———. "Hats, Shirts, and Spurs in Mexico." In Bowers, *Tales,* 465–68.

———. "A Jug of Pulque Is Heavy." In Bowers, *Tales,* 457–58.

———. "The Mexican Lower Classes." In Bowers, *Tales,* 435–38.

———. "Stephen Crane in Mexico—I." In Bowers, *Tales,* 438–43.

———. "Stephen Crane in Mexico—II." In Bowers, *Tales,* 450–56.

———. "Stephen Crane's Vivid Story of the Battle of San Juan." In Bowers, *Reports of War,* 154–66.

Davis, Richard Harding. *Cuba in War Time.* New York: R. H. Russell, 1898.

———. *Notes of a War Correspondent.* New York: Scribner's, 1910.

———. *With the Allies.* New York: Scribner's, 1918.

Dearborn, Mary V. *Queen of Bohemia: The Life of Louise Bryant.* Boston: Houghton Mifflin, 1996.

Dell, Floyd. Introduction to *Daughter of the Revolution and Other Stories,* v–ix.

Dickens, Charles. "A Visit to Newgate Prison." In *Sketches by Boz.* New York: Harper, 1954.

Didion, Joan. *Salvador.* New York: Simon & Schuster, 1983.

Duke, David C. *John Reed.* Boston: G. K. Hall, 1987.

Dunn, Robert. *Five Fronts: On the Firing Line with English-French, Austrian, German, and Russian Troops.* New York: Dodd, Mead, 1915.

———. *The Shameless Diary of an Explorer.* New York: Outing, 1907.

———. *World Alive: A Personal Story.* New York: Crown, 1956.

Eastman, Max. "Memoir." In *The Complete Poetry of John Reed,* ed. Jack Alan Robbins, 70–80. Lanham, Md.: University Press of America, 1983.

Eliot, T. S. "Tradition and the Individual Talent." In Richter, 466–71.

Finnegan, Jim. "Writing to Shake the World: The Historical Avant-Garde, Political Postmodernism, and the Post Avant-Garde." Diss., University of Illinois, 1998.

Fishkin, Shelley Fisher. *From Fact to Fiction: Journalism and Imaginative Writing in America.* Baltimore, Md.: Johns Hopkins University Press, 1985.

Flynn, Elizabeth Gurley. "Sabotage: The Conscious Withdrawal of the Workers' Industrial Efficiency." IWW Publishing Bureau. http://www.cat.org.au/dwu/sabotage.html.

Frus, Phyllis. *The Politics and Poetics of Journalistic Narrative.* Cambridge: Cambridge University Press, 1994.

Furst, Lillian. *All Is True: The Claims and Strategies of Realist Fiction.* Durham: Duke University Press, 1995.

Gelb, Barbara. *So Short a Time: The Autobiography of John Reed and Louise Bryant.* New York: Norton, 1973.

Gerard, Philip. *Creative Nonfiction: Researching and Crafting Stories of Real Life.* Cincinnati: Story Press, 1966.

Gold, Michael. "He Loved the People." *New Masses,* 22 Oct. 1940, 8–11.

Hartsock, John C. *A History of American Literary Journalism.* Amherst: University of Massachusetts Press, 2000.

Hellmann, John. *Fables of Fact: The New Journalism as New Fiction.* Urbana: University of Illinois Press, 1981.

Henderson, Harry III. "John Reed's Urban Comedy of Revolution." *Massachusetts Review* 14 (1973): 421–35.

Herr, Michael. *Dispatches.* New York: Avon, 1978.

Hicks, Granville. *John Reed: The Making of a Revolutionary.* New York: Macmillan, 1936.

"Hitting the Sawdust Trail." In Billy Graham Center Archives, 31 May 2000, http://www.wheaton.edu/bgc/archives/Sunday/suntxt01.html.

Homberger, Eric. *John Reed.* Manchester, Eng.: Manchester University Press, 1990.

———. "Proletarian Literature and the John Reed Clubs, 1929–35." *Journal of American Studies* 13 (1979): 221–44.

Homberger, Eric, and John Biggart, eds. *John Reed and the Russian Revolution: Uncollected Articles, Letters, and Speeches on Russia.* New York: St. Martin's, 1992.

Horace. "The Art of Poetry." In Richter, 21–29.

Hovey, Carl. Editorial in *Metropolitan Magazine,* Sept. 1913, 3.

———. "Fiction from an Editorial Viewpoint." *Metropolitan Magazine,* Aug. 1914, 2.

———. Letter to John Reed, 14 July 1914. JRP, bMS Am 1091:494.

———. Letter to John Reed, 28 July 1916. JRP, bMS Am 1091:496.

———. Letter to John Reed, 28 Sept. 1916. JRP, bMS Am 1091:497.

———. Letter to John Reed, 5 Feb. 1917. JRP, bMS Am 1091:500.

———. "Note" [to Reed's "La Tropa"]. *Metropolitan Magazine,* Apr. 1914, 10.

———. "Note" [to Reed's "With Villa in Mexico"]. *Metropolitan Magazine,* Feb. 1914, 72.

———. Telegram to John Reed. 17 Feb. 1914. JRP, bMS Am 1091:492.

Hovey, Tamara. *John Reed: Witness to Revolution.* Los Angeles: George Sand, 1975.

Humphrey, Robert E. "John Reed." *A Sourcebook of American Literary Journalism.* Ed. Thomas B. Connery. New York: Greenwood, 1992. 151–60.

"I.W.W. Arrests and Trials, The." *New International,* 1 Nov. 1917, 4.

Jacobs, Naomi. *The Character of Truth: Historical Figures in Contemporary Fiction*. Carbondale: Southern Illinois University Press, 1990.

"John Reed Is Reported Dead." *New York Call*, 18 Oct. 1920, 1.

Kaplan, Robert D. *Balkan Ghosts: A Journey through History*. New York: St. Martin's, 1993.

Katz, Friedrich. *The Life and Times of Pancho Villa*. Stanford: Stanford University Press, 1998.

Kramer, Mark. "Breakable Rules for Literary Journalists." In Sims and Kramer, 21–34.

Lande, Nathaniel. *Dispatches from the Front*. New York: Henry Holt, 1996.

Lehman, Daniel W. *Matters of Fact: Reading Nonfiction over the Edge*. Columbus: Ohio State University Press, 1997.

Leighton, George. "The Photographic History of the Mexican Revolution." In *The Wind that Swept Mexico*, ed. Amila Brenner, 287–92. New York: Harper, 1943.

Lippmann, Walter. "Legendary John Reed." *New Republic*, Dec. 1914, 15–16.

———. Letter to John Reed, 25 Mar. 1914. JRP, bMS Am 1091:568.

Lounsberry, Barbara. *The Art of Fact: Contemporary Artists of Nonfiction*. New York: Greenwood, 1990.

Lukacs, Georg. *History and Class Consciousness: Studies in Marxist Dialectics*. Cambridge: MIT Press, 1971.

"Mary Humphrey Ward." 20 June 2000. Spartacus Educational. http://www.spartacus.schoolnet.co.uk/wward.htm.

Mayhew, Henry. *London Labor and the London Poor*. 4 vols. London: Augustus M. Kelley, 1895.

Milton. John. "Paradise Lost." In *Complete Poems and Major Prose*, ed. Merritt Y. Hughes. Indianapolis: Odyssey, 1957.

Mott, Frank Luther. *American Journalism: A History of Newspapers in the United States*. New York: Macmillan, 1962.

Nochlin, Linda. "The Paterson Strike Pageant of 1913." In *Theatre for Working Class Audiences*, ed. Bruce MacOnachie and Daniel Friedman, 87–95. New York: Greenwood, 1985.

Pauley, John J. "The Politics of New Journalism." In Sims, 110–29.

Powell, C. Alexander. *Italy at War*. New York: Scribner's, 1917.

Pratt, Mary Louise. "Scratches in the Face of the Country; or, What Mr. Barrow Saw in the Land of the Bushmen." In *"Race," Writing, and Difference*, ed. Henry Louis Gates Jr., 138–62. Chicago: University of Chicago Press, 1985.

"Publisher's Note." Davis, *With the Allies*, vii–x.

Reed, Susan. "A Kinswoman of Famed Journalist John Reed Finds that *Ten Days* Still Shakes the Soviet Union." *People Weekly*, 6 Apr. 1987, 114–19.

Richter, David. *The Critical Tradition*. New York: St. Martin's, 1989.

Rideout, Walter. *The Radical Novel in the United States, 1900–1954*. New York: Columbia University Press, 1992.

Robertson, Michael. *Stephen Crane, Journalism, and the Making of Modern American Literature*. New York: Columbia University Press, 1997.

Rogers, Robert W. Letter to John Reed, June 1913. JRP, bMS Am 1091:752.

———. Letter to John Reed, 11 Jan. 1916. JRP, bMS Am 1091:756.

Roosevelt, Theodore. "Awake and Prepare." *Metropolitan Magazine*, Feb. 1916, 11.

Root, Robert L., Jr., and Michael Steinberg. *The Fourth Genre: Contemporary Writers of/on Creative Nonfiction*. Boston: Allyn & Bacon, 1999.

Rosenstone, Robert A. "Mabel Dodge." In *Affairs of the Mind: The Salon in Europe and America from the 19th to the 20th Century*, ed. Peter Quennell, 131–51. Washington, D.C.: New Republic, 1980.

———. "Reform and Radicalism: John Reed and the Limits of Reform." In *Reform and Reformers in the Progressive Era*, ed. David R. Colburn and George E. Pozzetta, 133–51. Westport, Conn.: Greenwood, 1983.

———. *Romantic Revolutionary: A Biography of John Reed*. New York: Vintage, 1975.

———. *Visions of the Past: The Challenge of Film to Our Idea of History*. Cambridge: Harvard University Press, 1995.

Sims, Norman. *Literary Journalism in the Twentieth Century*. Oxford: Oxford University Press, 1990.

Sims, Norman, and Mark Kramer, eds. *Literary Journalism*. New York: Ballantine, 1995.

Smucker, Philip. "Kosovo under Fire." *River Teeth: A Journal of Nonfiction Narrative* 1, no. 1 (1999): 122–36.

Stallman, R. W. *Stephen Crane: A Biography*. New York: G. Brazillier, 1968.

Stansell, Christine. *American Moderns: Bohemian New York and the Creation of a New Century*. New York: Henry Holt, 2000.

Startsev, Abel. "Writer and Revolutionary: On the Occasion of the 90th Anniversary of the Birth of John Reed." *Soviet Literature* 10 (1977): 165–68.

Steffens, Lincoln. Letter to John Reed, 17 June 1918. JRP, bMS Am 1091:854.

———. *John Reed under the Kremlin*. Chicago: Walden Book Shop, 1921.

Street, Julian. "A Soviet Saint: The Story of John Reed." *Saturday Evening Post*, Sept. 1930, 8+.

Tuck, Jim. *Pancho Villa and John Reed: Two Faces of Romantic Revolution*. Tucson: University of Arizona Press, 1984.

United States. House of Representatives. "Hearings before the Committee on Military Affairs, House of Representatives, 65th Congress, First Session on the Bill Authorizing the President to Increase Temporarily the Military Establishment of the United States," 31–33. 14 Apr. 1917.

Ward, Mary Humphrey. *England's Effort*. New York: Scribner's, 1917.

Wharton, Edith. *Fighting France, from Dunkerque to Belfort*. New York: Scribner's, 1915.

Whigham, H. J. "Are We a Nation of Slackers?" *Metropolitan Magazine*, Feb. 1916, 3.

———. Editorial in *Metropolitan Magazine*, July 1914, 3.

———. Editorial in *Metropolitan Magazine*, Dec. 1914, 2.

———. "Let Radicals Face Reality." *Metropolitan Magazine,* Nov. 1915, 3.

———. "What We Mean by Socialism." *Metropolitan Magazine,* Jan. 1914, 6.

White, Hayden. *The Content of the Form.* Baltimore, Md.: Johns Hopkins University Press, 1987.

Williams, Albert Rhys. *Journey into Revolution: Petrograd, 1917–1918.* Chicago: Quadrangle, 1969.

Wilson, Christopher P. "Broadway Nights: John Reed and the City." *Prospects: An Annual Journal of American Cultural Studies* 13 (1998): 273–94.

———. "Plotting the Border: John Reed, Pancho Villa, and *Insurgent Mexico.*" In *Cultures of United States Imperialism,* ed. Amy Kaplan and Donald E. Pease, 340–61. Durham, N.C.: Duke University Press, 1993.

Wilson, James C., ed. *John Reed for "The Masses."* Jefferson, N.C.: McFarland, 1987.

Wolfe, Tom. "The New Journalism." In *New Journalism,* ed. E. W. Johnson and Tom Wolfe, 3–52. New York: Harper and Row, 1973.

Index

213; comparisons of Reed's notes, type-scripts, and finished drafts, 35, 53–56, 60–61, 76–78, 80–84, 96–111, 148, 184–90, 196–97, 203–4, 213; the construction of history in narrative, 48–51, 63, 190–94, 212–13; critique of war representation, 115–16, 145–57, 208–9; descriptive power, 2, 4, 33, 38–45, 63, 65, 83, 92, 130, 151, 158–59, 162–63, 189, 193, 203–4, 215; irony (general) 75, 80, 92, 96, 164, 172, 191; ironic first-person narration, 2, 45–48, 63, 65–75, 80, 83–85, 88–89, 92–93, 112, 126–27, 149, 159, 213; polemical writing, 201–3; relationship of fiction and nonfiction, 45, 66–67, 76–85, 89, 92–93, 103, 105–11; relationship to reporting subjects, 95, 108–9; scene construction, 4, 29, 158, 189, 213; symbolism and metaphor, 59, 75, 89, 91, 122, 124–25, 129–31, 145, 151, 153, 159, 169, 170–71, 186, 201; themes, 6, 92, 129–31; use of dialogue, 65, 189, 213–14, 272 n; use of narrative structure, 63, 176–84; use of vivid verbs, 27, 33, 151; writing style, 4–5, 25–26, 35, 53, 63, 189

Reed, John, works of: "Across the War World," 170; *Adventures of a Young Man: Short Stories from Life,* 6; "Almost Thirty," 6–8, 11, 170–71, 173, 204, 217; "America 1918," 19, 39–40, 203–4; "Another Case of Ingratitude," 67–69, 73, 75, 84, 266–67 n, 269 n; "The Approach to War," 129–31, 144–46, 170; "Article on New York," 12; "Aspects of the Russian Revolution," 202; "Back of Billy Sunday," 5, 26–34, 48–49, 66, 240–61; "Bryan on Tour," 51–63; "The Capitalist," 69–72, 86–87, 267 n; "The Collapse of the II Socialist International," 141–44; *The Collected Works of John Reed,* 263 n; "The Colorado War," 15, 138–41, 143, 167; "Daughter of the Revolution" (story), 16, 79, 85–93; *Daughter of the Revolution and Other Stories,* 6, 40, 49, 66, 106; "The Dinner Guests of Big Tim," 12–14, 216; "Dynamite," 90–93, 271 n; *The Education of John Reed,* 6, 41; "El Paso," 109; "Essay on Chinese Servant," 8; "The Ever-Victorious," 215; "From Omaha to Broadway: A Sad True Tale of a New

Yorker," 134; "From the Inside Out: Thoughts Inspired by a New Magazine," 133–34; "German France," 149; "The Harvard Renaissance," 12–13; "The Head of the Family," 79; "Industrial Frightfulness in Bayonne," 166–68; "In Short," 266 n; *Insurgent Mexico,* 3, 5, 9, 15, 65, 80, 83, 94–128, 173, 175–76, 182, 194, 199, 207–8, 213, 263 n, 268 n, 269 n, 273 n; "In the German Trenches," 5, 150–55, 219–39; "Involuntary Ethics of Big Business: A Fable for Pessimists," 12; "The IWW Trial in Chicago," 49–50; *Kornilov to Brest-Litovsk,* 177, 215; "A Letter to Louise" (poem), 18; "Letter for Margaret Sanger," 19, 61; "Mac-American," 79, 89, 97, 106–7, 111, 118–19, 132, 169, 199, 208; "Mexican Notebooks," 41, 99–111, 135, 185; "A New Appeal," 200–202; "The Peripatetic Prince," 12; "The Rights of Small Nations," 79; "Roosevelt Sold Them Out," 166; "Russian Notebooks," 184–90; "Seeing Is Believing," 74–75, 124, 126, 269 n; *Shaking the World: John Reed's Revolutionary Journalism,* 270n; "Sheriff Radcliff's Hotel," 42, 45–47, 50–51, 66, 73, 136; "Shot at Sunrise," 76–85, 199, 269 n; "The Social Revolution in Court," 40–41; "Soviet Russia Now," 21; "Statement of Purpose for *The Masses,*" 134; "A Taste of Justice," 72–74, 84, 267 n, 269 n; *Ten Days That Shook the World,* 1, 20, 32, 52, 65, 80, 83, 94, 172–204, 207, 214–15, 263 n, 272 n, 274 n, 275 n; "The Thing to Do," 79; "This Unpopular War," 168–69, 271 n; "The Tides of Men," 215–16; "The Traders' War," 143–44; "A Visit to the Russian Army," 196–98; *The War in Eastern Europe,* 5, 42–45, 65, 155–64, 176, 205, 207, 209, 211, 213, 263 n, 266 n, 268 n, 272 n; "War in Paterson," 45–47, 50–51, 66, 73; "What Mr. Bryan Said," 52, 54, 58, 62; "Where the Heart Is," 269 n; "Why Political Democracy Must Go," 202; "Why They Hate Ford," 271 n; "With Gene Debs on the Fourth," 39; "With the Allies," 148–49; "The World Well Lost," 79; "The Worst Thing in Europe," 147